Integral Calculus

Hari Kishan

ATLANTIC
PUBLISHERS & DISTRIBUTORS (P) LTD

ATLANTIC
PUBLISHERS & DISTRIBUTORS (P) LTD
7/22, Ansari Road, Darya Ganj, New Delhi
Tel.: +91-11-4077 5252, 2327 3880
E-mail: orders@atlanticbooks.com
Web: www.atlanticbooks.com

Reprint 2026

Published by Atlantic Publishers & Distributors (P) Ltd.

Printed & bound in India by Atlantic Print Services

Preface

I feel great pleasure to place in the hands of readers my present book *Integral Calculus* that has been prepared with meticulous care. My experience of teaching this subject for a period of more than three decades has greatly contributed in making this book self-contained and easily accessible. It is primarily designed for B.Sc. and B.A. courses, introducing students to the full range of Integration and Determination. All the elementary principles and fundamental concepts have been rigorously explained, leaving no scope for illusion or confusion. The numerous, well-graded solved examples provided in the book have been mainly taken from the authoritative textbooks and question papers of various university and competitive examinations which will facilitate easy understanding of the various skills necessary in solving the problems. In addition, these examples will acquaint the readers with the type of questions usually set at the examinations. Furthermore, practice exercises of multiple varieties have also been given which would definitely prove useful to students in gaining confidence in the understanding of the subject. Answers provided to these questions have been verified thoroughly. The book will undoubtedly prove indispensable to the students of Mathematics.

In the preparation of this book, I have been particularly helped by my son Manish Goyal, an author and Lecturer in Mathematics, G.L.A.I.I.M., Mathura. His penetrating suggestions have enriched the quality of the book.

Last but not least, I express my gratitude to Dr. K.R. Gupta, Chairman, Atlantic Publishers & Distributors, for his encouragement and also for bringing out this book in record time.

Dr. Hari Kishan

198/A, Kachchi Mandi,
Kosi Kalan-281403
(05662) - 233339

Contents

Preface iii
1. Antiderivatives 1
2. Integration by Substitution Method 9
3. Integration by Parts 21
4. Integration by Trigonometrical Substitutions 29
5. Integration of Hyperbolic Functions 34
6. Integration of Rational Functions 38
7. Integration of Irrational Functions 62
8. Integration by Partial Fractions 79
9. Integration of Transcendental Functions 90
10. Definite Integrals 96
11. Reduction Formulae 119
12. Beta and Gamma Functions 192
13. Determination of Areas (Quadrature) 230
14. Determination of Lengths (Rectification) 287
15. Determination of Volumes and Surfaces of Solids of Revolution 313
16. Integration of Functions of Two and Three Variables 348
17. Change of Order of Integration 365

1

Antiderivatives

1.1 Integration

Integration is a process which is the inverse of differentiation.

In differential calculus, we find the differential coefficient of a function, while in Integral calculus, we find the function whose differential coefficient is given.

1.2 Definitions

If $\frac{d}{dx}F(x) = f(x)$, we say that $F(x)$ is an integral or a primitive or anti-derivative of $f(x)$. We write

$$\int f(x)\,dx = F(x)$$

Thus $$\int \cos x\,dx = \sin x$$

because $$\frac{d}{dx}(\sin x) = \cos x.$$

Similarly $$\int x^2 dx = \frac{x^3}{3},$$

$$\int e^x dx = e^x;\ \text{etc.}$$

The process of finding the integral of a function is called *integration*. We are said to integrate $f(x)$ when we find the integral of $f(x)$. The function to be integrated is called the *integrand*. Here $f(x)$ is the integrand.

The symbol "$\int$" denotes integration; dx indicates that the integration is to be performed *w.r.t.* x; x is called the variable of integration. Now if C is an arbitrary constant, which may assume different values, we also have

$$\frac{d}{dx}\{F(x)+C\} = f(x)$$

$$\Rightarrow \qquad \int f(x)\,dx = F(x) + C$$

It shows that the integral of a function is not unique, because by assigning different values to C, we will get several integrals of $f(x)$. It is for this reason that $F(x) + C$ is called the General Integral or Indefinite Integral of $f(x)$. C is called the constant of integration.

Note : The constant of integration is usually omitted from the result but it is always understood to exist with every indefinite integral.

1.3 Standard Integrals

We can find out the integrals of certain important functions keeping in mind that integration is a reverse process of differentiation.

(i) $\int x^n dx = \frac{x^{n+1}}{n+1}; n \neq -1 \qquad \because \frac{d}{dx}\left(\frac{x^{n+1}}{n+1}\right) = x^n$

(ii) $\int \frac{1}{x}\, dx = \log x; \qquad \because \frac{d}{dx}\log(x) = \frac{1}{x}$

(iii) $\int e^x\, dx = e^x; \qquad \because \frac{d}{dx}(e^x) = e^x$

(iv) $\int a^x\, dx = \frac{a^x}{\log_e^a}; \qquad \because \frac{d}{dx}\left(\frac{a^x}{\log_e^a}\right) = a^x$

(v) $\int \sin x\, dx = -\cos x \qquad \because \frac{d}{dx}(-\cos x) = \sin x$

(vi) $\int \cos x\, dx = \sin x \qquad \because \frac{d}{dx}(\sin x) = \cos x$

(vii) $\int \sec^2 x\, dx = \tan x \qquad \because \frac{d}{dx}(\tan x) = \sec^2 x$

(viii) $\int \text{cosec}^2 x\, dx = -\cot x \qquad \because \frac{d}{dx}(-\cot x) = \text{cosec}^2 x$

(ix) $\int \sec x \tan x\, dx = \sec x \qquad \because \frac{d}{dx}(\sec x) = \sec x \tan x$

(x) $\int \text{cosec } x \cot x \, dx$ $\quad \because \frac{d}{dx}(-\text{cosec } x)$

$= -\text{cosec } x$ $\quad = \text{cosec } x \cot x$

(xi) $\int 1 \, dx = x$ $\quad \because \frac{d}{dx}(x) = 1$

(xii) $\int 0 \, dx = C$ $\quad \because \frac{d}{dx}(C) = 0$

(xiii) $\int \frac{1}{\sqrt{1-x^2}} dx = \sin^{-1} x$ $\quad \because \frac{d}{dx}\left(\sin^{-1} x\right) = \frac{1}{\sqrt{1-x^2}}$

(xiv) $\int \frac{1}{1+x^2} dx = \tan^{-1} x$ $\quad \because \frac{d}{dx}\left(\tan^{-1} x\right) = \frac{1}{1+x^2}$

(xv) $\int \frac{1}{x\sqrt{x^2-1}} dx = \sec^{-1} x$ $\quad \because \frac{d}{dx}\left(\sec^{-1} x\right) = \frac{1}{x\sqrt{x^2-1}}$.

1.4 Fundamental Rules for Integration

Rule 1. The integral of the product of a constant and a function is equal to the product of the constant and the integral of the function, i.e., $\int cf(x)\,dx = c\int f(x)\,dx$.

Rule 2. The integral of the algebraic sum of two or more functions is equal to the algebraic sum of the integrals of those functions i.e.

$$\int (u \pm v \pm w \pm \ldots)\, dx = \int u \, dx \pm \int v \, dx \pm \int w \, dx \pm \ldots$$

where u, v, w, ... all are functions of x.

ILLUSTRATIVE EXAMPLES

Example 1. Integrate the following functions *w.r.t.* x :

(i) x^8 (ii) $x^{\frac{3}{2}}$ (iii) $\frac{1}{\sqrt{x}}$

(iv) $\frac{1}{\cos^2 x}$ (v) $\frac{\cos x}{\sin^2 x}$ (vi) $\left(1-x^2\right)^{1/2}$.

Solution :

(i) $\int x^8 dx = \frac{x^{8+1}}{8+1} = \frac{x^9}{9}$;

(ii) $\int x^{\frac{3}{2}} dx = \frac{x^{\frac{3}{2}+1}}{\frac{3}{2}+1} = \frac{2}{5} x^{\frac{5}{2}}$

(iii) $\int \frac{1}{\sqrt{x}} dx = \int x^{-\frac{1}{2}} dx = \frac{x^{-\frac{1}{2}+1}}{-\frac{1}{2}+1} = 2\sqrt{x}$

(iv) $\int \frac{1}{\cos^2 x} dx = \int \sec^2 x \, dx = \tan x$

(v) $\int \frac{\cos x}{\sin^2 x} dx = \int \frac{\cos x}{\sin x} \cdot \frac{1}{\sin x} dx = \int \cot x \operatorname{cosec} x \, dx = -\operatorname{cosec} x$

(vi) $\int \left(1 - x^2\right)^{-\frac{1}{2}} dx = \int \frac{1}{\sqrt{1 - x^2}} dx = \sin^{-1} x$.

Example 2. Integrate the following functions *w.r.t.* x :

(i) 0 (ii) 5 (iii) $2 - x^a$

(iv) $\sin x - \frac{2}{x} + e^x$ (v) $\frac{\sin x}{\sin(a - \alpha)}$.

Solution :

(i) $\int 0 \, dx = C$ where C is an arbitrary constant.

(ii) $\int 5 \, dx = 5 \int dx = 5x$

(iii) $\int \left(2 - x^a\right) dx = \int 2 \, dx - \int x^a dx$

$$= 2 \int dx - \int x^a dx$$

$$= 2x - \frac{x^{a+1}}{a+1}, \text{ where } a \neq -1$$

(If $a = -1$, then integral $= 2x - \log x$)

(iv) $$\int\left(\sin x-\frac{2}{x}+e^x\right)dx = \int \sin x\,dx-\int\frac{2}{x}\,dx+\int e^x\,dx$$

$$= -\cos x - 2\int\frac{1}{x}\,dx + e^x$$

$$= -\cos x - 2\log x + e^x$$

(v) $$\int\frac{\sin x}{\sin(a-\alpha)}\,dx = \frac{1}{\sin(a-\alpha)}\int \sin x\,dx$$

$$= \frac{-\cos x}{\sin(a-\alpha)}.$$

Example 3. Find $\int\sqrt{1+\sin 2x}\,dx.$

Solution :

$$\int\sqrt{1+\sin 2x}\,dx = \int\sqrt{\cos^2 x+\sin^2 x+2\sin x\cos x}\,dx$$

$$= \int\sqrt{(\cos x+\sin x)^2}\,dx$$

$$= \int(\cos x+\sin x)\,dx$$

$$= \int\cos x\,dx+\int\sin x\,dx$$

$$= \sin x - \cos x.$$

Example 4. Find $\int\frac{x^4}{1+x^2}\,dx.$

Solution :

$$\int\frac{x^4}{1+x^2}\,dx = \int\frac{x^4-1+1}{x^2+1}\,dx$$

$$= \int\frac{x^4-1}{x^2+1}\,dx+\int\frac{dx}{x^2+1}$$

$$= \int\frac{(x^2-1)(x^2+1)}{x^2+1}\,dx+\int\frac{dx}{x^2+1}$$

$$= \int(x^2-1)\,dx+\tan^{-1}x$$

$$= \int x^2 dx - \int dx + \tan^{-1} x$$

$$= \frac{x^3}{3} - x + \tan^{-1} x.$$

Example 5. If $f'(x) = \cos x + 4$ and $f(0) = 1$, then find $f(x)$.

Solution : By definition of integral

$$\int f'(x) dx = f(x)$$

$$\therefore \quad f(x) = \int (\cos x + 4)\, dx + C$$

$$= \int \cos x\, dx + \int 4\, dx + C$$

$$= \sin x + 4 \int dx + C$$

$$= \sin x + 4x + C$$

Put $x = 0$,

We get $\quad f(0) = C$

But $\quad f(0) = 1$

$\therefore \quad C = 1$

$\therefore \quad f(x) = \sin x + 4x + 1.$

EXERCISE 1.1

Find the integrals of the following functions with respect to x.

1. $6x^5$ **2.** 1

3. $\cot^2 x$ **4.** $\tan^2 x$

5. $\sqrt{x} - \frac{1}{\sqrt{x}}$ **6.** $ax^2 + bx + c$

7. $1 + x + \frac{x^2}{\lfloor 2} + \frac{x^3}{\lfloor 3} + \ldots$ **8.** $\frac{1}{x} + \sin x$

9. $\frac{5x + 7}{x} + e^x$ **10.** $\left(x - \frac{1}{x}\right)^2$

11. $\frac{4 - 5 \sin x}{\cos^2 x}$ **12.** $\frac{\cos 2x}{\cos^2 x}$

13. $\dfrac{1}{1-\sin x}$

14. $\dfrac{\cos x}{\sin^2 x}$

15. $\dfrac{\sin^2 x - \cos^2 x}{\sin^2 x \cos^2 x}$

16. $(\tan x + \cot x)^2$

17. $\dfrac{x^3 + 3x^2 + 4}{x^{\frac{1}{2}}}$

18. $\dfrac{\cos 2x + 2\sin^2 x}{\cos^2 x}$

19. $\sin x \sec^2 x$

20. $\dfrac{1}{1+\sin x}$

21. $\dfrac{\cos 2x - \cos 2\alpha}{\cos x - \cos \alpha}$

22. $\dfrac{\cos x - \sin x}{\cos x + \sin x}(1+\sin 2x)$

23. $\dfrac{\sin x + \cos x}{\sqrt{1+\sin 2x}}$

24. $\dfrac{\sin x + \operatorname{cosec} x}{\tan x}$

25. $10^x + 3e^x + x^3$

26. $\dfrac{(x+a)^3}{\sqrt{x}}$

27. $\dfrac{6}{\sqrt{1-x^2}} + 3\sec^2 x$

28. $\dfrac{(x^2+8)^2}{x^4}$

29. $(2x^3 + 3x - 7)\, x^{-\frac{2}{3}}$

30. $\dfrac{2}{1+x^2} + 3\,a^x$

31. If $\dfrac{dy}{dx} = 2x^2 + x - 1$ and $y = 0$ when $x = 0$, then find out a relation in y and x.

32. If $\dfrac{dy}{dx} = 1 - 5x^2$ and $y = 3$ when $x = 1$, then express y in terms of x.

ANSWERS

EXERCISE 1.1

1. x^6

2. x

3. $-\cot x - x$

4. $\tan x - x$

5. $\dfrac{2}{3}x^{\frac{3}{2}} - 2x^{\frac{1}{2}}$

6. $\dfrac{ax^3}{3} + \dfrac{bx^2}{2} + cx$

7. $x+\frac{x^2}{\lfloor 2}+\frac{x^3}{\lfloor 3}+\frac{x^4}{\lfloor 4}+\ldots$

8. $\log x-\cos x$

9. $5+7\log x+e^x$

10. $\frac{x^3}{3}-2x-\frac{1}{x}$

11. $4\tan x-5\sec x$

12. $2x-\tan x$

13. $\tan x+\sec x$

14. $-\operatorname{cosec} x$

15. $\tan x+\cot x$

16. $\tan x-\cot x$

17. $\frac{2}{7}x^{\frac{7}{2}}+\frac{6}{5}x^{\frac{5}{2}}+8\sqrt{x}$

18. $\tan x$

19. $\sec x$

20. $\tan x-\sec x$

21. $2(\sin x+x\cos\alpha)$

22. $\sin x\cos x$

23. x

24. $\sin x-\operatorname{cosec} x$

25. $\frac{10^x}{\log_e 10}+3e^x+\frac{1}{4}x^4$

26. $\frac{2}{7}x^{\frac{7}{2}}+\frac{6}{5}ax^{\frac{5}{2}}+2a^3x^{\frac{1}{2}}+2a^2x^{\frac{3}{2}}$

27. $6\sin^{-1}x+3\tan x$

28. $x-\frac{16}{x}-\frac{64}{3}x^{-3}$

29. $\frac{3}{5}x^{\frac{10}{3}}+\frac{9}{4}x^{\frac{4}{3}}-21x^{\frac{1}{3}}$

30. $2\tan^{-1}x+\frac{3a^x}{\log_e a}$

31. $y=\frac{2}{3}x^3+\frac{x^2}{2}-x$

32. $y=x-\frac{5}{3}x^3+\frac{11}{9}$

2

Integration by Substitution Method

2.1 Suppose we are required to integrate $f(x)$ *w.r.t.* x. Sometimes its direct integral is not easy or possible. In such a case we regard x as a suitable function of t say $x = \phi(t)$ so that $dx = \phi'(t)\, dt$. Now,

$$\int f(x)\, dx = \int f\{\phi(t)\}\, \phi'(t)\, dt$$

Now we evaluate this integal and putting the value of t in terms of x from $x = \phi(t)$, we express the result in term of x.

Note : There is no hard and fast rule for making suitable substitutions. It depends upon the nature of the integral. Experience will enable the students to think out a suitable institution. However, for the sake of convenience, we can learn certain suitable substitutions under the following headings :

(i) Function of a linear function of *x* :

For evaluating an integral of the type

$\int f(ax+b)\, dx$, we put $ax + b = t$ so that a $dx = dt$

$$\therefore dx = \frac{dt}{a}$$

$$\therefore \int f(ax+b)\, dx = \int f(t) \frac{dt}{a}$$

$$= \frac{1}{a} \int f(t)\, dt$$

which can be easily evaluated.

(ii) Functions involving $a^2 \pm x^2$.

In such cases the proper substitution is $x = at$.

(iii) Functions of x^n :

If we have an integral of the type

$\int f(x^n)\, x^{n-1} dx$, then the proper substitution is $x^n = t$.

(iv) Powers of a function :

Any power of a function when multiplied by the differential coefficient of the function can be immediately integrated by substituting t for the function.

(v) The integral of a function in which the numerator is the differential coefficient of the denominator is equal to the logarithm of the denominator, i.e.,

$$\int \frac{f'(x)}{f(x)}\, dx = \log f(x)$$

Note : Sometimes two or more substitutions in succession are used.

2.2 Remember the following results :

(i) $\int \sin(ax+b)\, dx = -\frac{\cos(ax+b)}{a}$

(ii) $\int \cos(ax+b)\, dx = \frac{\sin(ax+b)}{a}$

(iii) $\int \sec^2(ax+b)\, dx = \frac{\tan(ax+b)}{a}$

(iv) $\int e^{ax} dx = \frac{e^{ax}}{a}$

(v) $\int \frac{1}{ax+b}\, dx = \frac{1}{a} \log(ax+b)$

(vi) $\int (ax+b)^n\, dx = \frac{(ax+b)^{n+1}}{(n+1)\,a}, n \neq -1$

(vii) $\int \sec(ax+b) \tan(ax+b)\, dx = \frac{\sec(ax+b)}{a}$

(viii) $\int \frac{1}{a^2+x^2}\, dx = \frac{1}{a} \tan^{-1}\left(\frac{x}{a}\right)$

(ix) $\int \frac{1}{\sqrt{a^2 - x^2}} dx = \sin^{-1}\left(\frac{x}{a}\right)$

(x) $\int \frac{1}{x\sqrt{x^2 - a^2}} dx = \frac{1}{a}\sec^{-1}\left(\frac{x}{a}\right)$

(xi) $\int \tan x \, dx = \log \sec x = -\log \cos x$

(xii) $\int \cot x \, dx = \log \sin x$.

ILLUSTRATIVE EXAMPLES

Example 1. Evaluate $\int \frac{x^3}{\sqrt{1 - x^8}} dx$.

Solution :

Let $I = \int \frac{x^3}{\sqrt{1 - x^8}} dx$

Then $I = \int \frac{x^3}{\sqrt{1 - (x^4)^2}} dx$ Put $x^4 = t$

$\therefore \quad 4x^3 \, dx = dt$

$\therefore \quad x^3 \, dx = \frac{dt}{4}$

$\therefore \quad I = \frac{1}{4}\int \frac{dt}{\sqrt{1 - t^2}}$

$= \frac{1}{4}\sin^{-1} t$

$= \frac{1}{4}\sin^{-1}(x^4)$.

Example 2. Evaluate $\int \frac{a}{b + ce^x} dx$.

Solution :

Let $I = \int \frac{a}{b + ce^x} dx$

Then $I = \int \frac{ae^{-x}}{be^{-x} + c} dx$ | Dividing the numerator and denominator of the Integrand by e^x

Now put $be^{-x} + c = t$

$\therefore \quad -be^{-x}\,dx = dt$

$\therefore \quad e^{-x}\,dx = -\dfrac{dt}{b}$

$$\therefore \quad I = -\frac{a}{b}\int \frac{dt}{t}$$

$$= -\frac{a}{b}\log t$$

$$= -\frac{a}{b}\log\left(b\,e^{-x} + c\right)$$

$$= -\frac{a}{b}\log\left(\frac{b}{e^{x}} + c\right)$$

$$= -\frac{a}{b}\log\left(\frac{b + ce^{x}}{e^{x}}\right)$$

$$= \frac{a}{b}\log\left(\frac{e^{x}}{b + ce^{x}}\right).$$

Example 3. Evaluate $\displaystyle\int \frac{2x^3}{4 + x^8}\,dx.$

Solution :

Let $\quad I = \displaystyle\int \frac{2x^3}{4 + x^8}\,dx$

Then $\quad I = 2\displaystyle\int \frac{x^3}{4 + \left(x^4\right)^2}\,dx$

Put $x^4 = t$

$\therefore \quad 4x^3\,dx = dt$

$\therefore \quad x^3 dx = \dfrac{dt}{4}$

$$\therefore \quad I = \frac{2}{4}\int \frac{dt}{4 + t^2} = \frac{1}{2}\int \frac{dt}{t^2 + 2^2}$$

$$= \frac{1}{2}\cdot\frac{1}{2}\tan^{-1}\left(\frac{t}{2}\right) = \frac{1}{4}\tan^{-1}\left(\frac{t}{2}\right)$$

$$= \frac{1}{4}\tan^{-1}\left(\frac{x^4}{2}\right).$$

Example 4. Evaluate $\int \frac{1}{2\sqrt{x}\sqrt{1-x}}\, dx.$

Solution :

Let $\quad I = \int \frac{1}{2\sqrt{x}\sqrt{1-x}}\, dt$

Then $\quad I = \frac{1}{2}\int \frac{dx}{\sqrt{x}\sqrt{1-x}}$

Put $\quad \sqrt{x} = t$

$\therefore \quad \frac{1}{2}x^{-\frac{1}{2}}dx = dt$

$\therefore \quad \frac{1}{2\sqrt{x}}\, dx = dt$

$\therefore \quad \frac{dx}{\sqrt{x}} = 2\ dt$

$$\therefore \quad I = \frac{1}{2}\int \frac{2\, dt}{\sqrt{1-t^2}}$$

$$= \int \frac{dt}{\sqrt{1-t^2}}$$

$$= \sin^{-1} t = \sin^{-1}\left(\sqrt{x}\right)$$

Example 5. Evaluate $\int \frac{1}{1+3\sin^2 x}\, dx.$

Solution :

Let $\quad I = \int \frac{1}{1+3\sin^2 x}\, dx$

Divide Numerator & Denominator by $\cos^2 x$, we get

$$I = \int \frac{\sec^2 x}{\sec^2 x + 3\tan^2 x}\, dx$$

$$= \int \frac{\sec^2 x}{1+\tan^2 x + 3\tan^2 x}\, dx$$

$$= \int \frac{\sec^2 x\, dx}{1+4\tan^2 x}\, dx$$

$$= \frac{1}{4}\int \frac{\sec^2 x\, dx}{\frac{1}{4} + \tan^2 x} \qquad \text{Put } \tan x = t \quad \therefore \sec^2 x\, dx = dt$$

$$\therefore \qquad I = \frac{1}{4}\int \frac{dt}{\frac{1}{4} + t^2}$$

$$= \frac{1}{4}\int \frac{dt}{\left(\frac{1}{2}\right)^2 + t^2}$$

$$= \frac{1}{4} \cdot \frac{1}{\frac{1}{2}} \tan^{-1}\left(\frac{t}{\frac{1}{2}}\right)$$

$$= \frac{1}{2}\tan^{-1}(2t)$$

$$= \frac{1}{2}\tan^{-1}(2\tan x).$$

Example 6. Evaluate $\int \sqrt{1 + \sin x}\, dx$.

Solution :

$$I = \int \sqrt{1 + \sin x}\, dx$$

$$= \int \sqrt{\sin^2 \frac{x}{2} + \cos^2 \frac{x}{2} + 2\sin\frac{x}{2}\cos\frac{x}{2}}\, dx$$

$$= \int \sqrt{\left(\sin\frac{x}{2} + \cos\frac{x}{2}\right)^2}\, dx$$

$$= \int \left(\sin\frac{x}{2} + \cos\frac{x}{2}\right) dx$$

$$= \frac{-\cos\frac{x}{2}}{\frac{1}{2}} + \frac{\sin\frac{x}{2}}{\frac{1}{2}}$$

$$= -2\cos\frac{x}{2} + 2\sin\frac{x}{2}$$

$$= 2\left(\sin\frac{x}{2} - \cos\frac{x}{2}\right).$$

Example 7. Evaluate $\int \frac{\sin x \cos x \, dx}{a\cos^2 x + b\sin^2 x}$.

Solution :

Let $$I = \int \frac{\sin x \cos x \, dx}{a\cos^2 x + b\sin^2 x}$$

Put $a\cos^2 x + b\sin^2 x = t$

$\therefore (-2a\cos x \sin x$
$+ 2b \sin x \cos x)\, dx = dt$

$\therefore 2(b-a)\sin x \cos x \, dx = dt$

$\therefore \sin x \cos x \, dx = \dfrac{dt}{2(b-a)}$

$\therefore$ $$I = \frac{1}{2(b-a)}\int \frac{dt}{t}$$

$$= \frac{1}{2(b-a)}\log t$$

$$= \frac{1}{2(b-a)}\log\left(a\cos^2 x + b\sin^2 x\right).$$

Example 8. Evaluate $\int \frac{1}{\sin x + \cos x}\, dx$.

Solution :

$$I = \int \frac{1}{\sin x + \cos x}\, dx$$

$$= \frac{1}{\sqrt{2}}\int \frac{1}{\frac{1}{\sqrt{2}}\sin x + \frac{1}{\sqrt{2}}\cos x}\, dx$$

$$= \frac{1}{\sqrt{2}} \int \frac{1}{\sin \frac{\pi}{4} \sin x + \cos \frac{\pi}{4} \cos x} dx$$

$$= \frac{1}{\sqrt{2}} \int \frac{dx}{\cos\left(x - \frac{\pi}{4}\right)}$$

$$= \frac{1}{\sqrt{2}} \int \sec\left(x - \frac{\pi}{4}\right) dx \qquad \text{Put} \quad x - \frac{\pi}{4} = t$$

$$\therefore \quad dx = dt$$

$$\therefore \quad I = \frac{1}{\sqrt{2}} \int \sec t \, dt$$

$$= \frac{1}{\sqrt{2}} \int \frac{\sec t \left(\sec t + \tan t\right)}{\sec t + \tan t} dt$$

Again, put $\sec t + \tan t = z$

$\therefore$ $(\sec t \tan t + \sec^2 t) \, dt = \frac{1}{z}$

$\therefore$ $\sec t (\tan t + \sec t) \, dt = dz$

$$\therefore \quad I = \frac{1}{\sqrt{2}} \int \frac{dz}{z}$$

$$= \frac{1}{\sqrt{2}} \log z$$

$$= \frac{1}{\sqrt{2}} \log\left(\sec t + \tan t\right)$$

$$= \frac{1}{\sqrt{2}} \log\left[\sec\left(x - \frac{\pi}{4}\right) + \tan\left(x - \frac{\pi}{4}\right)\right].$$

Example 9. Evaluate $\frac{\sqrt{x}}{1+x} dx.$

Solution :

$$I = \int \frac{\sqrt{x}}{1+x} dx$$

$$= \int \frac{x\,dx}{\sqrt{x}(1+x)}$$

Put $\sqrt{x} = t$

$\therefore \quad \frac{1}{2}x^{-\frac{1}{2}}dx = dt$

$\therefore \quad \frac{dx}{\sqrt{x}} = 2dt$

$$\therefore \quad I = 2\int \frac{t^2 dt}{1+t^2}$$

$$= 2\int \frac{t^2+1-1}{1+t^2}dt$$

$$= 2\int \left(1 - \frac{1}{1+t^2}\right)dt$$

$$= 2\left[t - \tan^{-1} t\right]$$

$$= 2\left[\sqrt{x} - \tan^{-1}\left(\sqrt{x}\right)\right].$$

Example 10. Evaluate $\int \sin 2x \cos 3x\, dx.$

Solution :

$$I = \frac{1}{2}\int 2\sin 2x \cos 3x\, dx$$

$$= \frac{1}{2}\int (\sin 5x - \sin x)\, dx$$

$$= \frac{1}{2}\left[-\frac{\cos 5x}{5} + \cos x\right]$$

$$= \frac{5\cos x - \cos 5x}{10}.$$

EXERCISE 2.1

Integrate the following functions with respect to the variable of integration x :

1. $\frac{2x+3}{x^2+3x+7}$
2. $\frac{1-\sin x}{x+\cos x}$
3. $\frac{\cos x - \sin x}{\sin x + \cos x}$
4. $\frac{\sin x}{4+5\cos x}$

5. $\dfrac{x^{n-1}}{1+x^n}$

6. $\dfrac{x^3}{1+x^4}$

7. $\dfrac{\tan x}{\log \sec x}$

8. $\dfrac{\cot x}{\log \sin x}$

9. $\dfrac{\sec x \operatorname{cosec} x}{\log \tan x}$

10. $\dfrac{\operatorname{cosec}^2 x}{1+\cot x}$

11. $\dfrac{e^x - e^{-x}}{e^x + e^{-x}}$

12. $\dfrac{e^{2x}+1}{e^{2x}-1}$

13. $\dfrac{x^{n-1}}{a+bx^n}$

14. $\dfrac{\sin x}{a+b\cos x}$

15. $\dfrac{3x+2}{3x^2+4x+7}$

16. $\dfrac{x+1}{x^2+2x+2}$

17. $\dfrac{1}{x\log x}$

18. $\dfrac{1}{x(1+\log x)}$

19. $\dfrac{e^x}{3+e^x}$

20. $\dfrac{x^{e-1}+e^{x-1}}{x^e+e^x}$

21. $\dfrac{1}{(1+x^2)\tan^{-1} x}$

22. $\dfrac{1}{\sqrt{1-x^2}\sin^{-1} x}$

23. $\dfrac{1}{\sqrt{x}\left(1+\sqrt{x}\right)}$

24. $\dfrac{1}{x\log x\left[\log(\log x)\right]}$

25. $\operatorname{cosec} x$

26. $\dfrac{2x-1}{(x+1)^3}$

27. $\dfrac{x^2}{(a+bx)^2}$

28. $\dfrac{x}{1+x^4}$

29. $\dfrac{\cos\sqrt{x}}{\sqrt{x}}$

30. $x^2 \sin x^3$

31. $\cos\left(3x+\dfrac{\pi}{4}\right)$

32. $\dfrac{x^2}{\sqrt{1-x}}$

33. $e^x \cos e^x$

34. $x^{n-1} \sin x^n$

35. $\tan^4 x$

36. $\sec^4 x$

37. $\dfrac{x^3}{\left(1-x^4\right)^2}$

38. $\dfrac{\sin x}{\sin\left(x-a\right)}$

39. $\sin x \sin 2x \sin 3x$

40. $\text{cosec }(x-a) \text{ cosec }(x-b)$.

ANSWERS

EXERCISE 2.1

1. $\log (x^2 + 3x + 7)$

2. $\log (x + \cos x)$

3. $\log (\sin x + \cos x)$

4. $-\dfrac{1}{5}\log\left(4+5\cos x\right)$

5. $\dfrac{1}{n}\log\left(1+x^n\right)$

6. $\dfrac{1}{4}\log\left(1+x^4\right)$

7. $\log [\log (\sec x)]$

8. $\log [\log (\sin x)]$

9. $\log [\log (\tan x)]$

10. $-\log (1 + \cot x)$

11. $\log (e^x + e^{-x})$

12. $\log (e^x - e^{-x})$

13. $\dfrac{1}{b^n}\log\left(a+bx^n\right)$

14. $-\dfrac{1}{b}\log\left(a+b\cos x\right)$

15. $\dfrac{1}{2}\log\left(3x^2+4x+7\right)$

16. $\dfrac{1}{2}\log\left(x^2+2x+2\right)$

17. $\log \log x$

18. $\log (1 + \log x)$

19. $\log (3 + e^x)$

20. $\dfrac{1}{e}\log\left(x^e+e^x\right)$

21. $\log \tan^{-1} x$

22. $\log \sin^{-1} x$

23. $2 \log \left(1+\sqrt{x}\right)$

24. $\log [\log \{\log (x)\}]$

25. $\log (\text{cosec } x - \cot x)$ or $\log \tan \dfrac{x}{2}$

26. $-\dfrac{2}{x+1}+\dfrac{3}{2}\dfrac{1}{\left(x+1\right)^2}$

27. $\dfrac{1}{b^3}\left[\left(a+bx\right)-2a\log\left(a+bx\right)-a^3\left(a+bx\right)^{-1}\right]$

28. $\frac{1}{2}\tan^{-1} x^2$

29. $\sin \sqrt{x}$

30. $-\frac{1}{3}\cos x^3$

31. $\dfrac{\sin\left(3x+\frac{\pi}{4}\right)}{3}$

32. $2(1-x)^{\frac{1}{2}} - \frac{2}{5}(1-x)^{\frac{5}{2}} + \frac{4}{3}(1-x)^{\frac{3}{2}}$

33. $\sin e^x$

34. $-\frac{1}{n}\cos x^n$

35. $-\frac{1}{3}\tan^3 x - \tan x + x$

36. $\tan x + \frac{1}{3}\tan^3 x$

37. $\dfrac{1}{4\left(1-x^4\right)}$

38. $x \cos \alpha + \sin \alpha \log \sin (x - \alpha)$

39. $-\frac{1}{2}\left(\cos x + \frac{1}{2}\cos 5x\right)$

40. $\dfrac{1}{\sin(a-b)} \log \dfrac{\sin(x-a)}{\sin(x-b)}$.

3

Integration by Parts

3.1 Formula of Integration by Parts

If u and v are two functions of x, then

$$\int u\, v\, dx = u \int v\, dx - \int \frac{du}{dx}\left(\int v\, dx\right) dx$$

i.e. integral of the product of two functions = first function × integral of second function – integral of [differential coefficient of first function × integral of second function].

Integration with the help of this rule is called integration by parts. The success of the method depends upon choosing the first function in such a way that the second term on the right hand side may be easy to evaluate. There is no general rule for choosing first and second functions. However, the following points should be kept in mind while solving the questions by this method :

(i) Of the two functions, the one whose integral is not known should be taken as the first function.

(ii) If the integrals of both the functions are known, then the function which vanishes by successive differentiation be treated as the first function.

(iii) If the integral is a single function, then 1 should be treated as the second function.

(iv) If the integral of neither of the two functions reduces to zero by differentiating successively, then any of the given function can be treated as the first function. But if the integral on the right hand side reverts to the original form, then the value of the integral can be immediately inferred by transposing the former to the left hand side.

3.2 $\int e^x \{f(x)+f'(x)\}\,dx = e^x \cdot f(x)$

ILLUSTRATIVE EXAMPLES

Example 1. Evaluate $\int \frac{\log(\log x)}{x}\,dx.$

Solution :

$$I = \int \frac{\log(\log x)}{x}\,dx$$

$$I = \int \underset{\text{II}}{1}\ \underset{\text{I}}{\log t}\ dt$$

Put $\log x = t$

$\therefore \quad \frac{1}{x}\,dx = dt$

(integrating by parts)

$$= (\log t)\,t - \int \frac{1}{t}\cdot t\,dt$$

$$= t \log t - t$$

$$= \log x \log(\log x) - \log x$$

$$= \log x\,[\log(\log x) - 1]$$

$$= \log x\,[\log(\log x) - \log e]$$

$$= \log x \log\left(\frac{\log x}{e}\right).$$

Example 2. Evaluate $\int \tan^{-1} x\,dx.$

Solution :

$$I = \int \underset{\text{II}}{1}\ \underset{\text{I}}{\tan^{-1} x}\,dx$$

$$= \tan^{-1} x \cdot x - \int \frac{1}{1+x^2}\cdot x\,dx \text{ (integrating by parts)}$$

$$= x\tan^{-1} x - \frac{1}{2}\int \frac{2x}{1+x^2}\,dx$$

$$= x\tan^{-1} x - \frac{1}{2}\int \frac{d(1+x^2)}{1+x^2}$$

$$= x\tan^{-1} x - \frac{1}{2}\log(1+x^2).$$

Example 3. Evaluate $\int \sin^{-1} x\, dx$.

Solution :

$$I = \int \underset{\text{II}}{1} \underset{\text{I}}{\sin^{-1} x}\, dx$$

$$= \sin^{-1} x \cdot x - \int \frac{1}{\sqrt{1-x^2}} \cdot x\, dx$$

$$= x \sin^{-1} x - \int \frac{x}{\sqrt{1-x^2}}\, dx \qquad \text{(integrating by parts)}$$

Put $1 - x^2 = t^2$

$\therefore \quad -2x\, dx = 2tdt$

$\therefore \quad x\, dx = -\, tdt$

$$= x \sin^{-1} x + \int \frac{t\, dt}{t}$$

$$= x \sin^{-1} x + t$$

$$= x \sin^{-1} x + \sqrt{1-x^2}.$$

Example 4. Evaluate $\int \frac{xe^x}{(1+x^2)}\, dx$.

Solution :

$$I = \int \frac{xe^x}{(1+x^2)}\, dx$$

$$= \int \underset{\text{I}}{xe^x} \cdot \underset{\text{II}}{\frac{1}{(1+x)^2}}\, dx \qquad \text{(integrating by parts)}$$

$$= xe^x \left(-\frac{1}{1+x}\right) - \int \left(xe^x + e^x\right)\left(-\frac{1}{1+x}\right) dx$$

$$= \frac{-\, xe^x}{1+x} + e^x = e^x \left(1 - \frac{x}{1+x}\right) = \frac{e^x}{1+x}.$$

Example 5. Evaluate $\int e^{ax} \sin bx\, dx$.

Solution :

$$I = \int \underset{\text{I}}{e^{ax}} \underset{\text{II}}{\sin bx}\, dx$$

Integrating by parts

$$I = e^{ax}\left(-\frac{\cos bx}{b}\right) - \int a\, e^{ax}\left(-\frac{\cos bx}{b}\right) dx$$

$$= -\frac{e^{ax}\cos bx}{b} + \frac{a}{b}\int \underset{\text{I}}{e^{ax}}\ \underset{\text{II}}{\cos}\ bx\, dx$$

$$= -\frac{e^{ax}\cos bx}{b} + \frac{a}{b}\left[\frac{a^{ax}\sin bx}{b} - \int e^{ax} a\frac{\sin bx}{b}\, dx\right]$$

(again integrating by parts)

$$= -\frac{e^{ax}\cos bx}{b} + \frac{a}{b^2} e^{ax}\sin bx - \frac{a^2}{b^2}\int e^{ax}\sin bx\, dx$$

$$= -\frac{e^{ax}\cos bx}{b} + \frac{a}{b^2} e^{ax}\sin bx - \frac{a^2}{b^2} I$$

$$\therefore \quad I\left(1+\frac{a^2}{b^2}\right) = -\frac{e^{ax}\cos bx}{b} + \frac{a}{b^2} e^{ax}\sin bx$$

$$\therefore \quad I\left(\frac{a^2+b^2}{b^2}\right) = -\frac{e^{ax}\cos bx}{b} + \frac{ae^{ax}\sin bx}{b^2}$$

$$\therefore \quad I = -\frac{e^{ax}\cos bx}{a^2+b^2} + \frac{ae^{ax}\sin bx}{a^2+b^2}$$

$$\therefore \quad I = \frac{e^{ax}}{a^2+b^2}\left(a\sin bx - b\cos bx\right).$$

Example 6. Evaluate $\int e^x\left(1+\tan x\right)\sec x\, dx$.

Solution :

$$I = \int e^x\left(1+\tan x\right)\sec x\, dx$$

$$= \int \underset{\text{II}}{e^x}\ \underset{\text{I}}{\sec}\ x\, dx + \int e^x \sec x \tan x\, dx$$

$$= e^x \sec x - \int e^x \sec x\tan x\, dx + \int e^x \sec x \tan x\, dx$$

$$= e^x \sec x.$$

Example 7. Evaluate $\int \frac{x + \sin x}{1 + \cos x}\, dx.$

Solution :

$$I = \int \frac{x + \sin x}{1 + \cos x}\, dx$$

$$= \int \frac{x + 2\sin \frac{x}{2} \cos \frac{x}{2}}{2\cos^2 \frac{x}{2}}\, dx$$

$$= \frac{1}{2} \int \underset{\text{I}}{x} \ \underset{\text{II}}{\sec^2} \ \frac{x}{2}\, dx + \int \tan \frac{x}{2}\, dx$$

$$= \frac{1}{2}\left[x \cdot 2\tan \frac{x}{2} - \int 1 \cdot 2\tan \frac{x}{2}\, dx\right] + \int \tan \frac{x}{2}\, dx$$

$$= x \tan \frac{x}{2} - \int \tan \frac{x}{2}\, dx + \int \tan \frac{x}{2}\, dx$$

$$= x \tan \frac{x}{2}.$$

EXERCISE 3.1

Integrate the following functions :

1. xe^x

2. $x \sin x$

3. $x \cos x$

4. $x \sec^2 x$

5. $x \operatorname{cosec}^2 x$

6. $x \sin \frac{x}{2} \cos \frac{x}{2} \cos x$

7. $x \sin^2 x$

8. $x \cos^2 x$

9. $x \sin^3 x$

10. $x \cos^3 x$

11. $x \tan^2 x$

12. $x \cot^2 x$

13. $x \tan x \sec^2 x$

14. $x \cot x \operatorname{cosec}^2 x$

15. $x \sin x\ 2x \sin 3x$

16. $x \cos x \cos 2x \cos 3x$

17. $\log x$

18. $\log (1 + x^2)$

19. $\log \left\{x + \sqrt{a^2 + x^2}\right\}$

20. $\log x/(1 + x)^2$

21. $(\log x)^2$

22. $x^n \log x$

23. $x \log x$

24. $\dfrac{\log x}{x^2}$

25. $\dfrac{\log\left(1+x^2\right)}{x^2}$

26. $x^n (\log x)^2$

27. $x \tan^{-1} x$

28. $x^2 \tan^{-1} x$

29. $x^3 \tan^{-1} x$

30. $x \cot^{-1} x$

31. $e^{ax} \cos bx$

32. $e^x (\sin x + \cos x)$

33. $e^x \dfrac{1+x}{(2+x)^2}$

34. $e^x \dfrac{x^2+1}{(x+1)^2}$

35. $e^x \dfrac{1+\sin x}{1+\cos x}$

36. $e^x \dfrac{1-\sin x}{1-\cos x}$

37. $\dfrac{(1-x)e^x}{x^2}$

38. $\dfrac{e^x(1+x\log x)}{x}$

39. $\dfrac{\log x}{(1+\log x)^2}$

40. $\dfrac{x-\sin x}{1-\cos x}$.

ANSWERS

EXERCISE 3.1

1. $e^x (x-1)$

2. $-x \cos x + \sin x$

3. $x \sin x + \cos x$

4. $x \tan x + \log \cos x$

5. $-x \cot x + \log \sin x$

6. $\dfrac{1}{16}(\sin 2x - 2x \cos 2x)$

7. $\dfrac{x^2}{4} - \dfrac{x \sin 2x}{4} - \dfrac{\cos 2x}{8}$

8. $\dfrac{x^2}{2} + \dfrac{x \sin 2x}{4} + \dfrac{\cos 2x}{8}$

9. $\dfrac{1}{4}\left[-3x \cos x + 3 \sin x + \dfrac{x \cos 3x}{3} - \dfrac{\sin 3x}{9}\right]$

10. $\dfrac{1}{4}\left[3x \sin x + 3 \cos x + \dfrac{x \sin 3x}{3} + \dfrac{\cos 3x}{9}\right]$

11. $x \tan x + \log \cos x - \dfrac{x^2}{2}$

12. $-x \cot x + \log \sin x - \dfrac{x^2}{2}$

13. $\frac{1}{2}\left(x \tan^2 x - \tan x + x\right)$

14. $-\frac{1}{2}\left(x \cot^2 x + \cot x + x\right)$

15. $$\frac{1}{4}\left[-x\left(\frac{\cos 2x}{2}+\frac{\cos 4x}{4}-\frac{\cos 6x}{6}\right)+\left(\frac{\sin 2x}{4}+\frac{\sin 4x}{16}-\frac{\sin 6x}{36}\right)\right]$$

16. $$\frac{1}{8}\left[x^2 + x\left(\sin 2x+\frac{\sin 4x}{2}+\frac{\sin 6x}{3}\right)+\left(\frac{\cos 2x}{2}+\frac{\cos 4x}{8}+\frac{\cos 6x}{18}\right)\right]$$

17. $x \log x - x$

18. $x \log (1 + x^2) - 2x + 2 \tan^{-1} x$

19. $x \log\left(x+\sqrt{a^2+x^2}\right)-\sqrt{a^2+x^2}$

20. $-\frac{\log x}{1+x}+\log\frac{x}{1+x}$

21. $x (\log x)^2 - 2x \log x + 2x$

22. $\frac{x^{n+1}}{n+1}\left[\log x-\frac{1}{n+1}\right]$

23. $\frac{x^2}{2}\left(\log x-\frac{1}{2}\right)$

24. $-\frac{1}{x}(\log x+1)$

25. $-\frac{1}{x}\log\left(1+x^2\right)+2\tan^{-1} x$

26. $\frac{x^{n+1}}{n+1}\left[(\log x)^2-\frac{2}{n+1}\log x+\frac{2}{(n+1)^2}\right]$

27. $\frac{1}{2}\left[\left(x^2+1\right)\tan^{-1} x - x\right]$

28. $\frac{x^3}{3}\tan^{-1} x-\frac{x^2}{6}+\frac{1}{6}\log\left(x^2+1\right)$

29. $\frac{x^4}{4}\tan^{-1} x-\frac{1}{4}\left(\frac{x^3}{3}-x+\tan^{-1} x\right)$

30. $\frac{1}{2}\left[x+\left(x^2+1\right)\cot^{-1}x\right]$

31. $\frac{e^{ax}}{a^2+b^2}\left(a\cos bx+b\sin bx\right)$

32. $e^x \sin x$

33. $\frac{e^x}{2+x}$

34. $\frac{x-1}{x+1}e^x$

35. $e^x \tan\frac{x}{2}$

36. $-e^x \cot\frac{x}{2}$

37. $-\frac{1}{x}e^x$

38. $e^x \log x$

39. $\frac{x}{1+\log x}$

40. $-x\cot\frac{x}{2}$

4

Integration by Trigonometrical Substitutions

Example 1. Evaluate $\int \frac{x^2 \tan^{-1} x^3}{1+x^6} dx.$

Solution :

$$I = \int \frac{x^2 \tan^{-1} x^3}{1+x^6} dx \qquad \text{Put} \quad x^3 = t$$

$$\therefore \quad 3x^2\, dx = dt$$

$$\therefore \quad x^2\, dx = \frac{dt}{3}$$

$$\therefore \quad I = \frac{1}{3} \int \frac{\tan^{-1} t}{1+t^2} dt \qquad \text{Put} \quad t = \tan \theta$$

$$\therefore \quad dt = \sec^2 \theta\, d\theta$$

$$\therefore \quad I = \frac{1}{3} \int \frac{\tan^{-1} (\tan \theta) \sec^2 \theta}{1 + \tan^2 \theta} d\theta$$

$$= \frac{1}{3} \int \theta\, d\theta$$

$$= \frac{\theta^2}{6}$$

$$= \frac{\left(\tan^{-1} t\right)^2}{6}.$$

Example 2. Evaluate $\int \frac{x \tan^{-1} x}{\left(1+x^2\right)^{\frac{3}{2}}} dx.$

Solution :

$$I = \int \frac{x \tan^{-1} x}{\left(1+x^2\right)^{\frac{3}{2}}} dx \qquad \text{Put} \quad x = \tan \theta$$

$$\therefore \quad dx = \sec^2 \theta\, d\theta$$

$$\therefore \qquad I = \int \frac{\tan\theta \tan^{-1}(\tan\theta)\sec^2\theta \, d\theta}{(1+\tan^2\theta)^{\frac{3}{2}}}$$

$$= \int \frac{\tan\theta \cdot \theta}{\sec\theta} d\theta$$

$$= \int \underset{\text{I}}{\theta} \underset{\text{II}}{\sin\theta} \, d\theta \qquad \text{(integrate by parts)}$$

$$= \theta(-\cos\theta) - \int 1 \cdot (-\cos\theta) \, d\theta$$

$$= -\theta \cos\theta + \sin\theta$$

$$= -\tan^{-1} x \cdot \frac{1}{\sqrt{1+x^2}} + \frac{x}{\sqrt{1+x^2}}$$

$$= \frac{x - \tan^{-1} x}{\sqrt{1+x^2}}.$$

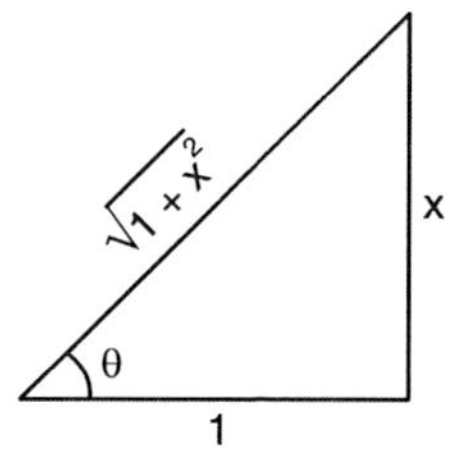

Example 3. Evaluate $\int \tan^{-1} \sqrt{\frac{1-x}{1+x}} \, dx.$

Solution :

$$I = \int \tan^{-1} \sqrt{\frac{1-x}{1+x}} \, dx \qquad \text{Put } x = \cos 2\theta$$

$$\therefore \quad dx = -2 \sin 2\theta \, d\theta$$

$$\therefore \qquad I = \int \tan^{-1} \sqrt{\frac{1-\cos 2\theta}{1+\cos 2\theta}} (-2\sin 2\theta) \, d\theta$$

$$= \int \tan^{-1} \sqrt{\frac{2\sin^2\theta}{2\cos^2\theta}} (-2\sin 2\theta) \, d\theta$$

$$= -2 \int \underset{\text{I}}{\theta} \underset{\text{II}}{\sin 2\theta} \, d\theta$$

$$= -2 \left[\theta \left(\frac{-\cos 2\theta}{2} \right) - \int 1 \cdot \left(\frac{-\cos 2\theta}{2} \right) d\theta \right]$$

$$= -2 \left[\frac{-\theta \cos 2\theta}{2} + \frac{1}{2} \frac{\sin 2\theta}{2} \right]$$

$$= -\left[-\theta\cos 2\theta + \frac{\sin 2\theta}{2}\right]$$

$$= \theta\cos 2\theta - \frac{\sin 2\theta}{2}$$

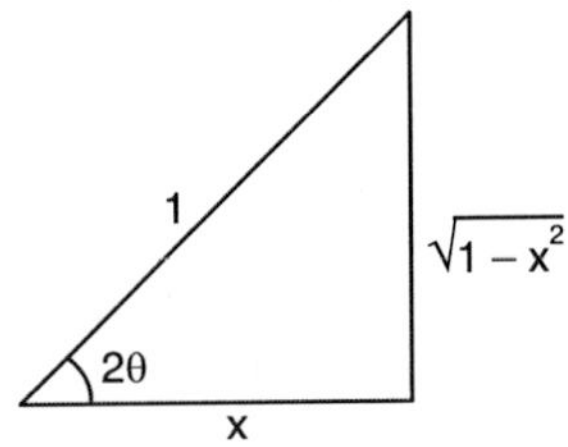

$$= \frac{1}{2}\cos^{-1}x\cdot x - \frac{1}{2}\cdot\sqrt{1-x^2}$$

$$= \frac{1}{2}\left[x\cos^{-1}x - \sqrt{1-x^2}\right].$$

Example 4. Evaluate $\int \frac{e^{m\sin^{-1}x}}{\sqrt{1-x^2}}\,dx.$

Solution :

$$I = \int \frac{e^{m\sin^{-1}x}}{\sqrt{1-x^2}}\,dx$$

Put $x = \sin\theta$

$\therefore\ dx = \cos\theta\, d\theta$

$$\therefore \quad I = \int \frac{e^{m\theta}}{\cos\theta}\cos\theta\, d\theta$$

$$= \int e^{m\theta}d\theta$$

$$= \frac{e^{m\theta}}{m}$$

$$= \frac{e^{m\sin^{-1}x}}{m}.$$

Example 5. Evaluate $\int \frac{\sec\left(\tan^{-1}x\right)}{1+x^2}\,dx.$

Solution :

$$I = \int \frac{\sec\left(\tan^{-1}x\right)}{1+x^2}\,dx$$

Put $x = \tan\theta$

$\therefore\ dx = \sec^2\theta\, d\theta$

$$I = \frac{\sec\left(\tan^{-1}\tan\theta\right)}{1+\tan^2\theta}\sec^2\theta\, d\theta$$

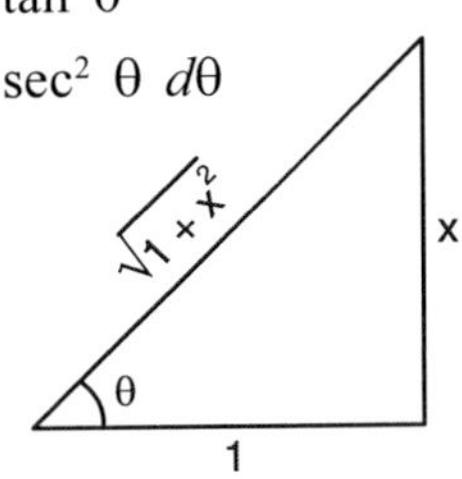

$$= \int \sec\theta\, d\theta$$

$$= \log(\sec\theta + \tan\theta)$$
$$= \left(\log\sqrt{1+x^2} + x\right).$$

EXERCISE 4.1

Integrate the following functions with respect to x :

1. $\dfrac{x\sin^{-1}x}{\sqrt{1-x^2}}$

2. $\dfrac{x^2\tan^{-1}x}{1+x^2}$

3. $\tan^{-1}\dfrac{2x}{1-x^2}$

4. $\sin^{-1}\dfrac{2x}{1+x^2}$

5. $\dfrac{\sin^{-1}x}{\left(1-x^2\right)^{\frac{3}{2}}}$

6. $\sin^{-1}\sqrt{\dfrac{x}{a+x}}$

7. $\cos^{-1}\left(\dfrac{1-x^2}{1+x^2}\right)$

8. $\tan^{-1}\left(\dfrac{3x-x^2}{1-3x^2}\right)$

9. $\dfrac{x\tan^{-1}x}{\left(1+x^2\right)^2}$

10. $\dfrac{1}{\left(a^2-b^2x^2\right)^{\frac{3}{2}}}$

11. $\dfrac{1}{\left(a^2+b^2x^2\right)^{\frac{3}{2}}}$

12. $\dfrac{1}{x^3\sqrt{x^2-1}}$.

ANSWERS

EXERCISE 4.1

1. $x-\sqrt{1-x^2}\,\sin^{-1}x$

2. $x\tan^{-1}x-\dfrac{1}{2}\log\left(1+x^2\right)-\dfrac{1}{2}\left(\tan^{-1}x\right)^2$

3. $2x\tan^{-1}x-2\log\left(\sqrt{1+x^2}\right)$

4. $2\left[x\tan^{-1}x-\dfrac{1}{2}\log\left(1+x^2\right)\right]$

5. $\dfrac{x\sin^{-1}x}{\sqrt{1-x^2}}+\dfrac{\log\left(1-x^2\right)}{2}$

6. $(a+x)\tan^{-1}\sqrt{\dfrac{x}{a}}-\sqrt{ax}$

7. $2x\tan^{-1}x-\log\left(1+x^2\right)$

8. $3\left[x\tan^{-1}x-\dfrac{1}{2}\log\left(1+x^2\right)\right]$

9. $\dfrac{1}{2}\left[-\dfrac{1}{2}\cdot\tan^{-1}x\cdot\left(\dfrac{2}{1+x^2}-1\right)+\dfrac{x}{1+x^2}\right]$

10. $\dfrac{x}{a^2\sqrt{a^2-b^2x^2}}$

11. $\dfrac{-x}{b^2\sqrt{a^2x^2-b^2}}$

12. $\dfrac{1}{2}\sec^{-1}x+\dfrac{\sqrt{x^2-1}}{2x^2}$

5

Integration of Hyperbolic Functions

5.1 There are six hyperbolic functions defined as under :

(i) $\sinh x = \dfrac{e^x - e^{-x}}{2}$

(ii) $\cosh x = \dfrac{e^x + e^{-x}}{2}$

(iii) $\tanh x = \dfrac{e^x - e^{-x}}{e^x + e^{-x}}$

(iv) $\coth x = \dfrac{e^x + e^{-x}}{e^x - e^{-x}}$

(v) $\text{sech } x = \dfrac{2}{e^x + e^{-x}}$

(vi) $\text{cosech } x = \dfrac{2}{e^x - e^{-x}}$

5.2

$$
\begin{aligned}
\sinh 0 &= 0 \\
\cosh 0 &= 1 \\
\cosh^2 x - \sinh^2 x &= 1 \\
\text{sech}^2 x &= 1 - \tanh^2 x \\
\text{cosech}^2 x &= -1 + \coth^2 x \\
\sinh 2x &= 2 \sinh x \cosh x \\
\cosh 2x &= \cosh^2 x + \sinh^2 x \\
&= 1 + 2 \sinh^2 x \\
&= 2 \cosh^2 x - 1.
\end{aligned}
$$

$$\tanh 2x = \frac{2\tanh x}{1+\tanh^2 x}$$

5.3 $$\sinh^{-1} x = \log\left(x+\sqrt{x^2+1}\right)$$

$$\cosh^{-1} x = \log\left(x+\sqrt{x^2-1}\right)$$

$$\tanh^{-1} x = \frac{1}{2}\log\frac{1+x}{1-x}$$

5.4 $\int \sinh x\, dx = \cosh x$

$\int \cosh x\, dx = \sinh x$

$\int \text{sech}^2\, x\, dx = \tanh x$

$\int \text{cosech}^2\, x\, dx = -\coth x$

$\int \text{sech}\, x \tanh x\, dx = -\text{sech}\, x$

$\int \text{cosech}\, x \coth x\, dx = -\text{cosech}\, x$

ILLUSTRATIVE EXAMPLES

Example 1. Evaluate $\int \frac{dx}{\sinh x}$.

Solution :

$$I = \int \frac{1}{\sinh x}\, dx$$

$$= \int \frac{2}{e^x - e^{-x}}\, dx$$

$$= 2\int \frac{1}{e^x - e^{-x}}\, dx$$

$$= 2\int \frac{e^{-x}}{1-e^{-2x}}\, dx$$

[Dividing N^r & D^r by e^x.

Put $e^{-x} = t$

$\therefore$ $-e^{-x}\, dx = dt$

$\therefore$ $e^{-x}\, dx = -dt$]

$$\therefore \qquad I = -2\int \frac{dt}{1-t^2}$$

$$= -2\int \frac{1}{(1-t)(1+t)}\,dt$$

$$= -\int \left(\frac{1}{1-t} + \frac{1}{1+t}\right) dt$$

$$= -[-\log(1-t) + \log(1+\text{t})]$$

$$= \log(1-t) - \log(1+t)$$

$$= \log\frac{1-t}{1+t}$$

$$= \log\frac{1-e^{-x}}{1+e^{-x}}$$

$$= \log\frac{1-\frac{1}{e^x}}{1+\frac{1}{e^x}}$$

$$= \log\left(\frac{e^x-1}{e^x+1}\right).$$

Example 2. Evaluate $\int \sinh 3x \cosh 3x\, dx$.

Solution :

$$I = \int \sinh 3x \cosh 3x\, dx$$

$$= \frac{1}{2}\int \sinh 6x\, dx$$

$$= \frac{1}{2}\cdot\frac{\cosh 6x}{6}$$

$$= \frac{\cosh 6x}{12}.$$

EXERCISE 5.1

Integrate the following functions :

1. $\cosh^2 x$

2. $\dfrac{1}{\left(e^x + e^{-x}\right)^2}$

3. $\left(\frac{e^x + e^{-x}}{e^x - e^{-x}}\right)^2$

4. $\left(e^x - e^{-x}\right)^2$

5. $\cosh(\log x)$

6. $\sin x \sinh x$

ANSWERS

EXERCISE 5.1

1. $\frac{1}{2}\left(x + \frac{\sinh 2x}{2}\right)$

2. $\frac{1}{4}\tanh x$

3. $x - \coth x$

4. $\sinh 2x - 2x$

5. $\frac{1}{2}\left(\frac{x^2}{2} + \log x\right)$

6. $\frac{1}{2}(\sin x \cosh x - \cos x \sinh x)$

6

Integration of Rational Functions

6.1 To evaluate $\int \frac{dx}{x^2 - a^2}$, $\int \frac{dx}{a^2 - x^2}$ and $\int \frac{dx}{a^2 + x^2}$

(i)
$$I = \int \frac{dx}{x^2 - a^2}, (x > a)$$
$$= \int \frac{dx}{(x-a)(x+a)}$$

First we shall break the integrand into partial fractions.

Let
$$\frac{1}{x^2 - a^2} = \frac{1}{(x-a)(x+a)} = \frac{A}{x-a} + \frac{B}{x+a}$$
$$\Rightarrow \quad 1 = A\ (x+a) + B\ (x-a)$$

Put $x = a$, we get
$$1 = A\ (a+a) = \text{A} \cdot 2a$$
$$\Rightarrow \quad A = \frac{1}{2a}$$

Then, put $x = -a$, we get
$$1 = B\ (-a-a) = B\ (-2a)$$
$$\Rightarrow \quad B = -\frac{1}{2a}$$
$$\therefore \quad \frac{1}{x^2 - a^2} = \frac{1}{2a}\left(\frac{1}{x-a} - \frac{1}{x+a}\right)$$
$$\therefore \int \frac{1}{x^2 - a^2}\, dx = \frac{1}{2a} \int \left(\frac{1}{x-a} - \frac{1}{x+a}\right) dx$$
$$= \frac{1}{2a}\left[\log(x-a) - \log(x+a)\right]$$

$$= \frac{1}{2a}\log\left(\frac{x-a}{x+a}\right)$$

(ii) $$I = \int \frac{dx}{a^2 - x^2}, (x < a)$$

First we shall break the integrand into partial fractions.

Let $$\frac{1}{a^2 - x^2} = \frac{1}{(a-x)(a+x)} = \frac{A}{a-x} + \frac{B}{a+x}$$

$$\Rightarrow \quad 1 = A\ (a + x) + B\ (a - x)$$

Put $x = a, - a$, we get

$$A = \frac{1}{2a}, B = \frac{1}{2a}$$

$$\therefore \quad \frac{1}{a^2 - x^2} = \frac{1}{2a}\left[\frac{1}{a-x} + \frac{1}{a+x}\right]$$

$$\therefore \quad \int \frac{dx}{a^2 - x^2} = \frac{1}{2a}\int\left(\frac{1}{a-x} + \frac{1}{a+x}\right)dx$$

$$= \frac{1}{2a}\left[-\log(a-x) + \log(a+x)\right]$$

$$= \frac{1}{2a}\log\left(\frac{a+x}{a-x}\right)$$

(iii) $$I = \int \frac{dx}{a^2 + x^2}$$

Put $x = a \tan\theta$

so that $dx = a \sec^2\theta\, d\theta$

$$\therefore \quad I = \int \frac{a\sec^2\theta\, d\theta}{a^2 + a^2\tan^2\theta}$$

$$= \frac{1}{a}\int d\theta$$

$$= \frac{\theta}{a}$$

$$= \frac{1}{a}\tan^{-1}\left(\frac{x}{a}\right)$$

ILLUSTRATIVE EXAMPLES

Example 1. Evaluate $\int \frac{dx}{x^2 - 64}$.

Solution :

$$\int \frac{dx}{x^2 - 64} = \int \frac{dx}{x^2 - (8)^2}$$

$$= \frac{1}{2.8} \log\left(\frac{x-8}{x+8}\right)$$

$$= \frac{1}{16} \log\left(\frac{x-8}{x+8}\right)$$

Example 2. Evaluate $\int \frac{dx}{9 - 4x^2}$.

Solution :

$$\int \frac{dx}{9 - 4x^2} = \frac{1}{4} \int \frac{dx}{\frac{9}{4} - x^2}$$

$$= \frac{1}{4} \int \frac{dx}{\left(\frac{3}{2}\right)^2 - x^2}$$

$$= \frac{1}{4} \cdot \frac{1}{2 \cdot \frac{3}{2}} \log\left(\frac{\frac{3}{2} + x}{\frac{3}{2} - x}\right)$$

$$= \frac{1}{12} \log\left(\frac{3+2x}{3-2x}\right)$$

Example 3. Evaluate $\int \frac{dx}{(2x+1)\sqrt{4x+3}}$.

Solution :

$$I = \frac{dx}{(2x+1)\sqrt{4x+3}}$$

Put $4x + 3 = t^2$

$\therefore \quad 4dx = 2t\ dt$

$\therefore \quad 2dx = t\ dt$

$\therefore \quad dx = \frac{1}{2} t\ dt$

$$\therefore \qquad I = \frac{1}{2}\int \frac{t\,dt}{\left(2\cdot\frac{t^2-3}{4}+1\right)t}$$

$$= \frac{1}{2}\int \frac{dt}{\frac{t^2-1}{2}}$$

$$= \int \frac{dt}{t^2-1}$$

$$= \frac{1}{2}\log\frac{t-1}{t+1}$$

$$= \frac{1}{2}\log\left[\frac{\sqrt{4x+3}-1}{\sqrt{4x+3}+1}\right]$$

Example 4. Evaluate $\int \frac{dx}{7+4x^2}$.

Solution :

$$\int \frac{dx}{7+4x^2} = \frac{1}{4}\int \frac{dx}{\frac{7}{4}+x^2}$$

$$= \frac{1}{4}\int \frac{dx}{\left(\frac{\sqrt{7}}{2}\right)^2 + x^2}$$

$$= \frac{1}{4}\cdot\frac{1}{\frac{\sqrt{7}}{2}}\tan^{-1}\left(\frac{x}{\frac{\sqrt{7}}{2}}\right)$$

$$= \frac{1}{2\sqrt{7}}\tan^{-1}\left(\frac{2x}{\sqrt{7}}\right)$$

EXERCISE 6.1

Integrate :

1. $\frac{1}{9x^2-4}$

2. $\frac{1}{9-4x^2}$

3. $\dfrac{x^2}{x^2 - a^2}$ **4.** $\dfrac{x^2}{4 + x^2}$

5. $\dfrac{2x - 3}{x^2 + 4}$ **6.** $\dfrac{x}{a^4 + x^4}$

7. $\dfrac{x}{x^4 - a^4}$ **8.** $\dfrac{\sec^2 x}{\tan^2 x + 4}$

ANSWERS

EXERCISE 6.1

1. $\dfrac{1}{12}\log\dfrac{3x-2}{3x+2}$ **2.** $\dfrac{1}{12}\log\dfrac{3+2x}{3-2x}$

3. $x + \dfrac{a}{2}\log\dfrac{x-a}{x+a}$ **4.** $x - 2\tan^{-1}\dfrac{x}{2}$

5. $\log\left(x^2 + 4\right) - \dfrac{3}{2}\tan^{-1}\dfrac{x}{2}$ **6.** $\dfrac{1}{2a^2}\tan^{-1}\left(\dfrac{x^2}{a^2}\right)$

7. $\dfrac{1}{4a^2}\log\dfrac{x^2-a^2}{x^2+a^2}$ **8.** $\dfrac{1}{2}\tan^{-1}\left(\dfrac{\tan x}{2}\right)$

6.2 To evaluate the integrals of the form $\int \frac{dx}{ax^2 + bx + c}$ where $ax^2 + bc + c$ is such a quadratic expression which cannot be factorized.

Method. First we transform $ax^2 + bx + c$ in either of the possible forms $X^2 + A^2$, $X^2 - A^2$ and $A^2 - X^2$, where X is one degree expression of x and A is a constant. Then we use the corresponding formula and evaluate the integral.

Example 1. Evaluate $\displaystyle\int \frac{dx}{2x^2 + x - 1}$.

Solution :

$$I = \int \frac{dx}{2x^2 + x - 1}$$

$$= \frac{1}{2}\int \frac{dx}{x^2 + \frac{x}{2} - \frac{1}{2}}$$

$$= \frac{1}{2}\int \frac{dx}{x^2 + \frac{x}{2} + \frac{1}{16} - \frac{1}{16} - \frac{1}{2}}$$

$$= \frac{1}{2}\int \frac{dx}{\left(x + \frac{1}{4}\right)^2 - \frac{9}{16}}$$

$$= \frac{1}{2}\int \frac{dx}{\left(x + \frac{1}{4}\right)^2 - \left(\frac{3}{4}\right)^2}$$

$$= \frac{1}{2}\cdot\frac{1}{2\cdot\frac{3}{4}}\log\left(\frac{x + \frac{1}{4} - \frac{3}{4}}{x + \frac{1}{4} + \frac{3}{4}}\right)$$

$$= \frac{1}{3}\log\left(\frac{x - \frac{1}{2}}{x + 1}\right)$$

$$= \frac{1}{3}\log\left\{\frac{2x - 1}{2(x + 1)}\right\}$$

Example 2. Evaluate $\int \frac{dx}{x^2 - x + 1}$.

Solution :

$$I = \int \frac{dx}{x^2 - x + 1}$$

$$= \int \frac{dx}{x^2 - x + \frac{1}{4} + 1 - \frac{1}{4}}$$

$$= \int \frac{dx}{\left(x - \frac{1}{2}\right)^2 + \left(\frac{\sqrt{3}}{2}\right)^2}$$

$$= \frac{1}{\left(\frac{\sqrt{3}}{2}\right)} \tan^{-1}\left(\frac{x - \frac{1}{2}}{\frac{\sqrt{3}}{2}}\right)$$

$$= \frac{3}{\sqrt{2}} \tan^{-1} \frac{2x-1}{\sqrt{3}}$$

EXERCISE 6.2

Integrate :

1. $\frac{1}{x^2+x+1}$ **2.** $\frac{1}{3-2x-x^2}$

3. $\frac{1}{2x^2+4x+3}$ **4.** $\frac{x}{x^4+2x^2+5}$

5. $\frac{1}{2x^2+x+1}$ **6.** $\frac{1}{x^2+6x+8}$

ANSWERS

EXERCISE 6.2

1. $\frac{2}{\sqrt{3}} \tan^{-1}\left(\frac{2x+1}{\sqrt{3}}\right)$ **2.** $\frac{1}{4} \log\left(\frac{3+x}{1-x}\right)$

3. $\frac{1}{\sqrt{2}} \tan^{-1}\left[\sqrt{2}\,(x+1)\right]$ **4.** $\frac{1}{4} \tan^{-1}\left(\frac{x^2+1}{2}\right)$

5. $\frac{2}{\sqrt{7}} \tan^{-1}\left(\frac{4x+1}{\sqrt{7}}\right)$ **6.** $\frac{1}{2} \log \frac{x+2}{x+4}$

6.3 To evaluate the integrals of the type $\int \frac{px+q}{ax^2+bx+c}\,dx$.

Method. We break $px + q$ into two parts in one of which is there is the differential coefficient of the denominator i.e. $ax^2 + bx + c$ and the other is a constant. Let,

$$px + q = M\frac{d}{dx}\left(ax^2+bx+c\right) + N,$$

where M and N are constants.

$\Rightarrow \quad px + q = M(2ax + b) + N$

Comparing the coefficients of equal powers of x, M and N can be determined.

Now the given integral breaks up into two integrals, one of which is of the form $\int \frac{f'(x)}{f(x)} dx$ which on evaluation gives $\log f(x)$ and other is of the form $\int \frac{1}{x^2 \pm a^2} dx$ or $\int \frac{dx}{a^2 - x^2}$ which can be evaluated by results given in article 6.1.

Hence the given integral can be completely evaluated.

Example 1. Evaluate $\int \frac{3x+1}{2x^2 - 2x + 3} dx.$

Solution :

$$\frac{d}{dx}\left(2x^2 - 2x + 3\right) = 4x - 2$$

Let $\quad 3x + 1 = M(4x - 2) + N$

where M and N are constants.

Comparing the coefficients of equal powers of x, we get

$$3 = 4M \qquad \Rightarrow \qquad M = \frac{3}{4}$$

$$1 = -2M + N$$

$$\Rightarrow \qquad 1 = -2 \cdot \frac{3}{4} + N$$

$$\Rightarrow \qquad 1 = -\frac{3}{2} + N$$

$$\Rightarrow \qquad N = 1 + \frac{3}{2} = \frac{5}{2}$$

$$\therefore \int \frac{3x+1}{2x^2 - 2x + 3} dx$$

$$= \int \frac{\frac{3}{4}(4x-2) + \frac{5}{2}}{2x^2 - 2x + 3} dx$$

$$= \frac{3}{4}\int \frac{4x-2}{2x^2-2x+3}\,dx + \frac{5}{2}\int \frac{dx}{2x^2-2x+3}$$

$$= \frac{3}{4}\log\left(2x^2-2x+3\right) + \frac{5}{4}\int \frac{dx}{x^2-x+\frac{3}{2}}$$

$$= \frac{3}{4}\log\left(2x^2-2x+3\right) + \frac{5}{4}\int \frac{dx}{x^2-x+\frac{1}{4}+\frac{3}{2}-\frac{1}{4}}$$

$$= \frac{3}{4}\log\left(2x^2-2x+3\right) + \frac{5}{4}\int \frac{dx}{\left(x-\frac{1}{2}\right)^2+\left(\frac{\sqrt{5}}{2}\right)^2}$$

$$= \frac{3}{4}\log\left(2x^2-2x+3\right) + \frac{5}{4}\cdot\frac{1}{\frac{\sqrt{5}}{2}}\tan^{-1}\left(\frac{x-\frac{1}{2}}{\frac{\sqrt{5}}{2}}\right)$$

$$= \frac{3}{4}\log\left(2x^2-2x+3\right) + \frac{\sqrt{5}}{2}\tan^{-1}\frac{2x-1}{\sqrt{5}}$$

EXERCISE 6.3

Integrate :

1. $\dfrac{3x+1}{2x^2+x+1}$

2. $\dfrac{x+1}{x^2+4x+5}$

3. $\dfrac{x}{2x^2+2x+3}$

4. $\dfrac{\cos x}{\sin^2 x+4\sin x+5}$

5. $\dfrac{4x+3}{2x^2+2x+5}$

6. $\dfrac{5x-2}{1+2x+3x^2}$

ANSWERS

EXERCISE 6.3

1. $\dfrac{3}{4}\log\left(x^2+2x+1\right)+\dfrac{1}{2\sqrt{7}}\tan^{-1}\left(\dfrac{4x+1}{\sqrt{7}}\right)$

2. $\dfrac{1}{2}\log\left(x^2+4x+5\right)-\tan^{-1}(x+2)$

3. $\frac{1}{2}\log\left(x^2+2x+3\right)-\frac{1}{\sqrt{2}}\tan^{-1}\left(\frac{x+1}{\sqrt{2}}\right)$

4. $\tan^{-1}(\sin x + 2)$

5. $\log\left(2x^2+2x+5\right)+\frac{1}{3}\tan^{-1}\left(\frac{2x+1}{3}\right)$

6. $\frac{5}{6}\log\left(3x^2+2x+1\right)-\frac{11}{3\sqrt{2}}\tan^{-1}\frac{3x+1}{\sqrt{2}}$

6.4 To evaluate the integrals of the type

(i) $\int\frac{dx}{a+b\cos^2 x}$ (ii) $\int\frac{dx}{a+b\sin^2 x}$

(iii) $\int\frac{dx}{a\sin^2 x+b\cos^2 x}$

(iv) $\int\frac{dx}{a\sin^2 x+b\sin x\cos x+c\cos^2 x}$

Method. We divide the numerator and denominator of the integrand by $\cos^2 x$ and then put $\tan x = t$.

Example 1. Evaluate $\int\frac{dx}{1+3\sin^2 x}$.

Solution :

$$I=\int\frac{dx}{1+3\sin^2 x}$$

$$=\int\frac{\sec^2 x}{\sec^2 x+3\tan^2 x}\,dx$$ | Dividing the numerator and denominator of the integrand by $\cos^2 x$.

$$=\int\frac{\sec^2 x\,dx}{1+4\tan^2 x}$$

Now put $\tan x = t$

$\therefore$ $\sec^2 x\,dx = dt$

$\therefore$ $$I=\int\frac{dt}{1+4t^2}$$

$$= \frac{1}{4}\int \frac{dt}{\frac{1}{4} + t^2}$$

$$= \frac{1}{4}\int \frac{dt}{\left(\frac{1}{2}\right)^2 + t^2}$$

$$= \frac{1}{4} \cdot \frac{1}{\frac{1}{2}} \tan^{-1}\left(\frac{t}{\frac{1}{2}}\right)$$

$$= \frac{1}{2}\tan^{-1}(2t)$$

$$= \frac{1}{2}\tan^{-1}(2\tan x)\cdot$$

Example 2. Evaluate $\int \frac{dx}{\sin^2 x + 4\cos^2 x}$.

Solution :

$$I = \int \frac{dx}{\sin^2 x + 4\cos^2 x}$$

$$= \int \frac{\sec^2 x}{\tan^2 x + 4}\,dx$$

| Dividing the numerator and denominator of integrand by $\cos^2 x$.

Put $\tan x = t$

$\therefore \quad \sec^2 x\, dx = dt$

$$\therefore \quad I = \int \frac{dt}{t^2 + 4}$$

$$= \int \frac{dt}{t^2 + 2^2}$$

$$= \frac{1}{2} \cdot \tan^{-1}\left(\frac{t}{2}\right)$$

$$= \frac{1}{2} \cdot \tan^{-1}\left(\frac{\tan x}{2}\right)$$

EXERCISE 6.4

Integrate :

1. $\dfrac{1}{1+\cos^2 x}$ **2.** $\dfrac{1}{a^2-b^2\cos^2 x}, a > b$

3. $\dfrac{1}{(2\sin x+\cos x)^2}$ **4.** $\dfrac{1}{(a\sin x+b\cos x)^2}$

5. $\dfrac{1}{a^2\cos^2 x+b^2\sin^2 x}$ **6.** $\dfrac{\cos x}{\cos 3x}$

7. $\dfrac{\sin x}{\sin 3x}$

ANSWERS

EXERCISE 6.4

1. $\dfrac{1}{\sqrt{2}}\tan^{-1}\left(\dfrac{\tan x}{\sqrt{2}}\right)$

2. $\dfrac{1}{a\sqrt{a^2-b^2}}\tan^{-1}\left(\dfrac{a\tan x}{\sqrt{a^2-b^2}}\right)$

3. $\dfrac{1}{2(2\tan x+1)}$ **4.** $\dfrac{-1}{a(\tan x+b)}$

5. $\dfrac{1}{ab}\tan^{-1}\left(\dfrac{b\tan x}{a}\right)$ **6.** $\dfrac{1}{\sqrt{3}}\log\left(\dfrac{\sqrt{3}+\tan x}{\sqrt{3}-\tan x}\right)$

7. $\dfrac{1}{2\sqrt{3}}\log\left(\dfrac{\sqrt{3}+\tan x}{\sqrt{3}-\tan x}\right)$

6.5 To evaluate integrals of the type $\displaystyle\int\frac{1}{a+b\cos x}\,dx$ and $\displaystyle\int\frac{1}{a+b\sin x}\,dx$

(i) $$I = \frac{1}{a+b\cos x}\,dx$$

$$= \int\frac{dx}{a\left(\cos^2\dfrac{x}{2}+\sin^2\dfrac{x}{2}\right)+b\left(\cos^2\dfrac{x}{2}-\sin^2\dfrac{x}{2}\right)}$$

$$= \int \frac{dx}{(a+b)\cos^2\frac{x}{2} + (a-b)\sin^2\frac{x}{2}}$$

$$= \int \frac{dx}{A\cos^2\frac{x}{2} + B\sin^2\frac{x}{2}}$$

where $a + b = A$

and $a - b = B$

$$\therefore \quad I = \int \frac{\sec^2\frac{x}{2}\,dx}{A + B\tan^2\frac{x}{2}}$$

$$= \frac{1}{B}\int \frac{\sec^2\frac{x}{2}\,dx}{\frac{A}{B} + \tan^2\frac{x}{2}}$$

Put $\tan\frac{x}{2} = t$

$$\therefore \quad \frac{1}{2}\sec^2\frac{x}{2}\,dx = dt$$

$$\therefore \quad \sec^2\frac{x}{2}\,dx = 2dt$$

$$\therefore \quad I = \frac{2}{B}\int \frac{dt}{\frac{A}{B} + t^2}$$

$$= \frac{2}{B}\int \frac{dt}{\left(\sqrt{\frac{A}{B}}\right) + t^2}$$

$$= \frac{2}{B}\cdot\frac{1}{\sqrt{\frac{A}{B}}}\tan^{-1}\left(\frac{t}{\sqrt{\frac{A}{B}}}\right)$$

$$= \frac{2}{\sqrt{AB}}\tan^{-1}\left(t\sqrt{\frac{B}{A}}\right)$$

$$= \frac{2}{\sqrt{AB}}\tan^{-1}\left(\sqrt{\frac{B}{A}}\cdot\tan\frac{x}{2}\right)$$

$$= \frac{2}{\sqrt{a^2 - b^2}}\tan^{-1}\left(\sqrt{\frac{a-b}{a+b}}\tan\frac{x}{2}\right)$$

(ii) $$I = \int \frac{1}{a + b\sin x}\,dx$$

$$= \int \frac{dx}{a\left(\cos^2\frac{x}{2} + \sin^2\frac{x}{2}\right) + 2b\sin\frac{x}{2}\cos\frac{x}{2}}$$

$$= \int \frac{\sec^2\frac{x}{2}\,dx}{a\left(1 + \tan^2\frac{x}{2}\right) + 2b\tan\frac{x}{2}}$$

Put $\tan\frac{x}{2} = t$

$\therefore \quad \frac{1}{2}\sec^2\frac{x}{2}\,dx = dt$

$\therefore \quad \sec^2\frac{x}{2}\,dx = 2dt$

$$\therefore \quad I = \int \frac{2dt}{a\left(1+t^2\right) + 2bt}$$

$$= \frac{2}{a}\int \frac{dt}{1 + t^2 + \frac{2b}{a}dt}$$

$$= \frac{2}{a}\int \frac{dt}{1 + t^2 + \frac{2b}{a}t + \frac{b^2}{a^2} - \frac{b^2}{a^2}}$$

$$= \frac{2}{a}\int \frac{dt}{1 - \frac{b^2}{a^2} + \left(t + \frac{b}{a}\right)^2}$$

$$= \frac{2}{a}\int \frac{dt}{\left(\frac{\sqrt{a^2 - b^2}}{a}\right)^2 + \left(t + \frac{b}{a}\right)^2}$$

$$= \frac{2}{a}\cdot\frac{1}{\frac{\sqrt{a^2 - b^2}}{a}}\tan^{-1}\left(\frac{t + \frac{b}{a}}{\frac{\sqrt{a^2 - b^2}}{a}}\right) \quad \text{if } a > b$$

$$= \frac{2}{\sqrt{a^2 - b^2}} \tan^{-1}\left(\frac{at + b}{\sqrt{a^2 - b^2}}\right) \text{if } a > b$$

$$= \frac{2}{\sqrt{a^2 - b^2}} \tan^{-1}\left(\frac{a \tan \frac{x}{2} + b}{\sqrt{a^2 - b^2}}\right)$$

Example 1. Evaluate $\int \frac{dx}{5 + 4 \cos x}$.

Solution :

$$I = \int \frac{dx}{5 + 4 \cos x}$$

$$= \int \frac{dx}{5\left(\cos^2 \frac{x}{2} + \sin^2 \frac{x}{2}\right) + 4\left(\cos^2 \frac{x}{2} - \sin^2 \frac{x}{2}\right)}$$

$$= \int \frac{dx}{9 \cos^2 \frac{x}{2} + \sin^2 \frac{x}{2}}$$

$$= \int \frac{\sec^2 \frac{x}{2}\, dx}{9 + \tan^2 \frac{x}{2}}$$

Put $\tan \frac{x}{2} = t$

$\therefore \quad \frac{1}{2} \sec^2 \frac{x}{2}\, dx = dt$

$\therefore \quad \sec^2 \frac{x}{2}\, dx = 2dt$

$$\therefore \quad I = \int \frac{2dt}{9 + t^2}$$

$$= 2 \int \frac{dt}{3^2 + t^2}$$

$$= \frac{2}{3} \tan^{-1}\left(\frac{t}{3}\right)$$

$$= \frac{2}{3}\tan^{-1}\left(\frac{\tan\frac{x}{2}}{3}\right)$$

Example 2. Evaluate $\int \frac{dx}{5+4\sin x}$.

Solution :

$$I = \int \frac{dx}{5+4\sin x}$$

$$= \int \frac{dx}{5\left(\cos^2\frac{x}{2}+\sin^2\frac{x}{2}\right)+8\sin\frac{x}{2}\cos\frac{x}{2}}$$

$$= \int \frac{\sec^2\frac{x}{2}\,dx}{5\left(1+\tan^2\frac{x}{2}\right)+8\tan\frac{x}{2}}$$

Put $\tan\frac{x}{2} = t$

$\therefore \quad \frac{1}{2}\sec^2\frac{x}{2}\,dx = dt$

$\therefore \quad \sec^2\frac{x}{2}\,dx = 2dt$

$$\therefore \quad I = 2\int \frac{dt}{5\left(1+t^2\right)+8t}$$

$$= \frac{2}{5}\int \frac{dt}{t^2+\frac{8}{5}t+1}$$

$$= \frac{2}{5}\int \frac{dt}{t^2+\frac{8}{5}t+\frac{16}{25}+1-\frac{16}{25}}$$

$$= \frac{2}{5}\int \frac{dt}{\left(t+\frac{4}{5}\right)^2+\left(\frac{3}{5}\right)^2}$$

$$= \frac{2}{5} \cdot \frac{1}{\frac{3}{5}} \tan^{-1}\left(\frac{t + \frac{4}{5}}{\frac{3}{5}}\right)$$

$$= \frac{2}{3} \tan^{-1}\left(\frac{5t + 4}{3}\right)$$

$$= \frac{2}{3} \tan^{-1}\left(\frac{5 \tan \frac{x}{2} + 4}{3}\right)$$

EXERCISE 6.5

Integrate :

1. $\dfrac{1}{4 + 5 \sin x}$

2. $\dfrac{1}{2 + \sin 2x}$

3. $\dfrac{1}{4 + 5 \cos x}$

4. $\dfrac{1}{2 + \cos x}$

5. $\dfrac{1}{1 + 2 \cos x}$

ANSWERS

EXERCISE 6.5

1. $\dfrac{1}{3} \log\left(\dfrac{2 \tan \frac{x}{2} + 1}{2 \tan \frac{x}{2} + 4}\right)$

2. $\dfrac{1}{\sqrt{3}} \tan^{-1}\left(\dfrac{1 + 2 \tan x}{\sqrt{3}}\right)$

3. $\dfrac{1}{3} \log\left(\dfrac{3 + \tan \frac{x}{2}}{3 - \tan \frac{x}{2}}\right)$

4. $\dfrac{2}{\sqrt{3}} \tan^{-1}\left(\dfrac{1}{\sqrt{3}} \tan \dfrac{x}{2}\right)$

5. $\dfrac{1}{\sqrt{3}} \log\left(\dfrac{\sqrt{3} + \tan \frac{x}{2}}{\sqrt{3} - \tan \frac{x}{2}}\right)$

6.6 To evaluate the integrals of the type $\int \frac{x^2+1}{x^4+kx^2+1}\,dx$, where k is a constant.

Method. Divide Numerator & Denominator of the integrand by x^2 and then put $x + \frac{1}{x} = t$ or $x - \frac{1}{x} = t$.

Example 1. Evaluate $\int \frac{x^2+1}{x^4+1}\,dx$.

Solution :

$$I = \int \frac{x^2+1}{x^4+1}\,dx$$

$$= \int \frac{1+\frac{1}{x^2}}{x^2+\frac{1}{x^2}}\,dx$$

$$= \int \frac{1+\frac{1}{x^2}}{\left(x^2+\frac{1}{x^2}-2\right)+2}\,dx$$

$$= \int \frac{1+\frac{1}{x^2}}{\left(x-\frac{1}{x^2}\right)^2+2}\,dx$$

Put $x - \frac{1}{x} = t$

$\therefore \left(1+\frac{1}{x^2}\right)dx = dt$

So, $$I = \int \frac{dt}{t^2+2}$$

$$= \frac{1}{\sqrt{2}} \tan^{-1} \frac{t}{\sqrt{2}}$$

$$= \frac{1}{\sqrt{2}} \tan^{-1}\left(\frac{x - \frac{1}{x}}{\sqrt{2}}\right)$$

$$= \frac{1}{\sqrt{2}} \tan^{-1}\left(\frac{x^2 - 1}{x\sqrt{2}}\right)$$

Example 2. Evaluate $\int \frac{dx}{x^4 + 1}$.

Solution :

$$I = \int \frac{dx}{x^4 + 1}$$

$$= \frac{1}{2} \int \frac{(x^2 + 1) - (x^2 - 1)}{x^4 + 1}\, dx$$

$$= \frac{1}{2} \int \frac{x^2 + 1}{x^4 + 1}\, dx - \frac{1}{2} \int \frac{x^2 - 1}{x^4 + 1}\, dx$$

$$= \frac{1}{2}(I_1 - I_2)$$

where $I_1 = \frac{1}{\sqrt{2}} \tan^{-1} \frac{x^2 - 1}{\sqrt{2}x}$ (by Example 1)

and $I_2 = \int \frac{x^2 - 1}{x^4 + 1}\, dx$

$$= \int \frac{1 - \frac{1}{x^2}}{x^2 + \frac{1}{x^2}}\, dx$$

$$= \int \frac{1 - \frac{1}{x^2}}{\left(x^2 + \frac{1}{x^2} + 2\right) - 2}\, dx$$

$$= \int \frac{1 - \frac{1}{x^2}}{\left(x + \frac{1}{x}\right)^2 - 2}\, dx$$

$$\text{Put} \qquad x + \frac{1}{x} = t$$

$$\therefore \quad \left(1 - \frac{1}{x^2}\right) dx = dt$$

$$\therefore \qquad I_2 = \int \frac{dt}{t^2 - 2}$$

$$= \frac{1}{2\sqrt{2}} \log\left(\frac{t - \sqrt{2}}{t + \sqrt{2}}\right)$$

$$= \frac{1}{2\sqrt{2}} \log\left(\frac{x + \frac{1}{x} - \sqrt{2}}{x + \frac{1}{x} + \sqrt{2}}\right)$$

$$= \frac{1}{2\sqrt{2}} \log\left(\frac{x^2 - \sqrt{2}\,x + 1}{x^2 + \sqrt{2}\,x + 1}\right)$$

$$\therefore \qquad I = \frac{1}{2}\left[\frac{1}{\sqrt{2}} \tan^{-1} \frac{x^2 - 1}{\sqrt{2}\,x} - \frac{1}{2\sqrt{2}} \log\left(\frac{x^2 - \sqrt{2}\,x + 1}{x^2 + \sqrt{2}\,x + 1}\right)\right]$$

Example 3. Evaluate $\int_0^{\pi/4} \sqrt{\tan \theta}\, d\theta$.

Solution :

$$I = \int_0^{\pi/4} \sqrt{\tan \theta}\, d\theta$$

$$\text{Put} \qquad \tan \theta = t^2$$

$$\therefore \quad \sec^2 \theta\, d\theta = 2t\, dt$$

$$\therefore \qquad d\theta = \frac{2t\, dt}{\sec^2 \theta}$$

$$= \frac{2t\, dt}{1 + \tan^2 \theta}$$

$$= \frac{2t\,dt}{1+t^4}$$

When $\theta = 0,\ t = 0$

When $\theta = \frac{\pi}{4},\ t = 1$

$$\therefore \quad I = \int_0^1 \frac{t \cdot 2t\,dt}{1+t^4}$$

$$= 2\int_0^1 \frac{t^2 dt}{1+t^4}$$

$$= 2\int_0^1 \frac{dt}{t^2+\frac{1}{t^2}}$$

$$= \frac{2}{2}\int_0^1 \frac{\left(1+\frac{1}{t^2}\right)+\left(1-\frac{1}{t^2}\right)}{t^2+\frac{1}{t^2}}\,dt$$

$$= \int_0^1 \frac{1+\frac{1}{t^2}}{\left(t-\frac{1}{t}\right)^2+2}\,dt + \int_0^1 \frac{1-\frac{1}{t^2}}{\left(t+\frac{1}{t}\right)^2-2}\,dt$$

$$= \int_0^1 \frac{d\left(t-\frac{1}{t}\right)}{\left(t-\frac{1}{t}\right)^2+2} + \int_0^1 \frac{d\left(t+\frac{1}{t}\right)}{\left(t+\frac{1}{t}\right)^2-2}$$

$$= \left[\frac{1}{\sqrt{2}}\tan^{-1}\left(\frac{t-\frac{1}{t}}{\sqrt{2}}\right)\right]_0^1 + \frac{1}{2\sqrt{2}}\left[\log\left(\frac{t+\frac{1}{t}\sqrt{2}}{t+\frac{1}{t}+\sqrt{2}}\right)\right]_0^1$$

$$= \frac{1}{2}\left[\tan^{-1}(0)-\tan^{-1}(-\infty)\right]$$

$$+ \frac{1}{2\sqrt{2}}\left[\log\left(\frac{t^2-\sqrt{2}\,t+1}{t^2+\sqrt{2}\,t+1}\right)\right]_0^1$$

$$= \frac{1}{2} \cdot \frac{\pi}{2} + \frac{1}{2\sqrt{2}} \left[\log \left(\frac{2-\sqrt{2}}{2+\sqrt{2}} \right) - \log 1 \right]$$

$$= \frac{\pi}{4} + \frac{1}{2\sqrt{2}} \log \left(\frac{\sqrt{2}-1}{\sqrt{2}+1} \right)$$

EXERCISE 6.6

Integrate :

1. $\dfrac{x^2 - 1}{x^4 + 1}$

2. $\dfrac{x^2 + 1}{x^4 - x^2 + 1}$

3. $\dfrac{x^2}{x^4 + 1}$

4. $\dfrac{x^2}{x^4 + x^2 + 1}$

5. $\dfrac{1}{x^4 + x^2 + 1}$

6. $\dfrac{x}{x^4 + x^2 + 1}$

7. $\displaystyle\int_0^{\pi/4} \sqrt{\cot \theta}\, d\theta$

ANSWERS

EXERCISE 6.6

1. $\dfrac{1}{\sqrt{2}} \log \left(\dfrac{x^2 - x\sqrt{2} + 1}{x^2 + x\sqrt{2} + 1} \right)$

2. $\tan^{-1} \left(\dfrac{x^2 - 1}{x} \right)$

3. $\dfrac{1}{2\sqrt{2}} \tan^{-1} \dfrac{x^2 - 1}{x\sqrt{2}} - \dfrac{4}{\sqrt{2}} \log \dfrac{x^2 - x\sqrt{2} + 1}{x^2 + x\sqrt{2} + 1}$

4. $\dfrac{1}{2\sqrt{3}} \tan^{-1} \dfrac{x^2 - 1}{x\sqrt{3}} + \log \dfrac{x^2 - x + 1}{x^2 + x + 1}$

5. $\dfrac{1}{2\sqrt{3}} \tan^{-1} \dfrac{x^2 - 1}{x\sqrt{3}} - \dfrac{1}{4} \log \dfrac{x^2 - x + 1}{x^2 + x + 1}$

6. $\frac{1}{\sqrt{3}} \tan^{-1} \frac{2x^2+1}{\sqrt{3}}$

7. $\frac{\pi}{2\sqrt{2}} - \frac{1}{2\sqrt{2}} \log \frac{\sqrt{2}-1}{\sqrt{2}+1}$

6.7 Problems based on a special method.

Example 1. Evaluate $\int \frac{\cos x \, dx}{a \cos x + b \sin x}$.

Solution :

Let $\cos x = A\,(a \cos x + b \sin x) + B \frac{d}{dx}(a \cos x + b \sin x)$

$\therefore$ $\cos x = A\,(a \cos x + b \sin x) + B\,(-a \sin x + b \cos x)$

$\Rightarrow$ $\cos x = (Aa + Bb) \cos x + (Ab - Ba) \sin x$

Comparing the coefficients of $\sin x$ and $\cos x$ on both sides, we get

$$1 = Aa + Bb, \qquad 0 = Ab - Ba$$

Solving these we get

$$A = \frac{a}{a^2+b^2}, \qquad B = \frac{b}{a^2+b^2}$$

Now,

$$\int \frac{\cos x \, dx}{a \cos x + b \sin x}$$

$$= \int \frac{A\left(a \cos x + b \sin x\right) + \left(-a \sin x + b \cos x\right)}{a \cos x + b \sin x} dx$$

$$= A \int dx + B \int \frac{-a \sin x + b \cos x}{a \cos x + b \sin x} dx$$

$$= A\,x + B \log\,(a \cos x + b \sin x)$$

$$= \frac{ax}{a^2+b^2} + \frac{b \log\left(a \cos x + b \sin x\right)}{a^2+b^2}$$

$$= \frac{ax + b \log\left(a \cos x + b \sin x\right)}{a^2+b^2}$$

EXERCISE 6.7

Integrate :

1. $\dfrac{\sin x}{\sqrt{3}\sin x + \cos x}$

2. $\dfrac{\sin x}{\sin x - \cos x}$

3. $\dfrac{1}{4 + 3\tan x}$

4. $\dfrac{1}{a + b\tan x}$

5. $\dfrac{2\sin x + 3\cos x}{3\sin x + 4\cos x}$

ANSWERS

EXERCISE 6.7

1. $\dfrac{\sqrt{3}}{4}x - \dfrac{1}{4}\log\left(\sqrt{3}\sin x + \cos x\right)$

2. $\dfrac{x}{2} + \dfrac{1}{2}\log(\sin x - \cos x)$

3. $\dfrac{4x}{25} + \dfrac{3}{25}\log(4\cos x + 3\sin x)$

4. $\dfrac{ax}{a^2 + b^2} + \dfrac{b}{a^2 + b^2}\log(a\cos x + b\sin x)$

5. $\dfrac{18}{25} + \dfrac{1}{25}(3\sin x + 4\cos x)$

7

Integration of Irrational Functions

7.1 To evaluate the integrals of the type $\int \frac{dx}{\sqrt{x^2+a^2}}$, $\int \frac{dx}{\sqrt{x^2-a^2}}$, $\int \frac{dx}{\sqrt{a^2-x^2}}$

(i) $$I = \int \frac{dx}{\sqrt{x^2+a^2}} \qquad \text{Put} \quad x = a\tan\theta$$

$$\therefore \quad dx = a\sec^2\theta\, d\theta$$

$$\therefore \quad I = \int \frac{a\sec^2\theta\, d\theta}{\sqrt{a^2\tan^2\theta + a^2}}$$

$$= \int \sec\theta\, d\theta$$

$$= \log(\sec\theta + \tan\theta)$$

$$= \log\left\{\sqrt{1+\tan^2\theta} + \tan\theta\right\}$$

$$= \log\left\{\sqrt{1+\frac{x^2}{a^2}} + \frac{x}{a}\right\}$$

$$= \log\left\{x + \sqrt{x^2+a^2}\right\} - \log a$$

$$= \log\left\{x + \sqrt{x^2+a^2}\right\}$$ leaving $-\log a$, it being a constant.

(ii) $$I = \int \frac{dx}{\sqrt{x^2-a^2}} \qquad \text{Put} \quad x = a\sec\theta$$

$$\therefore \quad dx = a\sec\theta\tan\theta\, d\theta$$

$$\therefore \quad I = \int \frac{a\sec\theta\tan\theta}{\sqrt{a^2\sec^2\theta - a^2}}\, d\theta$$

$$= \int \sec\theta\, d\theta$$

$$= \log(\sec\theta + \tan\theta)$$

$$= \log\left(\sec\theta + \sqrt{\sec^2\theta - 1}\right)$$

$$= \log\left(\frac{x}{a} + \sqrt{\frac{x^2}{a^2} - 1}\right)$$

$$= \log\left(x + \sqrt{x^2 - a^2}\right) - \log a$$

$$= \log\left(x + \sqrt{x^2 - a^2}\right)$$; leaving $-\log a$, it being a constant.

(iii) $I = \int \frac{dx}{\sqrt{a^2 - x^2}}$ Put $x = a\sin\theta$

$\therefore$ $dx = a\cos\theta\, d\theta$

$\therefore$ $$I = \frac{a\cos\theta\, d\theta}{\sqrt{a^2 - a^2\sin^2\theta}}$$

$$= \int d\theta = \theta = \sin^{-1}\frac{x}{a}$$

SUITABLE SUBSTITUTIONS

7.2

Form of Expression	**Suitable Substitution**
1. $a^2 - x^2$	$x = a\sin\theta$
2. $x^2 - a^2$	$x = a\sec\theta$
3. $\dfrac{a^2 - x^2}{a^2 + x^2}$	$x^2 = a^2\cos 2\theta$
4. $\dfrac{a - x}{a + x}$	$x = a\cos 2\theta$
5. $\sqrt{2ax - x^2}$	$x = a(1 - \cos\theta)$

Example 1. Evaluate $\int \frac{dx}{\sqrt{9 + 4x^2}}$.

Solution :

$$I = \int \frac{dx}{\sqrt{9 + 4x^2}} = \frac{1}{2}\int \frac{dx}{\sqrt{\frac{9}{4} + x^2}}$$

$$= \frac{1}{2}\int \frac{dx}{\sqrt{x^2 + \left(\frac{3}{2}\right)^2}}$$

$$= \frac{1}{2} . \log\left\{ x + \sqrt{x^2 + \left(\frac{3}{2}\right)^2} \right\}$$

$$= \frac{1}{2} \log\left\{ x + \sqrt{x^2 + \frac{9}{4}} \right\}$$

Example 2. Evaluate $\int \frac{x\,dx}{\sqrt{4 - x^4}}$.

Solution :

$$I = \int \frac{x\,dx}{\sqrt{4 - x^4}} \qquad \text{Put} \quad x^2 = t$$

$$\therefore \quad 2x\,dx = dt$$

$$\therefore \quad x\,dx = \frac{dt}{2}$$

$$\therefore \qquad I = \frac{1}{2}\int \frac{dt}{\sqrt{4 - t^2}}$$

$$= \frac{1}{2}\int \frac{dt}{\sqrt{2^2 - t^2}}$$

$$= \frac{1}{2}\sin^{-1}\frac{t}{2} = \frac{1}{2}\sin^{-1}\left(\frac{x^2}{2}\right)$$

Example 3. Evaluate $\int \sqrt{\frac{a + x}{a - x}}\, dx$.

Solution :

$$I = \int \sqrt{\frac{a + x}{a - x}}\, dx \qquad \text{Put} \quad x = a \cos\theta$$

$$\therefore \quad dx = -\, a \sin\theta\, d\theta$$

$$\therefore \qquad I = \int \sqrt{\frac{a + a\cos\theta}{a - a\cos\theta}}\,(-\,a\sin\theta)\,d\theta$$

$$= -a\int \sqrt{\frac{1 + \cos\theta}{1 - \cos\theta}}\,\sin\theta\, d\theta$$

$$= -a \int \sqrt{\frac{2\cos^2 \frac{\theta}{2}}{2\sin^2 \frac{\theta}{2}}} \cdot 2\sin\frac{\theta}{2}\cos\frac{\theta}{2}\,d\theta$$

$$= -2a \int \cos^2 \frac{\theta}{2}\,d\theta$$

$$= -a \int (1+\cos\theta)\,d\theta$$

$$= -a(\theta + \sin\theta)$$

$$= -a\left[\cos^{-1}\left(\frac{x}{a}\right) + \frac{\sqrt{a^2-x^2}}{a}\right] \quad \Big| \because \frac{x}{a} = \cos\theta$$

$$= -\left[a\cos^{-1}\frac{x}{a} + \sqrt{a^2-x^2}\right] \quad \Big| \because \sin\theta = \sqrt{1-\cos^2\theta} = \sqrt{1-\frac{x^2}{a^2}} = \sqrt{\frac{a^2-x^2}{a}}$$

Example 4. Evaluate $\int \frac{dx}{\sqrt{1-e^{2x}}}$.

Solution :

$$I = \int \frac{dx}{\sqrt{1-e^{2x}}}$$

$$= \int \frac{e^{-x}\,dx}{\sqrt{e^{-2x}-1}} \qquad \text{Put } e^{-x} = t$$

$$\therefore \quad -e^{-x}\,dx = dt$$

$$\therefore \quad I = -\int \frac{dt}{\sqrt{t^2-1}}$$

$$= -\log\left[t + \sqrt{t^2-1}\right]$$

$$= -\log\left[e^{-x} + \sqrt{e^{-2x}+1}\right]$$

EXERCISE 7.1

Integrate :

1. $\dfrac{1}{\sqrt{4-9x^2}}$

2. $\dfrac{1}{\sqrt{4x^2-1}}$

3. $\dfrac{3x^2}{\sqrt{9-16x^6}}$

4. $\dfrac{x+1}{\sqrt{x^2+1}}$

5. $\sqrt{\dfrac{1-x}{1+x}}$

6. $\dfrac{\cos x}{\sqrt{\dfrac{1}{4}-\cos^2 x}}$

7. $\dfrac{\sec^2 x}{\sqrt{\tan^2 x+4}}$

8. $\dfrac{\sin x}{\sqrt{4+\cos^2 x}}$

9. $\dfrac{\sin x}{\sqrt{4\cos^2 x-1}}$

10. $\dfrac{e^x}{\sqrt{4+e^{2x}}}$

11. $\dfrac{1}{\sqrt{1-e^x}}$

12. $\dfrac{2e^x}{\sqrt{4-e^{2x}}}$

ANSWERS

EXERCISE 7.1

1. $\dfrac{1}{3}\sin^{-1}\left(\dfrac{3x}{2}\right)$

2. $\dfrac{1}{2}\log\left[x+\sqrt{x^2-\dfrac{1}{4}}\right]$

3. $\dfrac{1}{4}\ \sin^{-1}\left(\dfrac{4x^3}{3}\right)$

4. $\sqrt{x^2-1}\ +\log\left[x+\sqrt{x^2+1}\right]$

5. $\sin^{-1} x+\sqrt{1-x^2}$

6. $\log\left(\sin x+\sqrt{\sin^2 x-\dfrac{3}{4}}\right)$

7. $\log\left(\tan x+\sqrt{\tan^2 x+4}\right)$

8. $-\log\left[\cos x+\sqrt{4+\cos^2 x}\right]$

9. $-\frac{1}{2}\log\left[2\cos x+\sqrt{4\cos^2 x-1}\right]$

10. $\log\left[e^x+\sqrt{4+e^{2x}}\right]$

11. $2\log\left[e^{-x/2}+\sqrt{e^{-x}-1}\right]$

12. $2\sin^{-1}\left(\frac{e^x}{2}\right)$

7.2 To evaluate the integrals of the form $\int\frac{dx}{\sqrt{ax^2+bx+c}}$.

Method. We express $\sqrt{ax^2+bx+c}$ in the form $\sqrt{X^2+A^2}$ or $\sqrt{X^2-A^2}$ or $\sqrt{A^2-X^2}$ where X is a linear function of x and A is a constant. Then using corresponding formulae derived in article 7.1, we evaluate the given integral.

Example 1. Evaluate $\int\frac{dx}{\sqrt{1-4x-2x^2}}$.

Solution :

$$I=\int\frac{dx}{\sqrt{1-4x-2x^2}}$$

$$=\int\frac{dx}{\sqrt{2}\sqrt{\frac{1}{2}-2x-x^2}}$$

$$=\frac{1}{\sqrt{2}}\int\frac{dx}{\sqrt{\frac{1}{2}-(x^2+2x)}}$$

$$=\frac{1}{\sqrt{2}}\int\frac{dx}{\sqrt{1+\frac{1}{2}-(x^2+2x+1)}}$$

$$=\frac{1}{\sqrt{2}}\int\frac{dx}{\sqrt{\left(\sqrt{\frac{3}{2}}\right)^2-(x+1)^2}}$$

Put $x+1=t$

$\therefore \quad dx=dt$

$$\therefore \qquad I = \frac{1}{\sqrt{2}} \int \frac{dt}{\sqrt{\left(\sqrt{\frac{3}{2}}\right)^2 - t^2}}$$

$$= \frac{1}{\sqrt{2}} \cdot \sin^{-1}\left(\frac{t}{\sqrt{\frac{3}{2}}}\right)$$

$$= \frac{1}{\sqrt{2}} \sin^{-1}\left\{(x+1)\sqrt{\frac{2}{3}}\right\}$$

7.3 To evaluate the integrals of the form $\int \frac{px+q}{\sqrt{ax^2+bx+c}}\, dx.$

Method. We write,

$$px + q = M \frac{d}{dx}\left(ax^2 + bx + c\right) + N$$

where M and N are constants. Then equating the coefficients of the equal powers of x on both sides we find M and N. Now the given integral breaks up into two parts :

First integral $= \int \frac{f'(x)}{\sqrt{f(x)}}\, dx = 2\sqrt{f(x)}$ and second integral assumes the form $\int \frac{dx}{\sqrt{x^2 \pm A^2}}$ or $\int \frac{dx}{\sqrt{A^2 - x^2}}$ which can be evaluated using results derived in article 7.1.

Example 1. Evaluate $\int \frac{x+8}{\sqrt{x^2+2x+5}}\, dx$.

Solution :

Here, $x + 8 = M \frac{d}{dx}\left(x^2 + 2x + 5\right) + N$

where M and N are constants.

$$\therefore \qquad x + 8 = M(2x + 2) + N$$

Equating the coefficients of equal powers of x on both sides, we get

$$1 = 2M$$

and $8 = 2M + N$

$\Rightarrow$ $M = \frac{1}{2}$ and $N = 8 - 2 \cdot \frac{1}{2} = 8 - 1 = 7$

$$\therefore \quad I = \int \frac{x+8}{\sqrt{x^2+2x+5}}\, dx$$

$$= \int \frac{\frac{1}{2}(2x+2)+7}{\sqrt{x^2+2x+5}}\, dx$$

$$= \frac{1}{2}\int \frac{2x+2}{\sqrt{x^2+2x+5}}\, dx + 7\int \frac{dx}{\sqrt{x^2+2x+5}}$$

$$= I_1 + I_2$$

Now, $I_1 = \frac{1}{2}\int \frac{2x+2}{\sqrt{x^2+2x+5}}$ Put $x^2 + 2x + 5 = t$

$\therefore$ $(2x + 2)\, dx = dt$

$$\therefore \quad I_1 = \frac{1}{2}\int \frac{dt}{\sqrt{t}}$$

$$= \frac{1}{2} \frac{t^{1/2}}{\frac{1}{2}}$$

$$= \sqrt{t}$$

$$= \sqrt{x^2+2x+5}$$

and

$$I_2 = 7\int \frac{dx}{\sqrt{x^2+2x+5}}$$

$$= 7\int \frac{dx}{\sqrt{(x+1)^2+2^2}}$$

$$= 7\log\left\{(x+1)+\sqrt{(x+1)^2+2^2}\right\}$$

$$= 7\log\left\{(x+1)+\sqrt{x^2+2x+5}\right\}$$

$$\therefore \quad \mathrm{I} = \sqrt{x^2+2x+5} + 7\left[\log\left\{(x+1)+\sqrt{x^2+2x+5}\right\}\right]$$

EXERCISE 7.2

Integrate :

1. $\dfrac{1}{\sqrt{x^2-4x+5}}$

2. $\dfrac{1}{\sqrt{x^2+2x}}$

3. $\dfrac{1}{\sqrt{x^2-2x+5}}$

4. $\dfrac{1}{\sqrt{2x^2-x+2}}$

5. $\dfrac{1}{\sqrt{4+8x-5x^2}}$

6. $\dfrac{x+1}{\sqrt{2x^2+x-3}}$

7. $\dfrac{2x+5}{\sqrt{x^2+2x+5}}$

8. $\dfrac{3x+1}{\sqrt{5-2x-x^2}}$

9. $\dfrac{2x}{\sqrt{x^2-x-1}}$

10. $\dfrac{4x+5}{\sqrt{x^2+4x+9}}$

ANSWERS

EXERCISE 7.2

1. $\log\left[x-2+\sqrt{x^2-4x+5}\right]$

2. $\log\left[x+1+\sqrt{x^2+2x}\right]$

3. $\log\left[x-1+\sqrt{x^2-2x+5}\right]$

4. $\dfrac{1}{\sqrt{2}}\log\left[x-\dfrac{1}{4}+\sqrt{\left(x-\dfrac{1}{4}\right)^2+\left(\dfrac{\sqrt{15}}{4}\right)^2}\right]$

5. $\dfrac{1}{\sqrt{5}}\sin^{-1}\left(\dfrac{5x-4}{6}\right)$

6. $\dfrac{1}{2}\sqrt{2x^2+x-3}+\dfrac{3}{4\sqrt{2}}\log\left[4x+1+\sqrt{2x^2+x-3}\right]$

7. $2\sqrt{x^2+2x+5}+3\log\left\{x+1+\sqrt{x^2+2x+5}\right\}$

8. $-3\sqrt{5-2x-x^2}-2\ \sin^{-1}\ \dfrac{x-1}{6}$

9. $2\sqrt{x^2-x-1}+\log\left[x-\frac{1}{2}+\sqrt{x^2-x-1}\right]$

10. $4\sqrt{x^2+4x+9}-3\log\left[(x+2)+\sqrt{x^2+4x+9}\right]$

7.4 To evaluate the integrals of the type $\int\sqrt{a^2-x^2}\,dx$, $\int\sqrt{x^2-a^2}\,dx$ and $\sqrt{x^2+a^2}\,dx$.

(i) $I = \int\sqrt{a^2-x^2}\,dx$ Put $x = a\sin\theta$

$\therefore\quad dx = a\cos\theta\,d\theta$

$$\therefore\quad I = \int\sqrt{a^2-a^2\sin^2\theta}\cdot a\cos\theta\,d\theta$$

$$= a^2\int\cos^2\theta\,d\theta$$

$$= \frac{a^2}{2}\int 2\cos^2\theta\,d\theta$$

$$= \frac{a^2}{2}\int(1+\cos 2\theta)\,d\theta$$

$$= \frac{a^2}{2}\left[\theta+\frac{\sin 2\theta}{2}\right]$$

$$= \frac{a^2}{2}[\theta+\sin\theta\cos\theta]$$

$$= \frac{a^2}{2}\left[\sin^{-1}\frac{x}{a}+\frac{x}{a}\sqrt{1-\frac{x^2}{a^2}}\right]$$

$$= \frac{1}{2}x\sqrt{a^2-x^2}+\frac{1}{2}a^2\sin^{-1}\frac{x}{a}$$

(ii) $I = \sqrt{x^2-a^2}\,dx$

$$= \int\underset{\text{I}}{\sqrt{x^2-a^2}}\,.\underset{\text{II}}{1}.\,dx$$

Integrating by parts

$$= \sqrt{x^2-a^2}\cdot x-\int\frac{1}{2}(x^2-a^2)^{-1/2}\cdot 2x\cdot x\,dx$$

$$= x\sqrt{x^2 - a^2} - \int \frac{x^2}{\sqrt{x^2 - a^2}}\, dx$$

$$= x\sqrt{x^2 - a^2} - \int \frac{(x^2 - a^2) + a^2}{\sqrt{x^2 - a^2}}\, dx$$

$$= x\sqrt{x^2 - a^2} - \int \sqrt{x^2 - a^2}\, dx - a^2 \int \frac{dx}{\sqrt{x^2 - a^2}}$$

$$= x\sqrt{x^2 - a^2} - I - a^2 \log\left[x + \sqrt{x^2 - a^2}\right]$$

$$\therefore \quad 2I = x\sqrt{x^2 - a^2} - a^2 \log\left[x + \sqrt{x^2 - a^2}\right]$$

$$\therefore \quad I = \frac{1}{2} x\sqrt{x^2 - a^2} - \frac{1}{2} a^2 \log\left[x + \sqrt{x^2 - a^2}\right].$$

(iii) $$I = \int \sqrt{x^2 + a^2}\, dx$$

$$= \int \underset{\text{I}}{\sqrt{x^2 + a^2}} \cdot \underset{\text{II}}{1}\, dx$$

Integrating by parts

$$= \sqrt{x^2 + a^2} \cdot x - \int \frac{1}{2}(x^2 + a^2)^{-1/2} \cdot 2x \cdot x\, dx$$

$$= x\sqrt{x^2 + a^2} - \int \frac{x^2}{\sqrt{x^2 + a^2}}\, dx$$

$$= x\sqrt{x^2 + a^2} - \int \frac{(x^2 + a^2) - a^2}{\sqrt{x^2 + a^2}}\, dx$$

$$= x\sqrt{x^2 + a^2} - \int \sqrt{x^2 + a^2}\, dx + a^2 \int \frac{dx}{\sqrt{x^2 + a^2}}$$

$$= x\sqrt{x^2 + a^2} - I + a^2 \log\left[x + \sqrt{x^2 + a^2}\right]$$

$$\therefore \quad 2I = x\sqrt{x^2 + a^2} + a^2 \log\left[x + \sqrt{x^2 + a^2}\right]$$

$$\therefore \quad I = \frac{1}{2} x\sqrt{x^2 + a^2} + \frac{1}{2} a^2 \log\left[x + \sqrt{x^2 + a^2}\right]$$

Example 1. Evaluate $\int \frac{x^2+1}{\sqrt{x^2+3}}\,dx \cdot$

Solution :

$$I = \int \frac{x^2+1}{\sqrt{x^2+3}}\,dx$$

$$= \frac{(x^2+3)-2}{\sqrt{x^2+3}}\,dx$$

$$= \int \sqrt{x^2+3}\,dx - 2\int \frac{dx}{\sqrt{x^2+3}}$$

$$= \frac{1}{2}x\sqrt{x^2+3} + \frac{3}{2}\log\left[x+\sqrt{x^2+3}\right] -2\log\left[x+\sqrt{x^2+3}\right]$$

$$= \frac{1}{2}x\sqrt{x^2+3} - \frac{1}{2}\log\left(x+\sqrt{x^2+3}\right)$$

$$= \frac{x\sqrt{x^2+3} - \log\left(x+\sqrt{x^2+3}\right)}{2}$$

Example 2. Evaluate $\int \sqrt{2-3x^2}\,dx \cdot$

Solution :

$$I = \int \sqrt{2-3x^2}\,dx$$

$$= \sqrt{3}\int \sqrt{\frac{2}{3}-x^2}\,dx$$

$$= \sqrt{3}\int \sqrt{\left(\sqrt{\frac{2}{3}}\right)^2 - x^2}\,dx$$

$$= \sqrt{3}\left[\frac{1}{2}x\sqrt{\frac{2}{3}-x^2} + \frac{1}{2}\cdot\frac{2}{3}\sin^{-1}\left(\frac{x}{\sqrt{\frac{2}{3}}}\right)\right]$$

$$= \sqrt{3}\left[\frac{1}{2}x\sqrt{\frac{2}{3}-x^2} + \frac{1}{3}\sin^{-1}\left(x\sqrt{\frac{3}{2}}\right)\right]$$

EXERCISE 7.3

Integrate :

1. $\sqrt{9-4x^2}$

2. $\sqrt{x^2-4}$

3. $\sqrt{4-25x^2}$

4. $\sec x \tan x\sqrt{\tan^2 x-4}$

5. $\sec x \tan x\sqrt{\sec^2 x+1}$

6. $\sin x\sqrt{\cos^2 x-4}$

7. $\cos x\sqrt{4-\sin^2 x}$

8. $x^2\sqrt{4-x^6}$

9. $e^x\sqrt{e^{2x}+1}$

10. $\sqrt{e^{4x}-e^{2x}}$

ANSWERS

EXERCISE 7.3

1. $\dfrac{1}{2}x\sqrt{\dfrac{9}{2}-4x^2}+\dfrac{9}{4}\sin^{-1}\dfrac{2x}{3}$

2. $\dfrac{1}{2}x\sqrt{x^2-4}-2\log\left(x+\sqrt{x^2-4}\right)$

3. $\dfrac{1}{2}x\sqrt{4-25x^2}+\dfrac{2}{5}\sin^{-1}\left(\dfrac{5x}{2}\right)$

4. $\dfrac{\sec x}{2}\sqrt{\sec^2 x+3}+\dfrac{3}{2}\log\left[\sec x+\sqrt{\sec^2 x+3}\right]$

5. $\dfrac{1}{2}\sec x\sqrt{\sec^2 x+1}+\dfrac{1}{2}\cdot\log\left[\sec x+\sqrt{\sec^2 x+1}\right]$

6. $-\left[\dfrac{1}{2}\cos x\sqrt{\cos^2 x-4}-2\log\left\{\cos x+\sqrt{\cos^2 x-4}\right\}\right]$

7. $\dfrac{1}{2}x\sqrt{4-\sin^2 x}+2\sin^{-1}\left(\dfrac{\sin x}{2}\right)$

8. $\dfrac{1}{3}\left[\dfrac{1}{2}x^3\sqrt{4-x^6}+2\sin^{-1}\dfrac{x^3}{2}\right]$

9. $\dfrac{1}{2}e^x\sqrt{e^{2x}+1}+\dfrac{1}{2}\log\left[e^x+\sqrt{e^{2x}+1}\right]$

10. $\dfrac{1}{2}e^x\sqrt{e^{2x}+1}-\dfrac{1}{2}\log\left[e^x+\sqrt{e^{2x}-1}\right]$

7.5 To evaluate an integral of the type $\int \sqrt{ax^2 + bx + c}\, dx$.

Method. We transform $\sqrt{ax^2 + bx + c}$ into either of the possible forms $\sqrt{A^2 + X^2}$ or $\sqrt{A^2 - X^2}$ or $\sqrt{X^2 - A^2}$ where X is a linear expression of x and A is a constant.

Example 1. Evaluate $\int \sqrt{5 - 4x - x^2}\, dx$.

Solution :

Here,

$$\begin{aligned} 5 - 4x - x^2 &= 5 - (4x + x^2) \\ &= 5 - (4x + x^2 + 4 - 4) \\ &= 5 + 4 - (x^2 + 4x + 4) \\ &= 9 - (x + 2)^2 \end{aligned}$$

$$\therefore \int \sqrt{5 - 4x - x^2}\, dx$$

$$= \int \sqrt{9 - (x+2)^2}\, dx \qquad \text{Put } x + 2 = t \quad \therefore dx = dt$$

$$= \int \sqrt{9 - t^2}\, dt$$

$$= \int \sqrt{3^2 - t^2}\, dt$$

$$= \frac{1}{2} \cdot t\sqrt{9 - t^2} + \frac{1}{2} \cdot 9 \cdot \sin^{-1}\left(\frac{t}{3}\right)$$

$$= \frac{x+2}{2}\sqrt{9 - (x+2)^2} + \frac{9}{2}\sin^{-1}\left(\frac{x+2}{3}\right)$$

$$= \frac{x+2}{2}\sqrt{5 - 4x - x^2} + \frac{9}{2}\sin^{-1}\left(\frac{x+2}{3}\right)$$

7.6 To evaluate an integral of the type $\int (px + q)\sqrt{ax^2 + bx + c}\, dx$.

Method. We break up $(px + q)$ into two parts in one of which there is the differential coefficient of $ax^2 + bx + c$ and the other a constant. Then the given integral can be easily evaluated.

Example 1. Evaluate $\int (2x-5)\sqrt{2+3x-x^2}\,dx.$

Solution :

Here $\dfrac{d}{dx}(2+3x-x^2)=3-2x$

$$\therefore \quad I = \int (2x-5)\sqrt{2+3x-x^2}\,dx$$

$$= -\int (5-2x)\sqrt{2+3x-x^2}\,dx$$

$$= -\int (3-2x)\sqrt{2+3x-x^2}\,dx - 2\int \sqrt{2+3x-x^2}\,dx$$

$$= I_1 + I_2 \qquad \text{(say)}$$

$$I_1 = \int (3-2x)\sqrt{2+3x-x^2}\,dx$$

Put $2 + 3x - x^2 = t$

$\therefore \quad (3 - 2x)\,dx = dt$

$$\therefore \quad I_1 = -\int \sqrt{t}\,dt$$

$$= -\frac{2}{3}t^{3/2}$$

$$= -\frac{2}{3}(2+3x-x^2)^{3/2}$$

and

$$I_2 = -2\int \sqrt{2+3x-x^2}\,dx$$

$$= -2\int \sqrt{2-\left(x^2-3x+\frac{9}{4}-\frac{9}{4}\right)}\,dx$$

$$= -2\int \sqrt{2+\frac{9}{4}-\left(x-\frac{3}{2}\right)^2}\,dx$$

$$= -2\int \sqrt{\left(\frac{\sqrt{17}}{2}\right)^2-\left(x-\frac{3}{2}\right)^2}\,dx$$

$$= -2\left[\frac{1}{2}\left(x-\frac{3}{2}\right)\sqrt{\left(\frac{\sqrt{17}}{2}\right)^2\left(x-\frac{3}{2}\right)^2} + \frac{1}{2}\cdot\frac{17}{4}\cdot\sin^{-1}\left(\frac{x-\frac{3}{2}}{\frac{\sqrt{17}}{2}}\right)\right]$$

$$= -\left[\frac{2x-3}{2}\sqrt{2+3x-x^2} + \frac{17}{4}\sin^{-1}\left(\frac{2x-3}{\sqrt{17}}\right)\right]$$

$$\therefore \qquad I = I_1 + I_2$$

$$= -\frac{2}{3}(2+3x-x^2)^{3/2} - \frac{2x-3}{2}\sqrt{2+3x-x^2} - \frac{17}{4}\sin^{-1}\left(\frac{2x-3}{\sqrt{17}}\right)$$

EXERCISE 7.4

Integrate :

1. $\sqrt{x^2 - x + 1}$ **2.** $(3x-2)\sqrt{x^2+x+1}$

3. $\sqrt{15-2x-x^2}$ **4.** $(2x+1)\sqrt{5-4x-x^2}$

5. $\sqrt{3-2x-2x^2}$ **6.** $(x+1)\sqrt{2x^2+3}$

7. $\sqrt{5+4x-x^2}$ **8.** $(2x+1)\sqrt{x^2+2x+5}$

9. $x^2\sqrt{x^6-1}$ **10.** $(x+1)\sqrt{x^2-x+1}$

ANSWERS

EXERCISE 7.4

1. $\frac{2x-1}{4}\sqrt{x^2-x+1} + \frac{3}{8}\log\left\{\frac{2x-1}{2} + \sqrt{x^2-x+1}\right\}$

2. $\frac{1}{8}(8x^2-6x+1)\sqrt{x^2+x+1} - \frac{21}{16}\log\left[\frac{2x+1}{\sqrt{3}} + \sqrt{\left(\frac{2x+1}{\sqrt{3}}\right)^2+1}\right]$

3. $\frac{1}{2}\left[(x+1)\sqrt{15-2x+x^2} + 16\sin^{-1}\left(\frac{x+1}{4}\right)\right]$

4. $-\frac{2}{3}(5-4x-x^2)^{3/2} - \frac{3}{2}\left[(x+2)\sqrt{5-4x-x^2} + 9\sin^{-1}\left(\frac{x+2}{3}\right)\right]$

5. $\frac{1}{2}\left[\left(x+\frac{1}{2}\right)\sqrt{3-2x-2x^2} + \frac{7}{2\sqrt{2}}\sin^{-1}\left(\frac{2x+1}{\sqrt{7}}\right)\right]$

6. $\frac{1}{6}(2x^2+3)^{3/2} + \frac{1}{2}x\sqrt{2x^2+3} + \frac{3\sqrt{2}}{4}\log\left[x\sqrt{\frac{2}{3}} + \sqrt{\frac{2}{3}x^2+1}\right]$

7. $\frac{1}{2}(x-2)\sqrt{5+4x-x^2}+9\sin^{-1}\left(\frac{x-2}{3}\right)$

8. $\frac{2}{3}(x^2+2x+5)^{3/2}-\frac{x+1}{2}\sqrt{x^2+2x+5}$

$$-2\log\left[x+1+\sqrt{x^2+2x+5}\right]$$

9. $\frac{1}{3}\left[\frac{1}{2}\sqrt{x^6-1}-\frac{1}{2}\log\left\{x^3+\sqrt{x^6-1}\right\}\right]$

10. $\frac{1}{24}(8x^2-10x+1)\sqrt{x^2-x+1}$

$$+\frac{9}{16}\log\left[\frac{2x-1}{\sqrt{3}}+\sqrt{\left(\frac{2x-1}{\sqrt{3}}\right)^2+1}\right]$$

8

Integration by Partial Fractions

8.1 A fraction of the form

$$\frac{a_0x^m + a_1x^{m-1} + \ldots\ldots. + a_m}{b_0x^n + b_1x^{n-1} + \ldots\ldots. b_n}$$

where a_0, a_1,..., a_m and b_0, b_1,..., b_n are constants and m, n are positive integers is called a *rational algebraic fraction.*

To integrate such fractions, we break them into partial fractions, for which we must remember the following points :

(1) The degree of the numerator of the given fraction should be less than the degree of the denominator of the given fraction. If it is not so, then it must be done by division. Such a form of fraction is called *Proper Fraction.*

(2) The terms of degree 2 or more in the denominator of the fraction should be resolved into possible real linear factors.

8.2 Methods of breaking a fraction into partial fraction

(1) *When the denominator is the product of only linear factors :* Then

$$\frac{f(x)}{(x+a)(x+b)(x+c)(x+d)} = \frac{A}{x+a} + \frac{B}{x+b} + \frac{C}{x+c} + \frac{D}{x+d}$$

(2) *When there is a repetition of a linear factor in the denominator* : Then

$$\frac{f(x)}{(x+a)^r(x+b)} = \frac{A_1}{x+a} + \frac{A_2}{(x+a)^2} + \ldots. + \frac{A_r}{(x+a)^r} + \frac{B}{x+b}$$

(3) *When the denominator contains a biquadratic factor* : Then

$$\frac{f(x)}{(x+a)(x^2+b^2)} = \frac{A}{x+a} + \frac{Bx+C}{x^2+b^2}$$

(4) *When there is a repetition of a quadratic factor in the denominator* : Then

$$\frac{f(x)}{(x^2+a^2)^2(x+b)}=\frac{Ax+B}{x^2+a^2}+\frac{Cx+D}{(x^2+a^2)^2}+\frac{E}{x+b}$$

ILLUSTRATIVE EXAMPLES

Case I. *When the denominator contains non-repeated linear factors only.*

Example 1. Evaluate $\int \frac{x^2}{(x+1)(x-2)(x+3)}dx\cdot$

Solution :

Let $\int \frac{x^2}{(x+1)(x-2)(x+3)}=\frac{A}{x+1}+\frac{B}{x-2}+\frac{C}{x+3}$

$\Rightarrow \quad x^2 = A\ (x-2)\ (x+3) + B\ (x+1)\ (x+3) + C\ (x+1)\ (x-2)$

Put $x = -1$, we get $\quad A = -\frac{1}{6}$

Put $x = 2$, we get $\quad B = \frac{4}{15}$

Put $x = -3$, we get $\quad C = \frac{9}{10}$

$\therefore \quad \int \frac{x^2}{(x+1)(x-2)(x+3)}dx$

$$= -\frac{1}{6}\int\frac{dx}{x+1}+\frac{4}{15}\int\frac{dx}{x-2}+\frac{9}{10}\int\frac{dx}{x+3}$$

$$= -\frac{1}{6}\log(x+1)+\frac{4}{15}\log(x-2)+\frac{9}{10}\log(x+3)$$

Example 2. Evaluate $\int \frac{x^2+1}{x^2-1}dx.$

Solution :

$$\frac{x^2+1}{x^2-1}=\frac{x^2-1+2}{x^2-1}=1+\frac{2}{x^2-1}=1+\frac{2}{(x-1)(x+1)}$$

Let $\dfrac{2}{(x-1)(x+1)} = \dfrac{A}{x-1} + \dfrac{B}{x+1}$

$\therefore \quad 2 = A\,(x+1) + B\,(x-1)$

Put $x = 1$, we get $A = 1$

Put $x = -1$, we get $B = -1$

$$\therefore \quad \int \frac{x^2+1}{x^2-1}\,dx = \int \left(1 + \frac{1}{x-1} - \frac{1}{x+1}\right) dx$$

$$= x + \log(x-1) - \log(x+1)$$

EXERCISE 8.1

Integrate :

1. $\dfrac{3x}{(x-2)(x+1)}$
2. $\dfrac{1}{(2x+1)(x+1)}$
3. $\dfrac{x}{(x-1)(x-2)}$
4. $\dfrac{1}{(x-1)(x^2-4)}$
5. $\dfrac{1}{x-x^2}$
6. $\dfrac{x^2+1}{x(x^2-1)}$
7. $\dfrac{x}{(x^2-a^2)(x^2-b^2)}$
8. $\dfrac{1}{(x+1)^2-4}$
9. $\dfrac{x^2+x+3}{(x-2)(x+1)}$
10. $\dfrac{x^2}{x^2+7x+12}$
11. $\dfrac{x^3+3}{x^3-3x}$
12. $\dfrac{x^2}{(x^2+1)(3x^2+1)}$

ANSWERS

EXERCISE 8.1

1. $2 \log (x-2) + \log (x+1)$
2. $\log (2x+1) - \log (x+1)$
3. $\log (x-1) + 2 \log (x-2)$
4. $-\dfrac{1}{3}\log(x-1) + \dfrac{1}{4}\log(x-2) + \dfrac{1}{12}\log(x-2)$
5. $\log x - \log (1-x)$

6. $\log\left(\dfrac{x^2-1}{x}\right)$

7. $\dfrac{1}{2(a^2-b^2)}\log\dfrac{x^2-a^2}{x^2-b^2}$

8. $\dfrac{1}{4}\log(x-1)-\dfrac{1}{4}\log(x+3)$

9. $x+3\log(x-2)-\log(x+1)$

10. $\dfrac{1}{2}x^2-7x-27\log(x+3)+64\log(x+4)$

11. $x+\dfrac{1}{2}\log\dfrac{x^2-3}{x^2}+\dfrac{\sqrt{3}}{2}\log\dfrac{x-\sqrt{3}}{x+\sqrt{3}}$

12. $\dfrac{1}{2}\tan^{-1}x-\dfrac{1}{2\sqrt{3}}\tan^{-1}\left(x\sqrt{3}\right)$

Case II. *When there is a repetition of a linear factor in the denominator.*

Example 1. Evaluate $\displaystyle\int\frac{x^2+1}{(x+1)^2(x-2)}\,dx$.

Solution :

Let $$\frac{x^2+1}{(x+1)^2(x-2)}=\frac{A}{x+1}+\frac{B}{(x+1)^2}+\frac{C}{x-2}$$

$\therefore$ $$x^2+1=A(x+1)(x-2)+B(x-2)+C(x+1)^2 \qquad \text{... (1)}$$

Put $x=-1$, we get

$$B=-\frac{2}{3}$$

Put $x=2$, we get

$$C=\frac{5}{9}$$

Equating the coefficients of x^2 on both sides, we get

$$1=A+C$$

$$\Rightarrow \quad A=1-C$$

$$\Rightarrow \quad A=1-\frac{5}{9}=\frac{4}{9}$$

Thus,

$$\int \frac{x^2+1}{(x+1)^2(x-1)}\,dx$$

$$= \frac{4}{9}\int \frac{1}{x+1}\,dx - \frac{2}{3}\int \frac{1}{(x+1)^2}\,dx + \frac{5}{9}\int \frac{1}{(x-2)}\,dx$$

$$= \frac{4}{9}\log(x-1) + \frac{2}{3}\ \frac{1}{x+1} + \frac{5}{9}\left(\log(x-2)\right)$$

EXERCISE 8.2

Integrate :

1. $\dfrac{x}{(x-1)^2(x-2)}$

2. $\dfrac{3x+1}{(x-1)^3(x+1)}$

3. $\dfrac{x^2+1}{(x+1)^3(x-2)}$

4. $\dfrac{1}{x^3-x^2-x+1}$

5. $\dfrac{x}{(x-1)^2(x+2)}$

6. $\dfrac{1}{(x+1)^2(x-1)}$

ANSWERS

EXERCISE 8.2

1. $\dfrac{1}{x+1} + \log\ \dfrac{x-2}{x-1}$

2. $\dfrac{1}{(x-1)^2} - \dfrac{1}{2(x-1)} + \dfrac{1}{4}\log\ \dfrac{x+1}{x-1}$

3. $-\dfrac{5}{27}\log(x+1) - \dfrac{4}{9}(x+1)^{-1} + \dfrac{1}{3}(x+1)^{-2} + \dfrac{5}{27}\log(x-2)$

4. $\dfrac{1}{4}\log(x+1) - \dfrac{1}{2}\cdot\dfrac{1}{x-1} - \dfrac{1}{4}\log(x-1)$

5. $-\dfrac{1}{3}\cdot\dfrac{1}{x-1} + \dfrac{2}{9}\log\dfrac{x-1}{x+2}$

6. $\log\dfrac{x-1}{x+2} + \dfrac{1}{2(x+1)}$

Case III. *When the denominator contains a non-repeated quadratic factor.*

Example 1. Evaluate $\int \frac{dx}{1+x+x^2+x^3}$.

Solution :

$$\int \frac{dx}{1+x+x^2+x^3} = \int \frac{dx}{1+x+x^2(1+x)}$$

$$= \int \frac{dx}{(1+x)(1+x^2)}$$

Let $\frac{1}{(1+x)(1+x^2)} = \frac{A}{1+x} + \frac{Bx+C}{1+x^2}$

$\therefore$ $1 = A(1+x^2) + (Bx + C)(1+x)$ ... (1)

In (1) Put $x = -1$, we get

$$A = \frac{1}{2}$$

Again (1) can be written as

$$1 = x^2(A+B) + x(B+C) + (A+C)$$

Equating the coefficients of equal powers of x on both sides, we get

$$A + B = 0 \Rightarrow B = -A = -\frac{1}{2}$$

$$B + C = 0$$

$$A + C = 1 \Rightarrow C = 1 - A = 1 - \frac{1}{2} = \frac{1}{2}$$

$$\therefore \int \frac{dx}{(1+x)(1+x^2)} = \frac{1}{2}\int \frac{dx}{1+x} - \frac{1}{2}\int \frac{x-1}{1+x^2}\,dx$$

$$= \frac{1}{2}\log(1+x) - \frac{1}{4}\int \frac{2x\,dx}{1+x^2} + \frac{1}{2}\int \frac{1}{1+x^2}\,dx$$

$$= \frac{1}{2}\log(x+1) - \frac{1}{4}\log(1+x^2) + \frac{1}{2}\tan^{-1}x$$

EXERCISE 8.3

Integrate :

1. $\frac{1}{(x-1)(x^2+4)}$

2. $\frac{x-1}{(x+1)(x^2+1)}$

3. $\dfrac{x^2}{(x+b)(x^2+a^2)}$

4. $\dfrac{1}{1-x^3}$

5. $\dfrac{1}{(x+1)^2(x^2+1)}$

6. $\dfrac{x^2}{(x-1)^2(x^2+1)}$

7. $\dfrac{1}{x(x^2+1)}$

ANSWERS

EXERCISE 8.3

1. $\frac{1}{5}\left[\log(x-1)-\frac{1}{2}\cdot\log(x^2+4)-\frac{1}{2}\tan^{-1}\left(\frac{x}{2}\right)\right]$
2. $-\log(x+1)+\frac{1}{2}\log(x^2+1)$
3. $\frac{1}{a^2+b^2}\left[\log(x+b)-\frac{1}{2}\log(x^2+a^2)+\frac{b}{a}\tan^{-1}\frac{x}{a}\right]$
4. $-\frac{1}{3}\log(1-x)+\frac{1}{6}\log(1+x+x^2)+\frac{1}{\sqrt{3}}\tan^{-1}\frac{2x+1}{\sqrt{3}}$
5. $\frac{1}{2}\log(x+1)-\frac{1}{2}\frac{1}{x+1}-\frac{1}{4}\log(x^2+1)$
6. $\frac{1}{2}\log(x-1)-\frac{1}{2(x-1)}-\frac{1}{4}\log(x^2+1)$
7. $\log x-\frac{1}{2}\log(x^2+1)$

Case IV. *Integration of fractions by partial fractions after using substitution method.*

Example 1. Evaluate $\int\frac{\cos x}{(1+\sin x)(2+\sin x)}dx$.

Solution :

$$I = \int\frac{\cos x}{(1+\sin x)(2+\sin x)}dx \quad \text{Put} \quad \sin x = t$$

$$\therefore \quad \cos dx = dt$$

$$\therefore \quad I = \int\frac{dt}{(1+t)(2+t)}$$

$$= \int \left(\frac{1}{1+t} - \frac{1}{2+t} \right) dt \quad \text{[resolving into partial fractions]}$$

$$= \int \frac{dt}{1+t} - \int \frac{dt}{2+t}$$

$$= \log (1 + t) - \log (2 + t)$$

$$= \log \left(\frac{1+t}{2+t} \right)$$

$$= \log \left(\frac{1+\sin x}{2+\sin x} \right)$$

Example 2. Evaluate $\int \frac{1+\sin x}{\sin x(1+\cos x)} dx.$

Solution :

$$I = \int \frac{1+\sin x}{\sin x(1+\cos x)} dx$$

$$= \frac{dx}{\sin x(1+\cos x)} + \int \frac{dx}{1+\cos x}$$

$$= \int \frac{\sin x\, dx}{\sin^2 x\,(1+\cos x)} + \frac{1}{2} \int \sec^2 \frac{x}{2}\, dx$$

$$= \int \frac{\sin x\, dx}{(1-\cos^2 x)(1+\cos x)} + \frac{1}{2} \cdot \frac{\tan \frac{x}{2}}{\frac{1}{2}}$$

$$= \int \frac{\sin x\, dx}{(1+\cos x)^2 (1-\cos x)} + \tan \frac{x}{2}$$

$$= I_1 + \tan \frac{x}{2}$$

Now, $\quad I_1 = \int \frac{\sin x\, dx}{(1+\cos x)^2 (1-\cos x)} \qquad$ Put $\cos x = t$

$\therefore -\sin x\, dx = dt$

$\therefore \quad I_1 = -\int \frac{dt}{(1+t)^2 (1-t)}$

$$= \int \frac{dt}{(t-1)(1+t)^2}$$

$$= \int \left\{ \frac{-1}{4(t+1)} - \frac{1}{2(t+1)^2} + \frac{1}{4(t+1)} \right\} dt$$

[resolving the integrand into partial fractions]

$$= -\frac{1}{4} \log(t+1) + \frac{1}{2(t+1)} + \frac{1}{4} \log(t-1)$$

$$= -\frac{1}{4} \log(\cos x + 1) + \frac{1}{2}(\cos x + 1)^{-1} + \frac{1}{4} \log(\cos x - 1)$$

$$\therefore \quad I = -\frac{1}{4} \log(\cos x + 1) + \frac{1}{2}(\cos x + 1)^{-1} + \frac{1}{4} \log(\cos x - 1) + \tan\frac{x}{2}$$

Example 3. Evaluate $\int \frac{1}{x(x^n+1)} dx.$

Solution :

$$I = \int \frac{1}{x(x^n+1)} dx$$

$$= \int \frac{x^{n-1}}{x^n(x^n+1)} dx$$

Put $x^n = t$

$\therefore nx^{n-1} dx = dt$

$\therefore x^{n-1} dx = \frac{dt}{n}$

$$\therefore \quad I = \int \frac{dt}{n\,t(t+1)}$$

$$= \frac{1}{n} \int \frac{dt}{t(t+1)}$$

$$= \frac{1}{n} \int \left(\frac{1}{t} - \frac{1}{t+1} \right) dt$$

(breaking into partial fractions)

$$= \frac{1}{n} [\log t - \log(t+1)]$$

$$= \frac{1}{n} \log\left(\frac{t}{t+1} \right)$$

$$= \frac{1}{n} \log\left(\frac{x^n}{x^n+1} \right)$$

Example 4. Integrate $\frac{1}{e^x - 1}$ $w.r.t.\ x.$

Solution :

$$I = \int \frac{dx}{e^x - 1}$$

$$= \int \frac{e^x dx}{e^x (e^x - 1)}$$

Put $e^x = t$

$\therefore \quad e^x\, dx = dt$

$$\therefore \quad I = \int \frac{dt}{t(t-1)}$$

$$= \int \left(\frac{1}{t-1} - \frac{1}{t} \right) dx$$

[breaking the integrand into partial fractions]

$$= \log(t-1) - \log t$$

$$= \log\left(\frac{t-1}{t}\right)$$

$$= \log\left(\frac{e^x - 1}{e^x}\right)$$

EXERCISE 8.4

Integrate :

1. $\frac{1}{\sin x(3 + 2\cos x)}$

2. $\frac{1}{\cos x(1 + \sin x)}$

3. $\frac{\sec x}{1 + \operatorname{cosec} x}$

4. $\frac{1 - \cos x}{\cos x(1 + \cos x)}$

5. $\frac{1}{\sin x + \sin 2x}$

6. $\frac{\sec^2 x}{(\tan x + 1)(\tan x + 2)}$

7. $\frac{1}{x(x^2 + 1)^3}$

8. $\frac{1}{(e^x - 1)^2}$

9. $\frac{1}{x(x^n - 1)}$

10. $\frac{1}{e^x + 1}$

11. $\frac{1}{x(x^4 + 1)}$

12. $\frac{1}{(x^2 + a^2)(x^2 + b^2)}$

ANSWERS

EXERCISE 8.4

1. $\frac{1}{10}\log(1-\cos x)-\frac{1}{2}\log(1+\cos x)+\frac{2}{5}\log(3+2\cos x)$

2. $\frac{1}{4}\left[\log\frac{1+\sin x}{1-\sin x}-\frac{2}{1+\sin x}\right]$

3. $\frac{1}{4}\left[\log\frac{1+\sin x}{1-\sin x}+\frac{2}{1+\sin x}\right]$

4. $\log(\sec x+\tan x)-2\tan\frac{x}{2}$

5. $\frac{1}{2}\log(1+\cos x)+\frac{1}{6}\log(1-\cos x)-\frac{2}{3}\log(1+2\cos x)$

6. $\log\left(\frac{1+\tan x}{2+\tan x}\right)$

7. $\frac{1}{4(x^2+1)^2}+\frac{1}{2(x^2+1)}-\frac{1}{2}\log(x^2+1)+\log x$

8. $x-\log(e^x-1)-\frac{1}{e^x-1}$

9. $\frac{1}{n}\log\frac{x^n-1}{x^n}$

10. $\log\frac{e^x}{e^x+1}$

11. $\frac{1}{4}\log\frac{x^4}{x^4+1}$

12. $\frac{1}{a^2-b^2}\left[\frac{1}{b}\tan^{-1}\frac{x}{b}-\frac{1}{a}\tan^{-1}\frac{x}{a}\right]$

9

Integration of Transcendental Functions

9.1 The functions which are not algebraic are called Transcendental Functions. They include Trigonometric Functions, Exponential Functions, Logarithmic Functions and Hyperbolic Functions, etc.

9.2 To evaluate $\int \sin^n x\,dx$ or $\int \cos^n x\,dx$ when n is an odd +ve integer.

Method.

(i) When the index of $\sin x$ is an odd +ve integer,

Put $\cos x = t$

(ii) When the index of $\cos x$ is an odd +ve integer,

Put $\sin x = t$

Example 1. Evaluate $\int \sin^3 x\,dx \cdot$

Solution :

$$I = \int \sin^3 x\,dx$$

$$= \int \sin^2 x \sin x\,dx$$

$$= \int \left(1-\cos^2 x\right)\sin x\,dx \qquad \text{Put } \cos x = t$$

$$\therefore\ -\sin x\,dx = dt$$

$$\therefore \qquad I = -\int \left(1-t^2\right)dt$$

$$= \int \left(t^2-1\right)dt$$

$$= \frac{t^3}{3} - t$$

$$= \frac{\cos^3 x}{3} - \cos x$$

Example 2. Evaluate $\int \cos^3 x\, dx$.

Solution :

$$I = \int \cos^3 x\, dx$$

$$= \int \cos^2 x \cdot \cos x\, dx$$

$$= \int (1 - \sin^2 x) \cos x\, dx \qquad \text{Put} \quad \sin x = t$$

$$\therefore \cos x\, dx = dt$$

$$\therefore \qquad I = \int (1 - t^2)\, dt$$

$$= t - \frac{t^3}{3}$$

$$= \sin x - \frac{\sin^3 x}{3}$$

9.3 To evaluate $\int \sin^n x\, dx$ or $\int \cos^2 x\, dx$ when n is a + ve even integer.

Method. We express $\sin^n x$ or $\cos^n x$ in a series of cosines of multiple angles of x by using the formulae

$$\sin^2 x = \frac{1 - \cos 2x}{2} \text{ and } \cos^2 x = \frac{1 + \cos 2x}{2}$$

and then integrate term by term.

Example 3. Evaluate $\int \sin^4 \theta\, d\theta$.

Solution :

$$I = \int \sin^4 \theta\, d\theta$$

$$= \int (\sin^2 \theta)^2\, d\theta$$

$$= \int \left(\frac{1 - \cos 2\theta}{2}\right)^2 d\theta$$

$$= \int \frac{1}{4}\left[1 - 2\cos 2\theta + \cos^2 2\theta\right] dx$$

$$= \frac{1}{4}\int\left(1 - 2\cos 2\theta + \frac{1+\cos 4\theta}{2}\right) d\theta$$

$$= \frac{1}{8}\int [3 - 4\cos 2\theta + \cos 4\theta]\, d\theta$$

$$= \frac{1}{8}\left[3\theta - 2\sin 2\theta + \frac{\sin 4\theta}{4}\right]$$

9.4 To evaluate $\int \sin^m x \cos^n x\, dx$

Method.

(i) If m is an odd positive integer, then put $\cos x = t$.

(ii) If n is an odd positive integer, then put $\sin x = t$.

(iii) If $(m + n)$ is an even negative integer, put $\tan x = t$.

Example 4. Evaluate $\int \sin^3 x \cos^2 x\, dx$.

Solution :

$$I = \int \sin^3 x \cos^2 x\, dx$$

$$= \int \sin^2 x \cos^2 x \cdot \sin x\, dx$$

$$= \int \left(1 - \cos^2 x\right)\cos^2 x \sin x\, dx \qquad \text{Put } \cos x = t$$

$$\therefore -\sin x\, dx = dt$$

$$\therefore \quad I = -\int \left(1 - t^2\right) t^2\, dt$$

$$= -\int \left(t^2 - t^4\right) dt$$

$$= \int \left(t^4 - t^2\right) dt$$

$$= \frac{t^5}{5} - \frac{t^3}{5}$$

$$= \frac{\cos^5 x}{5} - \frac{\cos^3 x}{3}$$

Example 5. Evaluate $\int \frac{dx}{\sin^3 x \cos^5 x}$.

Solution :

$$I = \int \frac{dx}{\sin^3 x \cos^5 x}$$

Here $m = -3$, $n = -5$

$\therefore\ m + n = -8$, an even –ve integer

$$= \int \frac{\sec^8 x}{\tan^3 x}\, dx$$

[Dividing numerator & denominator of the integrand by $\cos^8 x$]

$$= \int \frac{\sec^6 x \sec^2 x\, dx}{\tan^3 x}$$

$$= \int \frac{\left(1+\tan^2 x\right)^3 \sec^2 x\, dx}{\tan^3 x}$$

Put $\tan x = t$

$\therefore\ \sec^2 x\, dx = dt$

$$\therefore \qquad I = \int \frac{\left(1+t^2\right)^3}{t}\, dt$$

$$= \frac{1 + t^6 + 3t^2 + 3t^4}{t^3}\, dt$$

$$= \int \left(\frac{1}{t^3} + t^3 + \frac{3}{t} + 3t \right) dt$$

$$= -\frac{1}{2t^2} + \frac{t^4}{4} + 3 \log t + 3\frac{t^2}{2}$$

$$= -\frac{1}{2\tan^2 x} + \frac{\tan^4 x}{4} + 3 \log \tan x + \frac{3\tan^2 x}{2}$$

EXERCISE 9.1

Integrate :

1. $\sin^5 x$

2. $\cos^7 x$

3. $\cos^4 x$

4. $\sin^6 x$

5. $\sin^5 x \cos^4 x$

6. $\sin^2 x \cos^7 x$

7. $\sin^{\frac{2}{3}} x \cos^3 x$

8. $\sin^5 x \cos^3 x$

9. $\sin^3 x \cos^3 x$

10. $\sin^5 x \cos^{\frac{1}{2}} x$

11. $\sec x \tan^3 x$

12. $\sin^3 x \cos^2 2x$

13. $\dfrac{1}{\sin^2 x \cos^4 x}$

14. $\dfrac{\sin^2 x}{\cos^4 x}$

15. $\sec^{\frac{3}{4}} x \operatorname{cosec}^{\frac{5}{4}} x$

ANSWERS

EXERCISE 9.1

1. $-\cos x + \dfrac{2}{3}\cos^3 x - \dfrac{1}{5}\cos^5 x$

2. $\sin x - \sin^3 x + \dfrac{3}{5}\sin^5 x - \dfrac{1}{7}\sin^7 x$

3. $\dfrac{1}{8}\left[3x + 2\sin 2x + \dfrac{\sin 4x}{4}\right]$

4. $\dfrac{1}{32}\left[10x - \dfrac{15}{2}\sin 2x + \dfrac{3}{2}\sin 4x - \dfrac{1}{6}\sin x\right]$

5. $-\left[\dfrac{1}{5}\cos^5 x - \dfrac{2}{7}\cos^7 x + \dfrac{1}{9}\cos^9 x\right]$

6. $\dfrac{1}{3}\sin^3 x - \dfrac{3}{5}\sin^5 x + \dfrac{3}{7}\sin^7 x - \dfrac{1}{9}\sin^9 x$

7. $\dfrac{3}{5}\sin^{5/3} x - \dfrac{3}{11}\sin^{11/3} x$

8. $\dfrac{\sin^6 x}{6} - \dfrac{\sin^8 x}{8}$

9. $\dfrac{\sin^4 x}{4} - \dfrac{\sin^6 x}{6}$

10. $-\dfrac{2}{3}\cos^{3/2} x + \dfrac{4}{7}\cos^{7/2} x - \dfrac{2}{11}\cos^{11/2} x$

11. $\dfrac{1}{3}\sec^3 x - \sec x$

12. $-\cos x + \frac{5}{3}\cos^3 x - \frac{8}{5}\cos^5 x + \frac{4}{7}\cos^7 x$

13. $-\cot x + 2\tan x + \frac{1}{3}\tan^3 x$

14. $\frac{\tan^3 x}{3}$

15. $-4\cot^{\frac{1}{4}} x$

10

Definite Integrals

10.1 If $\frac{d}{dx} F(x) = f(x)$, then

$$\int f(x)\, dx = F(x)$$

$\int f(x)\, dx$ or $F(x)$ is called an indefinite integral or an antiderivative of $f(x)$.

Also $\int_a^b f(x)\; dx$ is called the definite integral of $f(x)$ between the limits a and b and is given by

$$\int_a^b f(x)\, dx = \left[F(x)\right]_a^b = F(b) - F(a)$$

Here a is called the lower limit of integration and b is called the upper limit of integration. The interval $[a, b]$ is called the range of integration.

Example 1. Evaluate $\int_0^1 \frac{1}{\sqrt{1-x^2}}\, dx$.

Solution :

$$I = \int_0^1 \frac{1}{\sqrt{1-x^2}}\, dx$$

$$= \left(\sin^{-1} x\right)_0^1$$

$$= \sin^{-1}(1) - \sin^{-1}(0) = \frac{\pi}{2} - 0 = \frac{\pi}{2}$$

Example 2. Evaluate $\int_0^1 \frac{\left(\tan^{-1} x\right)^2}{1+x^2}\, dx$.

Solution :

$$I = \int_0^1 \frac{\left(\tan^{-1} x\right)^2}{1+x^2}\, dx \qquad \text{Put } \tan^{-1} x = t$$

$$\therefore \frac{1}{1+x^2}\, dx = dt$$

When $x = 0$, then

$$t = \tan^{-1} 0 = 0$$

When $x = 1$, then

$$t = \tan^{-1} 1 = \frac{\pi}{4}$$

$$\therefore \qquad I = \int_0^{\pi/4} t^2\, dt$$

$$= \left(\frac{t^3}{3}\right)_0^{\pi/4}$$

$$= \frac{\pi^3}{192} - 0 = \frac{\pi^3}{192}$$

Example 3. Evaluate $\int_0^2 \sqrt{\frac{2+x}{2-x}}\, dx.$

Solution :

$$I = \int_0^2 \sqrt{\frac{2+x}{2-x}}\, dx$$

Put $x = 2 \cos 2\theta$

$\therefore \quad dx = -4 \sin 2\theta\, d\theta$

When $x = 0$, $2 \cos 2\theta = 0$

$$\therefore \qquad \cos 2\theta = 0 = \cos\frac{\pi}{2}$$

$$\therefore \qquad 2\theta = \frac{\pi}{2}$$

$$\therefore \qquad \theta = \frac{\pi}{4}$$

When $x = 2$, then

$$2 \cos 2\theta = 2$$

$$\therefore \qquad \cos 2\theta = 1 = \cos 0$$

$$\therefore \qquad 2\theta = 0$$

$$\therefore \qquad \theta = 0$$

$$\therefore \qquad I = \int_{\pi/4}^{0} \sqrt{\frac{2+2\cos 2\theta}{2-2\cos 2\theta}} (-4\sin 2\theta)\, d\theta$$

$$= -4\int_{\pi/4}^{0} \sqrt{\frac{1+\cos 2\theta}{1-\cos 2\theta}} \cdot \sin 2\theta\, d\theta$$

$$= -4\int_{\pi/4}^{0} \sqrt{\frac{2\cos^2\theta}{2\sin^2\theta}} 2\sin\theta\cos\theta\, d\theta$$

$$= -8\int_{\pi/4}^{0} \cos^2\theta\, d\theta = -4\int_{\pi/4}^{0} 2\cos^2\theta\, d\theta$$

$$= -4\int_{\pi/4}^{0} (1+\cos 2\theta)\, d\theta$$

$$= -4\left[\theta + \frac{\sin 2\theta}{2}\right]_{\pi/4}^{0}$$

$$= -4\left[(0+0) - \left(\frac{\pi}{4} + \frac{1}{2}\right)\right]$$

$$= 4\left(\frac{\pi}{4} + \frac{1}{2}\right) = \pi + 2$$

Example 4. Evaluate $\int_{1}^{3} \frac{\cos\log x}{x}\, dx.$

Solution :

$$I = \int_{1}^{3} \frac{\cos\log x}{x}\, dx$$

Put $\log x = t$

$\therefore \quad \frac{1}{x}\, dx = dt$

$$\therefore \qquad I = \int_{0}^{\log 3} \cos t\, dt$$

When $x = 1$, $t = \log 1 = 0$

When $x = 3$, $t = \log 3$

$$= (\sin t)_{0}^{\log 3}$$

$$= \sin\log 3 - \sin 0$$

$$= \sin\log 3 - 0 = \sin\log 3$$

EXERCISE 10.1

Evaluate :

1. $\int_0^{\pi/4} \sec x \tan x$

2. $\int_1^3 \frac{dx}{x}$

3. $\int_0^{\pi/2} x \cos x \, dx$

4. $\int_0^{\pi/2} \sin^3 x \, dx$

5. $\int_0^{\pi} \cos^3 x \, dx$

6. $\int_0^{\pi/2} \cos^4 x \, dx$

7. $\int_0^{\pi/3} \frac{\cos x}{3 + \sin x} dx$

8. $\int_0^{a} \left(a^2 - x^2\right) dx$

9. $\int_0^{\pi/4} \tan^2 x \, dx$

10. $\int_0^{\pi} \sin^3 x \, dx$

11. $\int_{-\pi/4}^{\pi/4} \operatorname{cosec}^2 x \, dx$

12. $\int_0^{\pi/8} \frac{\sec^2 2x}{2} dx$

13. $\int_0^{\infty} \frac{\sin \tan^{-1} x}{1 + x^2} dx$

14. $\int_0^{a} \frac{x\sqrt{a^2 - x^2}}{\sqrt{a^2 + x^2}} dx$

15. $\int_0^{1/2} \frac{x \sin^4 x}{\sqrt{1 - x^2}} dx$

16. $\int_0^{\pi/2} \frac{\cos x \, dx}{(1 + \sin x)(2 + \sin x)}$

17. $\int_0^{\pi/4} \cos\left(x + \frac{\pi}{4}\right) dx$

18. $\int_0^{\pi} x \sin^2 x \, dx$

19. $\int_0^{1} \frac{5x^3}{\sqrt{1 - x^8}} dx$

20. $\int_0^{\infty} \frac{x^2 \, dx}{\left(x^2 + a^2\right)\left(x^2 + b^2\right)}$

ANSWERS

EXERCISE 10.1

1. $\sqrt{2} - 1$

2. $\log 3$

3. $\frac{\pi}{2} - 1$

4. $\frac{2}{3}$

5. 0

6. $\frac{3\pi}{16}$

7. $\frac{1}{4}\left[\log\left(\frac{3 + 2\sqrt{3}}{3}\right)\right]$

8. $\frac{2}{3} a^3$

9. $1-\frac{\pi}{4}$

10. $\frac{2}{3}$

11. -2

12. $\frac{1}{4}$

13. 1

14. $a^2\frac{(\pi-2)}{4}$

15. $\frac{1}{2}-\sqrt{3}\frac{\pi}{12}$

16. $\log_e\left(\frac{4}{3}\right)$

17. $1-\frac{1}{\sqrt{2}}$

18. $\frac{\pi^2}{4}$

19. $\frac{5\pi}{8}$

20. $\frac{\pi}{2(a+b)}$

10.2 Properties of Definite Integrals

Property I

$$\int_a^b f(x)\,dx = \int_a^b f(t)\,dt$$

Proof

Let $\int_a^b f(x)\,dx = F(x) + c$

$$\text{Then } \int_a^b f(x)\,dx = [F(x)+c]_a^b$$

$$= [F(b)+c]-[F(a)+c]$$

$$= F(b) - F(a)$$

Similarly

$$\int_a^b f(t)\,dt = F(b) - F(a)$$

Property II

$$\int_a^b f(x)\,dx = -\int_b^a f(x)\,dx$$

Proof

$$\text{R.H.S.} = -\int_b^a f(x)\,dx$$

$$= -[F(x)+c]_b^a$$

$$= F(b) - F(a)$$

$$= \int_a^b f(x)\,dx$$

Hence Proved

Property III

$$\int_a^b f(x)\,dx = \int_a^c f(x)\,dx + \int_c^b f(x)\,dx$$

where $a < c < b$

Proof

$$\text{R.H.S.} = \int_a^c f(x)\,dx + \int_c^b f(x)\,dx$$

$$= \left[F(x) + C\right]_a^c + \left[F(x) + C\right]_c^b$$

$$= F(c) - F(a) + F(b) - F(c)$$

$$= F(b) - F(a)$$

$$= \int_a^b f(x)\,dx$$

Hence Proved

Property IV

$$\int_0^a f(x)\,dx = \int_0^a f(a-x)\,dx$$

Proof

Let $I = \int_0^a f(a-x)\,dx$

Put $a - x = t$

$\therefore \quad -dx = dt$

$\because \quad dx = -at$

When $x = 0$, $t = a - 0 = a$

$$\therefore \quad I = -\int_a^0 f(t)\,dt$$

$$= \int_0^a f(t)\,dt \qquad \text{by II}$$

$$= \int_0^a f(x)\,dx \qquad \text{by I}$$

$= \text{L.H.S.}$ Hence Proved

Property V

$$\int_{-a}^{+a} f(x)\,dx = 2\int_0^a f(x) \text{ if } f(x) \text{ is an even function of } x.$$

i.e. $f(-x) = f(x)$

$= 0$ if $f(x)$ is an odd function of x.

i.e. $f(-x) = -f(x)$

Proof

Since $-a < 0 < a$

$$\because \int_{-a}^{+a} f(x)\,dx = \int_{-a}^{0} f(x)\,dx + \int_0^a f(x)\,ax \qquad \text{by III}$$

In First integral put $x = -t$

$\therefore \quad dx = -dt$

when $x = -a$, $t = a$,

when $x = 0$, $t = 0$

$$= -\int_a^0 f(-t)\,dt + \int_0^a f(x)\,dx$$

$$= \int_0^a f(-t)\,dt + \int_0^a f(x)\,dx \qquad \text{by II}$$

$$= \int_0^a f(-x)\,dx + \int_0^a f(x)\,dx \qquad \text{by I}$$

(i) $$= \int_0^a f(x)\,dx + \int_0^a f(x)\,dx$$

when $f(x)$ is an even function of x

$$= 2\int_0^a f(x)\,dx$$

and (ii) $$= -\int_0^a f(x)\,dx + \int_0^a f(x)\,dx$$

when $f(x)$ is an odd function of x

$= 0$ Hence Proved

Property VI

$$\int_0^{2a} f(x)\,dx = 2\int_0^a f(x)\,dx \qquad \text{if } f(2a - x) = f(x)$$

if $f(2a - x) = -f(x)$

$= 0$

Proof

Since $0 < a < 2a$

$\therefore \quad \int_0^{2a} f(x)\,dx = \int_0^a f(x)\,dx + \int_a^{2a} f(x)\,dx$ by III

In second integral,

put $x = 2a - y$

$\therefore \quad dx = -\,dy$

when $x = a,\ y = a$

when $x = 2a,\ y = 0$

$\therefore$ Given integral

$$= \int_0^a f(x)\,dx - \int_a^0 f(2a-y)\,dy$$

$$= \int_0^a f(x)\,dx + \int_0^a f(2a-y)\,dy \qquad \text{by II}$$

$$= \int_0^a f(x)\,dx + \int_0^a f(2a-x)\,dx \qquad \text{by I}$$

(i) $$= \int_0^a f(x)\,dx + \int_0^a f(x)\,dx$$

if $f(2a - x) = f(x)$

$$= 2\int_0^a f(x)\,dx$$

and (ii) $$= \int_0^a f(x)\,dx + \int_0^a -f(x)\,dx$$

$$= 0 \qquad \text{if } f(2a - x) = -f(x)$$

Example 1. Prove that

$$\int_0^{\pi/2} \log \sin x\,dx = \int_0^{\pi/2} \log \cos x\,dx = -\frac{\pi}{2}\log_e 2$$

$$= \frac{\pi}{2}\log_e \frac{1}{2}$$

Solution :

$$I = \int_0^{\pi/2} \log \sin x\,dx \qquad \dots (1)$$

or, $$I = \int_0^{\pi/2} \log \sin\left(\frac{\pi}{2} - x\right) dx \qquad \text{by IV}$$

or, $$I = \int_0^{\pi/2} \log \cos x\,dx \qquad \dots (2)$$

Adding (1) and (2), we get

$$2I = \int_0^{\pi/2} \log \sin x \, dx + \int_0^{\pi/2} \log \cos x \, dx$$

$$= \int_0^{\pi/2} (\log \sin x + \log \cos x) \, dx$$

$$= \int_0^{\pi/2} (\log \sin x + \log \cos x + \log 2 - \log 2) \, dx$$

$$= \int_0^{\pi/2} \log (2 \sin x \cos x) \, dx - \int_0^{\pi/2} \log 2 \, dx$$

$$= \int_0^{\pi/2} \log \sin 2x \, dx - \log 2 \int_0^{\pi/2} dx$$

In first integral,

put $2x = \theta$

$\therefore \quad 2 \, dx = d\theta$

$\therefore \quad dx = \dfrac{d\theta}{2}$

when $x = 0, \ \theta = 0$

when $x = \dfrac{\pi}{2}, \ \theta = \pi$

$$\therefore \quad 2I = \frac{1}{2} \int_0^{\pi} \log \sin \theta \, d\theta - \log 2 \, (x)_0^{\pi/2}$$

$$= \frac{1}{2} \cdot 2 \int_0^{\pi/2} \log \sin \theta \, d\theta - (\log 2) \cdot \frac{\pi}{2} \qquad \text{by VI}$$

$$[\sin (\pi - \theta) = \sin \theta]$$

$$= \int_0^{\pi/2} \log \sin x \, dx - \frac{\pi}{2} \log 2 \qquad \text{by I}$$

$$= I - \frac{\pi}{2} \log 2$$

$$\therefore \quad 2I - I = -\frac{\pi}{2} \log 2$$

$$\therefore \quad I = -\frac{\pi}{2} \log_e 2$$

$$= \frac{\pi}{2} (\log_e 1 - \log_e 2) \qquad [\because \log_e 1 = 0]$$

$$= \frac{\pi}{2} \log_e (1/2)$$

Example 2. Prove that

$$\int_0^{\pi/2} \frac{\sqrt{\sin x}}{\sqrt{\sin x} + \sqrt{\cos x}}\, dx = \frac{\pi}{4}.$$

Solution :

$$I = \int_0^{\pi/2} \frac{\sqrt{\sin x}}{\sqrt{\sin x} + \sqrt{\cos x}}\, dx \qquad \text{... (1)}$$

or $$I = \int_0^{\pi/2} \frac{\sqrt{\sin\left(\frac{\pi}{2} - x\right)}}{\sqrt{\sin\left(\frac{\pi}{2} - x\right)} + \sqrt{\cos\left(\frac{\pi}{2} - x\right)}}\, dx \quad \text{by (IV)}$$

or $$I = \int_0^{\pi/2} \frac{\sqrt{\cos x}}{\sqrt{\cos x} + \sqrt{\sin x}}\, dx \qquad \text{... (2)}$$

Adding (1) and (2), we get

$$2I = \int_0^{\pi/2} \frac{\sqrt{\sin x}}{\sqrt{\sin x} + \sqrt{\cos x}}\, dx + \int_0^{\pi/2} \frac{\sqrt{\cos x}}{\sqrt{\sin x} + \sqrt{\cos x}}\, dx$$

$$= \int_0^{\pi/2} \frac{\sqrt{\sin x} + \sqrt{\cos x}}{\sqrt{\sin x} + \sqrt{\cos x}}\, dx$$

$$= \int_0^{\pi/2} 1\, dx = (x)_0^{\pi/2}$$

$$= \frac{\pi}{2}$$

$$\therefore \quad I = \frac{\pi}{4}$$

Example 3. Evaluate $\int_0^{\pi} \frac{x \sin x}{1 + \cos^2 x}\, dx.$

Solution :

$$I = \int_0^{\pi} \frac{x \sin x}{1 + \cos^2 x}\, dx \qquad \text{... (1)}$$

Using IV,

$$I = \int_0^{\pi} \frac{(\pi - x)\sin(\pi - x)\,dx}{1+\cos^2(\pi - x)}$$

or $$I = \int_0^{\pi} \frac{(\pi - x)\sin x}{1+\cos^2 x}\,dx \qquad \dots (2)$$

Adding (1) and (2), we get

$$2I = \int_0^{\pi} \frac{(x+\pi - x)\sin x}{1+\cos^2 x}\,dx$$

$$= \pi\int_0^{\pi} \frac{\sin x}{1+\cos^2 x}\,dx$$

Put $\cos x = t$

$\therefore \quad -\sin x\,dx = dt$

$\therefore \quad \sin x\,dx = -dt$

when $x = 0,\ t = \cos 0 = 1$

when $x = \pi,\ t = \cos \pi = -1$

$$\therefore \quad 2I = -\pi\int_1^{-1} \frac{dt}{1+t^2}$$

$$= \pi\int_{-1}^{1} \frac{dt}{1+t^2} \qquad \text{by II}$$

$$= 2\pi\int_0^{1} \frac{dt}{1+t^2} \qquad \text{by V}$$

$\because$ integrand is an even function of t

$$= 2\pi\left(\tan^{-1} t\right)_0^1$$

$$= 2\pi\left(\tan^{-1} 1 - \tan^{-1} 0\right)$$

$$= 2\pi\left(\frac{\pi}{4} - 0\right) = \frac{\pi^2}{2}$$

$$\therefore \quad I = \frac{\pi^2}{4}$$

Example 4. Show that

$$\int_0^{\pi/4} \log(1+\tan\theta)\,d\theta = \frac{\pi}{8}\log_e 2.$$

Solution :

$$I = \int_0^{\pi/4} \log(1+\tan\theta)\, d\theta \qquad \ldots (1)$$

Using IV

$$I = \int_0^{\pi/4} \log\left\{1+\tan\left(\frac{\pi}{4}-\theta\right)\right\} d\theta$$

$$= \int_0^{\pi/4} \log\left\{1+\frac{\tan\frac{\pi}{4}-\tan\theta}{1+\tan\frac{\pi}{4}\tan\theta}\right\} d\theta$$

$$= \int_0^{\pi/4} \log\left\{1+\frac{1-\tan\theta}{1+\tan\theta}\right\} d\theta$$

$$= \int_0^{\pi/4} \log\left(\frac{2}{1+\tan\theta}\right) d\theta$$

$$= \int_0^{\pi/4} \log 2\, d\theta - \int_0^{\pi/4} \log(1+\tan\theta)\, d\theta$$

$$= \log 2\left(\frac{\pi}{4}\right) - I$$

or, $$2I = \frac{\pi}{4}\log 2$$

or, $$I = \frac{\pi}{8}\log_e 2$$

EXERCISE 10.2

Evaluate :

1. $\int_0^{\pi/2} \frac{\sin x}{\sin x+\cos x}\, dx$

2. $\int_0^{\pi/2} \frac{\sqrt{\cot x}}{\sqrt{\cot x}+\sqrt{\tan x}}\, dx$

3. $\int_0^{\pi/2} \frac{dx}{1+\tan x}$

4. $\int_0^{\pi/2} \frac{dx}{1+\cot x}$

5. $\int_0^{\pi/2} \log\tan x\, dx$

6. $\int_0^{\pi} \sin^2 x\, dx$

7. $\int_0^{\pi} \cos^3 x\, dx$

8. $\int_0^{\pi} \sin^2\theta\,(1+2\cos\theta)\,(1+\cos\theta)^2\,d\theta$

9. $\int_0^{\pi} \frac{x\tan x\,dx}{\sec x+\tan x}$

10. $\int_0^{\pi/2} \frac{\sin^2 x\,dx}{\sin x+\cos x}$

11. $\int_0^{\infty} \log\left(x+\frac{1}{x}\right)\frac{dx}{1+x^2}$

12. $\int_0^{1} \frac{\log(1+x)}{1+x^2}\,dx$

13. $\int_0^{\pi} \frac{x}{a^2\cos^2 x+b^2\sin^2 x}\,dx$

14. $\int_0^{\pi} \frac{x\,dx}{1+\cos\alpha\sin x}$

15. $\int_0^{\pi/2} \frac{x\sin x\cos x\,dx}{\sin^4 x+\cos^4 x}$

ANSWERS

EXERCISE 10.2

1. $\frac{\pi}{4}$

2. $\frac{\pi}{4}$

3. $\frac{\pi}{4}$

4. $\frac{\pi}{4}$

5. 0

6. $\frac{4}{3}$

7. 0

8. $\frac{8}{3}$

9. $\pi\left(\frac{\pi}{2}-1\right)$

10. $\frac{1}{\sqrt{2}}\log\left(\sqrt{2}+1\right)$

11. $\pi\log_e 2$

12. $\frac{\pi}{8}\log_e 2$

13. $\frac{\pi^2}{2\,ab}$

14. $\pi\,\alpha\,\text{cosec}\,\alpha$

15. $\frac{\pi^2}{16}$

10.3 Definition of a definite integral as the limit of a sum

If $f(x)$ is a continuous and single valued function of x in the closed interval $[a, b]$ than

$$\text{Lt}_{h\to 0} h\left[f(a)+f(a+h)\ f(a+2h)+\ldots+f\left(a+\overline{n-1}\,h\right)\right]$$

where $nh = b - a$ is called the definite integral of $f(x)$ between the limits a and b and is written as $\int_a^b f(x)\,dx$.

Note 1. The above method of evaluating $\int_a^b f(x)\,dx$

i.e. $\int_a^b f(x)\,dx = \text{Lt}_{h\to 0}\left[f(a) + f(a+h) + f(a+2h) + \ldots + f\left(a - \overline{n-1}\,h\right)\right]$

where $nh = b - a$

is called the **integration by summation or integration from definition as the limit of a sum or integration from first principles or integration** *ab-initio*.

Note 2. Proceed to limit as $h \to 0$ only after putting $nh = b - a$.

Note 3. Sum of first n natural numbers

$$= 1 + 2 + 3 + \ldots + n = \frac{n(n+1)}{2}$$

$\therefore$ Sum of first $(n - 1)$ natural numbers

$$= 1 + 2 + 3 + \ldots + (n-1) = \frac{n(n-1)}{2}$$

Note 4. Sum of the squares of first n natural numbers

$$= 1^2 + 2^2 + 3^2 + \ldots + n^2$$

$$= \frac{n(n+1)(2n+1)}{6}$$

$\therefore$ Sum of the squares of first $(n - 1)$ natural numbers

$$= \frac{n(n-1)(2n-1)}{6}$$

Note 5. Sum of the cubes of first n natural numbers

i.e. $$= 1^3 + 2^3 + 3^3 + \ldots + n^3 = \left[\frac{n(n+1)}{2}\right]^2$$

$\therefore$ Sum of the subes of first $(n - 1)$ natural numbers

i.e. $$= 1^3 + 2^3 + 3^3 + \ldots + (n-1)^3 = \left[\frac{n(n-1)}{2}\right]^2$$

Example 1. Evaluate by definition of definite integral as the limit of a sum

$$\int_a^b x^2 dx.$$

Solution :

$$\int_a^b x^2 dx \qquad \text{[Here } f(x) = x^2\text{]}$$

$$= \text{Lt}_{h \to 0}\, h\Big[a^2 + (a-h)^2 + (a+2h)^2 + (a+3h)^2 + \ldots + \big(a + \overline{n-1}\,h\big)^2\Big]$$

where $nh = b - a$

$$= \text{Lt}_{h \to 0}\, h\Big[na^2 + 2ah\{1+2+3+\ldots+\overline{n-1}\} + h^2\{1^2+2^2+3^2+\ldots+(\overline{n-1})^2\}\Big]$$

where $nh = b - a$

$$= \text{Lt}_{h \to 0}\, h\left[na^2 + \frac{2ah\, n(n-1)}{2} + h^2\, \frac{n(n-1)(2n-1)}{6}\right]$$

where $nh = b - a$

$$= \text{Lt}_{h \to 0}\left[nh\, a^2 + nh(nh-h)\,a + nh(nh-h)\frac{\left(nh - \frac{h}{2}\right)}{3}\right]$$

where $nh = b - a$

$$= \text{Lt}_{h \to 0}\left[(b-a)\,a^2 + (b-a)(b-a-h)\,a + \frac{1}{3}(b-a)(b-a-h)\left(b-a-\frac{h}{2}\right)\right]$$

$$= (b-a)\,a^2 + (b-a)^2\, a + \frac{(b-a)^3}{3}$$

$$= (b-a)\left[a^2 + (b-a)\,a + \frac{(b-a)^2}{3}\right]$$

$$= (b-a)\left[a^2 + (b-a)\left\{a + \frac{b-a}{3}\right\}\right]$$

$$= (b-a)\left[a^2 + (b-a)\frac{(b+2a)}{3}\right]$$

$$= (b-a)\left[\frac{3a^2 + b^2 + 2ab - ab - 2a^2}{3}\right]$$

$$= \frac{(b-a)(a^2 + b^2 + ab)}{3}$$

$$= \frac{b^3 - a^3}{3}$$

EXERCISE 10.3

Evaluate the following definite integrals by definition of a definite integral as the limit of sum :

1. $\int_a^b x\,dx$

2. $\int_a^b e^x\,dx$

3. $\int_a^b \sin x\,dx$

4. $\int_a^b \cos x\,dx$

5. $\int_a^b \frac{1}{x^2}\,dx$

6. $\int_a^b \frac{1}{\sqrt{x}}\,dx$

ANSWERS

EXERCISE 10.3

1. $\frac{b^2 - a^2}{2}$

2. $e^b - e^a$

3. $\cos a - \cos b$

4. $\sin b - \sin a$

5. $\frac{1}{a} - \frac{1}{b}$

6. $2\left(\sqrt{b} - \sqrt{a}\right)$

10.4 Summation of Series

The definition of definite integral as the limit of sum enables us to express the limits of sums of series of a certain type as definite integrals and thus evaluate them.

We have seen that

$$\int_a^b f(x)\,dx = \text{Lt}_{h\to 0}\, h\left[f(a)+f(a+h)+f(a+2h) + \ldots + f\left(a+\overline{n-1}\,h\right)\right]$$

where $nh = b - a$

$$= \text{Lt}_{h\to 0} \sum_{r=0}^{n-1} hf\,(a+rh)$$

where $nh = b - a$

Now put $a = 0$ and $b = 1$

$$\therefore \int_0^1 f(x)\,dx = \text{Lt}_{h\to 0} \sum_{r=0}^{n-1} hf\,(rh)$$

where $nh = 1 - 0 = 1$

$$= \text{Lt}_{n\to\infty} \sum_{r=0}^{n-1} \frac{1}{n} f\left(\frac{r}{n}\right)$$

$\because \quad nh = 1$

$\Rightarrow \quad h = \frac{1}{n}$

and $\quad h \to 0$

$\Rightarrow \quad n \to \infty$

i.e. $\int_0^1 f(x)\,dx = \text{Lt}_{n\to\infty} \sum_{r=0}^{n-1} \frac{1}{n} f\left(\frac{r}{n}\right)$

Comparing the two sides of the above result we infer that in order to write down the corresponding definite integral, replace

(i) $\frac{r}{n}$ by x

(ii) $\frac{1}{n}$ by dx

and

(iii) $\text{Lt}_{n\to\infty} \sum$ by $\int$ sign.

The lower and upper limits of definite integral are the values of $\frac{r}{n}$ for the first and the last term (when $n \to \infty$, $h \to 0$).

Note. In order that a series my be capable of being summed up by the above formula, it must possess the following properties :

(i) It must be possible to write the terms in the form $\frac{1}{n} f\left(\frac{r}{n}\right)$, so that $\frac{1}{n}$, which tends to zero, is a factor of every term and all the terms are the functions of the same variable $\frac{r}{n}$, which form an A.P. whose common difference is $\frac{1}{n}$.

(ii) The number of terms should be n; but since each term tends to zero, the additions or omission of any finite number of terms will not change the required limit.

Example 1. Find the limit when $n \to \infty$, of the series

$$\frac{1}{n} + \frac{n^2}{(n+1)^3} + \frac{n^2}{(n+2)^3} + \ldots + \frac{1}{8n}.$$

Solution :

$$\text{Lt}_{n \to \infty} \left[\frac{1}{n} + \frac{n^2}{(n+1)^3} + \frac{n^2}{(n+2)^3} + \ldots + \frac{1}{8n} \right]$$

$$= \text{Lt}_{n \to \infty} \left[\frac{n^2}{(n+0)^3} + \frac{n^2}{(n+1)^3} + \frac{n^2}{(n+2)^3} + \ldots + \frac{n^2}{(n+n)^3} \right]$$

$$= \text{Lt}_{n \to \infty} \sum_{r=0}^{n} \frac{n^2}{(n+r)^3}$$

$$= \text{Lt}_{n \to \infty} \sum_{r=0}^{n} \frac{n^2}{n^3 \left(1 + \frac{r}{n}\right)^3}$$

$$= \text{Lt}_{n \to \infty} \sum_{r=0}^{n} \frac{1}{n} \frac{1}{\left(1 + \frac{r}{n}\right)^3}$$

$$= \int_0^1 \frac{dx}{(1+x)^3}$$

$$= \left[-\frac{1}{2(1+x)^2}\right]_0^1$$

$$= -\frac{1}{2}\left(\frac{1}{4}-1\right)$$

$$= \frac{3}{8}$$

Example 2. Find the limit when $n \to \infty$ of the series

$$\frac{1}{n}+\frac{1}{n+1}+\frac{1}{n+2}+\frac{1}{n+3}+\ldots+\frac{1}{3n}.$$

Solution :

$$\text{Lt}_{n\to\infty}\left[\frac{1}{n}+\frac{1}{n+1}+\frac{1}{n+2}+\frac{1}{n+3}+\ldots+\frac{1}{3n}\right]$$

$$= \text{Lt}_{n\to\infty}\left[\frac{1}{n+0}+\frac{1}{n+1}+\frac{1}{n+2}+\ldots+\frac{1}{n+n}\right]$$

$$+ \text{Lt}_{n\to\infty}\left[\frac{1}{2n+1}+\frac{1}{2n+2}+\frac{1}{2n+3}+\ldots+\frac{1}{2n+n}\right]$$

$$= \text{Lt}_{n\to\infty}\sum_{r=0}^{n}\frac{1}{n+r}+\text{Lt}_{n\to\infty}\sum_{r=1}^{n}\frac{1}{2n+r}$$

$$= \text{Lt}_{n\to\infty}\sum_{r=0}^{n}\frac{1}{n}\cdot\frac{1}{1+\frac{r}{n}}+\text{Lt}_{n\to\infty}\sum_{r=0}^{n}\frac{1}{n\left(2+\frac{r}{n}\right)}$$

$$= \int_0^1\frac{dx}{1+x}+\int_0^1\frac{dx}{2+x}$$

$$= \left[\log(1+x)\right]_0^1+\left[\log(2+x)\right]_0^1$$

$$= \log 2 - \log 1 + \log 3 - \log 2$$

$$= \log_e 3$$

Example 3. Prove that

$$\text{Lt}_{h\to\infty}\left[\left(1+\frac{1}{n^2}\right)\left(1+\frac{2^2}{n^2}\right)\left(1+\frac{3^2}{n^2}\right)\ldots\left(1+\frac{n^2}{n^2}\right)\right]^{1/n} = 2e^{(\pi-4)/2}$$

Solution :

Let,

$$P = \text{Lt}_{n\to\infty}\left[\left(1+\frac{1}{n^2}\right)\left(1+\frac{2^2}{n^2}\right)\left(1+\frac{3^2}{n^2}\right)\ldots\left(1+\frac{n^2}{n^2}\right)\right]^{1/n}$$

$$\therefore \quad \log P = \text{Lt}_{n\to\infty}\frac{1}{n}\left[\log\left(1+\frac{1^2}{n^2}\right)+\log\left(1+\frac{2^2}{n^2}\right) + \log\left(1+\frac{3^2}{n^2}\right)+\ldots+\log\left(1+\frac{n^2}{n^2}\right)\right]$$

$$= \text{Lt}_{n\to\infty}\frac{1}{n}\sum_{r=0}^{n}\log\left(1+\frac{r^2}{n^2}\right)$$

$$= \int_0^1 \underset{\text{II}}{1}\cdot \underset{\text{I}}{\log\left(1+x^2\right)}\,dx$$

$$= \left[\log\left(1+x^2\right)x\right]_0^1 - \int_0^1\frac{2x}{1+x^2}\cdot x\,dx$$

$$= \log 2 - 2\int_0^1\frac{\left(x^2+1\right)-1}{1+x^2}\,dx$$

$$= \log 2 - 2\int_0^1\left(1-\frac{1}{1+x^2}\right)dx$$

$$= \log 2 - 2\left[x-\tan^{-1}x\right]_0^1$$

$$= \log 2 - 2\left[1-\tan^{-1}1\right]$$

$$= \log 2 - 2 + 2\tan^{-1}1$$

$$= \log 2 - 2 + 2\cdot\frac{\pi}{4}$$

$$= \log 2 - 2 + \frac{\pi}{2}$$

$$\therefore \log P - \log 2 = \frac{\pi}{2} - 2 = \frac{\pi-4}{2}$$

$$\Rightarrow \quad \log\frac{P}{2} = \frac{\pi-4}{2}$$

$$\Rightarrow \quad \frac{P}{2} = e^{\frac{\pi-4}{2}}$$

$$\Rightarrow \quad P = 2e^{\frac{\pi-4}{2}}$$

Example 4. Apply the definition of a definite integral as the limit of a sum to evaluate $\text{Lt}_{n\to\infty}\left(\frac{n!}{n^n}\right)^{1/n}$.

Solution :

$$\text{Let} \qquad P = \text{Lt}_{n\to\infty}\left(\frac{n!}{n^n}\right)^{1/n}$$

$$= \text{Lt}_{n\to\infty}\left(\frac{1, 2, 3.....n}{n, n, n.....n}\right)^{1/n}$$

$$\therefore \qquad \log P = \text{Lt}_{n\to\infty}\frac{1}{n}\left[\log\frac{1}{n}+\log\frac{2}{n}+\log\frac{3}{n}+...+\log\frac{n}{n}\right]$$

$$= \text{Lt}_{n\to\infty}\frac{1}{n}\sum_{r=1}^{n}\log\frac{r}{n}$$

$$= \int_0^1 \underset{\text{II}}{1}\cdot \underset{\text{I}}{\log x}\,dx$$

$$= [\log x\cdot x]_0^1 - \int_0^1 \frac{1}{x}\cdot x\,dx$$

$$= 0 - \int_0^1 1\cdot dx$$

$$= -(x)_0^1$$

$$= -1$$

$$\therefore \qquad P = e^{-1} = \frac{1}{e}$$

EXERCISE 10.4

Find the limit when $n \to \infty$ of the series :

1. $\frac{1}{n+1}+\frac{1}{n+2}+\frac{1}{n+3}+...+\frac{1}{2n}$

2. $\frac{1}{n^3}+\frac{4}{n^3}+\frac{9}{n^3}+\frac{16}{n^3}+...+\frac{n^2}{n^3}$

3. $\frac{n}{(n+1)^2}+\frac{n}{(n+2)^2}+...+\frac{n}{(n+n)^2}$

4. $\frac{n}{n^2}+\frac{n}{n^2+1^2}+\frac{n}{n^2+1^2}+...+\frac{n}{n^2+(n-1)^2}$

5. $\dfrac{1^2}{1^2+n^3}+\dfrac{2^2}{2^3+n^3}+\ldots+\dfrac{n^2}{n^3+n^3}$

6. $\dfrac{n^{1/2}}{n^{3/2}}+\dfrac{n^{1/2}}{(n+3)^{3/2}}+\dfrac{n^{1/2}}{(n+6)^{3/2}}+\ldots+\dfrac{n^{1/2}}{[n+3(n-1)]^{3/2}}$

7. $\dfrac{1}{n^2}\sec^2\dfrac{1}{n^2}+\dfrac{2}{n^2}\sec^2\dfrac{4}{n^2}+\dfrac{3}{n^2}\sec^2\dfrac{9}{n^2}+\ldots+\dfrac{1}{n}\sec^2\dfrac{n^2}{n^2}$

8. $\dfrac{1}{n}\left[\sin^{2k}\dfrac{\pi}{2n}+\sin^{2k}\dfrac{2\pi}{2n}+\sin^{2k}\dfrac{2\pi}{2n}+\ldots+\sin^{2k}\dfrac{\pi}{2}\right]$

9. Evaluate

$$\text{Lt}_{n\to\infty}\sum_{r=1}^{n-1}\frac{1}{n}\sqrt{\frac{n+r}{n-r}}$$

10. Evaluate

$$\text{Lt}_{n\to\infty}\sum_{r=0}^{n-1}\frac{1}{\sqrt{n^2-r^2}}$$

11. Evaluate

$$\text{Lt}_{n\to\infty}\sum_{r=1}^{n}\frac{r^3}{r^4+n^4}$$

12. Evaluate

$$\text{Lt}_{n\to\infty}\left[\tan\frac{\pi}{2n}\tan\frac{2\pi}{2n}\tan\frac{3\pi}{2n}\ldots\tan\frac{n\pi}{2n}\right]^{1/n}$$

13. Evaluate

$$\text{Lt}_{n\to\infty}\left[\left(1+\frac{1}{n}\right)\left(1+\frac{2}{n}\right)\left(1+\frac{3}{n}\right)\ldots\left(1+\frac{n}{n}\right)\right]^{1/n}$$

14. Evaluate

$$\text{Lt}_{n\to\infty}\sum_{r=1}^{n}\frac{\sqrt{n}}{\sqrt{r}\left[3\sqrt{r}+4\sqrt{n}\right]^2}$$

15. Evaluate

$$\text{Lt}_{n\to\infty}\left[\left(1+\frac{1}{n}\right)\left(1+\frac{2}{n}\right)^{1/2}\left(1+\frac{3}{n}\right)^{1/3}\left(1+\frac{4}{n}\right)^{1/4}\ldots\left(1+\frac{n}{n}\right)^{1/n}\right]$$

ANSWERS

EXERCISE 10.4

1. $\log_e 2$
2. $\frac{1}{3}$
3. $\frac{1}{2}$
4. $\frac{\pi}{4}$
5. $\frac{1}{3}\log_e 2$
6. $\frac{1}{3}$
7. $\frac{1}{2}\tan 1$
8. $\frac{(2k)!}{\left[2^k (k!)\right]^2}$
9. $\frac{\pi}{2+1}$
10. $\frac{\pi}{2}$
11. $\frac{1}{4}\log_e 2$
12. 1
13. $\frac{4}{e}$
14. $\frac{1}{14}$
15. $e^{\pi^2/12}$

11

Reduction Formulae

11.1 Definition

A formula which connects an integral with another in which the integrand is of the same type, but is of lower degree or is otherwise easier to integrate, is called a *Reduction Formula*.

Usually the reduction formula has to be used repeated to arrive at the integral of the given function. This method of integration is called *Integration by successive reduction*.

Reduction formulae are usually obtained by the method of integration by parts and are useful when the integral cannot be otherwise immediately obtained.

11.2 Reduction formula for $\int \sin^n x\, dx$ where n is a positive integer

Let
$$I_n = \int \sin^n x\, dx$$
$$= \int \underset{\text{I}}{\sin^{n-1} x}\; \underset{\text{II}}{\sin x}\, dx$$

Taking $\sin^{n-1}$ as the first function and $\sin x$ as the second function and integrating by parts,

$$= \sin^{n-1} x\,(-\cos x) - \int (n-1)\sin^{n-2} x \cos x\,(-\cos x)\, dx$$
$$= -\sin^{n-1} x \cos x + (n-1)\int \sin^{n-2} x \cos^2 x\, dx$$
$$= -\sin^{n-1} x \cos x + (n-1) \int \sin^{n-2} x\,(1-\sin^2 x)\, dx$$

$$= -\sin^{n-1} x \cos x + (n-1) \int \sin^{n-2} x \, dx - (n-1) \int \sin^n x \, dx$$

$$\Rightarrow \left(1 + \overline{n-1}\right) \int \sin^n x \, dx = -\sin^{n-1} x \cos x + (n-1) \int \sin^{n-2} x \, dx$$

$$\Rightarrow n \int \sin^n x \, dx = -\sin^{n-1} x \cos x + (n-1) \int \sin^{n-2} x \, dx$$

$$\Rightarrow \int \sin^n x \, dx = -\frac{\sin^{n-1} x \cos x}{n} + \frac{n-1}{n} \int \sin^{n-2} x \, dx$$

This is the required reduction formula.

11.3 Reduction formula for $\int \cos^n x \, dx$ where *n* is a positive integer

Let $$I_n = \int \cos^n x \, dx$$

$$= \int \underset{\text{I}}{\cos^{n-1} x} \, \underset{\text{II}}{\cos x} \, dx$$

Taking $\cos^{n-1} x$ as the first function and $\cos x$ as the second function and integrating by parts,

$$= \cos^{n-1} x \cdot \sin x - \int (n-1) \cos^{n-2} x \cdot (-\sin x) \cdot \sin x \cdot dx$$

$$= \cos^{n-1} \cdot \sin x + (n-1) \int \cos^{n-2} x \cdot \sin^2 x \, dx$$

$$= \cos^{n-1} x \cdot \sin x + (n-1) \int \cos^{n-2} x \cdot \left(1 - \cos^2 x\right) dx$$

$$= \cos^{n-1} x \cdot \sin x + (n-1) \int \cos^{n-2} x \, dx - (n-1) \int \cos^n x \, dx$$

$$\Rightarrow \left(1 + \overline{n-1}\right) \int \cos^n x \, dx = \cos^{n-1} x \sin x + (n-1) \int \cos^{n-2} x \, dx$$

$$\Rightarrow \quad n\int \cos^n x\,dx = \cos^{n-1} x \sin x + (n-1)\int \cos^{n-2} x\,dx$$

$$\Rightarrow \quad \int \cos^n x\,dx = \frac{\cos^{n-1} x \sin x}{n} + \frac{n-1}{n}\int \cos^{n-2} x\,dx$$

This is the required reduction formula.

11.4 Walli's Formula

If n is a +ve integer then $\int_0^{\pi/2} \sin^n x\,dx = \int_0^{\pi/2} \cos^n x\,dx$ has the value

$$\frac{n-1}{n}\cdot\frac{n-3}{n-2}\cdot\frac{n-5}{n-4}\cdots\cdots\frac{2}{3} \quad \text{if } n \text{ is odd}$$

and the value

$$\frac{n-1}{n}\cdot\frac{n-3}{n-2}\cdot\frac{n-5}{n-4}\cdots\cdots\frac{3}{4}\,\frac{1}{2}\cdot\frac{\pi}{2} \quad \text{if } n \text{ is even}$$

Proof

Let
$$I_n = \int_0^{\pi/2} \sin^n x\,dx$$

$$= \int_0^{\pi/2} \sin^n\left(\frac{\pi}{2} - x\right)dx \qquad \left|\ \because \int_0^a f(x)\,dx = \int_0^a f(a-x)\,dx\right.$$

$$= \int_0^{\pi/2} \cos^n x\,dx$$

$$= \left[\frac{\cos^{n-1} x \sin x}{n}\right]_0^{\pi/2} + \frac{n-1}{n}\int_0^{\pi/2} \cos^{n-2} x\,dx$$

| using art. 11.2

$$\Rightarrow \quad I_n = \frac{n-1}{n} I_{n-2} \qquad \ldots (1)$$

Replacing n by $n - 2$, we get

$$I_{n-2} = \frac{n-3}{n-2} I_{n-4} \qquad \ldots (2)$$

Putting the value of I_{n-2} from (2) in (1), we get

$$I_n = \frac{n-1}{n}\cdot\frac{n-3}{n-2} I_{n-4} \qquad \ldots (3)$$

Replace n by $n - 4$ in (1), we get

$$I_{n-4} = \frac{n-5}{n-4} I_{n-6} \qquad \dots (4)$$

Putting the value of I_{n-4} from (4) in (3), we get

$$I_n = \frac{n-1}{n} \cdot \frac{n-3}{n-2} \cdot \frac{n-5}{n-4} I_{n-6}$$

Proceeding in this manner, we see that two cases arise :

Case I. When n is odd, then

$$I_n = \frac{n-1}{n} \cdot \frac{n-3}{n-2} \cdot \frac{n-5}{n-4} \dots\dots \frac{2}{3} \cdot I_1$$

Now
$$I_1 = \int_0^{\pi/2} \sin x \, dx$$
$$= (-\cos x)_0^{\pi/2}$$
$$= 1$$

$\therefore$
$$I_n = \frac{n-1}{n} \cdot \frac{n-3}{n-2} \cdot \frac{n-5}{n-4} \dots\dots \frac{2}{3}$$

Case II. When n is even, then

$$I_n = \frac{n-1}{n} \cdot \frac{n-3}{n-2} \cdot \frac{n-5}{n-4} \dots\dots \frac{1}{2} \cdot I_0$$

Now
$$I_0 = \int_0^{\pi/2} \sin^0 x \, dx$$
$$= (x)_0^{\pi/2}$$
$$= \frac{\pi}{2}$$

$\therefore$
$$I_n = \frac{n-1}{n} \cdot \frac{n-3}{n-2} \cdot \frac{n-5}{n-4} \dots\dots \frac{1}{2} \cdot \frac{\pi}{2}$$

11.5 Reduction formula for $\int \tan^n x \, dx$ where n is a positive integer

Let
$$I_n = \int \tan^n x \, dx$$
$$= \int \tan^{n-2} x \tan^2 x \, dx$$
$$= \int \tan^{n-2} x \left(\sec^2 x - 1\right) dx$$

$$= \int \tan^{n-2} x \sec^2 x \, dx - \int \tan^{n-2} x \, dx$$

Put $\tan x = t$

$\therefore \sec^2 x \, dx = dt$

$$= \int t^{n-2} dt - \int \tan^{n-2} x \, dx$$

$$= \frac{t^{n-1}}{n-1} - \int \tan^{n-2} x \, dx$$

$$\Rightarrow \int \tan^n x \, dx = \frac{\tan^{n-1} x}{n-1} - \int \tan^{n-2} x \, dx$$

This is the required reduction formula.

11.6 Reduction formula for $\int \cot^n x \, dx$ where *n* is a positive integer

Let $I_n = \int \cot^n x \, dx$

$$= \int \cot^{n-2} x \cdot \cot^2 x \, dx$$

$$= \int \cot^{n-2} x \left(\operatorname{cosec}^2 x - 1\right) dx$$

$$= \int \cot^{n-2} x \operatorname{cosec}^2 x \, dx - \int \cot^{n-2} x \, dx$$

Put $\cot x = t$

$\therefore \; -\operatorname{cosec}^2 x \, dx = dt$

$$= -\int t^{n-2} dt - \int \cot^{n-2} x \, dx$$

$$= -\frac{t^{n-1}}{n-1} - \int \cot^{n-2} x \, dx$$

$$\Rightarrow \int \cot^n x \, dx = -\frac{\cot^{n-1} x}{n-1} - \int \cot^{n-2} x \, dx$$

This is the required reduction formula.

11.7 Reduction formula for $\int \sec^n x \, dx$ where *n* is a positive integer

Let $I_n = \int \sec^n x \, dx$

$$= \int \underset{\text{I}}{\sec^{n-2} x} \cdot \underset{\text{II}}{\sec^2 x} \, dx$$

Taking $\sec^{n-2} x$ as the first finction and $\sec^2 x$ as the second function and integrating by parts,

$$= \sec^{n-2} x \cdot \tan x$$

$$- \int (n-2) \sec^{n-3} x \cdot \sec x \tan x \cdot \tan x \, dx$$

$$= \sec^{n-2} x \tan x - (n-2) \int \sec^{n-2} x \tan^2 x \, dx$$

$$= \sec^{n-2} x \tan x - (n-2)$$

$$\int \sec^n dx + (n-2) \int \sec^{n-2} x \, dx$$

$$\Rightarrow \quad (1 + n - 2) \int \sec^n x \, dx$$

$$= \sec^{n-2} x \tan x + (n-2) \int \sec^{n-2} x \, dx$$

$$\Rightarrow \quad (n-1) \int \sec^n x \, dx$$

$$= \sec^{n-2} x \tan x + (n-2) \int \sec^{n-2} x \, dx$$

$$\Rightarrow \int \sec^n x \, dx = \frac{\sec^{n-2} x \tan x}{n-1} + \frac{n-2}{n-1} \int \sec^{n-2} x \, dx$$

This is the required reduction formula.

11.8 Reduction formula for $\int \mathbf{cosec}^n x \, dx$ where n is a positive integer

Let $\quad I_n = \int \operatorname{cosec}^n x \, dx$

$$= \int \underset{\text{I}}{\operatorname{cosec}^{n-2} x} \cdot \underset{\text{II}}{\operatorname{cosec}^2 x} \, dx$$

Taking $\operatorname{cosec}^{n-2} x$ as the first function and $\operatorname{cosec}^2 x$ as the second function and integrating by parts,

$$= \operatorname{cosec}^{n-2} x \cdot (-\cot x)$$

$$- \int (n-2) \operatorname{cosec}^{n-3} x \cdot \{-\operatorname{cosec} x \cot x\} \cdot (-\cot x) \, dx$$

$$= -\operatorname{cosec}^{n-2} x \cot x - (n-2) \int \operatorname{cosec}^{n-2} x \cot^2 x \, dx$$

$$= -\operatorname{cosec}^{n-2} x \cot x - (n-2)$$

$$\int \operatorname{cosec}^{n-2} x \left(\operatorname{cosec}^2 x - 1\right) dx$$

$$= -\operatorname{cosec}^{n-2}x \cot x - (n-2)\int \operatorname{cosec}^n x \, dx + (n-2)\int \operatorname{cosec}^{n-2} x \, dx$$

$$\Rightarrow \quad (1+n-2)\int \operatorname{cosec}^n x \, dx = -\operatorname{cosec}^{n-2}x \cot x + (n-2)\int \operatorname{cosec}^{n-2} x \, dx$$

$$\Rightarrow \quad (n-1)\int \operatorname{cosec}^n x \, dx = -\operatorname{cosec}^{n-2}x \cot x + (n-2)\int \operatorname{cosec}^{n-2} x \, dx$$

$$\Rightarrow \quad \int \operatorname{cosec}^n x \, dx = -\frac{\operatorname{cosec}^{n-2}x \cot x}{n-1} + \frac{n-2}{n-1}\int \operatorname{cosec}^{n-2} x \, dx$$

This is the required reduction formula.

ILLUSTRATIVE EXAMPLES

Example 1. Evaluate $\int \sin^6 x \, dx$.

Solution : We know that

$$\int \sin^n x \, dx = -\frac{\sin^{n-1} x \cos x}{n} + \frac{n-1}{n}\int \sin^{n-2} x \, dx$$

Put $n = 6, 4, 2$ in succession, we get

$$\int \sin^6 x \, dx = -\frac{\sin^5 x \cos x}{6} + \frac{5}{6}\int \sin^4 x \, dx$$

$$\int \sin^4 x \, dx = -\frac{\sin^3 x \cos x}{4} + \frac{3}{4}\int \sin^2 x \, dx$$

$$\int \sin^2 x \, dx = -\frac{\sin x \cos x}{2} + \frac{1}{2}\int \sin^0 x \, dx$$

$$= -\frac{\sin x \cos x}{2} + \frac{1}{2} \cdot x$$

Hence,

$$\int \sin^6 x \, dx = -\frac{\sin^5 x \cos x}{6} + \frac{5}{6}\int \sin^4 x \, dx$$

$$= -\frac{\sin^5 x \cos x}{6} + \frac{5}{6}\left[-\frac{\sin^3 x \cos x}{4} + \frac{3}{4}\int \sin^2 x \, dx\right]$$

$$= -\frac{\sin^5 x \cos x}{6} - \frac{5}{24}\sin^3 x \cos x + \frac{5}{8}\int \sin^2 x \, dx$$

$$= -\frac{\sin^5 x \cos x}{5} - \frac{5}{24}\sin^3 x \cos x + \frac{5}{8}\left[-\frac{\sin x \cos x}{2} + \frac{x}{2}\right]$$

$$= -\frac{\sin^5 x \cos x}{6} - \frac{5}{24}\sin^3 x \cos x - \frac{5}{16}\sin x \cos x + \frac{5x}{16}$$

Example 2. Evaluate $\int \cos^6 x \, dx$.

Solution : We know that

$$\int \cos^n x \, dx = \frac{\cos^{n-1} x \sin x}{6} + \frac{n-1}{n}\int \cos^{n-2} x \, dx$$

Put $n = 6, 4, 2$ in succession, we get

$$\int \cos^6 x \, dx = \frac{\cos^5 x \sin x}{6} + \frac{5}{6}\int \cos^4 x \, dx$$

$$\int \cos^4 x \, dx = \frac{\cos^3 x \sin x}{4} + \frac{3}{4}\int \cos^2 x \, dx$$

$$\int \cos^2 x \, dx = \frac{\cos x \sin x}{2} + \frac{1}{2}\int \cos^0 x \, dx$$

$$= \frac{\cos x \sin x}{2} + \frac{1}{2} \cdot x$$

Hence,

$$\int \cos^6 x \, dx = \frac{\cos^5 x \sin x}{6} + \frac{5}{6}\int \cos^4 x \, dx$$

$$= \frac{\cos^5 x \sin x}{6} + \frac{5}{6}\left[\frac{\cos^3 x \sin x}{4} + \frac{3}{4}\int \cos^2 x \, dx\right]$$

$$= \frac{\cos^5 x \sin x}{6} + \frac{5}{24}\cos^3 x \sin x + \frac{5}{8}\int \cos^2 x \, dx$$

$$= \frac{\cos^5 x \sin x}{6} + \frac{5}{24}\cos^3 x \sin x$$

$$+ \frac{5}{8}\left[\frac{\cos x \sin x}{2} + \frac{x}{2}\right]$$

$$= \frac{\cos^5 x \sin x}{6} + \frac{5}{24}\cos^3 x \sin x + \frac{5}{16}\cos x \sin x + \frac{5}{16}x$$

Example 3. Evaluate $\int_0^a (a^2 + x^2)^{5/2}\, dx.$

Solution :

$$I = \int_0^a (a^2 + x^2)^{5/2}\, dx \qquad \text{Put} \quad x = a \tan\theta$$

$$\therefore \quad dx = a \sec^2\theta\, d\theta$$

$$= \int_0^{\pi/4} (a^2 + a^2\tan^2\theta)^{5/2} \cdot a\sec^2\theta\, d\theta$$

$$= a^6 \int_0^{\pi/4} \sec^7\theta\, d\theta$$

$$= a^6 \left[\left(\frac{\sec^5\theta \tan\theta}{6} \right)_0^{\pi/4} + \frac{5}{6}\int_0^{\pi/4} \sec^5\theta\, d\theta \right]$$

$$= a^6 \left[\frac{2\sqrt{2}}{3} + \frac{5}{6}\int_0^{\pi/4} \sec^5\theta\, d\theta \right]$$

$$= a^6 \left[\frac{2\sqrt{2}}{3} + \frac{5}{6}\left\{ \left(\frac{\sec^3\theta + \tan\theta}{4} \right)_0^{\pi/4} + \frac{3}{4}\int_0^{\pi/4} \sec^3\theta\, d\theta \right\} \right]$$

$$= a^6 \left[\frac{2\sqrt{2}}{3} + \frac{5}{6}\left\{ \frac{2\sqrt{2}}{4} + \frac{3}{4}\int_0^{\pi/4} \sec^3\theta\, d\theta \right\} \right]$$

$$= a^6 \left[\frac{2\sqrt{2}}{3} + \frac{5\sqrt{2}}{12} + \frac{5}{8}\int_0^{\pi/4} \sec^3\theta\, d\theta \right]$$

$$= a^6 \left[\frac{2\sqrt{2}}{3} + \frac{5\sqrt{2}}{12} + \frac{5}{8}\left\{ \left(\frac{\sec\theta \tan\theta}{2} \right)_0^{\pi/4} + \frac{1}{2}\int_0^{\pi/4} \sec\theta\, d\theta \right\} \right]$$

$$= a^6 \left[\frac{2\sqrt{2}}{3} + \frac{5\sqrt{2}}{12} + \frac{5}{8}\left\{ \frac{\sqrt{2}}{2} + \frac{1}{2}\{\log(\sec\theta + \tan\theta)\}_0^{\pi/4} \right\} \right]$$

$$= a^6 \left[\frac{2\sqrt{2}}{3} + \frac{5\sqrt{2}}{12} + \frac{5\sqrt{2}}{16} + \frac{5}{16}\log\left(\sqrt{2} + 1\right) \right]$$

$$= a^6\left[\frac{32\sqrt{2}}{48}+\frac{20\sqrt{2}}{48}+\frac{15\sqrt{2}}{48}+\frac{5}{16}\log\left(\sqrt{2}+1\right)\right]$$

$$= a^6\left[\frac{32\sqrt{2}+20\sqrt{2}+15\sqrt{2}}{48}+\frac{5}{16}\log\left(\sqrt{2}+1\right)\right]$$

$$= a^6\left[\frac{67\sqrt{2}}{48}+\frac{5}{16}\log\left(\sqrt{2}+1\right)\right]$$

$$= \frac{a^6}{48}\left[67\sqrt{2}+15\log\left(\sqrt{2}+1\right)\right]$$

Example 4. Evaluate $\int \frac{d\theta}{\sin^4 \frac{\theta}{2}}$.

Solution :

$$I = \int \frac{d\theta}{\sin^4 \frac{\theta}{2}} \qquad \text{Put} \quad \frac{\theta}{2} = t \quad \Rightarrow \quad d\theta = 2dt$$

$$= 2\int \frac{dt}{\sin^4 t}$$

$$= 2\int \operatorname{cosec}^4 t\, dt$$

$$= 2\left[-\frac{\operatorname{cosec}^2 t \cot t}{3}+\frac{2}{3}\int \operatorname{cosec}^2 t\, dt\right]$$

$$= -\frac{2}{3}\operatorname{cosec}^2 t \cot t - \frac{4}{3}\cot t$$

$$= -\frac{2}{3}\cot t\left[\operatorname{cosec}^2 t + 2\right]$$

$$= -\frac{2}{3}\cot\frac{\theta}{2}\left[\operatorname{cosec}^2\frac{\theta}{2}+2\right]$$

Example 5. Evaluate $\int_0^{\pi/4} \tan^5\theta\, d\theta$.

Solution :

$$I = \int_0^{\pi/4} \tan^5\theta\, d\theta$$

$$= \left(\frac{\tan^4 \theta}{4}\right)_0^{\pi/4} - \int_0^{\pi/4} \tan^3 \theta \, d\theta$$

$$= \frac{1}{4} - \int_0^{\pi/4} \tan^3 \theta \, d\theta$$

$$= \frac{1}{4} - \left[\left(\frac{\tan^2 \theta}{2}\right)_0^{\pi/4} - \int_0^{\pi/4} \tan \theta \, d\theta\right]$$

$$= \frac{1}{4} - \left[\frac{1}{2} - (\log \sec \theta)_0^{\pi/4}\right]$$

$$= \frac{1}{4} - \left[\frac{1}{2} - \log \sqrt{2}\right]$$

$$= -\frac{1}{4} + \log \sqrt{2}$$

$$= -\frac{1}{4} + \frac{1}{2} \log 2$$

Example 6. Evaluate $\int \cot^4 x \, dx$.

Solution :

$$I = \int \cot^4 x \, dx$$

$$= -\frac{\cot^3 x}{3} - \int \cot^2 x \, dx$$

$$= -\frac{\cot^3 x}{2} - \int (\operatorname{cosec}^2 x - 1) \, dx$$

$$= -\frac{\cot^3 x}{3} - (-\cot x - x)$$

$$= -\frac{\cot^3 x}{3} + \cot x + x$$

Example 7. If $\varphi(n) = \int_0^{\pi/4} \tan^n x \, dx$, show that $\varphi(n) + \varphi(n-2) = \frac{1}{n-1}$ and deduce the value of $\varphi(5)$.

Solution :

$$\varphi(n) = \int_0^{\pi/4} \tan^n x\, dx$$

$$= \left(\frac{\tan^{n-1} x}{n-1}\right)_0^{\pi/4} - \int_0^{\pi/4} \tan^{n-2} x\, dx$$

$$= \frac{1}{n-1} - \varphi_{n-2}$$

$$\Rightarrow \varphi_n + \varphi_{n-2} = \frac{1}{n-1} \qquad \text{Proved}$$

Now

$$\varphi(5) = \frac{1}{4} - \varphi_3$$

$$= \frac{1}{4} - \left[\frac{1}{2} - \varphi_1\right]$$

$$= -\frac{1}{4} + \varphi_1$$

$$= -\frac{1}{4} + \int_0^{\pi/4} \tan x\, dx$$

$$= -\frac{1}{4} + (\log \sec x)_0^{\pi/4}$$

$$= -\frac{1}{4} + \log \sqrt{2}$$

$$= -\frac{1}{4} + \frac{1}{2}\log 2$$

Example 8. Show that $\int_0^{\pi/8} \cos^3 4x\, dx = \frac{1}{6}$.

Solution :

$$I = \int_0^{\pi/8} \cos^3 4x\, dx \qquad \text{Put } 4x = t$$

$$\therefore \quad 4dx = dt$$

$$= \int_0^{\pi/2} \cos^3 t \frac{dt}{4} \qquad \therefore \quad dx = \frac{dt}{4}$$

$$= \frac{1}{4}\int_0^{\pi/2} \cos^3 t\, dt$$

$$= \frac{1}{4} \cdot \frac{2}{3} \qquad \text{Using Walli's formula}$$

$$= \frac{1}{6}$$

Example 9. Evalute $\int_0^{2a} x^{9/2} (2a - x)^{-1/2} \, dx$.

Solution :

$$I = \int_0^{2a} x^{9/2} (2a - x)^{-1/2} \, dx$$

Put $x = 2a \sin^2 \theta$

$\therefore$ $dx = 4a \sin \theta \cos \theta \, d\theta$

$$= \int_0^{\pi/2} (2a)^{9/2} \sin^9 \theta \left(2a - 2a \sin^2 \theta\right)^{-1/2} \cdot 4a \sin \theta \cos \theta \, d\theta$$

$$= \int_0^{\pi/2} (2a)^{9/2} \cdot \sin^9 \theta \cdot (2a)^{-1/2} \cos^{-1} \theta \cdot 4a \sin \theta \cos \theta \, d\theta$$

$$= (2a)^4 \cdot 4a \cdot \int_0^{\pi/2} \sin^{10} \theta \, d\theta$$

$$= 64 \, a^5 \, \frac{9}{10} \cdot \frac{7}{8} \cdot \frac{5}{6} \cdot \frac{3}{4} \cdot \frac{1}{2} \cdot \frac{\pi}{2} \qquad \text{Using Walli's formula}$$

$$= \frac{63 \, \pi \, a^5}{8}$$

Example 10. If $I_n = \int_0^a \left(a^2 - x^2\right)^n dx$, and $n > 0$, prove that $I_n = \dfrac{2na^2}{2n+1} I_{n-1}$.

Solution : We have

$$I_n = \int_0^a \left(a^2 - x^2\right)^n dx$$

Put $x = a \sin \theta$

$\therefore$ $dx = a \cos \theta \, d\theta$

$$= \int_0^{\pi/2} \left(a^2 - a^2 \sin^2 \theta\right)^n \left(a \cos \theta\right) d\theta$$

$$= a^{2n+1} \int_0^{\pi/2} \cos^{2n+1} \theta \, d\theta$$

$$= a^{2n+1} \left[\left(\frac{\cos^{2n} \theta \sin \theta}{2n+1} \right)_0^{\pi/2} + \frac{2n}{2n+1} \int_0^{\pi/2} \cos^{2n-1} \theta \, d\theta \right]$$

$$= \frac{2n}{2n+1} a^{2n+1} \int_0^{\pi/2} \cos^{2n-1} \theta \, d\theta$$

$$= \frac{2na^2}{2n+1} \left\{ a^{2n-1} \int_0^{\pi/2} \cos^{2n-1} \theta \, d\theta \right\}$$

$$= \frac{2na^2}{2n+1} I_{n-1}$$

EXERCISE 11.1

Integrate :

1. $\sin^2 x$

2. $\sin^3 x$

3. $\sin^8 x$

4. $\sin^4 x$

5. $\sin^5 x$

6. $\cos^2 x$

7. $\cos^3 x$

8. $\cos^4 x$

9. $\cos^5 x$

10. $\cos^7 x$

11. $\tan^3 x$

12. $\tan^4 x$

13. $\tan^5 x$

14. $\cot^5 x$

15. $\cos^6 x$

16. $\text{cosec}^3 x$

17. $\int_0^{\pi/4} \sec^3 x \, dx$

18. $\int (1+x^2)^{3/2} \, dx$

19. $\int \frac{\sin^2 x}{\cos^3 x} \, dx$

20. $\int_0^{\pi/2} \sin^6 x \, dx$

21. $\int_0^{\pi/2} \sin^8 x \, dx$

22. $\int_0^{\pi/2} \sin^{10} x \, dx$

23. $\int_0^{\pi/2} \sin^7 \theta \, d\theta$

24. $\int_0^{\pi/2} \sin^{15} \theta \, d\theta$

25. $\int_0^{\pi/2} \cos^4 \theta \, d\theta$

26. $\int_0^{\pi/2} \cos^9 \theta \, d\theta$

27. $\int_0^{\pi/4} \sin^4 \theta \, d\theta$

28. $\int_0^{\pi/4} \sin^4 2\theta \, d\theta$

29. $\int_0^{\pi/4} \cos^2 2\theta \, d\theta$

30. $\int_0^{\pi/12} \sin^5 6\theta \, d\theta$

31. $\int_0^{\pi} \sin^7 \frac{\theta}{2} \, d\theta$

32. $\int_0^{\infty} \frac{dx}{(1+x^2)^4}$

33. $\int_0^\infty \frac{dx}{(a^2+x^2)^4}$

34. $\int_0^{\pi/2} \sin^4 x \cos^2 x \, dx$

35. $\int_0^1 x^6 (1-x^2)^{1/2} \, dx$

36. $\int_0^3 \left(\frac{x^3}{3-x}\right)^{1/2} dx$

37. $\int_0^a \frac{x^4}{\sqrt{a^2-x^2}} \, dx$

38. $\int_0^a x^2 \left(\frac{a-x}{a+x}\right)^{1/2} dx$

39. $\int_0^{\pi/2} \sin^{2n} x \, dx$

40. $\int_0^a \frac{x^n dx}{\sqrt{ax-x^2}}$

ANSWERS

EXERCISE 11.1

1. $\frac{1}{2}x - \frac{1}{4}\sin 2x$

2. $\frac{1}{12}\cos 3x - \frac{3}{4}\cos x$

3. $-\frac{1}{8}\sin^7 x \cos x + \frac{7}{8}\left\{-\frac{1}{6}\sin^5 x \cos x - \frac{5}{24}\sin^3 x \cos x - \frac{5}{16}\sin x \cos x + \frac{5x}{16}\right\}$

4. $-\frac{1}{4}\sin^3 x \cos x - \frac{3}{8}\sin x \cos x + \frac{3}{8}x$

5. $-\frac{1}{5}\sin^4 x \cos x - \frac{4}{15}(\sin^2 x + 2)\cos x$

6. $\frac{1}{2}x + \frac{1}{4}\sin 2x$

7. $\frac{3}{4}\sin x + \frac{1}{12}\sin 3x$

8. $\frac{1}{4}\cos^3 x \sin x + \frac{3}{8}(\cos x \sin x + x)$

9. $\frac{1}{5}\cos^4 x \sin x + \frac{4}{15}\cos^2 x \sin x + \frac{8}{15}\sin x$

10. $\sin x - \sin^3 x + \frac{3}{5}\sin^5 x - \frac{1}{7}\sin^7 x$

OR

$$-\frac{1}{7}\cos^6 x\sin x+\frac{6}{7}\frac{\cos^4 x\sin x}{5}+\frac{4}{5}\left\{\frac{\cos^2 x\sin x}{3}+\frac{2}{3}\sin x\right\}$$

11. $\frac{1}{2}\tan^2 x+\log\cos x$

12. $\frac{1}{3}\tan^3 x-(\tan x-x)$

13. $\frac{1}{4}\tan^4 x-\frac{1}{2}\tan^2 x-\log\cos x$

14. $-\frac{1}{4}\cot^4 x+\frac{1}{2}\cot^2 x+\log\sin x$

15. $-\frac{\cot^5 x}{5}-\left\{-\frac{\cot^3 x}{3}+\cot x+x\right\}$

16. $-\frac{\operatorname{cosec} x\cot x}{2}+\frac{1}{2}\log\tan\frac{x}{2}$

17. $\frac{1}{2}\left[\sqrt{2}+\log\left(1+\sqrt{2}\right)\right]$

18. $\frac{1}{4}x\left(1+x^2\right)^{3/2}+\frac{3x}{8}\left(1+x^2\right)^{1/2}+\frac{3}{8}\log\left(x+\sqrt{1+x^2}\right)$

19. $\frac{1}{2}\left[\sec x\tan x-\log(\sec x+\tan x)\right]$

20. $\frac{5\pi}{32}$

21. $\frac{35\pi}{256}$

22. $\frac{63\pi}{512}$

23. $\frac{16}{35}$

24. $\frac{\lfloor 15}{(15\cdot 13\cdot 11\cdot 9\cdot 7\cdot 5\cdot 3)^2}$

25. $\frac{3\pi}{16}$

26. $\frac{128}{315}$

27. $\frac{1}{8}\left(\frac{3\pi}{4}-2\right)$

28. $\frac{3\pi}{32}$

29. $\frac{\pi}{8}$

30. $\frac{4}{45}$

31. $\frac{32}{35}$

32. $\dfrac{5\pi}{32}$

33. $\dfrac{5\pi}{32\,a^7}$

34. $\dfrac{\pi}{32}$

35. $\dfrac{5\pi}{256}$

36. $\dfrac{9\pi}{8}$

37. $\dfrac{3\pi\, a^4}{16}$

38. $a^3\left(\dfrac{\pi}{4}-\dfrac{2}{3}\right)$

39. $\dfrac{\lfloor 2n}{\left(2^n \lfloor n\right)^2}\,\dfrac{\pi}{2}$

40. $\dfrac{\pi \cdot a^n \cdot \{1.3.5.....(2n-1)\}}{2.4.6.....2n}$

11.9 Reduction formula for $\int \sin^m x \cos^n x\, dx$

This integral may be connected with any one of the following :

(i) $\int \sin^{m-2} x \cos^n x\, dx$

(ii) $\int \sin^m x \cos^{n-2} x\, dx$

(iii) $\int \sin^{m+2} x \cos^n x\, dx$

(iv) $\int \sin^m x \cos^{n+2} x\, dx$

(v) $\int \sin^{m-2} x \cos^{n+2} x\, dx$

(vi) $\int \sin^{m+2} x \cos^{n-2} x\, dx$

Proofs

Let $$I_{m,\,n} = \int \sin^m x \cos^n x\, dx \qquad \text{... (1)}$$

$$= \int \underset{I}{\sin^{m-1} x} \cdot \underset{II}{\cos^n x \sin x}\, dx$$

Taking $\sin^{m-1} x$ as the first function and $\cos^n x \sin x$ as the second function and integrating by parts,

$$= \sin^{m-1} x \cdot \left(-\frac{\cos^{n+1} x}{n+1}\right)$$

$$-\int (m-1)\cdot \sin^{m-2} x \cdot \cos x \cdot \left(-\frac{\cos^{n+1} x}{n+1}\right) dx$$

$$= -\frac{\sin^{m-1} x \cos^{n+1} x}{n+1} + \frac{m-1}{n+1} \int \sin^{m-2} x \cos^{n+2} x \, dx \quad \text{... (2)}$$

$$= -\frac{\sin^{m-1} x \cos^{n+1} x}{n+1} + \frac{m-1}{n+1} \int \sin^{m-2} x \cos^{n} x \left\{1 - \sin^2 x\right\} dx$$

$$= -\frac{\sin^{m-1} x \cos^{n+1} x}{n+1} + \frac{m-1}{n+1} \int \sin^{m-2} x \cos^{n} x \, dx - \frac{m-1}{n+1} \int \sin^{m} x \cos^{n} x \, dx$$

$$\Rightarrow \quad I_{m,n} \left\{1 + \frac{m-1}{n+1}\right\} = -\frac{\sin^{m-1} x \cos^{n+1} x}{n+1} + \frac{m-1}{n+1} I_{m-2,\, n}$$

$$\Rightarrow \quad I_{m,\, n} \left\{\frac{m+n}{n+1}\right\} = -\frac{\sin^{m-1} x \cos^{n+1} x}{n+1} + \frac{m-1}{n+1} I_{m-2,\, n}$$

$$\Rightarrow \quad I_{m,\, n} = -\frac{\sin^{m-1} x \cos^{n+1} x}{m+n} + \frac{m-1}{m+n} I_{m-2,\, n} \quad \text{... (3)}$$

Writing $m + 2$ for m in (3), we get

$$I_{m+2,\, n} = -\frac{\sin^{m+1} x \cos^{n+1} x}{m+n+2} + \frac{m+1}{m+n+2} I_{m,\, n}$$

$$\Rightarrow \quad (m+n+2)\, I_{m+2,\, n} = -\sin^{m+1} x \cos^{n+1} x + (m+1)\, I_{m,\, n}$$

$$\Rightarrow \quad (m+1)\, I_{m,\, n} = \sin^{m+1} x \cos^{n+1} x + (m+n+2)\, I_{m+2,\, n}$$

Dividing by $(m + 1)$, we get

$$I_{m,\, n} = \frac{\sin^{m+1} x \cos^{n+1} x}{m+1} + \frac{m+n+2}{m+1} I_{m+2,\, n} \quad \text{... (4)}$$

(2), (3) and (4) above give the required connections.

Again,

$$I_{m,\,n} = \int \sin^m x \cos^n x \, dx$$

$$= \int \underset{II}{\sin^m x \cos x} \cdot \underset{I}{\cos^{n-1} x} \, dx$$

Taking $\cos^{n-1} x$ as the first function, $\sin^m x \cos x$ as the second function and integrating by parts,

$$= \cos^{n-1} x \cdot \frac{\sin^{m+1} x}{m+1} - \int (n-1) \cos^{n-2} x \cdot (-\sin x) \cdot \frac{\sin^{m+1} x}{m+1} \, dx$$

$$= \frac{\sin^{m+1} x \cos^{n-1} x}{m+1} + \frac{n-1}{m+1} \int \sin^{m+2} x \cos^{n-2} x \, dx \qquad \text{... (5)}$$

$$= \frac{\sin^{m+1} x \cos^{n-1} x}{m+1} + \frac{n-1}{m+1} \int \sin^m x \cos^{n-2} x \left\{1 - \cos^2 x\right\} dx$$

$$= \frac{\sin^{m+1} x \cos^{n-1} x}{m+1} + \frac{n-1}{m+1} \int \sin^m x \cos^{n-2} x \, dx - \frac{n-1}{m+1} \int \sin^m x \cos^n x \, dx$$

$$\Rightarrow \quad \left(1 + \frac{n-1}{m+1}\right) I_{m,\,n} = \frac{\sin^{m+1} x \cos^{n-1} x}{m+1} + \frac{n-1}{m+1} I_{m,\,n-2}$$

$$\Rightarrow \quad \left(\frac{m+n}{m+1}\right) I_{m,\,n} = \frac{\sin^{m+1} x \cos^{n-1} x}{m+1} + \frac{n-1}{m+1} I_{m,\,n-2}$$

$$\Rightarrow \quad I_{m,\,n} = \frac{\sin^{m+1} x \cos^{n-1} x}{m+n} + \frac{n-1}{m+n} I_{m,\,n-2} \qquad \text{... (6)}$$

Writing $n + 2$ for n in (6), we get

$$I_{m,\,n+2} = \frac{\sin^{m+1} x \cos^{n+1} x}{m+n+2} + \frac{n+1}{m+n+2} I_{m,\,n}$$

$$\Rightarrow \quad \frac{n+1}{m+n+2} I_{m,\,n}$$

$$= -\frac{\sin^{m+1} x \cos^{n+1} x}{m+n+2} + I_{m,\,n+2}$$

$$\Rightarrow \quad I_{m,\,n} = -\frac{\sin^{m+1} x \cos^{n+1} x}{n+1} + \frac{m+n+2}{n+1} I_{m,\,n+2} \quad \text{... (7)}$$

(5), (6) and (7) give the required connections.

Alternative Method

To connect $\int \sin^m x \cos^n x \, dx$ with any one of the six integrals given below :

(i) $\int \sin^{m-2} x \cos^n x \, dx$

(ii) $\int \sin^m x \cos^{n-2} x \, dx$

(iii) $\int \sin^{m+2} x \cos^n x \, dx$

(iv) $\int \sin^m x \cos^{n+2} x \, dx$

(v) $\int \sin^{m-2} x \cos^{n+2} x \, dx$

(vi) $\int \sin^{m+2} x \cos^{n-2} x \, dx$

We follow the following steps :

Step I. Take $P = \sin^{\lambda+1} x \cos^{\mu+1} x$ where λ is smaller of the two indices of $\sin x$ and μ is smaller of the two indices of $\cos x$ in the two integrals which are to be connected.

Step II. Find $\dfrac{dP}{dx}$ and express it as a linear function of the two integrands whose integrals are being connected.

Step III. Integrate both sides *w.r.t.* x, transpose and solve for the given integral.

ILLUSTRATIVE EXAMPLES

Example 1. Connect $\int \sin^m x \cos^n x\, dx$ with $\int \sin^{m-2} x \cos^{n+2} x\, dx$.

Solution :

Let $\quad P = \sin^{(m-2)+1} x \cos^{(n)+1} x$

$\Rightarrow \quad P = \sin^{m-1} x \cos^{n+1} x$

$$\therefore \quad \frac{dP}{dx} = (m-1) \sin^{m-2} x \cos x \cdot \cos^{n+1} x + \sin^{m-1} x \cdot (n+1) \cos^n x (-\sin x)$$

$$= (m-1) \sin^{m-2} x \cos^{n+2} x - (n+1) \sin^m x \cos^n x$$

Integate both sides *w.r.t.* x, we get

$$P = (m-1)\int \sin^{m-2} x \cos^{n+2} x\, dx - (n+1)\int \sin^m x \cos^n x\, dx$$

$$\Rightarrow \quad (n+1)\int \sin^m x \cos^n x\, dx = -P + (m-1)\int \sin^{m-2} x \cos^{n+2} x\, dx$$

$$\Rightarrow \quad (n+1)\int \sin^m x \cos^n x\, dx = -\sin^{m-1} x \cos^{n+1} x + (m-1)\int \sin^{m-2} x \cos^{n+2} x\, dx$$

$$\Rightarrow \quad \int \sin^m x \cos^n x\, dx = -\frac{\sin^{m-1} x \cos^{n+1} x}{n+1} + \frac{m-1}{n+1}\int \sin^{m-2} x \cos^{n+2} x\, dx$$

Example 2. Evaluate $\int \frac{\sin^4 x}{\cos^2 x} dx$.

Solution : We shall connect $\int \sin^4 x \cos^{-2} x\, dx$ with $\int \sin^2 x\, dx$

Let $\quad P = \sin^3 x \cos^{-1} x$

$$\therefore \quad \frac{dP}{dx} = 3 \sin^2 x + \sin^3 x \cos^{-2} x \sin x$$

$$= 3 \sin^2 x + \sin^4 x \cos^{-2} x$$

Integrate both sides *w.r.t.* x, we get

$$P = 3\int \sin^2 x\, dx + \int \sin^4 x \cos^{-2} x\, dx$$

$$\Rightarrow \quad \int \sin^4 x \cos^{-2} x\, dx$$

$$= P - 3\int \sin^2 x\, dx$$

$$\Rightarrow \int \frac{\sin^4 x}{\cos^2 x}\, dx = \frac{\sin^3 x}{\cos x} - \frac{3}{2}\int 2\sin^2 x\, dx$$

$$= \frac{\sin^3 x}{\cos x} - \frac{3}{2}\int (1 - \cos 2x)\, dx$$

$$= \frac{\sin^3 x}{\cos x} - \frac{3}{2}\left(x - \frac{\sin 2x}{2}\right)$$

$$= \frac{\sin^3 x}{\cos x} + \frac{3}{2}\sin x \cos x - \frac{3}{2}x$$

EXERCISE 11.2

1. Connect $\int \sin^m x \cos^n x\, dx$ with each of the following :

(i) $\int \sin^{m-2} x \cos^n x\, dx$ (ii) $\int \sin^m x \cos^{n-2} x\, dx$

(iii) $\int \sin^{m+2} x \cos^n x\, dx$ (iv) $\int \sin^m x \cos^{n+2} x\, dx$

(v) $\int \sin^{m+2} x \cos^{n-2} x\, dx$

2. Evaluate $\int \sin^2 x \cos^4 x\, dx$

3. Evaluate $\int \sin^4 x \cos^2 x\, dx$

4. Evaluate $\int \sin^2 x \cos^6 x\, dx$

5. Evaluate $\int_0^{\pi/4} \sin^5 x \cos^2 x\, dx$

ANSWERS

EXERCISE 11.2

1. (i) $\int \sin^m x \cos^n x\, dx$

$$= -\frac{\sin^{m-1} x \cos^{n+1} x}{m+n} + \frac{m-1}{m+n}\int \sin^{m-2} x \cos^n x\, dx$$

(ii) $\int \sin^m x \cos^n x\, dx$

$$= \frac{\sin^{m+1} x \cos^{n-1} x}{m+n} + \frac{n-1}{m+n}\int \sin^m x \cos^{n-2} x\, dx$$

(iii) $\int \sin^m x \cos^n x\, dx$

$$= \frac{\sin^{m+1} x \cos^{n+1} x}{m+1} + \frac{m+n+2}{m+1} \int \sin^{m+2} x \cos^n x\, dx$$

(iv) $\int \sin^m x \cos^n x\, dx$

$$= -\frac{\sin^{m+1} x \cos^{n+1} x}{n+1} + \frac{m+n+2}{n+1} \int \sin^m x \cos^{n+2} x\, dx$$

(v) $\int \sin^m x \cos^n x\, dx$

$$= \frac{\sin^{m+1} x \cos^{n-1} x}{m+1} + \frac{n-1}{m+1} \int \sin^{m+2} x \cos^{n-2} x\, dx$$

2. $\frac{1}{6} \sin^3 x \cos^3 x + \frac{1}{8} \sin^3 x \cos x - \frac{1}{16} \sin x \cos x + \frac{x}{16}$

3. $-\frac{1}{6} \sin^3 x \cos^3 x - \frac{1}{8} \sin x \cos^3 x + \frac{1}{6} \sin x \cos x + \frac{x}{16}$

4. $\frac{1}{8}\left(-\cos^7 x + \frac{1}{6} \cos^5 x + \frac{5}{24} \cos^3 x + \frac{5}{16} \cos x\right) \sin x + \frac{5x}{128}$

5. $\frac{128 - 71\sqrt{2}}{1680}$

11.10 To show that

$$\int_0^{\pi/2} \sin^m x \cos^n x\, dx = \frac{\left|\overline{\frac{m+1}{2}}\right. \left|\overline{\frac{n+1}{2}}\right.}{2\left|\overline{\frac{m+n+2}{2}}\right.}$$

where m and n are integers.

Proof

Case I. When $n = 0$. Then

$$\int_0^{\pi/4} \sin^m x \cos^n x\, dx$$

$$= \int_0^{\pi/2} \sin^m x\, dx$$

$$= \left[-\frac{\sin^{m-1} x \cos x}{m}\right]_0^{\pi/2} + \frac{m-1}{m} \int_0^{\pi/2} \sin^{m-2} x\, dx$$

$$= \frac{m-1}{m} \int_0^{\pi/2} \sin^{m-2} x\, dx$$

Now two cases arise

Case (i) When m is even. Then

$$= \frac{m-1}{m} \cdot \frac{m-3}{m-2} \cdot \frac{m-5}{m-4} \cdots\cdots \frac{1}{2} \int_0^{\pi/2} \sin^0 x \, dx$$

$$= \frac{m-1}{m} \cdot \frac{m-3}{m-2} \cdot \frac{m-5}{m-4} \cdots\cdots \frac{1}{2} \cdot \frac{\pi}{2}$$

$$= \frac{\left\{\frac{m-1}{2} \cdot \frac{m-3}{2} \cdot \frac{m-5}{2} \cdots\cdots \frac{1}{2} \cdot \Gamma\frac{1}{2}\right\} \sqrt{\pi}}{\left\{\frac{m}{2} \cdot \frac{m-2}{2} \cdot \frac{m-4}{2} \cdots\cdots \frac{2}{2} \cdot \Gamma 1\right\} 2}$$

$$= \frac{\Gamma\frac{m+1}{2} \sqrt{\pi}}{2\,\Gamma\frac{m+2}{2}} \qquad \because \quad \Gamma\frac{1}{2} = \sqrt{\pi}, \quad \Gamma(P+1) = P\,\Gamma P \ \forall\, P, \quad \Gamma 1 = 1$$

$$= \frac{\Gamma\frac{m+1}{2}\,\Gamma\frac{0+1}{2}}{2\,\Gamma\frac{m+0+2}{2}}$$

$$= \frac{\Gamma\frac{m+1}{2}\,\Gamma\frac{n+1}{2}}{2\,\Gamma\frac{m+n+2}{2}} \qquad \text{where } n = 0$$

Case (ii) When m is odd. Then

$$= \frac{m-1}{m} \cdot \frac{m-3}{m-2} \cdot \frac{m-5}{m-4} \cdots\cdots \frac{2}{3} \int_0^{\pi/2} \sin x \, dx$$

$$= \frac{m-1}{m} \cdot \frac{m-3}{m-2} \cdot \frac{m-5}{m-4} \cdots\cdots \frac{2}{3} \cdot 1$$

$$= \frac{\frac{m-1}{2} \cdot \frac{m-3}{2} \cdot \frac{m-5}{2} \cdots\cdots \frac{2}{2} \sqrt{\pi}}{\frac{m}{2} \cdot \frac{m-2}{2} \cdot \frac{m-4}{2} \cdots\cdots \frac{3}{2} \cdot \frac{1}{2}\,\Gamma\frac{1}{2} \cdot 2}$$

$$= \frac{\Gamma\left(\frac{m+1}{2}\right)\sqrt{\pi}}{\Gamma\left(\frac{m+2}{2}\right)\cdot 2}$$

$$= \frac{\Gamma\left(\frac{m+1}{2}\right)\Gamma\left(\frac{0+1}{2}\right)}{2\Gamma\left(\frac{m+0+2}{2}\right)}$$

$$= \frac{\Gamma\left(\frac{m+1}{2}\right)\Gamma\left(\frac{n+1}{2}\right)}{2\Gamma\left(\frac{m+n+2}{2}\right)} \qquad \text{when } n = 0$$

Case II. When $m = 0$. Then exactly as case I,

$$\int_0^{\pi/2} \sin^m x \cos^n x \, dx$$

$$= \int_0^{\pi/2} \cos^n x \, dx$$

$$= \frac{\Gamma\left(\frac{n+1}{2}\right)\Gamma\left(\frac{0+1}{2}\right)}{2\Gamma\left(\frac{n+0+2}{2}\right)}$$

$$= \frac{\Gamma\left(\frac{m+1}{2}\right)\Gamma\left(\frac{n+1}{2}\right)}{2\Gamma\left(\frac{m+n+2}{2}\right)} \qquad \text{when } m = 0$$

Case III. When m and n both are even positive integers. Then let $m = 2p$, $n = 2q$; $p, q \in I$

$$\therefore \quad \int_0^{\pi/2} \sin^m x \cos^n x \, dx$$

$$= \int_0^{\pi/2} \sin^{2p} x \cos^{2q} x \, dx$$

$$= \left[\frac{\sin^{2p+1} x \cos^{2q-1}}{2p+2q}\right]_0^{\pi/2} + \frac{2q-1}{2p+2q}\int_0^{\pi/2} \sin^{2p} x \cos^{2q-2} x \, dx$$

$$= \frac{2q-1}{2p+2q} \int_0^{\pi/2} \sin^{2p} x \cos^{2q-2} x \, dx$$

$$= \frac{(2q-1)(2q-3).....3.1}{(2p+2q)(2p+2q-2).....(2p+2)} \int_0^{\pi/2} \sin^{2p} x \, dx$$

$$= \frac{(2q-1)(2q-3).....3.1}{(2p+2q)(2p+2q-2).....(2p+2)} \cdot \frac{(2p-1)(2p-3).....3\cdot 1}{2p(2p-2).....4\cdot 2} \cdot \frac{\pi}{2}$$

$$= \frac{\left\{\frac{2q-1}{2}\cdot\frac{2q-3}{2}\cdot.....\frac{3}{2}\cdot\frac{1}{2}\cdot\sqrt{\pi}\right\} \left\{\frac{2p-1}{2}\cdot\frac{2p-3}{2}\cdot.....\frac{3}{2}\cdot\frac{1}{2}\cdot\sqrt{\pi}\right\}}{2\cdot\{(p+q)(p+q-1)..........2\cdot 1\}}$$

$$= \frac{\Gamma\left(\frac{2q+1}{2}\right)\Gamma\left(\frac{2p+1}{2}\right)}{2\,\Gamma\left(\frac{2p+2q+2}{2}\right)}$$

$$= \frac{\Gamma\left(\frac{m+1}{2}\right)\Gamma\left(\frac{n+1}{2}\right)}{2\,\Gamma\left(\frac{m+n+2}{2}\right)}$$

Case IV. When m is odd and n is an even integer.

Let $m = 2p + 1$, $n = 2q$; $p, q \in I$

$$\therefore \quad \int_0^{\pi/2} \sin^m x \cos^n x \, dx$$

$$= \int_0^{\pi/2} \sin^{2p+1} x \cos^{2q} x \, dx$$

$$= \left[\frac{\sin^{2p+2} x \cos^{2q-1} x}{2p+1+2q}\right]_0^{\pi/2} + \frac{2q-1}{2p+1+2q}\int_0^{\pi/2} \sin^{2p+1} x \cos^{2q-2} x \, dx$$

$$= \frac{2q-1}{2p+2q+1} \cdot \int_0^{\pi/2} \sin^{2p+1} x \cos^{2q-2} x \, dx$$

$$= \frac{2q-1}{2p+2q+1} \cdot \frac{2q-3}{2p+2q-1} \cdot \ldots\ldots \frac{3}{2p+5} \cdot \frac{1}{2p+3} \int_0^{\pi/2} \sin^{2p+1} x \, dx$$

$$= \left\{\frac{2q-1}{2p+2q+1} \cdot \frac{2q-3}{2p+2q-1} \cdot \ldots\ldots \frac{3}{2p+5} \cdot \frac{1}{2p+3}\right\} \left\{\frac{2p}{2p+1} \cdot \frac{2p-2}{2p-1} \cdot \ldots\ldots \frac{4}{5} \cdot \frac{2}{3}\right\}$$

$$= \frac{\left\{\frac{2q-1}{2} \cdot \frac{2q-3}{2} \cdot \ldots\ldots \frac{3}{2} \cdot \frac{1}{2} \cdot \sqrt{\pi}\right\}\{p(p-1) \ldots\ldots 2 \cdot 1\}}{\left(p+q+\frac{1}{2}\right)\left(p+q-\frac{1}{2}\right) \ldots\ldots \frac{5}{2} \cdot \frac{3}{2} \cdot \frac{1}{2} \cdot \sqrt{\pi} \cdot 2}$$

$$= \frac{\Gamma\left(\frac{2q+1}{2}\right) \Gamma(p+1)}{2\,\Gamma\left(p+q+\frac{3}{2}\right)}$$

$$= \frac{\Gamma\left(\frac{n+1}{2}\right) \Gamma\left(\frac{m-1}{2}+1\right)}{2\,\Gamma\left(\frac{m-1}{2}+\frac{n}{2}+\frac{3}{2}\right)}$$

$$= \frac{\Gamma\left(\frac{m+1}{2}\right) \Gamma\left(\frac{n+1}{2}\right)}{2\,\Gamma\left(\frac{m+n+2}{2}\right)}$$

Case V. When m is even and n is an odd integer.

Proceed exactly as in case IV.

Case VI. When m and n both are odd positive integers.

Let $m = 2p + 1$, $n = 2q + 1$

$$\therefore \int_0^{\pi/2} \sin^m x \cos^n x \, dx$$

$$= \int_0^{\pi/2} \sin^{2p+1} x \cos^{2q+1} x \, dx$$

$$= \left[\frac{\sin^{2p+2} x \cos^{2q} x}{2p+1+2q+1} \right]_0^{\pi/2} + \frac{2q}{2p+2q+2} \int_0^{\pi/2} \sin^{2p+1} x \cos^{2q-1} x \, dx$$

$$= \frac{2q}{2p+2q+2} \cdot \int_0^{\pi/2} \sin^{2p+1} x \cos^{2q-1} x \, dx$$

$$= \frac{2q}{2p+2q+2} \cdot \frac{2q-2}{2p+2q} \cdot \frac{2q-4}{2p+2q-2} \cdots\cdots \frac{2}{2p+4} \int_0^{\pi/2} \sin^{2p+1} x \cos x \, dx$$

$$= \frac{2q}{2p+2q+2} \cdot \frac{2q-2}{2p+2q} \cdots\cdots \frac{2}{2p+4} \cdot \left(\frac{\sin^{2p+2} x}{2p+2} \right)_0^{\pi/2}$$

$$= \frac{2q}{2p+2q+2} \cdot \frac{2q-2}{2p+2q} \cdots\cdots \frac{2}{2p+4} \cdot \frac{1}{2p+2}$$

$$= \frac{\left\{ \frac{2q}{2} \cdot \frac{2q-2}{2} \cdots\cdots \frac{2}{2} \right\} \{ p(p-1)(p-2) \ldots\ldots 1 \}}{2 \left\{ \frac{2p+2q+2}{2} \cdot \frac{2p+2q}{2} \cdots\cdots \frac{2p+4}{2} \right\} (p+1) \{ p(p-1)(p-2) \ldots\ldots 1 \}}$$

$$= \frac{\{ q \cdot (q-1) \ldots\ldots 1 \} \{ p(p-1) \ldots\ldots 1 \}}{2 \{ (p+q+1)(p+q) \ldots\ldots 1 \}}$$

$$= \frac{\lceil q+1 \lceil p+1}{2 \lceil p+q+2}$$

$$= \frac{\Gamma\left(\frac{n+1}{2}\right)\Gamma\left(\frac{m+1}{2}\right)}{2\,\Gamma\left(\frac{m+n+2}{2}\right)} \qquad \text{Proved}$$

ILLUSTRATIVE EXAMPLES

Example 1. Evaluate $\int_0^{\pi/6} \cos^6 3\theta \sin^2 6\theta \, d\theta$

Solution :

$$I = \int_0^{\pi/6} \cos^6 3\theta \sin^2 6\theta \, d\theta \qquad \text{Put } 3\theta = t$$

$$\text{so that } 3d\theta = dt \quad \Rightarrow \quad d\theta = \frac{dt}{3}$$

$$= \int_0^{\pi/6} \cos^6 3\theta \,(2\sin 3\theta \cos 3\theta)^2 \, d\theta$$

$$= 4\int_0^{\pi/6} \sin^2 3\theta \cos^8 3\theta \, d\theta$$

$$= \frac{4}{3}\int_0^{\pi/2} \sin^2 t \cot^8 t \, dt$$

$$= \frac{4\,\Gamma\left(\frac{2+1}{2}\right)\Gamma\left(\frac{8+1}{2}\right)}{3\cdot 2\,\Gamma\left(\frac{2+8+2}{2}\right)} = \frac{2\,\Gamma\left(\frac{3}{2}\right)\Gamma\left(\frac{9}{2}\right)}{3\,\Gamma(6)}$$

$$= \frac{2\cdot\frac{1}{2}\cdot\sqrt{\pi}\cdot\frac{7}{2}\cdot\frac{5}{2}\cdot\frac{3}{2}\cdot\frac{1}{2}\cdot\sqrt{\pi}}{3\cdot 5\cdot 4\cdot 3\cdot 2\cdot 1}$$

$$= \frac{105\,\pi}{3\cdot 16\times 120} = \frac{7\pi}{3\cdot 128} = \frac{7\pi}{384}$$

Example 2. Prove that $\int_0^1 x^{3/2}(1-x)^{3/2}\, dx = \frac{3\pi}{128}$.

Solution :

$$I = \int_0^1 x^{3/2}(1-x)^{3/2}\, dx \qquad \text{Put } x = \sin^2\theta$$

$$\therefore \quad dx = 2\sin\theta\cos\theta\, d\theta$$

$$= \int_0^{\pi/2} \sin^3\theta \cos^3\theta \cdot 2\sin\theta\cos\theta \, d\theta$$

$$= 2\int_0^{\pi/2} \sin^4\theta \cos^4\theta \, d\theta$$

$$= \frac{2\,\Gamma\left(\frac{4+1}{2}\right)\Gamma\left(\frac{4+1}{2}\right)}{2\,\Gamma\left(\frac{4+4+2}{2}\right)}$$

$$= \frac{\Gamma\left(\frac{5}{2}\right)\Gamma\left(\frac{5}{2}\right)}{\Gamma(5)}$$

$$= \frac{\frac{3}{2} - \frac{1}{2}\cdot\sqrt{\pi}\cdot\frac{3}{2}\cdot\frac{1}{2}\cdot\sqrt{\pi}}{4\cdot 3\cdot 2\cdot 1}$$

$$= \frac{3\pi}{128}$$

Example 3. Evaluate $\int_0^{2a} x^3 \left(2ax - x^2\right)^{3/2} dx.$

Solution :

$$I = \int_0^{2a} x^3 \left(2ax - x^2\right)^{3/2} dx$$

$$= \int_0^{2a} x^{9/2} \left(2a - x\right)^{3/2} dx$$

Put $x = 2a\sin^2\theta$

$\therefore \quad dx = 4a \sin\theta \cos\theta \, d\theta$

$$= \int_0^{\pi/2} (2a)^{9/2} \sin^9\theta \,(2a)^{3/2} \cos^3\theta \cdot 4a \sin\theta \cos\theta \, d\theta$$

$$= (2a)^6 \cdot 4a \int_0^{\pi/2} \sin^{10}\theta \cos^4\theta \, d\theta$$

$$= 256\, a^7 \frac{\Gamma\left(\frac{11}{2}\right)\Gamma\left(\frac{5}{2}\right)}{2\,\Gamma(8)}$$

$$= 128\, a^7 \frac{\frac{9}{2}\cdot\frac{7}{2}\cdot\frac{5}{2}\cdot\frac{3}{2}\cdot\frac{1}{2}\cdot\sqrt{\pi}\cdot\frac{3}{2}\cdot\frac{1}{2}\cdot\sqrt{\pi}}{7\cdot 6\cdot 5\cdot 4\cdot 3\cdot 2\cdot 1}$$

$$= \frac{9\pi a^7}{16}$$

EXERCISE 11.3

Evaluate :

1. $\int_0^{\pi/2} \sin^4\theta \cos^2\theta \, d\theta$

2. $\int_0^{\pi/2} \sin^2\theta \cos^4\theta \, d\theta$

3. $\int_0^{\pi/2} \sin^5\theta \cos^2\theta \, d\theta$

4. $\int_0^{\pi/2} \sin^5\theta \cos^4\theta \, d\theta$

5. $\int_0^{\pi/2} \sin^5\theta \cos^6\theta \, d\theta$

6. $\int_0^{\pi/2} \sin^5\theta \cos^8\theta \, d\theta$

7. $\int_0^{\pi/2} \sin^3\theta \cos^3\theta \, d\theta$

8. $\int_0^{\pi/2} \sin^2 x \,(1+\cos x)^3 \, dx$

9. $\int_0^{\pi} \sin^4 x \,(1+\cos x)^3 \, dx$

10. $\int_0^{\pi/6} \cos^4 3\varphi \sin^2 6\varphi \, d\varphi$

11. $\int_0^{\pi/4} \sin^n (2x)\, dx$

12. $\int_0^{\pi/2} \sin^{2n} x \, dx$

13. $\int_0^1 x^2 (1-x^2)^{3/2} \, dx$

14. $\int_0^1 x^6 (1-x^2)^{1/2} \, dx$

15. $\int_0^1 x^4 (1-x^2)^{5/2} \, dx$

16. $\int_0^1 x^{3/2} \sqrt{1-x} \, dx$

17. $\int_0^a x^2 (ax-x^2)^{1/2} \, dx$

18. $\int_0^a x^4 \sqrt{a^2-x^2} \, dx$

19. $\int_0^a \dfrac{x^4}{\sqrt{a^2-x^2}} \, dx$

20. $\int_0^\infty \dfrac{x^4 dx}{(a^2+x^2)^4}$

21. $\int_0^a \dfrac{x^4 dx}{(a^2+x^2)^4}$

22. $\int_0^{2a} x^3 \sqrt{2ax-x^2} \, dx$

23. $\int_0^{2a} x^{9/2} (2a-x)^{-1/2} \, dx$

24. $\int_0^a x^3 (2ax-x^2)^{3/2} \, dx$

25. $\int_0^{\pi/8} \cos^3 4x \, dx$

ANSWERS

EXERCISE 11.3

1. $\dfrac{\pi}{32}$

2. $\dfrac{\pi}{32}$

3. $\dfrac{8}{105}$

4. $\dfrac{8}{315}$

5. $\dfrac{8}{693}$

6. $\dfrac{8}{1287}$

7. $\dfrac{1}{12}$

8. $\dfrac{7\pi}{8}$

9. $\dfrac{9\pi}{16}$

10. $\dfrac{5\pi}{192}$

11. $\dfrac{\sqrt{\pi}}{4} \cdot \dfrac{\left|\dfrac{n+1}{2}\right.}{\left|\dfrac{n+2}{2}\right.}$

12. $\dfrac{2n-1}{2n} \cdot \dfrac{2n-3}{2n-2} \cdots\cdots \dfrac{3}{4} \cdot \dfrac{1}{2} \cdot \dfrac{\pi}{2}$

13. $\dfrac{\pi}{32}$

14. $\dfrac{5\pi}{256}$

15. $\dfrac{3\pi}{512}$

16. $\dfrac{\pi}{16}$

17. $\dfrac{5\pi a^4}{128}$

18. $\dfrac{\pi a^6}{32}$

19. $\dfrac{3\pi a^4}{16}$

20. $\dfrac{\pi}{32 a^3}$

21. $\dfrac{1}{16}\left(\dfrac{\pi}{4} - \dfrac{1}{3}\right)\dfrac{1}{a^3}$

22. $\dfrac{7\pi a^5}{8}$

23. $\dfrac{63}{8}\pi a^5$

24. $\left(\dfrac{9\pi}{32} - \dfrac{23}{35}\right) a^7$

25. $\dfrac{1}{6}$

11.11 Reduction formula for $\int x^n \sin mx\, dx$

$$I = \int \underset{\text{I}}{x^n} \underset{\text{II}}{\sin mx}\, dx$$

Taking x^n as the first function and $\sin mx$ as the second function and integrating by parts,

$$= x^n\left(\frac{-\cos mx}{m}\right) - \int nx^{n-1}\left(\frac{-\cos mx}{m}\right)dx$$

$$= \frac{-x^n \cos mx}{m} + \frac{n}{m}\int \underset{\text{I}}{x^{n-1}} \underset{\text{II}}{\cos mx}\, dx$$

Again taking x^{n-1} as the first function and cos mx as the second function and integrating by parts,

$$= \frac{-x^n \cos mx}{m} + \frac{n}{m}\left[x^{n-1}\frac{\sin mx}{m} - \int (n-1)x^{n-2}\cdot\frac{\sin mx}{m}dx\right]$$

$$= \frac{-x^n \cos mx}{m} + \frac{n}{m^2}x^{n-1}\sin mx - \frac{n(n-1)}{m^2}\int x^{n-2}\sin mx\, dx$$

This is the required reduction formula.

11.12 Reduction formula for $\int x^n \cos mx\, dx$

Proceeding exactly as in art. 11.11, we can get the required reduction formula as follows :

$$\int x^n \cos mx\, dx = \frac{x^n \sin mx}{m} + \frac{nx^{n-1}\cos mx}{m^2} - \frac{n(n-1)}{m^2}\int x^{n-2}\cos mx\, dx$$

11.13 Reduction formula for $\int x \sin^n x\, dx$

$$I = \int x \sin^n x\, dx$$

$$= \int \underset{I}{\left(x \sin^{n-1} x\right)} \underset{II}{\sin x}\, dx$$

$$= x\sin^{n-1} x(-\cos x) - \int \{\sin^{n-1} x + x\cdot(n-1)\sin^{n-2} x\cdot\cos x\}(-\cos x)dx$$

$$= -x \sin^{n-1} x \cos x + \int \sin^{n-1} x \cos x \, dx$$
$$+ (n-1) \int x \sin^{n-2} x \cos^2 x \, dx$$

$$= -x \sin^{n-1} x \cos x + \frac{\sin^n x}{n} + (n-1)$$
$$\int x \sin^{n-2} x \cdot (1 - \sin^2 x) \, dx$$

$$= -x \sin^{n-1} x \cos x + \frac{\sin^n x}{n} + (n-1)$$
$$\int x \sin^{n-2} x \, dx - (n-1) \int x \sin^n x \, dx$$

$$\Rightarrow \quad (1 + n - 1) \int x \sin^n x \, dx$$
$$= -x \sin^{n-1} x \cos x + \frac{\sin^n x}{n} + (n-1) \int x \sin^{n-2} x \, dx$$

$$\Rightarrow \quad \int x \sin^n x \, dx$$
$$= \frac{-x \sin^{n-1} x \cos x}{n} + \frac{\sin^n x}{n^2} + \frac{n-1}{n} \int x \sin^{n-2} x \, dx$$

This is the required reduction formula.

11.14 Reduction formula for $\int x \cos^n x \, dx$

Proceeding exactly as in art. 11.13, we can get the required reduction formula as follows :

$$\int x \cos^n x \, dx = \frac{x \cos^{n-1} x \sin x}{n} + \frac{\cos^n x}{n^2} + \frac{n-1}{n} \int x \cos^{n-2} x \, dx$$

ILLUSTRATIVE EXAMPLES

Example 1. If $u_n = \int_0^{\pi/2} x^n \sin mx \, dx$, then prove that

$$u_n = \frac{n}{m^2} \left(\frac{\pi}{2}\right)^{n-1} - \frac{n(n-1)}{m^2} u_{n-2}$$

where m is of the form $4r + 1$.

Solution :

We know that

$$\int x^n \sin mx\, dx = -\frac{x^n \cos mx}{m} + \frac{nx^{n-1}\sin mx}{m^2} - \frac{n(n-1)}{m^2}\int x^{n-2}\sin mx\, dx$$

$$\Rightarrow \quad \int_0^{\pi/2} x^n \sin mx\, dx$$

$$= \left[\frac{-x^n \cos mx}{m}\right]_0^{\pi/2} + \left[\frac{nx^{n-1}\sin mx}{m^2}\right]_0^{\pi/2} - \frac{n(n-1)}{m^2}\int_0^{\pi/2} x^{n-2}\sin mx\, dx$$

$$\Rightarrow \quad u_n = -\left(\frac{\pi}{2}\right)^n \frac{1}{m}\cos\left(m\frac{\pi}{2}\right) + n\left(\frac{\pi}{2}\right)^{n-1}\frac{1}{m^2}\sin\frac{m\pi}{2} - \frac{n(n-1)}{m^2}u_{n-2}$$

$$\text{Now, } \cos\frac{m\pi}{2} = \cos\left\{(4r+1)\frac{\pi}{2}\right\} = \cos\left(2r\pi + \frac{\pi}{2}\right) = \cos\frac{\pi}{2} = 0$$

$$\text{and} \quad \sin\frac{m\pi}{2} = \sin\left\{(4r+1)\frac{\pi}{2}\right\} = \sin\left(2r\pi + \frac{\pi}{2}\right) = \sin\frac{\pi}{2} = 1$$

$$\therefore \quad u_n = \frac{n}{m^2}\left(\frac{\pi}{2}\right)^{n-1} - \frac{n(n-1)}{m^2}u_{n-2}$$

Example 2. If $u_n = \int_0^{\pi/2} \theta \sin^n \theta \, d\theta$ and $n > 1$, then prove that

$$u_n = \frac{1}{n^2} + \frac{n-1}{n} u_{n-2}$$

Hence deduce that $u_5 = \dfrac{149}{225}$

Solution :

We know that

$$\int \theta \sin^n \theta \, d\theta = -\frac{\theta \sin^{n-1} \theta \cos \theta}{n} + \frac{\sin^n \theta}{n^2} + \frac{n-1}{n} \int \theta \sin^{n-2} \theta \, d\theta$$

$$\therefore \quad \int_0^{\pi/2} \theta \sin^n \theta \, d\theta = \left(\frac{-\theta \sin^{n-1} \theta \cos \theta}{n} \right)_0^{\pi/2} + \left(\frac{\sin^n \theta}{n^2} \right)_0^{\pi/2} + \frac{n-1}{n} \int_0^{\pi/2} \theta \sin^{n-2} \theta \, d\theta$$

$$\Rightarrow \quad u_n = \frac{1}{n^2} + \frac{n-1}{n} u_{n-2} \qquad \text{Proved}$$

Put $n = 5$

$$\therefore \quad u_5 = \frac{1}{25} + \frac{4}{5} u_3$$

$$= \frac{1}{25} + \frac{4}{5} \left[\frac{1}{9} + \frac{2}{3} u_1 \right]$$

$$= \frac{1}{25} + \frac{4}{45} + \frac{8}{15} u_1$$

$$= \frac{1}{25} + \frac{4}{45} + \frac{8}{15} \int_0^{\pi/2} \underset{\text{I}}{\theta} \underset{\text{II}}{\sin \theta} \, d\theta$$

$$= \frac{1}{25} + \frac{4}{45} + \frac{8}{15} \left[\{\theta(-\cos\theta)\}_0^{\pi/2} - \int_0^{\pi/2} 1 \cdot (-\cos\theta) \, d\theta \right]$$

$$= \frac{1}{25} + \frac{4}{45} + \frac{8}{15}[\sin\theta]_0^{\pi/2}$$

$$= \frac{1}{25} + \frac{4}{45} + \frac{8}{15}$$

$$= \frac{9+20+120}{225}$$

$$= \frac{149}{225}$$

EXERCISE 11.4

Evaluate :

1. $\int x^2 \sin 2x \, dx$

2. $\int x^2 \cos 2x \, dx$

3. $\int x \sin^2 x \, dx$

4. $\int x \sin^3 x \, dx$

5. $\int x \cos^5 x \, dx$

6. $\int_0^{\pi/2} x^3 \sin 3x \, dx$

7. $\int_0^{\pi} \theta \sin^2 \theta \cos \theta \, d\theta$

8. If $u_n = \int_0^{\pi/2} x^n \sin x \, dx$, and $n > 1$, prove that

$$u_n + n(n-1)u_{n-2} = n\left(\frac{\pi}{2}\right)^{n-1}$$

Hence evaluate

$$\int_0^{\pi/2} x^5 \sin x \, dx$$

9. If $I_n = \int_0^{\pi/2} x^n \sin(2p+1)x \, dx$, then prove that

$$I_n + \frac{n(n-1)I_n - 2}{(2p+1)^2} = (-1)^p \frac{n}{(2p+1)^2}\left(\frac{\pi}{2}\right)^{n-1}$$

where n and p are positive integers. Hence evaluate

$$\int_0^{\pi/2} x^4 \sin 3x \, dx$$

10. Prove that $\int_0^a \sqrt{a^2 - x^2}\left\{\cos^{-1}\left(\frac{x}{a}\right)\right\}^2 dx = \frac{\pi a^2}{8}\left(\frac{\pi^2}{6} + 1\right)$

ANSWERS

EXERCISE 11.4

1. $\left(\frac{1}{4}-\frac{1}{2}x^2\right)\cos 2x+\frac{1}{2}x\sin 2x$

2. $\frac{1}{2}x^2\sin 2x+\frac{1}{2}x\cos 2x-\frac{1}{4}\sin 2x$

3. $\frac{1}{4}x^2-\frac{1}{4}x\sin 2x-\frac{1}{8}\cos 2x$

4. $-\frac{x\sin^2 x\cos x}{3}+\frac{1}{9}\sin^3 x+\frac{2}{3}(\sin x-x\cos x)$

5. $I_5=\frac{1}{5}\left(x\sin x\cos^4 x+\frac{1}{5}\cos^5 x+4\,I_3\right)$ = etc.

6. $\frac{2}{27}-\frac{\pi^2}{12}$

7. $-\frac{4}{9}$

8. $5\left(\frac{\pi}{2}\right)^4-60\left(\frac{\pi}{2}\right)^2+120$

11.15 Reduction formula for $\int e^{ax}\sin^n bx\,dx$

$$I=\int \underset{\text{II}}{e^{ax}}\,\underset{\text{I}}{\sin^n bx}\,dx$$

$$=\sin^n bx\frac{e^{ax}}{a}-\int n\sin^{n-1}bx\cdot\cos bx\cdot b\frac{e^{ax}}{a}dx$$

$$=\frac{e^{ax}\sin^n bx}{a}-\frac{nb}{a}\int \underset{\text{I}}{\left(\sin^{n-1}bx\cos bx\right)}\underset{\text{II}}{e^{ax}}dx$$

$$=\frac{e^{ax}\sin^n bx}{a}-\frac{nb}{a}\left[\frac{\sin^{n-1}bx\cos bx\,e^{ax}}{a}\right.$$
$$-\int\left\{(n-1)\sin^{n-2}bx\cdot\cos^2 bx\cdot b\right.$$
$$\left.\left.-\sin^{n-1}bx\cdot\sin bx\cdot b\right\}\cdot\frac{e^{ax}}{a}dx\right]$$

$$= \frac{e^{ax}\sin^n bx}{a} - \frac{nb}{a^2} e^{ax}\sin^{n-1} bx \cos bx + \frac{nb^2}{a^2}$$
$$\int \{(n-1)\sin^{n-2} bx \cos^2 bx - \sin^n bx\} e^{ax} dx$$

$$= \frac{e^{ax}\sin^n bx}{a} - \frac{nb}{a^2} e^{ax}\sin^{n-1} bx \cos bx + \frac{nb^2}{a^2}$$
$$\int \{(n-1)\sin^{n-2} bx \left(1-\sin^2 bx\right) - \sin^n bx\} e^{ax} dx$$

$$= \frac{e^{ax}\sin^n bx}{a} - \frac{nb}{a^2} e^{ax}\sin^{n-1} bx \cos bx + \frac{nb^2}{a^2}$$
$$\int \{(n-1)\sin^{n-2} bx - (n-1)\sin^n bx - \sin^n bx\} e^{ax} dx$$

$$= \frac{e^{ax}\sin^n bx}{a} - \frac{nb}{a^2} e^{ax}\sin^{n-1} bx \cos bx + \frac{nb^2}{a^2}$$
$$\int \{(n-1)\sin^{n-2} bx - n\sin^n bx\} x^{ax} dx$$

$$= \frac{e^{ax}\sin^n bx}{a} - \frac{nb}{a^2} e^{ax}\sin^{n-1} bx \cos bx + \frac{n(n-1)b^2}{a^2}$$
$$\int e^{ax}\sin^{n-2} bx\, dx - \frac{n^2b^2}{a^2}\int e^{ax}\sin^n bx\, dx$$

$$\Rightarrow \left(1+\frac{n^2b^2}{a^2}\right)\int e^{ax}\sin^n bx\, dx$$
$$= \frac{e^{ax}\sin^n bx}{a} - \frac{nb}{a^2} e^{ax}\sin^{n-1} bx \cos bx$$
$$+ \frac{n(n-1)b^2}{a^2}\int e^{ax}\sin^{n-2} bx\, dx$$

$$\Rightarrow \left(\frac{a^2+n^2b^2}{a^2}\right)\int e^{ax}\sin^n bx\, dx$$
$$= \frac{e^{ax}\sin^n bx}{a} - \frac{nb}{a^2} e^{ax}\sin^{n-1} bx \cos bx$$
$$+ \frac{n(n-1)b^2}{a^2}\int e^{ax}\sin^{n-2} bx\, dx$$

$$\Rightarrow \quad \int e^{ax} \sin^n bx\, dx = \frac{e^{ax} \sin^{n-1} bx \{a \sin bx - nb \cos bx\}}{a^2 + n^2 b^2} + \frac{n(n-1) b^2}{a^2 + n^2 b^2} \int e^{ax} \sin^{n-2} bx\, dx$$

This is the required reduction formula. Similarly,

$$\int e^{ax} \cos^n bx\, dx = \frac{e^{ax} \cos^{n-1} bx\,(a \cos bx + nb \sin bx)}{a^2 + n^2 b^2} + \frac{n(n-1) b^2}{a^2 + n^2 b^2} \int e^{ax} \cos^{n-2} bx\, dx$$

11.16 Reduction formula for $\int x^n e^{ax} \sin bx\, dx$

We know that

$$\int e^{ax} \sin bx\, dx = \frac{e^{ax}}{\sqrt{a^2 + b^2}} \sin(bx - \alpha)$$

where $\alpha = \tan^{-1}\left(\frac{b}{a}\right)$

$$\therefore \quad \int \underset{\text{I}}{x^n} \underset{\text{II}}{(e^{ax} \sin bx)}\, dx$$

$$= x^n \frac{e^{ax}}{\sqrt{a^2 + b^2}} \sin(bx - \alpha) - \int \frac{n\, x^{n-1} e^{ax} \sin(bx - \alpha)}{\sqrt{a^2 + b^2}}\, dx$$

$$= \frac{x^n e^{ax} \sin(bx - \alpha)}{\sqrt{a^2 + b^2}} - \frac{n}{\sqrt{a^2 + b^2}} \int x^{n-1} e^{ax} \sin(bx - \alpha)\, dx$$

This is the required reduction formula. Similarly,

$$\int x^n (e^{ax} \cos bx)\, dx = \frac{x^n e^{ax} \cos(bx - \alpha)}{\sqrt{a^2 + b^2}} - \frac{n}{\sqrt{a^2 + b^2}} \int x^{n-1} e^{ax} \cos(bx - \alpha)\, dx$$

ILLUSTRATIVE EXAMPLES

Example 1. Integrating by parts twice, or otherwise, obtain a reduction formula for

$$I_m = \int_0^\infty e^{-x} \sin^m x \, dx$$

where $m \geq 2$ in the form

$$(1 + m^2)\, I_m = m\,(m - 1)\, I_{m-2}$$

Hence evaluate I_4

Solution :

$$I_m = \int_0^\infty \underset{\text{II}}{e^{-x}}\, \underset{\text{I}}{\sin^m x}\, dx$$

$$= \left[\sin^m x\left(-e^{-x}\right)\right]_0^\infty - \int_0^\infty m \sin^{m-1} x \cos x \left(-e^{-x}\right) dx$$

$$= m \int_0^\infty \underset{\text{II}}{e^{-x}}\, \underset{\text{I}}{\sin^{m-1} x \cos x}\, dx$$

$$= m\Big[\left\{\sin^{m-1} x \cos x\left(-e^{-x}\right)\right\}_0^\infty$$

$$- \int_0^\infty \left\{(m-1)\sin^{m-2} x \cos x \cdot \cos x\right.$$

$$\left. + \sin^{m-1} x\,(-\sin x)\right\}\left(-e^{-x}\right) dx\Big]$$

$$= m \int_0^\infty \left\{(m-1)\sin^{m-2} x\left(1 - \sin^2 x\right) - \sin^m x\right\} e^{-x} dx$$

$$= m \int_0^\infty \left\{(m-1)\sin^{m-2} x - (m-1)\sin^m x - \sin^m x\right\} e^{-x} dx$$

$$= m \int_0^\infty \left\{(m-1)\sin^{m-2} x - m \sin^m x\right\} e^{-x} dx$$

$$= m\,(m-1)\int_0^\infty e^{-x} \sin^{m-2} x \, dx - m^2 \int_0^\infty e^{-x} \sin^m x \, dx$$

$$\Rightarrow \quad \left(1 + m^2\right) \int_0^\infty e^{-x} \sin^m x \, dx$$

$$= m\,(m-1)\int_0^\infty e^{-x} \sin^{m-2} x \, dx$$

$$\Rightarrow \quad \left(1 + m^2\right) I_m = m\,(m-1)\, I_{m-2}$$

Put $m = 4$

$$17\ I_4 = 12\ I_2$$

$$\Rightarrow \qquad I_4 = \frac{12}{17} I_2$$

$$= \frac{12}{17}\left[\frac{2}{5} I_0\right]$$

$$= \frac{24}{85} I_0$$

$$= \frac{24}{85}\int_0^{\infty} e^{-x}\,dx$$

$$= \frac{24}{85}$$

EXERCISE 11.5

Integrate :

1. $e^{2x}\cos^3 x$

2. $e^{ax}\sin^3 x$

3. $x^2 e^{3x}\sin 4x$

4. $e^x\left(x\cos x + \sin x\right)$

5. $e^{ax}\cos^4 x$

6. $x^3 e^x \sin x$

7. $\int_0^{\infty} x\,e^{-2x}\cos 2x\,dx$

ANSWERS

EXERCISE 11.5

1. $\frac{1}{4}e^{2x}\left\{\frac{1}{\sqrt{13}}\cos\left(3x - \tan^{-1}\frac{3}{2}\right) + \frac{3}{\sqrt{5}}\cos\left(x - \tan^{-1}\frac{1}{2}\right)\right\}$

2. $\frac{1}{4}e^{ax}\left\{\frac{3}{\sqrt{1+a^2}}\sin\left(x - \cot^{-1} a\right) - \frac{1}{\sqrt{a^2+9}}\sin\left(3x - \cot^{-1}\frac{a}{3}\right)\right\}$

3. $\frac{1}{5}\left[x^2 e^{3x}\sin\left(4x-\tan^{-1}\frac{4}{3}\right)-\frac{2}{5}x\,e^{3x}\sin\left(4x-2\tan^{-1}\frac{4}{3}\right)\right]$

$$+\frac{2}{25}\cdot\frac{1}{5}\cdot e^{3x}\sin\left(4x-3\tan^{-1}\frac{4}{3}\right)$$

4. $\frac{1}{2}e^x\{x(\cos x+\sin x)-\cos x\}$

5. $\frac{e^{ax}\cos^3 x(a\cos x+4\sin x)}{a^2+16}+\frac{12(a\cos x+2\sin x)\cos x\,e^{ax}}{(a^2+16)(a^2+4)}$

$$+\frac{24\,e^{ax}}{(a^2+16)(a^2+4)\,a}$$

6. $x^3\frac{1}{\sqrt{2}}e^x\sin\left(x-\frac{\pi}{4}\right)-\frac{3x^2}{2}e^x\sin\left(x-\frac{\pi}{2}\right)$

$$+6x\,2^{-3/2}e^x\sin\left(x-3\frac{\pi}{4}\right)-6\,2^{-2}e^x\sin(x-\pi)$$

7. $\frac{3}{25}$

11.17 Reduction formula for $\int \sin^m x \sin nx\, dx$

$$I = \int \underset{\text{I}}{\sin^m x}\ \underset{\text{II}}{\sin nx}\, dx$$

$$= \sin^m x\left(-\frac{\cos nx}{n}\right) - \int m\sin^{m-1}x\cos x\left(-\frac{\cos nx}{n}\right)dx$$

$$= -\frac{\sin^m x\cos nx}{n}+\frac{m}{n}\int \underset{\text{I}}{(\sin^{m-1}x\cos x)}\ \underset{\text{II}}{\cos nx}\,dx$$

$$= -\frac{\sin^m x\cos nx}{n}+\frac{m}{n}\left[\frac{\sin^{m-1}x\cos x\sin nx}{n} - \int\{(m-1)\sin^{m-2}x\cos^2 x-\sin^m x\}\frac{\sin nx}{n}\,dx\right]$$

$$= -\frac{\sin^m x \cos nx}{n} + \frac{m \sin^{m-1} x \cos x \sin nx}{n^2}$$

$$- \frac{m}{n^2} \int \left\{ (m-1) \sin^{m-2} x \left(1 - \sin^2 x\right) - \sin^m x \right\} \sin nx \, dx$$

$$= -\frac{\sin^m x \cos nx}{n} + \frac{m \sin^{m-1} x \cos x \sin nx}{n^2}$$

$$- \frac{m}{n^2} \int \left\{ (m-1) \sin^{m-2} x - m \sin^m x \right\} \sin nx \, dx$$

$$= -\frac{\sin^m x \cos nx}{n} + \frac{m \sin^{m-1} x \cos x \sin nx}{n^2}$$

$$- \frac{m}{n^2} (m-1) \int \sin^{m-2} x \sin nx \, dx + \frac{m^2}{n^2}$$

$$\int \sin^m x \cdot \sin nx \, dx$$

$$\Rightarrow \quad \left(1 - \frac{m^2}{n^2}\right) \int \sin^m x \sin nx \, dx$$

$$= \frac{m \sin^{m-1} x \cos x \sin nx - n \sin^m x \cos nx}{n^2}$$

$$- \frac{m(m-1)}{n^2} \int \sin^{m-2} x \sin nx \, dx$$

$$\Rightarrow \quad \int \sin^m x \sin nx \, dx$$

$$= \frac{n \sin^m x \cos nx - m \sin^{m-1} x \cos x \sin nx}{m^2 - n^2}$$

$$+ \frac{m(m-1)}{m^2 - n^2} \int \sin^{m-2} x \sin nx \, dx$$

This is the required reduction formula. Similarly,

$$\int \sin^m x \cos nx \, dx$$

$$= -\frac{n \sin^m x \sin nx + m \sin^{m-1} x \cos x \cos nx}{m^2 - n^2}$$

$$+ \frac{m(m-1)}{m^2 - n^2} \int \sin^{m-2} x \cos nx \, dx$$

11.18 Reduction formula for $\int \cos^m x \sin nx\, dx$

$$I = \int \underset{\text{I}}{\cos^m x} \underset{\text{II}}{\sin nx}\, dx$$

$$= \cos^m x\left(-\frac{\cos nx}{n}\right) - \int m \cos^{m-1} x\,(1 - \sin x)\left(-\frac{\cos nx}{n}\right) dx$$

$$= -\frac{\cos^m x \cos nx}{n} - \frac{m}{n} \int \cos^{m-1} x \sin x \cos nx\, dx$$

Now,

$\sin (n - 1)\, x = \sin nx \cos x - \cos nx \sin x$

$\Rightarrow \quad \sin x \cos nx$

$$= \sin nx \cos x - \sin (n - 1)\, x$$

$$\therefore \qquad I = -\frac{\cos^m x \cos nx}{n} - \frac{m}{n} \int \cos^{m-1} x \{\sin nx \cos x - \sin (n-1)\, x\}\, dx$$

$$\Rightarrow \qquad I = -\frac{\cos^m x \cos nx}{n} - \frac{m}{n} \int \cos^m x \sin nx\, dx + \frac{m}{n} \int \cos^{m-1} x \sin (n-1)\, x\, dx$$

$$\Rightarrow \quad I\left\{1 + \frac{m}{n}\right\} = -\frac{\cos^m x \cos nx}{n} + \frac{m}{n} \int \cos^{m-1} x \sin (n-1)\, x\, dx$$

$$\Rightarrow \quad \int \cos^m x \sin nx\, dx = -\frac{\cos^m x \cos nx}{m+n} + \frac{m}{m+n} \int \cos^{m-1} x \sin (n-1)\, x\, dx$$

This is the required reduction formula.

Similarly,

$$\int \cos^m x \cos nx \, dx$$

$$= \frac{\cos^m x \sin nx}{m+n} + \frac{m}{m+n} \int \cos^{m-1} x \sin (n-1) x \, dx$$

ILLUSTRATIVE EXAMPLES

Example 1. Prove that

$$\int_0^{\pi/2} \cos^m x \sin mx \, dx = \frac{1}{2^{m+1}} \left\{ 2 + \frac{2^2}{2} + \frac{2^3}{3} + \ldots\ldots + \frac{2^m}{m} \right\}$$

Solution :

We know that

$$\int_0^{\pi/2} \cos^m x \sin mx \, dx$$

$$= \left[-\frac{\cos^m x \cos mx}{m+m} \right]_0^{\pi/2} + \frac{m}{m+m} \int_0^{\pi/2} \cos^{m-1} x \sin (m-1) x \, dx$$

$$\Rightarrow \qquad I_{m,\, m} = \frac{1}{2m} + \frac{1}{2} I_{m-1,\, m-1}$$

Put $m - 1$ for m,

$$I_{m-1,\, m-1} = \frac{1}{2(m-1)} + \frac{1}{2} I_{m-2,\, m-2}$$

$$\therefore \qquad I_{m,\, m} = \frac{1}{2m} + \frac{1}{2}\left[\frac{1}{2(m-1)} + \frac{1}{2} I_{m-2,\, m-2} \right]$$

$$= \frac{1}{2m} + \frac{1}{2^2(m-1)} + \frac{1}{2^2} I_{m-2,\, m-2}$$

$$= \frac{1}{2m} + \frac{1}{2^2(m-1)} + \frac{1}{2^3(m-2)} + \frac{1}{2^3} I_{m-3,\, m-3}$$

| Proceeding similarly

$$= \frac{1}{2m} + \frac{1}{2^2(m-1)} + \frac{1}{2^3(m-2)} + \ldots\ldots + \frac{1}{2^m \{m-(m-1)\}} + \frac{1}{2^m} I_{m-m,\, m-m}$$

$$= \frac{1}{2m} + \frac{1}{2^2(m-1)} + \frac{1}{2^3(m-2)} + \ldots\ldots + \frac{1}{2^m 1} + \frac{1}{2^m} I_{o,o}$$

$$= \frac{1}{2m} + \frac{1}{2^2(m-1)} + \frac{1}{2^3(m-2)} + \ldots\ldots + \frac{1}{2^m \cdot 1} + \frac{1}{2^m} \int_0^{\pi/2} o\, dx$$

Now $\int_0^{\pi/2} o\, dx = [c]_0^{\pi/2} = c - c = o$

$$\therefore \quad I_{m,\, m} = \frac{1}{2m} + \frac{1}{2^2(m-1)} + \frac{1}{2^3(m-2)} + \ldots\ldots + \frac{1}{2^m \cdot 1}$$

Writing the series in the reverse order

$$= \frac{1}{2^m \cdot 1} + \frac{1}{2^{m-1} \cdot 2} + \frac{1}{2^{m-2} \cdot 3} + \ldots\ldots + \frac{1}{2m}$$

$$= \frac{1}{2^{m+1}} \left[\frac{2^{m+1}}{2^m \cdot 1} + \frac{2^{m+1}}{2^{m-1} \cdot 2} + \frac{2^{m+1}}{2^{m-2} \cdot 3} + \ldots\ldots + \frac{2^{m+1}}{2m} \right]$$

$$= \frac{1}{2^{m+1}} \left[\frac{2}{1} + \frac{2^2}{2} + \frac{2^3}{3} + \ldots\ldots + \frac{2^m}{m} \right]$$

Example 2. Prove that

$$\int_0^{\pi/2} \cos^n x \cos nx\, dx = \frac{\pi}{2^{n+1}}.$$

Solution :

$$I_{mn} = \int_0^{\pi/2} \cos^n x \cos nx\, dx$$

$$= \left(\frac{\cos^n x \sin nx}{n+n} \right)_0^{\pi/2} + \frac{n}{n+n} I_{n-1,\, n-1}$$

$$= \frac{1}{2} I_{n-1,\, n-1}$$

$$= \frac{1}{2} \cdot \frac{1}{2} I_{n-2,\, n-2}$$

$$= \frac{1}{2^2} I_{n-2,\, n-2}$$

Proceeding in this manner

$$= \frac{1}{2^n} I_{n-n,\, n-n}$$

$$= \frac{1}{2^n} I_{o,\, o}$$

$$= \frac{1}{2^n} \int_0^{\pi/2} 1 \cdot dx$$

$$= \frac{1}{2^n} \cdot \frac{\pi}{2}$$

$$= \frac{\pi}{2^{n+1}}$$

Example 3. Prove that $\int_0^{\pi/2} \cos^{n-2} x \sin nx\, dx = \frac{1}{n-1}$; n being an integer greater than unity.

Solution :

$$I = \int_0^{\pi/2} \cos^{n-2} x \sin nx\, dx$$

$$= \int_0^{\pi/2} \cos^{n-2} x \sin \{(n-1)\,x + x\}\, dx$$

$$= \int_0^{\pi/2} \cos^{n-2} x\, \{\sin (n-1)\, x \cos x + \cos (n-1)\, x \sin x\}\, dx$$

$$= \int_0^{\pi/2} \underset{\text{I}}{\cos^{n-1} x}\, \underset{\text{II}}{\sin (n-1)\, x}\, dx + \int_0^{\pi/2} \cos^{n-2} x \cos (n-1)\, x \sin x\, dx$$

Integrating the first integral only by parts

$$= \left\{\cos^{n-1} x - \frac{\cos (n-1)\, x}{n-1}\right\}_0^{\pi/2} - \int_0^{\pi/2} (n-1) \cos^{n-2} x\, (-\sin x) \cdot \left\{-\frac{\cos (n-1)\, x}{n-1}\right\} dx + \int_0^{\pi/2} \cos^{n-2} x \cos (n-1)\, x \sin x\, dx$$

$$= \frac{1}{n-1} - \int_0^{\pi/2} \cos^{n-2} x \cos(n-1) x \sin x \, dx$$
$$+ \int_0^{\pi/2} \cos^{n-2} x \cos(n-1) x \sin x \, dx$$

$$= \frac{1}{n-1}$$

EXERCISE 11.6

1. Prove that

$$\int_0^{\pi/2} \cos^m x \sin nx \, dx = \frac{1}{m+n} + \frac{m}{m+n}$$
$$\int_0^{\pi/2} \cos^{m-1} x \cdot \sin(n-1)x \, dx$$

Hence evaluate

$$\int_0^{\pi/2} \cos^5 x \sin 3x \, dx$$

2. If $I_{m,n} = \int_0^{\pi/2} \cos^m x \cos nx \, dx$, then prove that

$$I_{m,n} = \frac{m(m-1)}{m^2 - n^2} I_{m-2,n}$$

3. If $f(m,n) = \int_0^{\pi/2} \cos^m x \cos nx \, dx$, then prove that

$$f(m,n) = \frac{m}{m-n} f(m-1, n+1) = \frac{m}{m+n} f(m-1, n-1)$$

4. Prove that

$$\int_0^{\pi} \sin^m x \sin nx \, dx = \frac{m(m-1)}{m^2 - n^2} \int_0^{\pi} \sin^{m-2} x \sin nx \, dx$$

ANSWERS

EXERCISE 11.6

1. $\frac{1}{3}$

11.19 Reduction formula for $\int x^m \left(a + bx^n\right)^p dx$

The integral $\int x^m \left(a + bx^n\right)^p dx$ can be connected with any one of the following six integrals :

(i) $\int x^{m-n} \left(a + bx^n\right)^p dx$

(ii) $\int x^{m+n} \left(a + bx^n\right)^p dx$

(iii) $\int x^m \left(a + bx^n\right)^{p-1} dx$

(iv) $\int x^m \left(a + bx^n\right)^{p+1} dx$

(v) $\int x^{m-n} \left(a + bx^n\right)^{p+1} dx$

(vi) $\int x^{m+n} \left(a + bx^n\right)^{p-1} dx$

Proofs

$$I = \int x^m \left(a + bx^n\right)^p \quad \text{... (1)}$$

$$= \int \underset{\text{I}}{x^{m-n+1}} \underset{\text{II}}{\left\{\left(a + bx^n\right)^p \cdot x^{n-1}\right\}} dx$$

$$= x^{m-n+1} \frac{\left(a + bx^n\right)^{p+1}}{(p+1)\,nb}$$

$$- \int (m-n+1)\, x^{m-n} \frac{\left(a + bx^n\right)^{p+1}}{(p+1)\,nb} dx \quad \text{... (2)}$$

$$= \frac{x^{m-n+1}\left(a + bx^n\right)^{p+1}}{(p+1)\,nb} - \frac{m-n+1}{nb\,(p+1)}$$

$$\int x^{m-n}\left(a + bx^n\right)\left(a + bx^n\right)^p dx$$

$$= \frac{x^{m-n+1}\left(a + bx^n\right)^{p+1}}{(p+1)\,nb} - \frac{a\,(m-n+1)}{nb\,(p+1)}$$

$$\int x^{m-n}\left(a + bx^n\right)^p dx - \frac{m-n+1}{n\,(p+1)}$$

$$\int x^m \left(a + bx^n\right)^p dx$$

$$\Rightarrow \quad \left\{1 + \frac{m-n+1}{n(p+1)}\right\} I$$

$$= \frac{x^{m-n+1}(a+bx^n)^{p+1}}{nb(p+1)}$$

$$- \frac{a(m-n+1)}{nb(p+1)} \int x^{m-n}(a+bx^n)^p \, dx$$

$$\Rightarrow \quad \int x^m (a+bx^n)^p \, dx$$

$$= \frac{x^{m-n+1}(a+bx^n)^{p+1}}{b(np+m+1)}$$

$$- \frac{a(m-n+1)}{b(np+m+1)} \int x^{m-n}(a+bx^n)^p \, dx \qquad \ldots (3)$$

Writing $m + n$ for m in (2), we get

$$\int x^{m+n}(a+bx^n)^p \, dx$$

$$= \frac{x^{m+1}(a+bx^n)^{p+1}}{(p+1)nb} - \frac{m+1}{(p+1)nb} \int x^m (a+bx^n)^{p+1} \, dx$$

$$= \frac{x^{m+1}(a+bx^n)^{p+1}}{(p+1)nb} - \frac{m+1}{(p+1)nb}$$

$$\int x^m (a+bx^n)(a+bx^n)^p \, dx$$

$$= \frac{x^{m+1}(a+bx^n)^{p+1}}{(p+1)nb} - \frac{(m+1)a}{(p+1)nb}$$

$$\int x^m (a+bx^n)^p \, dx - \frac{(m+1)}{(p+1)n} \int x^{m+n}(a+bx^n)^p \, dx$$

$$\Rightarrow \quad \frac{(m+1)a}{(p+1)nb} \int x^m (a+bx^n)^p \, dx$$

$$= \frac{x^{m+1}(a+bx^n)^{p+1}}{(p+1)nb}$$

$$- \int x^{m+n}(a+bx^n)^p \, dx \cdot \left\{1 + \frac{m+1}{(p+1)n}\right\}$$

$$\Rightarrow \quad \frac{(m+1)\,a}{(p+1)\,nb}\int x^m \left(a+bx^n\right)^p dx$$

$$= \frac{x^{m+1}\left(a+bx^n\right)^{p+1}}{(p+1)\,nb}$$

$$- \frac{np+n+m+1}{(p+1)\,n}\int x^{m+n}\left(a+bx^n\right)^p dx$$

$$\Rightarrow \quad \int x^m \left(a+bx^n\right)^p dx$$

$$= \frac{x^{m+1}\left(a+bx^n\right)^{p+1}}{(m+1)\,a} - \frac{(np+n+m+1)\,b}{(m+1)\,a}$$

$$\int x^{m+n}\left(a+bx^n\right)^p dx \qquad \ldots (4)$$

Again $\quad I = \int \underset{\text{II}}{x^m} \underset{\text{I}}{\left(a+bx^n\right)^p} dx$

$$= \left(a+bx^n\right)^p \frac{x^{m+1}}{m+1}$$

$$-\int p\left(a+bx^n\right)^{p-1} bn\, x^{n-1} \cdot \frac{x^{m+1}}{m+1}\, dx$$

$$= \frac{\left(a+bx^n\right)^p x^{m+1}}{m+1} - \frac{pbn}{m+1}$$

$$\int x^{m+n}\left(a+bx^n\right)^{p-1} dx \qquad \ldots (5)$$

$$= \frac{\left(a+bx^n\right)^p x^{m+1}}{m+1} - \frac{pn}{m+1}$$

$$\int x^m - bx^n \cdot \left(a+bx^n\right)^{p-1} dx$$

$$= \frac{\left(a+bx^n\right)^p x^{m+1}}{m+1} - \frac{pn}{m+1}$$

$$\int x^m \left(a+bx^n - a\right)\left(a+bx^n\right)^{p-1} dx$$

$$= \frac{\left(a+bx^n\right)^p x^{m+1}}{m+1} - \frac{pn}{m+1}\int x^m \left(a+bx^n\right)^p dx$$

$$+ \frac{pna}{m+1}\int x^m \left(a+bx^n\right)^{p-1} dx$$

$$\Rightarrow \left(1+\frac{pn}{m+1}\right)\int x^m\left(a+bx^n\right)^p dx$$

$$= \frac{x^{m+1}\left(a+bx^n\right)^p}{m+1}+\frac{anp}{m+1}\int x^m\left(a+bx^n\right)^{p-1} dx$$

$$\Rightarrow \int x^m\left(a+bx^n\right)^p dx$$

$$= \frac{x^{m+1}\left(a+bx^n\right)^p}{np+m+1}+\frac{anp}{np+m+1}\int x^m\left(a+bx^n\right)^{p-1} dx \quad \text{... (6)}$$

Writing $p + 1$ for p in (6), we get

$$\int x^m\left(a+bx^n\right)^{p+1} dx$$

$$= \frac{x^{m+1}\left(a+b\,x^n\right)^{p+1}}{np+m+n+1}+\frac{an\left(p+1\right)}{np+n+m+1}\int x^m\left(a+bx^n\right)^p dx$$

$$\Rightarrow \frac{an\left(p+1\right)}{np+n+m+1}\int x^m\left(a+bx^n\right)^p dx$$

$$= -\frac{x^{m+1}\left(a+bx^n\right)^{p+1}}{np+m+n+1}+\int x^m\left(a+bx^n\right)^{p+1} dx$$

$$\Rightarrow \int x^m\left(a+bx^n\right)^p dx$$

$$= -\frac{x^{m+1}\left(a+bx^n\right)^{p+1}}{an\left(p+1\right)}+\frac{np+n+m+1}{an\left(p+1\right)}\int x^m\left(a+bx^n\right)^{p+1} dx \quad \text{... (7)}$$

Equations (2), (3), (4), (5), (6) and (7) respectively give the connections of $\int x^m\left(a+bx^n\right)^p dx$ with the integrals (v), (i), (ii), (vi), (iii) and (iv).

Alternative Method

The integral $\int x^m\left(a+bx^n\right)^p dx$ can be connected with any one of the following six integrals :

(i) $\int x^{m-n}\left(a+bx^n\right)^p dx$

(ii) $\int x^{m+n}\left(a+bx^n\right)^p dx$

(iii) $\int x^{m}\left(a+bx^n\right)^{p-1} dx$

(iv) $\int x^{m}\left(a+bx^n\right)^{p+1} dx$

(v) $\int x^{m-n}\left(a+bx^n\right)^{p+1} dx$

(vi) $\int x^{m+n}\left(a+bx^n\right)^{p-1} dx$

according to the following rule whose steps are given below :

Step 1. Let $P = x^{\lambda+1}(a+b\,x^n)^{\mu+1}$

where λ is the smaller of the two indices of x and μ is the smaller of the two indices of $(a+bx^n)$ in the two integrals which are to be connected.

Step 2. Find $\frac{dP}{dx}$ and express it as a linear function of the two integrands whose integrals are to be connected.

Step 3. Integrate both sides *w.r.t.* x, transpose and solve for the given integral.

Example 1. Connect $\int x^m\left(a+bx^n\right)^p dx$ with $\int x^{m-n}\left(a+bx^n\right)^{p+1} dx$.

Solution :

Let $\quad P = x^{(m-n)+1}(a+bx^n)^{(p)+1}$

Then
$$\frac{dP}{dx} = x^{m-n+1}\cdot(p+1)(a+bx^n)^p\,bnx^{n-1} + (m-n+1)\,x^{m-n}(a+bx^n)^{p+1}$$
$$= (p+1)\,nb\,x^m(a+bx^n)^p + (m-n+1)\,x^{m-n}(a+bx^n)^{p+1}$$

Integrate both sides *w.r.t.* x, we get

$$P = (p+1)\,nb\int x^m\left(a+bx^n\right)^p dx + (m-n+1)\int x^{m-n}\left(a+bx^n\right)^{p+1} dx$$

$$\Rightarrow \quad x^{m-n+1}(a+bx^n)^{p+1} = (p+1)nb\int x^m(a+bx^n)^p\,dx + (m-n+1)\int x^{m-n}(a+bx^n)^{p+1}\,dx$$

$$\Rightarrow \quad (p+1)nb\int x^m(a+bx^n)^p\,dx = x^{m-n+1}(a+bx^n)^{p+1} - (m-n+1)\int x^{m-n}(a+bx^n)^{p+1}\,dx$$

$$\Rightarrow \quad \int x^m(a+bx^n)^p\,dx = \frac{x^{m-n+1}(a+bx^n)^{p+1}}{(p+1)nb} - \frac{m-n+1}{(p+1)nb}\int x^{m-n}(a+bx^n)^{p+1}\,dx$$

Example 2. Connect $\int x^m(a+bx^n)^p\,dx$ with $\int x^{m-n}(a+bx^n)^p\,dx.$

Solution :

Let $\qquad P = x^{m-n+1}(a+bx^n)^{p+1}$

Differentiating *w.r.t.* x, we get

$$\begin{aligned}\frac{dP}{dx} &= (m-n+1)x^{m-n}(a+bx^n)^{p+1} + x^{m-n+1}(p+1)(a+bx^n)^p\,bnx^{n-1}\\ &= (m-n+1)x^{m-n}(a+bx^n)(a+bx^n)^p + (p+1)nb\,x^m(a+bx^n)^p\\ &= (m-n+1)a\,x^{m-n}(a+bx^n)^p + (m-n+1)bx^m(a+bx^n)^p + (p+1)nb\,x^m(a+bx^m)^p\\ &= (m-n+1)ax^{m-n}(a+bx^n)^p + \{(m-n+1)b+(p+1)nb\}\,x^m(a+bx^n)^p\\ &= (m-n+1)ax^{m-n}(a+bx^n)^p + b(m-n+1+np+n)\,x^m(a+bx^n)^p\\ &= (m-n+1)ax^{m-n}(a+bx^n)^p + b(m+np+1)\,x^m(a+bx^n)^p\end{aligned}$$

Integrating both sides *w.r.t.* x, we get

$$P = (m - n + 1)\ a \int x^{m-n}\left(a+bx^n\right)^p dx + b\ (m + np + 1) \int x^m \left(a+bx^n\right)^p dx$$

$$\Rightarrow \quad x^{m-n+1}\ (a + bx^n)^{p+1} = (m - n + 1)\ a \int x^{m-n}\left(a+bx^n\right)^p dx + b\ (m + np + 1) \int x^m \left(a+bx^n\right)^p dx$$

$$\Rightarrow \quad b\ (m + np + 1) \int x^m \left(a+bx^n\right)^p dx = x^{m-n+1}\ (a + bx^n)^{p+1} - (m - n + 1)\ a \int x^{m-n}\left(a+bx^n\right)^p dx$$

$$\Rightarrow \quad \int x^m \left(a+bx^n\right)^p dx = \frac{x^{m-n+1}\left(a+bx^n\right)^{p+1}}{b\left(m+np+1\right)} - \frac{a\left(m-n+1\right)}{b\left(m+np+1\right)} \int x^{m-n}\left(a+bx^n\right)^p dx$$

Example 3. If $I_n = \int_0^1 x^p \left(1-x^q\right)^n dx$ where p, q and n are positive, prove that $(nq + p + 1)\ I_n = nq\ I_{n-1}$. Evaluate I_n when n is a +ve integer.

Solution :

Let $\qquad P = x^{p+1}\ (1 - x^q)^{n-1+1} = x^{p+1}\ (1 - x^q)^n$

Differentiating we get

$$\frac{dP}{dx} = (p + 1)\ x^p\ (1 - x^q)^n + x^{p+1}\ n\ (1 - x^q)^{n-1}\ (-qx^{q-1})$$

$$= (p + 1)\ x^p\ (1 - x^q)^n - nq\ x^{p+q}\ (1 - x^q)^{n-1}$$

$$= (p + 1)\ x^p\ (1 - x^q)^n + nq\ x^p\ (1 - x^q - 1)\ (1 - x^q)^{n-1}$$

$$= (p + 1)\ x^p\ (1 - x^q)^n + nq\ x^p\ (1 - x^q)^n - nq\ x^p\ (1 - x^q)^{n-1}$$

$$= (nq + p + 1)\ x^p\ (1 - x^q)^n - nq\ x^p\ (1 - x^q)^{n-1}$$

Integrating both sides *w.r.t.* x, we get

$$P = (nq + p + 1) \int x^p (1 - x^q)^n \, dx - nq \int x^p (1 - x^q)^{n-1} \, dx$$

$$\Rightarrow \quad (nq + p + 1) \int x^p (1 - x^q)^n \, dx = P + nq \int x^p (1 - x^q)^{n-1} \, dx$$

$$\Rightarrow \quad (nq + p + 1) \int x^p (1 - x^q)^n \, dx = x^{p+1} (1 - x^q)^n + nq \int x^p (1 - x^q)^{n-1} \, dx$$

$$\Rightarrow \quad (nq + p + 1) \int_0^1 x^p (1 - x^q)^n \, dx = \left[x^{p+1} (1 - x^q)^n \right]_0^1 + nq \int_0^1 x^p (1 - x^q)^{n-1} \, dx$$

$$\Rightarrow \quad (nq + p + 1) \int_0^1 x^p (1 - x^q)^n \, dx = nq \int_0^1 x^p (1 - x^q)^{n-1} \, dx$$

$$\Rightarrow \quad (nq + p + 1) \, I_n = nq \, I_{n-1}$$

Proved

$$\Rightarrow \quad I_n = \frac{nq}{nq + p + 1} I_{n-1}$$

$$\Rightarrow \quad I_n = \frac{nq}{nq + p + 1} \cdot \frac{(n-1)q}{(n-1)q + p + 1} I_{n-2}$$

$$= \frac{nq}{nq + p + 1} \cdot \frac{(n-1)q}{(n-1)q + p + 1} \cdots\cdots \frac{(2-1)q}{(2-1)q + p + 1} I_0$$

$$= \frac{q^n \underline{|n}}{(p + 1 + nq)(p + 1 + \overline{n-1}\, q) \cdots\cdots (p + 1 + q)} I_0$$

Now $\quad I_0 = \int_0^1 x^p dx$

$$= \left(\frac{x^{p+1}}{p+1} \right)_0^1$$

$$= \frac{1}{p+1}$$

$$\therefore \quad I_n = \frac{q^n \lfloor n}{(p+1+nq)(p+1+\overline{n-1}\,q)\ldots..(p+1+q)} \frac{1}{p+1}$$

Example 4. If $I_n = \int x^n (a-x)^{1/2} dx$, prove that $(2n + 3) I_n = 2an I_{n-1} - 2x^n (a - x)^{3/2}$ and evaluate $\int_0^a x^2 \sqrt{ax - x^2} dx$.

Solution :

$$\because \quad I_n = \int x^n (a-x)^{1/2} dx$$

$$\therefore \quad I_{n-1} = \int x^{n-1} (a-x)^{1/2} dx$$

So let $\quad P = x^{n-1+1} (a-x)^{1/2+1}$

$$\Rightarrow \quad P = x^n (a-x)^{3/2}$$

$$\therefore \quad \frac{dP}{dx} = nx^{n-1} (a-x)^{3/2} + \frac{3}{2} x^n (a-x)^{1/2} (-1)$$

$$= nx^{n-1} (a-x)(a-x)^{1/2} - \frac{3}{2} x^n (a-x)^{1/2}$$

$$= nax^{n-1} (a-x)^{1/2} - nx^n (a-x)^{1/2} - \frac{3}{2} x^n (a-x)^{1/2}$$

$$= nax^{n-1} (a-x)^{1/2} - \left(n + \frac{3}{2}\right) x^n (a-x)^{1/2}$$

Integrating, we get

$$P = na \int x^{n-1} (a-x)^{1/2} dx - \left(n + \frac{3}{2}\right) \int x^n (a-x)^{1/2} dx$$

$$\Rightarrow \quad 2P = 2na\, I_{n-1} - (2n + 3)\, I_n$$

$$\Rightarrow \quad (2n + 3)\, I_n = 2an\, I_{n-1} - 2P$$

$$\Rightarrow \quad (2n + 3)\, I_n = 2an\, I_{n-1} - 2x^n (a-x)^{3/2} \qquad \text{Proved}$$

$$\Rightarrow \quad (2n+3) \int_0^a x^n (a-x)^{1/2} dx$$

$$= 2an \int_0^a x^{n-1} (a-x)^{1/2} dx - 2\left[x^n (a-x)^{3/2}\right]_0^a$$

$$\Rightarrow \quad (2n+3)\int_0^a x^n (a-x)^{1/2}\,dx = 2an\int_0^a x^{n-1}(a-x)^{1/2}\,dx$$

Put $n = \dfrac{5}{2}$

$$\Rightarrow \quad 8\int_0^a x^{5/2}(a-x)^{1/2}\,dx = 5a\int_0^a x^{3/2}(a-x)^{1/2}\,dx$$

$$\Rightarrow \quad \int_0^a x^{5/2}(a-x)^{1/2}\,dx = \frac{5a}{8}\int_0^a x^{3/2}(a-x)^{1/2}\,dx$$

$$= \frac{5a}{8}\cdot\frac{2a\cdot\frac{3}{2}}{3\times 3}\int_0^a x^{1/2}(a-x)^{1/2}\,dx$$

$$= \frac{5a^2}{16}\int_0^a x^{1/2}(a-x)^{1/2}\,dx$$

Put $x = a\sin^2\theta$

$\therefore \qquad dx = 2a\sin\theta\cos\theta$

$$= \frac{5a^2}{16}\int_0^{\pi/2} a^{1/2}\sin\theta\, a^{1/2}\cos\theta\cdot 2a\sin\theta\cos\theta\,d\theta$$

$$= \frac{5a^4}{8}\int_0^{\pi/2}\sin^2\theta\cos^2\theta\,d\theta$$

$$= \frac{5a^4}{8}\,\frac{\Gamma\left(\frac{3}{2}\right)\Gamma\left(\frac{3}{2}\right)}{2\,\Gamma(3)}$$

$$= \frac{5a^4}{16}\,\frac{\frac{1}{2}\sqrt{\pi}\,\frac{1}{2}\sqrt{\pi}}{2}$$

$$= \frac{5\pi a^4}{128}$$

Example 5. Connect $\int x^{m-1}(a+bx^n)^p\,dx$ with $\int x^{m-n-1}(a+bx^n)^p\,dx$ and evaluate $\int \frac{x^8}{(1-x^3)^{1/3}}\,dx$.

Solution :

Let $P = x^{m-n}(a+bx^n)^{p+1}$

$$\therefore \quad \frac{dP}{dx} = (m-n)\,x^{m-n-1}(a+bx^n)^{p+1} + x^{m-n}(p+1)(a+bx^n)^p(nbx^{n-1})$$

$$= (m-n)\,x^{m-n-1}(a+bx^n)(a+bx^n)^p + x^{m-1}(p+1)\,nb\,(a+bx^n)^p$$

$$= (m-n)\,ax^{m-n-1}(a+bx^n)^p + (m-n)\,b\,x^{m-1}(a+bx^n)^p + x^{m-1}(p+1)\,nb\,(a+bx^n)^p$$

$$= (m-n)\,ax^{m-n-1}(a+bx^n)^p + b\,(a+bx^n)^p\,x^{m-1}\{m-n+np+n\}$$

$$= (m-n)\,a\,x^{m-n-1}(a+bx^n)^p + b\,(m+np)\,x^{m-1}(a+bx^n)^p$$

Integrating, we get

$$P = (m-n)\,a\int x^{m-n-1}(a+bx^n)^p\,dx + b(m+np)\int x^{m-1}(a+bx^n)^p\,dx$$

$$\Rightarrow \quad b\,(m+np)\int x^{m-1}(a+bx^n)^p\,dx = x^{m-n}(a+bx^n)^{p+1} - (m-n)\,a\int x^{m-n-1}(a+bx^n)^p\,dx$$

$$\Rightarrow \quad \int x^{m-1}(a+bx^n)^p\,dx = \frac{x^{m-n}(a+bx^n)^{p+1}}{b(m+np)} - \frac{a(m-n)}{b(m+np)}\int x^{m-n-1}(a+bx^n)^p\,dx$$

Put $m - 1 = 8$, $a = 1$, $b = -1$, $n = 3$, $p = -\frac{1}{3}$, we get

$$\int x^8 \left(1-x^3\right)^{-\frac{1}{3}} dx$$

$$= -\frac{x^6\left(1-x^3\right)^{\frac{2}{3}}}{8} + \frac{3}{4}\int x^5\left(1-x^3\right)^{-\frac{1}{3}} dx$$

$$= -\frac{x^6\left(1-x^3\right)^{\frac{2}{3}}}{8} + \frac{3}{4}\left[-\frac{1}{5}x^3\left(1-x^3\right)^{\frac{2}{3}} + \frac{3}{5}\int x^2\left(1-x^3\right)^{-\frac{1}{3}} dx\right]$$

$$= -\frac{x^6\left(1-x^3\right)^{\frac{2}{3}}}{8} - \frac{3x^3\left(1-x^3\right)^{\frac{2}{3}}}{20} + \frac{9}{20}\int x^2\left(1-x^3\right)^{-\frac{1}{3}} dx$$

$$= -\frac{x^6\left(1-x^3\right)^{\frac{2}{3}}}{8} - \frac{3x^3}{20}\left(1-x^3\right)^{\frac{2}{3}} - \frac{9}{20}\cdot\frac{1}{3}\cdot\frac{\left(1-x^3\right)^{\frac{2}{3}}}{\frac{2}{3}}$$

$$= -\frac{1}{40}\left(1-x^3\right)^{\frac{2}{3}}\left[5x^6 + 6x^3 + 9\right]$$

EXERCISE 11.7

1. Prove that

$$\int\left(a^2+x^2\right)^{\frac{n}{2}} dx = \frac{x\left(a^2+x^2\right)^{\frac{n}{2}}}{n+1} + \frac{na^2}{n+1}\int\left(a^2+x^2\right)^{\frac{n}{2}-1} dx$$

2. Evaluate $\int\left(a^2+x^2\right)^{\frac{5}{2}} dx$.

3. If $I_n = \int_0^a \left(a^2-x^2\right)^n dx$ and $n > 0$, prove that

$$I_n = \frac{2na^2}{2n+1} I_{n-1}$$

Hence evaluate $\int_0^a \left(a^2-x^2\right)^3 dx$

4. If $U_n = \int x^n \sqrt{a^2 - x^2}\, dx$, then prove that

$$U_n = -\frac{x^{n-1}\left(a^2 - x^2\right)^{3/2}}{n+2} + \frac{n-1}{n+2} a^2 U_{n-2}$$

Hence evaluate

$$\int_0^a x^4 \sqrt{a^2 - x^2}\, dx$$

5. Investigate a formula of reduction applicable to

$$\int x^m \left(1 + x^2\right)^{n/2} dx$$

where m and n are +ve integers, and complete the integration if $m = 5$, $n = 7$

6. If m in a +ve integer, find a reduction formula for

$$\int x^m \sqrt{2ax - x^2}\, dx$$

Hence obtain the value of

$$\int_0^{2a} x^3 \sqrt{2ax - x^2}\, dx$$

7. Prove that

$$\int_0^1 x^{-1/4}\left(1 - x^{1/2}\right)^{5/2} dx = \frac{5}{16}\int_0^1 x^{-1/4}\left(1 - x^{1/2}\right)^{1/2} dx$$

8. If $U_n = \int x^n \left(1 + x^4\right)^{-1/2} dx$, prove that

$$U_n = \frac{x^{n-2}\left(1 + x^4\right)^{1/2}}{n-1} - \frac{n-3}{n-1} U_{n-4}$$

9. If $I_n = \int \frac{dx}{\left(x^2 + K\right)^n}$ where n is a +ve integer, prove that

$$I_n = \frac{x}{\left(x^2 + K\right)^{n-1}(2n-2)K} + \frac{2n-3}{(2n-2)K} I_{n-1}$$

10. Evaluate $\int_0^\infty \frac{dx}{\left(1 + x^2\right)^{n + 1/2}}$ where n is a +ve integer.

ANSWERS

EXERCISE 11.7

2. $\frac{1}{48} x\left[8x^4 + 26a^2x^2 + 33a^4\right]\sqrt{x^2 + a^2} + \frac{5}{16} a^6 \sin h^{-1}\left(\frac{x}{a}\right)$

3. $\frac{16}{35} a^7$

4. $\frac{\pi a^6}{32}$

5. $I_{m, n} = \frac{x^{m-1}\left(1 + x^2\right)^{n/2 + 1} - (m-1) I_{m-2, n}}{m + n + 1}$

where $I_{m, n}$ is the given integral.

$I_{5,7} = \left\{\frac{x^4}{13} - \frac{4x^2}{13.11} + \frac{4.2}{13.11.9}\right\}\left(1 + x^2\right)^{9/2}$

6. $(m + 2)\, I_m = (2m + 1)\, a\, I_{m-1} - x^{m-1}\, (2ax - x^2)^{3/2}$ where

$I_m = \int x^m \sqrt{2ax - x^2}\, dx;\ \frac{7\pi a^5}{8}$

10. $\frac{2^{2n-2}\left(\lfloor n - 1\right)^2}{\lfloor 2n - 1}$

11.20 Reduction formula for $\int \frac{e^{mx}}{x^n} dx$, where n > 0

$$I = \int \frac{e^{mx}}{x^n} dx$$

$$= \int \underset{\text{I}}{e^{mx}}\, \underset{\text{II}}{x^{-n}}\, dx$$

Integrate by parts,

$$= e^{mx} \frac{x^{-n+1}}{-n+1} - \int m e^{mx} \frac{x^{-n+1}}{-n+1} dx$$

$$= -\frac{e^{mx}}{(n-1)\, x^{n-1}} + \frac{m}{n-1} \int \frac{e^{mx}}{x^{n-1}} dx$$

This is the required reduction formula.

11.21 Reduction formula for $\int x^m (\log x)^n\, dx$

$$I = \int x^m (\log x)^n\, dx$$
$$\quad\;\; \text{II} \quad\; \text{I}$$

Integrating by parts

$$= (\log x)^n \frac{x^{m+1}}{m+1} - \int n (\log x)^{n-1} \cdot \frac{1}{x} \frac{x^{m+1}}{m+1}\, dx$$

$$= \frac{x^{m+1} (\log x)^n}{m+1} - \frac{n}{m+1} \int x^m (\log x)^{n-1}\, dx$$

This is the required reduction formula.

11.22 Reduction formula for $\int \frac{x^m}{(\log x)^n}\, dx$

$$I = \int \frac{x^m}{(\log x)^n}\, dx$$

$$= \int x^{m+1} \left\{ \frac{1}{x (\log x)^n} \right\} dx$$
$$\quad\;\; \text{I} \qquad\quad \text{II}$$

$$= -\frac{x^{m+1}}{(n-1)(\log x)^{n-1}}$$
$$\qquad - \int (m+1)\, x^m \left\{ -\frac{1}{(n-1)(\log x)^{n-1}} \right\} dx$$

$$= -\frac{x^{m+1}}{(n-1)(\log x)^{n-1}} + \frac{m+1}{n-1} \int \frac{x^m}{(\log x)^{n-1}}\, dx$$

ILLUSTRATIVE EXAMPLES

Example 1. Prove that $\int_0^\infty e^{-x} x^n dx = \lfloor n$

Solution :

$$I_n = \int_0^\infty e^{-x} x^n\, dx$$
$$\qquad\; \text{II} \;\; \text{I}$$

Integrating by parts

$$= \left[x^n - e^{-x}\right]_0^\infty + \int_0^\infty nx^{n-1}e^{-x}dx$$

$$= n\int_0^\infty x^{n-1}e^{-x}dx$$

$$\because \lim_{x\to\infty} e^{-x}x^n = \lim_{x\to\infty}\frac{x^n}{e^x}$$

$$= \lim_{x\to\infty}\frac{n(n-1)(n-2).....1}{e^x}$$

$$= \lim_{x\to\infty}\frac{\lfloor n}{e^x} = \frac{\lfloor n}{\infty} = 0$$

By applying De L' Hospital's rule n times

$$= n\, I_{n-1}$$

$$= n\,(n-1)\, I_{n-2}$$

$$= n\,(n-1)\,(n-2)\, I_{n-3}$$

$$= n\,(n-1)\,(n-2)\, ...\, 3.2.1.\, I_0$$

$$= \lfloor n\, I_0$$

$$= \lfloor n \int_0^\infty e^{-x}dx$$

$$= \lfloor n \cdot 1$$

$$= \lfloor n$$

Example 2. Evaluate $\int_0^1 x^m (\log x)^n\, dx$ where $m \geq 0$ and n is a positive integer.

Solution : We know that

$$\int x^m (\log x)^n\, dx$$

$$= \frac{x^{m+1}(\log x)^n}{m+1} - \frac{n}{m+1}\int x^m (\log x)^{n-1}\, dx$$

$$\therefore \quad \int_0^1 x^m (\log x)^n\, dx$$

$$= \left[\frac{x^{m+1}(\log x)^n}{m+1}\right]_0^1 - \frac{n}{m+1}\int_0^1 x^m (\log x)^{n-1}\, dx$$

$$\Rightarrow \qquad I_n = -\frac{n}{m+1} I_{n-1}$$

$$= -\frac{n}{m+1} \cdot \frac{-(n-1)}{m+1} I_{n-2}$$

$$= -\frac{n}{m+1} \cdot \frac{-(n-1)}{m+1} \cdot \frac{-(n-2)}{m+1} \cdots\cdots \frac{-1}{m+1} I_0$$

$$= \frac{(-1)^n \lfloor n}{(m+1)^n} I_0$$

$$= \frac{(-1)^n \lfloor n}{(m+1)^n} \int_0^1 x^m dx$$

$$= \frac{(-1)^n \lfloor n}{(m+1)^n} \frac{1}{m+1}$$

$$= \frac{(-1)^n \lfloor n}{(m+1)^{n+1}}$$

Example 3. If m and n be positive integers, prove that

$$\int_0^1 x^{n-1} (\log x)^m \, dx = -\frac{m}{n} \int_0^1 x^{n-1} (\log x)^{m-1} \, dx$$

Hence deduce that

$$\int_0^1 x^{n-1} (\log x)^m \, dx = \frac{(-1)^m \lfloor m}{n^{m+1}}$$

Solution :

$$\int_0^1 x^{n-1} (\log x)^m \, dx$$

II I

Integrate by parts

$$= \left[(\log x)^m \frac{x^n}{n} \right]_0^1 - \int_0^1 m (\log x)^{m-1} \cdot \frac{1}{x} \cdot \frac{x^n}{n} dx$$

$$= -\frac{m}{n} \int_0^1 x^{n-1} (\log x)^{m-1} \, dx \qquad \text{Proved}$$

$$\Rightarrow \qquad I_{m,\, n} = -\frac{m}{n} I_{m-1,\, n}$$

$$= -\frac{m}{n} \cdot \frac{-m-1}{n} I_{m-2,\, n}$$

$$= -\frac{m}{n} \cdot \frac{-m-1}{n} \cdot \frac{-m-2}{n} \ldots\ldots \frac{-1}{n} I_{0,\,n}$$

$$= \frac{(-1)^m \lfloor m}{n^m} I_{0,\,n}$$

$$= \frac{(-1)^m \lfloor m}{n^m} \int_0^1 x^{n-1} dx$$

$$= \frac{(-1)^m \lfloor m}{n^m} \frac{1}{n}$$

$$= \frac{(-1)^m \lfloor m}{n^{m+1}}$$

EXERCISE 11.8

1. Evaluate $\int x^3 (\log x)^3 \, dx.$
2. Evaluate $\int x^m (\log x)^2 \, dx.$
3. Evaluate $\int_0^1 x^m (\log x)^3 \, dx.$
4. Evaluate $\int_0^1 x^m (\log x)^4 \, dx.$
5. Evaluate $\int_0^1 x^m (\log x)^5 \, dx.$

ANSWERS

EXERCISE 11.8

1. $\frac{x^4}{4}\left[(\log x)^3 - \frac{3}{4}(\log x)^2 + \frac{3}{8}\log x - \frac{3}{32}\right]$
2. $\frac{x^{m+1}}{m+1}\left[(\log x)^2 - \frac{2}{m+1}\log x + \frac{2}{(m+1)^2}\right]$
3. $-\frac{6}{(m+1)^4}$
4. $\frac{24}{(m+1)^5}$
5. $-\frac{120}{(m+1)^6}$

HARDER SOLVED EXAMPLES

Example 1. Find a reduction formula for $\int \frac{\sin nx}{\sin x}\,dx$ and prove that $\int_0^{\pi} \frac{\sin nx}{\sin x}\,dx = \pi \text{ or } 0$ according as n is odd or even positive integer.

Solution :

We know that

$$\sin nx - \sin (n-2)x = 2 \sin x \cos (n-1) x$$

$$\Rightarrow \quad \frac{\sin nx}{\sin x} - \frac{\sin (n-2) x}{\sin x} = 2 \cos (n-1) x$$

$$\Rightarrow \quad \frac{\sin nx}{\sin x} = 2 \cos (n-1) x + \frac{\sin (n-2) x}{\sin x}$$

$$\Rightarrow \int \frac{\sin nx}{\sin x}\,dx = \int 2 \cos (n-1) x\,dx + \int \frac{\sin (n-2) x}{\sin x}\,dx$$

$$\Rightarrow \int \frac{\sin nx}{\sin x}\,dx = \frac{2 \sin (n-1) x}{n-1} + \int \frac{\sin (n-2) x}{\sin x}\,dx \qquad \text{... (1)}$$

This is the required reduction formula.

Let $\quad I_n = \int_0^{\pi} \frac{\sin nx}{\sin x}\,dx$

then $\quad I_n = \left[\frac{2 \sin (n-1) x}{n-1}\right]_0^{\pi} + \int_0^{\pi} \frac{\sin (n-2) x}{\sin x}\,dx$ | From (1)

$\Rightarrow \quad I_n = I_{n-2}$

$\Rightarrow \quad I_n = I_{n-4}$

$\quad = I_{n-6}$

$\quad = \ldots\ldots\ldots \begin{cases} = I_1 \text{ if } n \text{ is odd} \\ = I_0 \text{ if } n \text{ is even} \end{cases}$

Now $\quad I_1 = \int_0^{\pi} \frac{\sin x}{\sin x}\,dx = \pi$

and $$I_0 = \int_0^{\pi} \frac{0}{\sin x}\, dx = 0$$

Hence $$I_n = \pi \text{ if } n \text{ is odd}$$
$$= 0 \text{ if } n \text{ is even}$$

Example 2. By a reduction formula or otherwise, prove that $\int_0^{\pi} \frac{\sin^2 n\theta}{\sin^2 \theta}\, d\theta = n\pi$ where n is a +ve integer.

Solution :

Let $$I_n = \int_0^{\pi} \frac{\sin^2 n\theta}{\sin^2 \theta}\, d\theta$$

Then $$I_{n-1} = \int_0^{\pi} \frac{\sin^2 (n-1)\theta}{\sin^2 \theta}\, d\theta$$

$$\therefore \quad I_n - I_{n-1} = \int_0^{\pi} \frac{\sin^2 n\theta}{\sin^2 \theta}\, d\theta - \int_0^{\pi} \frac{\sin^2 (n-1)\theta}{\sin^2 \theta}\, d\theta$$

$$= \int_0^{\pi} \frac{\sin^2 n\theta - \sin^2 (n-1)\theta}{\sin^2 \theta}\, d\theta$$

$$= \int_0^{\pi} \frac{\sin (2n-1)\theta \sin \theta}{\sin^2 \theta}\, d\theta$$

$$= \int_0^{\pi} \frac{\sin (2n-1)\theta}{\sin \theta}\, d\theta$$

$$= \pi \qquad \text{| by Ex. 1}$$

$$\Rightarrow \quad I_n = \pi + I_{n-1}$$
$$= 2\pi + I_{n-2}$$
$$= 3\pi + I_{n-3}$$
$$\cdots\cdots\cdots$$
$$\cdots\cdots\cdots$$
$$= n\pi + I_{n-n}$$
$$= n\pi + I_0$$
$$= n\pi + 0$$
$$= n\pi$$

Example 3. If $I_n = \int x^n e^{1/x} dx,$ then prove that

$$\underline{|n+1}\, I_n = I_0 + e^{1/x}\left\{\underline{|1}\, x^2 + \underline{|2}\, x^3 + \ldots.. + \underline{|n}\, x^{n+1}\right\}$$

Solution :

$$I_n = \int \underset{\text{II}}{x^n} \underset{\text{I}}{e^{1/x}} dx$$

Integrating by parts

$$= e^{1/x} \frac{x^{n+1}}{n+1} - \int e^{1/x}\left(-\frac{1}{x^2}\right)\frac{x^{n+1}}{n+1} dx$$

$$= \frac{e^{1/x}\, x^{n+1}}{n+1} + \frac{1}{n+1}\int e^{1/x}\, x^{n-1}\, dx$$

$$\Rightarrow \qquad I_n = \frac{e^{1/x}\, x^{n+1}}{n+1} + \frac{1}{n+1} I_{n-1}$$

$$\therefore \qquad I_n = \frac{e^{1/x}\, x^{n+1}}{n+1} + \frac{1}{n+1}\left[\frac{e^{1/x} x^n}{n} + \frac{1}{n} I_{n-2}\right]$$

$$= \frac{e^{1/x}\, x^{n+1}}{n+1} + \frac{e^{1/x} x^n}{(n+1)\, n} + \frac{1}{(n+1)\, n} I_{n-2}$$

Proceeding in this manner

$$= \frac{e^{1/x}\, x^{n+1}}{n+1} + \frac{e^{1/x} \cdot x^n}{(n+1)\, n} + \ldots.. + \frac{e^{1/x} \cdot x^2}{(n+1)\, n\, (n-1) \ldots 2} + \frac{1}{(n+1)\, n\, (n-1) \ldots 2} I_0$$

$$\Rightarrow \quad \underline{|n+1}\, I_n = e^{1/x}\left[\frac{x^{n+1}}{n+1}\underline{|n+1} + \frac{x^n}{(n+1)\, n}\underline{|n+1} + \ldots.. + \frac{x^2}{(n+1)\, n\, (n-1) \ldots 2}\underline{|n+1}\right] + \frac{\underline{|n+1}}{(n+1) \cdot n \cdot (n-1) \ldots 2} I_0$$

$$= e^{1/x}\left[\underline{|n}\, x^{n+1} + \underline{|n-1}\, x^{n} + \ldots.. + \underline{|2}\, x^{3} + \underline{|1}\, x^{2}\right] + I_0$$

$$= I_0 + e^{1/x}\left[\underline{|1}\, x^{2} + \underline{|2}\, x^{3} + \ldots.. + \underline{|n}\, x^{n+1}\right] \text{ Proved}$$

EXERCISE 11.9

1. Obtain a reduction formula for $\int \tan h^n x\, dx$ and deduce the value of $\int \tan h^3 x\, dx$.

2. If $I_n = \int_0^{\pi/4} \tan^n \theta\, d\theta$, prove that

$$n\left[I_{n-1} + I_{n+1}\right] = 1$$

3. Prove that

$$\int_0^a x^5 \left(2a^2 - x^2\right)^{-3} dx = \frac{1}{2}\left(\log 2 - \frac{1}{2}\right)$$

4. Prove that

$$\int \frac{1}{\cos^n \theta}\, d\theta = \frac{\sin \theta}{(n-1)\cos^{n-1}\theta} + \frac{n-2}{n-1}\int \frac{1}{\cos^{n-2}\theta}\, d\theta$$

5. Prove that

$$\int \operatorname{cosec}^{2n+1}\phi\, d\phi = -\frac{1}{2n}\cot\phi\, \operatorname{cosec}^{2n-1}\phi + \left(1 - \frac{1}{2n}\right)\int \operatorname{cosec}^{2n-1}\phi\, d\phi$$

6. Prove that

$$\int_0^\infty \frac{du}{\cos h^n u} = \frac{n-2}{n-1}\int_0^\infty \frac{du}{\cos h^{n-2} u};\; n > 2$$

7. If $U_n = \int \frac{\sin nx}{\sin x}\, dx$, prove that

$$U_n = \frac{2\sin(n-1)x}{n-1} + U_{n-2}$$

Hence evaluate

$$\int_0^{\pi/2} \frac{\sin 7x}{\sin x}\, dx$$

8. If $S_n = \int_0^{\pi/2} \frac{\sin(2n-1)x}{\sin x}\,dx$, $V_n = \int_0^{\pi/2} \left(\frac{\sin nx}{\sin x}\right)^2 dx$ where n is an integer, show that

$$S_{n+1} - S_n = 0,$$
$$V_{n+1} - V_n = S_{n+1}$$

9. Evaluate $\int_{-\pi/2}^{+\pi/2} \frac{\cos^5 x}{\sin^2 x}\,dx$

10. Evaluate $\int_0^1 x^5 \sin^{-1} x\,dx$

11. Prove that $\int_0^1 \frac{1}{x} \log\left(\frac{1+x}{1-x}\right) dx = \frac{\pi^2}{4}$

12. Evaluate $\int_0^\infty \frac{dx}{(a^2+x^2)^{n+1/2}}$, where n is a +ve integer.

13. Evaluate $\int_0^{2a} x^m \sqrt{2ax - x^2}\,dx$, where m is a +ve integer.

14. If m and n are positive integers, prove that

$$\int_a^b (x-a)^m (b-x)^n\,dx = \frac{\underline{|m}\,\underline{|n}\,(b-a)^{m+n+1}}{\underline{|m+n+1}}$$

15. If m and n are positive, prove that

$$\int_0^1 x^{m-1}(1-x)^{n-1}\,dx = \frac{\Gamma m\,\Gamma n}{\Gamma(m+n)}$$

16. Evaluate $\int_0^a x^2 \sqrt{\frac{a-x}{a+x}}\,dx$

17. Evaluate $\int_0^1 \frac{x^{2n}\,dx}{\sqrt{1-x^2}}$

18. Prove that

$$\int_0^\infty e^{-ax} x^n\,dx = \frac{\underline{|n}}{a^{n+1}},$$ where n is a +ve integer.

19. Find a reduction formula for $\int \frac{x}{\sin^n x}\,dx$.

20. Evaluate $\int_0^1 \frac{x^3 \sin^{-1} x}{(1-x^2)^{1/2}}\, dx$

ANSWERS

EXERCISE 11.9

1. $\int \tan h^n x\, dx = -\frac{\tan h^{n-1} x}{n-1} + \int \tan h^{n-2} x\, dx;$

$$-\frac{\tan h^2 x}{2} + \log \cos hx$$

7. $\frac{\pi}{2}$

9. $-\frac{16}{3}$

10. $\frac{11\pi}{192}$

12. $\frac{\{\lfloor n-1\}^2\, 2^{2n-2}}{\lfloor 2n-1\, a^{2n}}$

13. $\frac{\lfloor 2m+1\, \pi\, a^{m+2}}{\lfloor m \lfloor m+2\, 2^m}$

16. $a^3\left(\frac{\pi}{4} - \frac{2}{3}\right)$

17. $\frac{\Gamma\left(n+\frac{1}{2}\right)\sqrt{\pi}}{2\,\Gamma(n+1)}$

19. $\int \frac{x}{\sin^n x}\, dx = -\frac{x \cos x}{(n-1)\sin^{n-1} x} - \frac{1}{(n-1)(n-2)\sin^{n-2} x}$

$$+\frac{n-2}{n-1}\int \frac{x}{\sin^{n-2} x}\, dx$$

20. $\frac{7}{9}$

12
Beta and Gamma Functions

12.1 Definitions

Euler, a great mathematician, gave two definite integrals which after his name are styled as Eulerian integral of first kind (or First Eulerian Integral) and Eulerian integral of second kind (or Second Eulerian Integral). These integrals are of fundamental importance in the theory of definite integrals. They are respectively given as follows :

(1) $\beta(l, m) = \int_0^1 x^{l-1}(1-x)^{m-1}\,dx$

where l, m are positive numbers, integrals or fractional.

It is read as "**Beta *l*, *m***", and

(2) $\Gamma n = \int_0^\infty e^{-x} x^{n-1}dx$, where $n > 0$.

It is read as "**Gamma *n***".

These integrals are known as Beta and Gamma Functions respectively.

12.2 Evaluation of Beta Function

We know that

$$\beta(l, m) = \int_0^1 x^{l-1}(1-x)^{m-1}\,dx$$

Case I. *Let m be a positive integer*, then integrating by parts taking $(1-x)^{m-1}$ as the first function and x^{l-1} as the second function, we get

$$\beta\ (l,\ m) = \left[(1-x)^{m-1}\frac{x^l}{l}\right]_0^1 - \int_0^1 -(m-1)(1-x)^{m-2}\frac{x^l}{l}\,dx$$

$$= \frac{m-1}{l}\int_0^1 x^l(1-x)^{m-2}\,dx$$

Again integrating by parts taking $(1 - x)^{m-2}$ as the first function and x^l as the second function, we get

$$= \frac{m-1}{l}\left[\left\{(1-x)^{m-2}\frac{x^{l+1}}{l+1}\right\}_0^1 - \int_0^1 -(m-2)(1-x)^{m-3}\frac{x^{l+1}}{l+1}dx\right]$$

$$= \frac{m-1}{l}\cdot\frac{m-2}{l+1}\int_0^1(1-x)^{m-3}x^{l+1}dx$$

Proceeding in this manner, we obtain

$$= \frac{m-1}{l}\cdot\frac{m-2}{l+1}\cdot\frac{m-3}{l+2}\cdots\cdots\frac{1}{l+m-2}\int_0^1(1-x)^{m-m}\cdot x^{l+m-2}dx$$

$$= \frac{m-1}{l}\cdot\frac{m-2}{l+1}\cdot\frac{m-3}{l+2}\cdots\cdots\frac{1}{l+m-2}\cdot\left(\frac{x^{l+m-1}}{l+m-1}\right)_0^1$$

$$= \frac{m-1}{l}\cdot\frac{m-2}{l+1}\cdot\frac{m-3}{l+2}\cdots\cdots\frac{1}{l+m-2}\cdot\frac{1}{l+m-1}$$

$$= \frac{(m-1)!}{l(l+1)(l+2)\ldots(l+m-1)}$$

If l also is a +ve integer, then

$$= \frac{(m-1)!(l-1)!}{(l-1)!\{l(l+1)(l+2)\ldots(l+m-1)\}}$$

$$= \frac{(m-1)!(l-1)!}{(l+m-1)!}$$

Case II. *Let l be a positive integer*, then integrating by parts taking x^{l-1} as the first function and $(l - x)^{m-1}$ as the second function, we get

$$\beta\,(l, m) = \left[-x^{l-1}\frac{(1-x)^m}{m}\right]_0^1 + \int_0^1(l-1)x^{l-2}\frac{(1-x)^m}{m}dx$$

$$= \frac{l-1}{m}\int_0^1 x^{l-2}(1-x)^m\,dx$$

Again integrating by parts taking x^{l-2} as the first function and $(1 - x)^m$ as the second function, we get

$$= \frac{l-1}{m}\left[\left[\left\{-x^{l-2}\frac{(1-x)^{m+1}}{m+1}\right\}_0^1 + \int_0^1 (l-2)\,x^{l-3}\frac{(1-x)^{m+1}}{m+1}\,dx\right]\right.$$

$$= \frac{l-1}{m}\cdot\frac{l-2}{m+1}\int_0^1 x^{l-3}(1-x)^{m+1}\,dx$$

Proceeding in this manner, we get

$$= \frac{l-1}{m}\cdot\frac{l-2}{m+1}\cdot\frac{l-3}{m+2}\cdots\cdots\frac{1}{m+l-2}\int_0^1 x^{l-1}(1-x)^{m+l-2}\,dx$$

$$= \frac{l-1}{m}\cdot\frac{l-2}{m+1}\cdots\cdots\frac{1}{m+l-2}\left[-\frac{(1-x)^{m+l-1}}{m+l-1}\right]_0^1$$

$$= \frac{l-1}{m}\cdot\frac{l-2}{m+1}\cdots\cdots\frac{1}{m+l-2}\cdot\frac{1}{m+l-1}$$

$$= \frac{(l-1)!}{m(m+1)\cdots\cdots(m+l-1)}$$

If m also is a +ve integer, then

$$= \frac{(l-1)!(m-1)!}{(m-1)!\{m(m+1)\cdots\cdots(m+l-1)\}}$$

$$= \frac{(l-1)!(m-1)!}{(l+m-1)!}$$

12.3 Transformations of Beta Function

(i) **$\beta(l, m) = \beta(m, l)$**

We have

$$\beta(l, m) = \int_0^1 x^{l-1}(1-x)^{m-1}\,dx$$

$$= \int_0^1 (1-x)^{l-1}\{1-(1-x)\}^{m-1}\,dx$$

$$\left[\because \int_0^a f(x)\,dx = \int_0^a f(a-x)\,dx\right]$$

$$= \int_0^1 x^{m-1}(1-x)^{l-1}\,dx = \beta(m, l)$$

Aliter. We have

$$\beta\,(l,\,m) = \int_0^1 x^{l-1}(1-x)^{m-1}\,dx$$

[Put $x = 1 - y \therefore dx = -dy$]

$$= \int_1^0 (1-y)^{l-1}\left(1-\overline{1-y}\right)^{m-1}(-dy)$$

$$= \int_0^1 y^{m-1}(1-y)^{l-1}\,dy$$

$$= \beta\,(m,\,l)$$

(ii) $\beta\,(\boldsymbol{l},\,\boldsymbol{m}) = \int_0^\infty \frac{\boldsymbol{x}^{l-1}}{(1+\boldsymbol{x})^{l+m}}\,\boldsymbol{dx}$

We have

$$\beta\,(l,\,m) = \int_0^1 x^{l-1}(1-x)^{m-1}\,dx$$

$$\left[\text{Put } x = \frac{1}{1+y} \therefore dx = -\frac{1}{(1+y)^2}\,dy\right]$$

$$= -\int_\infty^0 \frac{1}{(1+y)^{l-1}}\,\frac{y^{m-1}}{(1+y)^{m-1}}\,\frac{1}{(1+y)^2}\,dx$$

$$= \int_0^\infty \frac{y^{m-1}}{(1+y)^{m+l}}\,dy$$

$$= \int_0^\infty \frac{x^{m-1}}{(1+x)^{m+l}}\,dx \qquad \dots (1)$$

$$\left[\because \int_a^b f(x)\,dt = \int_a^b f(t)\,dt\right]$$

$$\therefore \beta\,(m,\,l) = \int_0^\infty \frac{x^{l-1}}{(1+x)^{m+l}}\,dx \qquad \dots (2)$$

But

$$\beta\,(l,\,m) = \beta\,(m,\,l)$$

$$\therefore \beta\,(l,\,m) = \int_0^\infty \frac{x^{l-1}}{(1+x)^{l+m}}\,dx$$

(iii) $\boldsymbol{\beta}$ **(l, m)** $= \mathbf{2\int_0^{\pi/2} \sin^{2l-1}\theta \cos^{2m-1}\theta\, d\theta}$

We have

$$\beta\ (l,\ m) = \int_0^1 x^{l-1}(1-x)^{m-1}\, dx$$

[Put $x = \sin^2\theta \therefore dx = 2 \sin\theta \cos\theta\, d\theta$]

$$\therefore \beta\ (l,\ m) = \int_0^{\pi/2} \sin^{2l-2}\theta \cos^{2m-2}\theta \cdot 2 \sin\theta \cos\theta\, d\theta$$

$$= 2\int_0^{\pi/2} \sin^{2l-1}\theta \cos^{2m-1}\theta\, d\theta$$

12.4 Evaluation of Gamma Function

We have

$$\Gamma n = \int_0^\infty e^{-x} x^{n-1} dx$$

Integrating by parts taking x^{n-1} as the first function and e^{-x} as the second function, we get

$$\Gamma n = \left\{x^{n-1}\left(-e^{-x}\right)\right\}_0^\infty - \int_0^\infty (n-1)\, x^{n-2}\left(-e^{-x}\right) dx$$

$$= (n-1)\int_0^\infty e^{-x} x^{n-2} dx$$

$$= (n-1)\int_0^\infty e^{-x} x^{(n-1)^{-1}} dx$$

$$= (n-1)\,\Gamma(n-1) \qquad \text{... (1)}$$

$\because \quad \text{Lt}_{x\to\infty}\left(-x^{n-1}e^{-x}\right)$

$$= \text{Lt}_{x\to\infty}\left(-\frac{x^{n-1}}{e^x}\right)$$

$$= \text{Lt}_{x\to\infty}\left(\frac{-x^{n-1}}{1 + x + \dfrac{x^2}{2!} + ...}\right)$$

$$= 0$$

In (1) replacing n by $(n - 1)$, we get

$$\Gamma(n-1) = (n-2)\,\Gamma(n-2) \qquad \text{... (2)}$$

From (2) putting the value of $\Gamma(n - 1)$ in (1), we get

$$\Gamma n = (n-1)(n-2)\,\Gamma(n-2)$$

If n is a +ve integer, then continuing this process, we get

$$\Gamma n = (n-1)(n-2)(n-3)\ .....\ 1\ \Gamma 1$$

But $\quad \Gamma 1 = \int_0^\infty e^{-x} x^{1-1} dx \qquad$ [putting $n = 1$ in Γn]

$$= \int_0^\infty e^{-x} dx$$

$$= \left(-e^{-x}\right)_0^\infty$$

$$= 1$$

$\therefore \quad \Gamma n = (n-1)(n-2)\ .....\ 1 = (n-1)\,!$

Thus $\quad \Gamma n = (n-1)\,\Gamma(n-1)\ \forall\ n$

and $\quad \Gamma n = (n-1)\,! \qquad$ [if n is a +ve integer]

12.5 Recurrence Formula for Gamma Function

We know that for all values of n,

$$\Gamma n = (n-1)\,\Gamma(n-1)$$

Replace n by $n + 1$, we get

$$\boxed{\Gamma(n+1) = n\Gamma n}$$

This is known as recurrence formula for the gamma function.

12.6 Generalization of Gamma Function

Applying the process of analytic continuation, we can generalize Γn for $n < 0$ by using recurrence formula in the form

$$\Gamma n = \frac{\Gamma(n+1)}{n}$$

Two values

(i) Put $\quad n = 0$

$$\Gamma 0 = \frac{\Gamma 1}{0} = \frac{1}{0} = \infty$$

(ii) Let $n = -p$ where p is a positive integer, then

$$\Gamma(-p) = \frac{\Gamma(-p+1)}{-p}$$

$$= \frac{(-p)!}{-p} \qquad \left[\Gamma(p+1) = p\,\Gamma p\ \forall\ p\right]$$

$$= \infty$$

Note : We know that

$$^{n}P_{r} = \frac{n!}{n-r!} \qquad \text{[Put } n = 0\text{]}$$

$$\therefore \quad {}^{0}P_{r} = \frac{0!}{0-r!} = \frac{0!}{-r!}$$

But $\quad {}^{n}P_{r} = n\ (n-1)\ .....\ (n-r+1)$

$$\therefore \quad {}^{0}P_{r} = 0$$

$$\therefore \quad 0 = \frac{0!}{-r!} \qquad ...\ (1)$$

Value of 0!

$$^{n}p_{r} = \frac{n!}{n-r!} \qquad \text{[Put } r = n\text{]}$$

$$\therefore \quad {}^{n}p_{n} = \frac{n!}{n-n!} = \frac{n!}{0!}$$

$$\Rightarrow \quad n! = \frac{n!}{0!}$$

$$\Rightarrow \quad 0! = 1$$

Hence from (1),

$$0 = \frac{1}{-r!}$$

$$\Rightarrow \quad -r! = \frac{1}{0} = \infty$$

where r is a +ve integer.

12.7 Transformations of Gamma Function

(i) We have

$$\Gamma n = \int_{0}^{\infty} e^{-x} x^{n-1} dx \qquad \text{[Put } x = ky \text{ so that } dx = kdy\text{]}$$

$$\therefore \quad \Gamma n = \int_{0}^{\infty} e^{-ky} (ky)^{n-1}\, k\, dy$$

$$= k^{n} \int_{0}^{\infty} e^{-ky} y^{n-1} dy$$

$$\Rightarrow \quad \frac{\Gamma n}{k^{n}} = \int_{0}^{\infty} e^{-ky} y^{n-1} dy$$

(ii) We have

$$\Gamma n = \int_0^\infty e^{-x} x^{n-1} dx \qquad \left[\text{Put } x^n = y \text{ so that } nx^{n-1}\,dx = dy \quad \therefore\ x^{n-1}\,dx = \frac{dy}{n}\right]$$

$$= \frac{1}{n}\int_0^\infty e^{-y^{1/n}}\,dy$$

Put $n = \frac{1}{2}$

$$\Gamma\frac{1}{2} = 2\int_0^\infty e^{-y^2}\,dy = 2\,\frac{\sqrt{\pi}}{2} = \sqrt{\pi}$$

(iii) We have

$$\Gamma n = \int_0^\infty e^{-x} x^{n-1} dx \qquad \left[\text{Put } e^{-x} = y \text{ so that } -e^{-x}\,dx = dy\right]$$

$$= -\int_1^0 \left(\log\frac{1}{y}\right)^{n-1} dy$$

$$= \int_0^1 \left(\log\frac{1}{y}\right)^{n-1} dy$$

12.8 Relation between beta and gamma functions

To prove that

$$\beta\ (m,\ n) = \frac{\Gamma m\,\Gamma n}{\Gamma(m+n)}$$

where m, n are positive numbers.

We know that

$$\Gamma n = \int_0^\infty e^{-zx} x^{n-1} z^n dx$$

$$\therefore \Gamma n\ e^{-z} z^{m-1} = \int_0^\infty e^{-z(1+x)} z^{m+n-1} x^{n-1} dx$$

Integrating both sides with respect to z between the limits 0 to ∞, we get

$$\Gamma n \int_0^\infty e^{-z} z^{m-1} dz$$

$$= \int_0^\infty x^{n-1} \left\{\int_0^\infty e^{-z(1+x)} z^{m+n-1} dz\right\} dx$$

[Put $z\ (1 + x) = y$ so that

$z = \dfrac{y}{1+x}$ and $dz\ (1 + x) = dy$

$\therefore \quad dz = \dfrac{dy}{1+x}$]

$$= \int_0^\infty x^{n-1}\left\{\int_0^\infty e^{-y}\frac{y^{m+n-1}}{(1+x)^{m+n-1}}\cdot\frac{dy}{1+x}\right\}dx$$

$$= \int_0^\infty \frac{x^{n-1}}{(1+x)^{m+n}}\left\{\int_0^\infty e^{-y}y^{m+n-1}dy\right\}dx$$

$$= \int_0^\infty \frac{x^{n-1}}{(1+x)^{m+n}}\Gamma(m+n)\,dx$$

$$= \Gamma(m+n)\int_0^\infty \frac{x^{n-1}}{(1+x)^{m+n}}dx$$

$$= \Gamma(m+n)\beta(m,n)$$

$$\therefore \quad \beta\ (m,\ n) = \frac{\Gamma m\,\Gamma n}{\Gamma(m+n)};(m,n>0)$$

12.9 Prove that

$$\Gamma n\ \Gamma(1-n) = \frac{\pi}{\sin n\pi}, 0<n<1$$

Proof. We know that

$$\beta\ (m,\ n) = \frac{\Gamma m\,\Gamma n}{\Gamma(m+n)}$$

$$\Rightarrow \int_0^\infty \frac{x^{n-1}}{(1+x)^{m+n}}dx = \frac{\Gamma m\,\Gamma n}{\Gamma(m+n)}$$

Put $m + n = 1$ so that $m = 1 - n$, we have

$$\int_0^\infty \frac{x^{n-1}}{1+x}dx = \frac{\Gamma(1-n)\Gamma n}{\Gamma 1}$$

$$= \Gamma n\ \Gamma(1-n) \qquad [\because \Gamma 1 = 1]$$

$$\therefore \quad \Gamma n\ \Gamma(1-n) = \frac{\pi}{\sin n\pi}, 0<n<1$$

$$\left[\because \int_0^\infty \frac{x^{n-1}}{1+x}dx = \frac{\pi}{\sin n\pi}, 0<n<1\right]$$

Aliter. We know that

$$\int_0^\infty \frac{x^{n-1}}{1+x}\,dx = \frac{\pi}{\sin n\pi}; 0 < n < 1$$

Put $\dfrac{x}{1+x} = y$

$\therefore \quad x = y + yx$

$\therefore \quad x(1 - y) = y$

$\therefore \quad x = \dfrac{y}{1-y}$

$$\therefore \quad dx = \frac{(1-y)1 - y(-1)}{(1-y)^2}\,dy = \frac{1}{(1-y)^2}\,dy$$

$$= \int_0^1 \frac{y^{n-1}}{(1-y)^{n-1}} \cdot \frac{1}{1+\frac{y}{1-y}} \frac{1}{(1-y)^2}\,dy$$

$$= \int_0^1 \frac{y^{n-1}}{(1-y)^n}\,dy$$

$$= \int_0^1 y^{n-1}(1-y)^{-n}\,dy$$

$$= \int_0^1 y^{n-1}(1-y)^{(1-n)-1}\,dy$$

$$= \beta(n, 1-n)$$

$$= \frac{\Gamma n\,\Gamma(1-n)}{\boxed{n+1-n}}$$

$$= \frac{\Gamma n\,\Gamma(1-n)}{\Gamma 1}$$

$$= \Gamma n\,\Gamma(1-n) \qquad [\because \Gamma 1 = 1]$$

12.10 Duplication Formula

If m is positive, then

$$\Gamma m \Gamma\left(m + \frac{1}{2}\right) = \frac{\sqrt{\pi}\,\Gamma 2m}{2^{2m-1}}$$

Proof. We know that

$$\beta(m, n) = \frac{\Gamma m\,\Gamma n}{(m+n)!} \qquad \ldots (1)$$

$$\Rightarrow \quad 2\int_0^{\pi/2} \sin^{2m-1}\theta \cos^{2n-1}\theta \, d\theta = \frac{\Gamma m \, \Gamma n}{(m+n)!} \qquad \ldots (2)$$

Putting $2n - 1 = 0$ i.e. $n = \frac{1}{2}$ in (2), we get

$$2\int_0^{\pi/2} \sin^{2m-1}\theta \, d\theta = \frac{\Gamma m \, \Gamma \frac{1}{2}}{\Gamma\left(m + \frac{1}{2}\right)}$$

$$\Rightarrow \quad 2\int_0^{\pi/2} \sin^{2m-1}\theta \, d\theta = \frac{\Gamma m \sqrt{\pi}}{\Gamma\left(m + \frac{1}{2}\right)} \qquad \ldots (3)$$

Again putting $n = m$ in (2), we get

$$2\int_0^{\pi/2} \sin^{2m-1}\theta \cos^{2m-1}\theta \, d\theta = \frac{\Gamma m \, \Gamma m}{\Gamma(m+m)}$$

$$\Rightarrow \frac{2}{2^{2m-1}} \int_0^{\pi/2} 2^{2m-1} \sin^{2m-1}\theta \cos^{2m-1}\theta \, d\theta = \frac{(\Gamma m)^2}{\Gamma(2m)}$$

$$\Rightarrow \quad \frac{2}{2^{2m-1}} \int_0^{\pi/2} (2\sin\theta\cos\theta)^{2m-1} \, d\theta = \frac{(\Gamma m)^2}{\Gamma(2m)}$$

$$\Rightarrow \quad \frac{2}{2^{2m-1}} \int_0^{\pi/2} \sin^{2m-1} 2\theta \, d\theta = \frac{(\Gamma m)^2}{\Gamma(2m)}$$

Put $2\theta = \phi$, so that $2d\theta = d\phi$

$$\Rightarrow \quad \frac{1}{2^{2m-1}} \int_0^{\pi} \sin^{2m-1}\phi \, d\phi = \frac{(\Gamma m)^2}{\Gamma(2m)}$$

$$\Rightarrow \quad \frac{2}{2^{2m-1}} \int_0^{\pi/2} \sin^{2m-1}\phi \, d\phi = \frac{(\Gamma m)^2}{\Gamma(2m)}$$

$$\Rightarrow \quad \int_0^{\pi/2} \sin^{2m-1}\phi \, d\phi = 2^{2m-2} \frac{(\Gamma m)^2}{\Gamma(2m)} \qquad \ldots (4)$$

From (3) and (4), we obtain

$$\frac{\Gamma m \sqrt{\pi}}{2\Gamma\left(m + \frac{1}{2}\right)} = \frac{2^{2m-2} (\Gamma m)^2}{\Gamma(2m)}$$

$$\Rightarrow \qquad \Gamma m\, \Gamma\left(m+\frac{1}{2}\right) = \frac{\sqrt{\pi}\,\Gamma(2m)}{2^{2m-1}}$$

12.11 Value of $\Gamma\frac{1}{6}$

From Duplication Formula, we know that

$$\Gamma m\, \Gamma\left(m+\frac{1}{2}\right) = \frac{\sqrt{\pi}\,\Gamma 2m}{2^{2m-1}}$$

Put $\qquad m = \frac{1}{6}$

$$\Gamma\frac{1}{6}\,\Gamma\left(\frac{1}{6}+\frac{1}{2}\right) = \frac{\sqrt{\pi}\,\Gamma\frac{1}{3}}{2^{-2/3}}$$

$$\Rightarrow \qquad \Gamma\frac{1}{6}\,\Gamma\frac{2}{3} = \frac{\sqrt{\pi}\,\Gamma\frac{1}{3}}{2^{-2/3}}$$

$$\Rightarrow \qquad \Gamma\frac{1}{6}\,\Gamma\frac{1}{3}\,\Gamma\frac{2}{3} = \frac{\sqrt{\pi}\left(\Gamma\frac{2}{3}\right)^2}{2^{-2/3}}$$

$$\Rightarrow \qquad \Gamma\frac{1}{6}\,\Gamma\frac{1}{3}\,\Gamma\left(1-\frac{1}{3}\right) = \frac{\sqrt{\pi}\left(\Gamma\frac{1}{3}\right)^2}{2^{-2/3}}$$

$$\Rightarrow \qquad \Gamma\frac{1}{6}\,\frac{\pi}{\sin\frac{\pi}{3}} = \sqrt{\pi}\,\frac{\left(\Gamma\frac{1}{3}\right)^2}{2^{-2/3}}$$

$$\Rightarrow \qquad \Gamma\frac{1}{6}\,\frac{2\pi}{\sqrt{3}} = \sqrt{\pi}\left(\Gamma\frac{1}{3}\right)^2 2^{2/3}$$

$$\Rightarrow \qquad \boxed{\Gamma\frac{1}{6} = 2^{-1/3}3^{1/2}\pi^{-1/2}\left(\Gamma\frac{1}{3}\right)^2}$$

12.12 To prove that

$$\Gamma\frac{1}{n}\,\Gamma\frac{2}{n}\,\Gamma\frac{3}{n}\,.....\,\Gamma\frac{n-1}{n} = \frac{(2\pi)^{\frac{n-1}{2}}}{n^{1/2}}$$

where n is a +ve integer greater than 1.

Proof. Let

$$P = \Gamma\frac{1}{n}\Gamma\frac{2}{n}\Gamma\frac{3}{n}.....\Gamma\frac{n-1}{n}$$

Writing the value of P in the reverse order

$$P = \Gamma\frac{n-1}{n}\Gamma\frac{n-2}{n}\Gamma\frac{n-3}{n}.....\Gamma\frac{1}{n}$$

Multiplying the two values of P, we obtain

$$P^2 = \left\{\Gamma\frac{1}{n}\Gamma 1-\frac{1}{n}\right\}\left\{\Gamma\frac{2}{n}\Gamma 1-\frac{2}{n}\right\}\left\{\Gamma\frac{3}{n}\Gamma 1-\frac{3}{n}\right\}.....\left\{\Gamma\frac{n-1}{n}\Gamma 1-\frac{n-1}{n}\right\}$$

$$= \frac{\pi}{\sin\frac{\pi}{n}}\cdot\frac{\pi}{\sin\frac{2\pi}{n}}\cdot\frac{\pi}{\sin\frac{3\pi}{n}}.....\frac{\pi}{\sin\frac{n-1}{n}\pi}$$

$$= \frac{\pi^{n-1}}{\sin\frac{\pi}{n}\cdot\sin\frac{2\pi}{n}\cdot\sin\frac{3\pi}{n}.....\sin\frac{n-1}{n}\pi} \qquad ... (1)$$

Now we know that

$$\frac{\sin n\theta}{\sin\theta} = 2^{n-1}\sin\left(\theta+\frac{\pi}{n}\right)\sin\left(\theta+\frac{2\pi}{n}\right).....\sin\left(\theta+\frac{n-1}{n}\pi\right)$$

Taking limit as $\theta \to 0$, we get

$$\text{L.H.S.} = \text{Lt}_{\theta\to 0}\frac{\sin n\theta}{\sin\theta}$$

$$= \text{Lt}_{\theta\to 0}\left\{\frac{\sin n\theta}{\sin\theta}\right\}n\left\{\frac{\theta}{\sin\theta}\right\}=1\cdot n\cdot 1=n$$

$\therefore$ In limit

$$n = 2^{n-1}\sin\frac{\pi}{n}\cdot\sin\frac{2\pi}{n}\cdot\sin\frac{3\pi}{n}.....\sin\frac{n-1}{n}\pi$$

$$\Rightarrow \quad \sin\frac{\pi}{n}\cdot\sin\frac{2\pi}{n}.....\sin\frac{n-1}{n}\pi = \frac{n}{2^{n-1}}$$

From (1) $$P^2 = \frac{\pi^{n-1} \cdot 2^{n-1}}{n} = \frac{(2\pi)^{n-1}}{n}$$

$$\Rightarrow \qquad P = \frac{(2\pi)^{\left(n-\frac{1}{2}\right)}}{n^{\frac{1}{2}}}$$

12.13 To evaluate the integrals

$$\int_0^\infty e^{-ax} \cos bx \, x^{m-1} dx$$

and $$\int_0^\infty e^{-ax} \sin bx \, x^{m-1} dx$$

We know from 11.7 (i) that

$$\int_0^\infty e^{-zx} x^{m-1} dx = \frac{\Gamma m}{z^m}$$

Put $z = a - ib$

$$\int_0^\infty e^{-(a-ib)x} x^{m-1} dx = \frac{\Gamma m}{(a-ib)^m}$$

$$= \frac{\Gamma m \, (a+ib)^m}{(a-ib)^m \, (a+ib)^m}$$

$$= \frac{\Gamma m \, (a+ib)^m}{\left(a^2+b^2\right)^m}$$

$$\Rightarrow \qquad \int_0^\infty e^{-az} e^{ibx} x^{m-1} dx = \frac{\Gamma m \, (a+ib)^m}{\left(a^2+b^2\right)^m}$$

Put $a = r \cos \theta$, $b = r \sin \theta$

then $$r = \sqrt{a^2+b^2}$$

and $$\theta = \tan^{-1}\left(\frac{b}{a}\right)$$

$$\therefore \qquad \int_0^\infty e^{-az} x^{ibx} x^{m-1} dx = \frac{\Gamma m \left(a^2+b^2\right)^{\frac{m}{2}} [\cos\theta + i \sin\theta]^m}{\left(a^2+b^2\right)^m}$$

$$\Rightarrow \qquad \int_0^\infty e^{-az} x^{m-1} (\cos bx + i \sin bx) \, dx$$

$$= \frac{\Gamma m \, (\cos m\theta + i \sin m\theta)}{\left(a^2+b^2\right)^{\frac{m}{2}}}$$

Equating real and imaginary parts, we get

$$\int_0^\infty e^{-az} x^{m-1} \cos bx \, dx = \frac{\Gamma m \cos m\theta}{\left(a^2+b^2\right)^{m/2}} \qquad \text{... (1)}$$

and $$\int_0^\infty e^{-az} x^{m-1} \sin bx \, dx = \frac{\Gamma m \sin m\theta}{\left(a^2+b^2\right)^{m/2}} \qquad \text{... (2)}$$

where $\theta = \tan^{-1}\left(\frac{b}{a}\right)$

Deductions : Put $a = 0$ so that $\theta = \pi/2$ in (1) and (2), we obtain

$$\int_0^\infty x^{m-1} \cos bx \, dx = \frac{\Gamma m}{b^m} \cos \frac{m\pi}{2}$$

and $$\int_0^\infty x^{m-1} \sin bx \, dx = \frac{\Gamma m}{b^m} \sin \frac{m\pi}{2}$$

12.14 To evaluate $\int_0^\infty \cos\left(bx^{1/n}\right) dx$

Let $$I = \int_0^\infty \cos\left(bx^{1/n}\right) dx \qquad \left[\text{Put } x = z^n \quad \therefore \; dx = nz^{n-1}\, dz\right]$$

$$\therefore \quad I = \int_0^\infty \cos(bz)\, nz^{n-1} dz$$

$$= n\int_0^\infty z^{n-1} \cos(bz)\, dz$$

$$= n\frac{\Gamma n}{b^n} \cos\frac{n\pi}{2}$$

$$= \frac{\Gamma(n+1)}{b^n} \cos\frac{n\pi}{2}$$

12.15 To evaluate $\int_0^\infty \sin\left(bx^{1/n}\right) dx$

Let $$I = \int_0^\infty \sin\left(bx^{1/n}\right) dx \qquad \left[\text{Put } x = z^n \quad \therefore \; dx = nz^{n-1}\, dz\right]$$

$$\therefore \quad I = n\int_0^\infty \sin(bz)\, z^{n-1} dz$$

$$= n\frac{\Gamma n}{b^n} \frac{\sin n\pi}{2}$$

$$= \frac{\Gamma(n+1)}{b^n} \sin\left(\frac{n\pi}{2}\right)$$

ILLUSTRATIVE EXAMPLES

Example 1. The value of $\Gamma n\ \Gamma(1-n)$ is

(i) $\beta\ (n, 1)$ (ii) $\beta\ (n, 1-n)$

(iii) $\beta\ (n, 1-2n)$ (iv) $\beta\ (1-n, 1-n)$.

Solution :

The value of $\Gamma n\ \Gamma\ (1-n)$ is $\beta\ (n, 1-n)$

Example 2. The value of $\int_0^\infty e^{-x^2}\,dx$ is

(i) π (ii) $\frac{\sqrt{\pi}}{2}$

(iii) $\sqrt{\pi}$ (iv) $\frac{n\sqrt{\pi}}{2}$.

Solution :

The value of $\int_0^\infty e^{-x^2}\,dx$ is $\frac{\sqrt{\pi}}{2}$

Example 3. Express $\int_0^1 x^m\left(1-x^n\right)^p dx$ in terms of the beta function, and hence evaluate $\int_0^1 x^5\left(1-x^3\right)^{10} dx$.

Solution :

$$\int_0^1 x^m\left(1-x^n\right)^p dx$$

[Put $x^n = y$

$\therefore\quad x = y^{1/n}$

$\therefore\quad dx = \frac{1}{n} y^{1/n-1} dy$]

$$= \frac{1}{n}\int_0^1 y^{m/n}\left(1-y\right)^p y^{1/n-1} dy$$

$$= \frac{1}{n}\int_0^1 y^{\frac{m+1}{n}-1}\left(1-y\right)^{(p+1)-1} dy$$

$$= \frac{1}{n}\beta\left(\frac{m+1}{n}, p+1\right)$$

Put $m = 5$, $n = 3$, $p = 10$, we get

$$\int_0^1 x^5\left(1-x^3\right)^{10} dx = \frac{1}{3}\beta\left(\frac{5+1}{3}, 10+1\right)$$

$$= \frac{1}{3}\beta(2,11)$$

$$= \frac{1}{3}\frac{\Gamma 2\,\Gamma 11}{\Gamma(2+11)}$$

$$= \frac{1}{3}\frac{\Gamma 2\,\Gamma 11}{\Gamma 13}$$

$$= \frac{1!(10)!}{3(12)!}$$

$$= \frac{1}{3.12.11}$$

$$= \frac{1}{396}$$

Example 4. Evaluate $\Gamma\left(-\frac{1}{2}\right), \Gamma\left(-\frac{3}{2}\right), \Gamma\left(-\frac{5}{2}\right)$

Solution : We know that

$$\Gamma n\,\Gamma(1-n) = \frac{\pi}{\sin n\pi} \qquad \ldots (1)$$

(i) Put $n = -\frac{1}{2}$ in (1), we get

$$\Gamma\left(-\frac{1}{2}\right)\Gamma\left(\frac{3}{2}\right) = \frac{\pi}{\sin\left(-\frac{1}{2}\pi\right)} = -\pi$$

$$\Rightarrow \quad \Gamma\left(-\frac{1}{2}\right) = \frac{-\pi}{\Gamma\frac{3}{2}}$$

$$= \frac{-\pi}{\frac{1}{2}\Gamma\frac{1}{2}}$$

$$= \frac{-\pi}{\frac{1}{2}\sqrt{\pi}} = -2\sqrt{\pi}$$

(ii) Put $n = -\frac{3}{2}$ in (1), we get

$$\Gamma\left(-\frac{3}{2}\right)\Gamma\frac{5}{2} = \frac{\pi}{\sin\left(-\frac{3\pi}{2}\right)}$$

$$= -\frac{\pi}{\sin\frac{3\pi}{2}}$$

$$= \pi$$

$$\Rightarrow \quad \Gamma\left(-\frac{3}{2}\right) = \frac{\pi}{\Gamma\frac{5}{2}} = \frac{\pi}{\frac{3}{2}\cdot\frac{1}{2}\cdot\sqrt{\pi}} = 4\frac{\sqrt{\pi}}{3}$$

(iii) Put $n = -\dfrac{5}{2}$ in (1), we get

$$\Gamma\left(-\frac{5}{2}\right)\Gamma\frac{7}{2} = \frac{\pi}{\sin\left(-\frac{5\pi}{2}\right)}$$

$$= -\frac{\pi}{\sin\frac{5\pi}{2}}$$

$$= -\pi$$

$$\Rightarrow \quad \Gamma\left(-\frac{5}{2}\right) = -\frac{\pi}{\Gamma\frac{7}{2}}$$

$$= -\frac{\pi}{\frac{5}{2}\cdot\frac{3}{2}\cdot\frac{1}{2}\cdot\sqrt{\pi}}$$

$$= -\frac{8\sqrt{\pi}}{15}$$

Aliter. *Let us use recurrence formula generalized to negative values.*

i.e., $$\Gamma n = \frac{\Gamma(n+1)}{n} \qquad \text{... (1)}$$

(i) Put $n = -\dfrac{1}{2}$ in (1), we obtain

$$\Gamma -\frac{1}{2} = \frac{\Gamma \frac{1}{2}}{-\frac{1}{2}} = -2\sqrt{\pi}$$

(ii) Put $n = -\frac{3}{2}$ in (1), we obtain

$$\Gamma -\frac{3}{2} = \frac{\Gamma -\frac{1}{2}}{-\frac{3}{2}} = -\frac{2\sqrt{\pi}}{-\frac{3}{2}} = \frac{4\sqrt{\pi}}{3}$$

(iii) Put $n = -\frac{5}{2}$ in (1), we obtain

$$\Gamma -\frac{5}{2} = \frac{\Gamma -\frac{3}{2}}{-\frac{5}{2}} = \frac{4\sqrt{\pi}}{3 \cdot -\frac{5}{2}} = -\frac{8\sqrt{\pi}}{15}$$

Example 5. Evaluate $\int_0^\infty x^4 e^{-x} dx.$

Solution :

$$\begin{aligned}\int_0^\infty x^4 e^{-x} dx &= \int_0^\infty e^{-x} x^{5-1} dx \\ &= \Gamma 5 \\ &= 4! \\ &= 4 \cdot 3 \cdot 2 \cdot 1 \\ &= 24\end{aligned}$$

Example 6. Evaluate $\int_0^\infty e^{-4x} x^{5/2} dx.$

Solution :

Let $\quad I = \int_0^\infty e^{-4x} x^{5/2} dx$

[Put $4x = y$

$\therefore \quad 4dx = dy$

$\therefore \quad dx = \frac{dy}{4}$]

$$= \int_0^\infty e^{-y} \frac{y^{5/2}}{4^{5/2}} \frac{dy}{4}$$

$$= \frac{1}{4^{7/2}} \int_0^\infty e^{-y} y^{7/2-1} dy$$

$$= \frac{1}{2^7} \Gamma\left(\frac{7}{2}\right)$$

$$= \frac{\frac{5}{2} \cdot \frac{3}{2} \cdot \frac{1}{2} \cdot \Gamma\frac{1}{2}}{2^7}$$

$$= \frac{15\sqrt{\pi}}{1024}$$

Example 7. Prove that $\int_0^1 x^2 (1-x)^3 \, dx = \frac{1}{60}$.

Solution :

$$\int_0^1 x^2 (1-x)^3 \, dx = \int_0^1 x^{3-1} (1-x)^{4-1} \, dx$$

$$= \beta\ (3,\ 4)$$

$$= \frac{\Gamma 3\, \Gamma 4}{\Gamma(3+4)}$$

$$= \frac{\Gamma 3\, \Gamma 4}{\Gamma 7}$$

$$= \frac{2!\,3!}{6!}$$

$$= \frac{(2.1)(3.2.1)}{(6.5.4.3.2.1)}$$

$$= \frac{1}{60}$$

Example 8. Evaluate $\int_0^a \frac{x^2}{\sqrt{a-x}} \, dx$.

Solution :

Let $I = \int_0^a \frac{x^2}{\sqrt{a-x}} \, dx$

[Put $x = ay$

$\therefore \quad dx = a\,dy$]

$$= \int_0^1 \frac{a^2 y^2 a dy}{\sqrt{a - ay}}$$

$$= a^{5/2} \int_0^1 y^2 (1-y)^{-1/2} dy$$

$$= a^{5/2} \int_0^1 y^{3-1} (1-y)^{1/2 - 1} dy$$

$$= a^{5/2} \beta\left(3, \frac{1}{2}\right)$$

$$= a^{5/2} \frac{\Gamma 3 \, \Gamma \frac{1}{2}}{\Gamma 3 + \frac{1}{2}}$$

$$= a^{5/2} \frac{\Gamma 3 \, \Gamma \frac{1}{2}}{\Gamma \frac{7}{2}}$$

$$= a^{5/2} \frac{2! \sqrt{\pi}}{\frac{5}{2} \cdot \frac{3}{2} \cdot \frac{1}{2} \cdot \sqrt{\pi}}$$

$$= \frac{16 a^{5/2}}{15}$$

Example 9. Evaluate $\int_0^\infty \frac{dx}{1+x^4}$

Solution :

Let $I = \int_0^\infty \frac{dx}{1+x^4}$ [Put $x^4 = y$

$\therefore \quad x = y^{1/4}$

$\therefore \quad dx = \frac{1}{4} y^{-3/4} dy$]

$$\therefore \quad I = \int_0^\infty \frac{\frac{1}{4} y^{-3/4} dy}{1+y}$$

$$= \frac{1}{4} \int_0^\infty \frac{y^{1/4 - 1}}{(1+y)^{1/4 + 3/4}} dy$$

$$= \frac{1}{4}\beta^{\left(\frac{1}{4},\frac{3}{4}\right)}$$

$$= \frac{1}{4}\frac{\Gamma\frac{1}{4}\Gamma\frac{3}{4}}{\Gamma\left(\frac{1}{4}+\frac{3}{4}\right)}$$

$$= \frac{1}{4}\frac{\Gamma\frac{1}{4}\left(1-\frac{1}{4}\right)}{\Pi}$$

$$= \frac{1}{4}\frac{\pi}{\sin\frac{\pi}{4}} \qquad [\because \Gamma 1 = 1]$$

$$= \frac{\pi}{4\cdot\frac{1}{\sqrt{2}}}$$

$$= \frac{\pi\sqrt{2}}{4}$$

Example 10. Evaluate $\int_0^{\pi/2} \tan^n x\, dx.$

Solution :

Let $$I = \int_0^{\pi/2} \tan^n x\, dx$$

$$= \int_0^{\pi/2} \sin^n x \cos^{-n} x\, dx$$

$$= \int_0^{\pi/2} \sin^{2\left(\frac{n+1}{2}\right)-1} x \cdot \cos^{2\left(\frac{1-n}{2}\right)-1} x\, dx$$

$$= \frac{1}{2}\beta\left(\frac{n+1}{2}, \frac{1-n}{2}\right)$$

$$= \frac{\Gamma\left(\frac{n+1}{2}\right)\Gamma\left(\frac{1-n}{2}\right)}{2\Gamma\left(\frac{n+1}{2}+\frac{1-n}{2}\right)}$$

$$= \frac{1}{2}\Gamma\left(\frac{n+1}{2}\right)\Gamma\left[1-\left(\frac{n+1}{2}\right)\right] \qquad [\because \Gamma 1 = 1]$$

$$= \frac{1}{2} \frac{\pi}{\sin\left(\frac{n+1}{2}\pi\right)}$$

$$= \frac{1}{2} \frac{\pi}{\cos\frac{n\pi}{2}}$$

$$= \frac{\pi}{2} \sec\frac{n\pi}{2}$$

Example 11. Show that

(i) $\int_0^{\pi/2} \sin^{2m-1}\theta \cos^{2n-1}\theta \, d\theta = \dfrac{\Gamma m \, \Gamma n}{2\Gamma(m+n)}$

(ii) $\int_0^{\pi/2} \sin^p\theta \cos^q\theta \, d\theta = \dfrac{\Gamma\left(\frac{p+1}{2}\right)\Gamma\left(\frac{q+1}{2}\right)}{2\Gamma\left(\frac{p+q+2}{2}\right)}$

Solution :

(i) $\int_0^{\pi/2} \sin^{2m-1}\theta \cos^{2n-1}\theta \, d\theta$

$$= \frac{1}{2}\beta(m, n)$$

$$= \frac{1}{2} \frac{\Gamma m \, \Gamma n}{\Gamma(m+n)}$$

(ii) $\int_0^{\pi/2} \sin^p\theta \cos^q\theta \, d\theta$

$$= \int_0^{\pi/2} \sin^{2\left(\frac{p+1}{2}\right)-1} \cos^{2\left(\frac{q+1}{2}\right)-1} \theta \, d\theta$$

$$= \frac{1}{2}\beta\left(\frac{p+1}{2}, \frac{q+1}{2}\right)$$

$$= \frac{\Gamma\left(\frac{p+1}{2}\right)\Gamma\left(\frac{q+1}{2}\right)}{2\Gamma\left(\frac{p+1}{2}+\frac{q+1}{2}\right)}$$

$$= \frac{\Gamma\left(\frac{p+1}{2}\right)\Gamma\left(\frac{q+1}{2}\right)}{2\Gamma\left(\frac{p+q+2}{2}\right)}$$

Example 12. Show that

$$2^p\Gamma\left(\frac{p+1}{2}\right)\Gamma\left(\frac{p+2}{2}\right) = \sqrt{\pi}\,\Gamma(p+1).$$

Solution : By Duplication Formula, we know that

$$\Gamma p\,\Gamma\left(p+\frac{1}{2}\right) = \frac{\sqrt{\pi}\,\Gamma(2p)}{2^{2p-1}}$$

Replacing p by $\frac{p+1}{2}$, we get

$$\Gamma\left(\frac{p+1}{2}\right)\Gamma\left(\frac{p+2}{2}\right) = \frac{\sqrt{\pi}\,\Gamma\left[2\cdot\left(\frac{p+1}{2}\right)\right]}{2\left(\frac{p+1}{2}\right)-1}$$

$$= \frac{\sqrt{\pi}\,\Gamma(p+1)}{2^p}$$

$$\Rightarrow \quad 2^p\Gamma\left(\frac{p+1}{2}\right)\Gamma\left(\frac{p+2}{2}\right) = \sqrt{\pi}\,\Gamma(p+1)$$

Example 13. Prove that

$\beta(m, n) = \beta(m+1, n) + \beta(m, n+1)$.

Solution :

$$\text{R.H.S.} = \beta(m+1, n) + \beta(m, n+1)$$

$$= \frac{\Gamma(m+1)\Gamma n}{\Gamma(m+1+n)} + \frac{\Gamma m\,\Gamma(n+1)}{\Gamma(m+n+1)}$$

$$= \frac{m\,\Gamma m\,\Gamma n}{(m+n)\Gamma(m+n)} + \frac{\Gamma m\,n\Gamma n}{(m+n)\Gamma(m+n)}$$

$$= \frac{\Gamma m\,\Gamma n}{\Gamma(m+n)}\left[\frac{m}{m+n} + \frac{n}{m+n}\right]$$

$$= \frac{\Gamma m \, \Gamma n}{\Gamma(m+n)}$$
$$= \beta\ (m,\ n)$$

Example 14. Prove that $\int_0^\infty \frac{x^c}{c^x}\,dx = \frac{\Gamma(c+1)}{(\log c)^{c+1}}; c > 1.$

Solution :

Let
$$I = \int_0^\infty \frac{x^c}{c^x}\,dx$$
$$= \int_0^\infty x^c c^{-x}\,dx$$
$$= \int_0^\infty x^c e^{-x} \log_e c\,dx \qquad \left[\because c^{-x} = e^{-z} \log_e c\right]$$

[Put $x \log_e c = y$

$\therefore \quad dx \log_e c = dy$

$\therefore \quad dx = \dfrac{dy}{\log_e c}$]

$$= \int_0^\infty \frac{y^c}{(\log_e c)^c} e^{-y} \frac{dy}{\log_e c}$$
$$= \frac{1}{(\log_e c)^{c+1}} \int_0^\infty e^{-y} y^c\,dy$$
$$= \frac{1}{(\log_e c)^{c+1}} \int_0^\infty e^{-y} y^{(c+1)-1}\,dy$$
$$= \frac{\Gamma(c+1)}{(\log_e c)^{c+1}}$$

Example 15. Evaluate

(i) $\int_0^\infty \frac{x^8(1-x^6)}{(1+x)^{24}}\,dx$

(ii) $\int_0^\infty \frac{x^4(1+x^5)}{(1+x)^{15}}\,dx$

Solution :

(i)
$$I = \int_0^\infty \frac{x^8(1-x^6)}{(1+x)^{24}}\,dx$$

$$= \int_0^\infty \frac{x^8}{(1+x)^{24}}\, dx - \int_0^\infty \frac{x^{14}}{(1+x)^{24}}\, dx$$

$$= \int_0^\infty \frac{x^{9-1}}{(1+x)^{9+15}}\, dx - \int_0^\infty \frac{x^{15-1}}{(1+x)^{15+9}}\, dx$$

$$= \beta\ (9,\ 15) - \beta\ (15,\ 9)$$

$$= 0 \qquad [\because \beta(l, m) = \beta(m, l)]$$

(ii) $$I = \int_0^\infty \frac{x^4(1+x^5)}{(1+x)^{15}}\, dx$$

$$= \int_0^\infty \frac{x^4}{(1+x)^{15}}\, dx + \int_0^\infty \frac{x^9}{(1+x)^{15}}\, dx$$

$$= \int_0^\infty \frac{x^{5-1}}{(1+x)^{5+10}}\, dx + \int_0^\infty \frac{x^{10-1}}{(1+x)^{10+5}}\, dx$$

$$= \beta\ (5,\ 10) + \beta\ (10,\ 5)$$

$$= 2\beta\ (5,\ 10) \qquad [\because \beta(l, m) = \beta(m, l)]$$

$$= \frac{2\Gamma 5\, \Gamma 10}{\Gamma(5+10)}$$

$$= \frac{2\Gamma 5\, \Gamma 10}{\Gamma 15}$$

$$= \frac{24!9!}{14!}$$

$$= \frac{2.(4.3.2.1)(9.8.7.6.5.4.3.2.1)}{14.13.12.11.10.9.8.7.6.5.4.3.2.1}$$

$$= \frac{1}{5005}$$

Example 16. Evaluate Γ.1 Γ.2 Γ.3......Γ.9.

Solution : We know that

$$\Gamma\frac{1}{n}\Gamma\frac{2}{n}\Gamma\frac{3}{n}.....\Gamma\left(\frac{n-1}{n}\right) = \frac{(2\pi)^{\left(n-\frac{1}{2}\right)}}{n^{\frac{1}{2}}}$$

Put $n = 10$, we get

$$\Gamma.1\,\Gamma.2\,\Gamma.3.....\Gamma.9 \equiv \frac{(2\pi)^{9/2}}{\sqrt{10}}$$

Example 17. Show that

$$\int_0^{\pi/2} \frac{dx}{\sqrt{\sin x}} \times \int_0^{\pi/2} \sqrt{\sin x}\, dx = \pi.$$

Solution :

$$\int_0^{\pi/2} \frac{dx}{\sqrt{\sin x}} \times \int_0^{\pi/2} \sqrt{\sin x}\, dx$$

$$= \int_0^{\pi/2} \sin^{-1/2} x\, dx \int_0^{\pi/2} \sin^{1/2} x\, dx$$

$$= \int_0^{\pi/2} \sin^{2(1/4)-1} x \cos^{2(1/2)-1} x\, dx \times \int_0^{\pi/2} \sin^{2(3/4)-1} x \cos^{2(1/2)-1} x\, dx$$

$$= \frac{1}{2}\beta\left(\frac{1}{4}, \frac{1}{2}\right) \cdot \frac{1}{2}\beta\left(\frac{3}{4}, \frac{1}{2}\right)$$

$$= \frac{1}{2} \frac{\Gamma\frac{1}{4}\Gamma\frac{1}{2}}{\Gamma\left(\frac{1}{4}+\frac{1}{2}\right)} \cdot \frac{1}{2} \frac{\Gamma\frac{3}{4}\Gamma\frac{1}{2}}{\Gamma\left(\frac{3}{4}+\frac{1}{2}\right)}$$

$$= \frac{1}{2} \cdot \frac{\Gamma\frac{1}{4}\sqrt{\pi}}{\Gamma\frac{3}{4}} \cdot \frac{1}{2} \frac{\Gamma\frac{3}{4}\sqrt{\pi}}{\Gamma\frac{5}{4}}$$

$$= \frac{\Gamma\frac{1}{4} \cdot \pi}{4\Gamma\frac{5}{4}}$$

$$= \frac{\Gamma\frac{1}{4} \cdot \pi}{4 \cdot \frac{1}{4}\Gamma\frac{1}{4}}$$

$$= \pi$$

Example 18. Prove that

$$\int_0^1 \frac{x^2}{\left(1-x^4\right)^{1/2}}\,dx \cdot \int_0^1 \frac{dx}{\left(1+x^4\right)^{1/2}}\,dx = \frac{\pi}{4\sqrt{2}}.$$

Solution :

$$I_1 = \int_0^1 \frac{x^2}{\left(1-x^4\right)^{1/2}}\,dx$$

[Put $x^4 = \sin^2\theta$

$\Rightarrow \quad x^2 = \sin\theta$

$\Rightarrow \quad x = \sin^{1/2}\theta$

$\Rightarrow \quad dx = \dfrac{1}{2}\sin^{1/2}\theta\cos\theta\,d\theta$]

$$\therefore \qquad I_1 = \int_0^{\pi/2} \frac{\sin\theta \cdot \frac{1}{2}\sin^{-1/2}\theta\cos\theta\,d\theta}{\cos\theta}$$

$$= \frac{1}{2}\int_0^{\pi/2} \sin^{1/2}\theta\,d\theta$$

$$= \frac{1}{2}\int_0^{\pi/2} \sin^{2(3/4)-1}\theta\cos^{2(1/2)-1}\theta\,d\theta$$

$$= \frac{1}{2}\cdot\frac{1}{2}\beta\left(\frac{3}{4},\frac{1}{2}\right)$$

$$= \frac{1}{4}\,\frac{\Gamma\frac{3}{4}\,\Gamma\frac{1}{2}}{\Gamma\left(\frac{3}{4}+\frac{1}{2}\right)}$$

$$= \frac{\frac{1}{2}\Gamma\frac{3}{4}\sqrt{\pi}}{\Gamma\frac{5}{4}}$$

$$= \frac{\frac{1}{4}\Gamma\frac{3}{4}\sqrt{\pi}}{\frac{1}{4}\Gamma\frac{1}{4}}$$

$$= \frac{\sqrt{\pi}\,\Gamma\frac{3}{4}}{\Gamma\frac{1}{4}} \qquad \ldots (1)$$

$$I_2 = \int_0^1 \frac{dx}{(1+x^4)^{1/2}}$$

$$\left[\text{Put } x^4 = \tan^2\phi \quad \therefore x^2 = \tan\phi \quad \therefore x = \tan^{1/2}\phi \quad \therefore dx = \frac{1}{2}\tan^{-1/2}\phi\sec^2\phi\, d\phi\right]$$

$$= \int_0^{\pi/4} \frac{\frac{1}{2}\tan^{-1/2}\phi\sec^2\phi\, d\phi}{\sec\phi}$$

$$= \frac{1}{2}\int_0^{\pi/4} \frac{\sec\phi}{\sqrt{\tan\phi}}\, d\phi$$

$$= \frac{1}{2}\int_0^{\pi/4} \frac{1}{\cos\phi\sqrt{\frac{\sin\phi}{\cos\phi}}}\, d\phi$$

$$= \frac{1}{2}\int_0^{\pi/4} \frac{d\phi}{\sqrt{\sin\phi\cos\phi}}$$

$$= \frac{1}{\sqrt{2}}\int_0^{\pi/4} \frac{d\phi}{\sqrt{2\sin\phi\cos\phi}}$$

$$= \frac{1}{\sqrt{2}}\int_0^{\pi/4} \frac{d\phi}{\sqrt{\sin 2\phi}}$$

$$\left[\text{Put } 2\phi = \alpha \quad \therefore 2d\phi = d\alpha \quad \therefore d\phi = \frac{d\alpha}{2}\right]$$

$$= \frac{1}{\sqrt{2}}\int_0^{\pi/2} \frac{d\alpha}{2\sqrt{\sin\alpha}}$$

$$= \frac{1}{2\sqrt{2}}\int_0^{\pi/2} \sin^{-1/2}\alpha\, d\alpha$$

$$= \frac{1}{2\sqrt{2}}\int_0^{\pi/2} \sin^{2(1/4)-1}\alpha\cos^{2(1/2)-1}\alpha\, d\alpha$$

$$= \frac{1}{2\sqrt{2}} \frac{1}{2} \beta\left(\frac{1}{4}, \frac{1}{2}\right)$$

$$= \frac{1}{2\sqrt{2}} \frac{\Gamma\frac{1}{4}\Gamma\frac{1}{2}}{2\Gamma\left(\frac{1}{4}+\frac{1}{2}\right)}$$

$$= \frac{1}{2\sqrt{2}} \frac{\Gamma\frac{1}{4}\Gamma\frac{1}{2}}{2\Gamma\frac{3}{4}}$$

$$= \frac{\sqrt{\pi}}{4\sqrt{2}} \frac{\Gamma\frac{1}{4}}{\Gamma\frac{3}{4}} \qquad \text{... (2)}$$

$$\therefore \qquad I_1 \times I_2 = \frac{\sqrt{\pi}\,\Gamma\frac{3}{4}}{\Gamma\frac{1}{4}} \cdot \frac{\sqrt{\pi}\,\Gamma\frac{1}{4}}{4\sqrt{2}\,\Gamma\frac{3}{4}}$$

$$= \frac{\pi}{4\sqrt{2}}$$

Example 19. Show that

$$\int_0^1 \frac{x^{m-1} + x^{n-1}}{(1+x)^{m+n}}\, dx = \beta\,(m, n).$$

Solution :

$$\int_0^1 \frac{x^{m-1} + x^{n-1}}{(1+x)^{m+n}}\, dx$$

$$= \int_0^1 \frac{x^{m-1}}{(1+x)^{m+n}}\, dx + \int_0^1 \frac{x^{n-1}}{(1+x)^{m+n}}\, dx$$

In the second integral.

Put $\qquad x = \frac{1}{y}$

$\therefore \qquad dx = -\frac{1}{y^2}\, dy$

$$\therefore \quad \int_0^1 \frac{x^{m-1} + x^{n-1}}{(1+x)^{m+n}}\, dx$$

$$= \int_0^1 \frac{x^{m-1}}{(1+x)^{m+n}}\, dx + \int_0^1 \frac{\left(\frac{1}{y}\right)^{n-1}}{\left(1+\frac{1}{y}\right)^{m+n}} \left(-\frac{1}{y^2}\right) dy$$

$$= \int_0^1 \frac{x^{m-1}}{(1+x)^{m+n}}\, dx + \int_1^\infty \frac{y^{m-1}}{(1+y)^{m+n}}\, dy$$

$$= \int_0^1 \frac{x^{m-1}}{(1+x)^{m+n}}\, dx + \int_1^\infty \frac{x^{m-1}}{(1+x)^{m+n}}\, dx$$

$$\left[\because \int_a^b f(x)\, dx = \int_a^b f(t)\, dt\right]$$

$$= \int_0^\infty \frac{x^{m-1}}{(1+x)^{m+n}}\, dx$$

$$= \beta\ (m,\ n)$$

Example 20. Show that

$$\int_0^1 \frac{dx}{\sqrt{1-x^6}} = \frac{\sqrt{3}}{2} \int_0^1 \frac{dx}{\sqrt{1-x^3}}$$

$$= \frac{\left(\Gamma \frac{1}{3}\right)^3}{2^{7/3} \cdot \pi}.$$

Solution :

$$I_1 = \int_0^1 \frac{dx}{\sqrt{1-x^6}}$$

[Put $x^6 = \sin^2 \theta$

$\Rightarrow \ x = \sin^{1/3} \theta$

$\Rightarrow \ dx = \dfrac{1}{3} \sin^{-2/3} \theta \cos \theta \ d\theta$]

$$= \int_0^{\pi/2} \frac{\frac{1}{2} \sin^{-2/3} \theta \cos \theta \, d\theta}{\cos \theta}$$

$$= \frac{1}{3} \int_0^{\pi/2} \sin^{-2/3} \theta \, d\theta$$

$$= \frac{1}{3}\int_0^{\pi/2} \sin^{2(1/6)-1}\theta \cos^{2(1/2)-1}\theta \, d\theta$$

$$= \frac{1}{3}\frac{1}{2}\beta\left(\frac{1}{6}, \frac{1}{2}\right)$$

$$= \frac{1}{6}\frac{\Gamma\frac{1}{6}\Gamma\frac{1}{2}}{\Gamma\left(\frac{1}{6}+\frac{1}{2}\right)}$$

$$= \frac{1}{6}\frac{\Gamma\frac{1}{6}\sqrt{\pi}}{\Gamma\frac{2}{3}}$$

$$= \frac{1}{6}\cdot\frac{2^{-1/3}\sqrt{3}\left(\Gamma\frac{1}{3}\right)^2\sqrt{\pi}}{\sqrt{\pi}\,\Gamma\frac{2}{3}}$$

$$= \frac{\sqrt{3}}{6\cdot 2^{1/3}}\frac{\left(\Gamma\frac{1}{3}\right)^2\Gamma\frac{1}{3}}{\Gamma\frac{2}{3}\Gamma\frac{1}{3}}$$

$$= \frac{\sqrt{3}}{6\cdot 2^{1/3}}\frac{\left(\Gamma\frac{1}{3}\right)^3}{\Gamma\left(1-\frac{1}{3}\right)\Gamma\frac{1}{3}}$$

$$= \frac{\sqrt{3}}{6\cdot 2^{1/3}}\frac{\left(\Gamma\frac{1}{3}\right)^3}{\frac{\pi}{\sin \pi/3}}$$

$$= \frac{\sqrt{3}\left(\Gamma\frac{1}{3}\right)^3\cdot\sqrt{3}}{6\cdot 2^{1/3}\pi\cdot 2}$$

$$= \frac{\left(\Gamma\frac{1}{3}\right)^3}{2^{7/3}\pi}$$

Again $$I_2 = \frac{\sqrt{3}}{2}\int_0^1 \frac{dx}{\sqrt{1-x^3}}$$

[Put $x^3 = \sin^2\theta$

$\therefore \quad x = \sin^{2/3}\theta$

$\therefore \quad dx = \frac{2}{3}\sin^{-1/3}\theta\cos\theta\, d\theta$]

$$\therefore \qquad I_2 = \frac{\sqrt{3}}{2}\int_0^{\pi/2} \frac{\frac{2}{3}\cdot\sin^{-1/3}\theta\cos\theta\, d\theta}{\cos\theta}$$

$$= \frac{1}{\sqrt{3}}\int_0^{\pi/2}\sin^{-1/3}\theta\, d\theta$$

$$= \frac{1}{\sqrt{3}}\int_0^{\pi/2}\sin^{2(1/3)-1}\theta\cos^{2(1/2)-1}\theta\, d\theta$$

$$= \frac{1}{\sqrt{3}}\frac{1}{2}\beta\left(\frac{1}{3},\frac{1}{2}\right)$$

$$= \frac{1}{2\sqrt{3}}\frac{\Gamma\frac{1}{3}\Gamma\frac{1}{2}}{\Gamma\left(\frac{1}{3}+\frac{1}{2}\right)}$$

$$= \frac{\sqrt{\pi}}{2\sqrt{3}}\frac{\Gamma\frac{1}{3}\Gamma\frac{1}{6}}{\Gamma\frac{5}{6}\Gamma\frac{1}{6}}$$

$$= \frac{\sqrt{\pi}}{2\sqrt{3}}\frac{\Gamma\frac{1}{3}2^{-1/3}\sqrt{3}\left(\Gamma\frac{1}{2}\right)^2}{\left[\Gamma\left(1-\frac{1}{6}\right)\Gamma\frac{1}{6}\right]\sqrt{\pi}}$$

$$= \frac{\left(\Gamma\frac{1}{2}\right)^3}{2^{4/3}\dfrac{\pi}{\sin\pi/6}}$$

$$= \frac{\left(\Gamma\frac{1}{3}\right)^3}{2^{4/3}\,\frac{\pi}{1/2}}$$

$$= \frac{\left(\Gamma\frac{1}{3}\right)^3}{2^{7/3}\,\pi}$$

EXERCISE 12.1

1. Express the following integrals in terms of Beta functions

(a) $\int_0^1 x^m \left(1-x^2\right)^n dx$

(b) $\int_0^1 \frac{x^2}{\sqrt{1-x^5}}\, dx$

(c) $\int_0^2 (8-x)^{-1/3}\, dx.$

2. Show that

$$\frac{\left(\Gamma\frac{1}{3}\right)^2}{\Gamma\frac{1}{6}} = \frac{\sqrt{\pi}\, 2^{1/3}}{3^{1/2}}.$$

3. Show that

$$\Gamma\frac{1}{9}\Gamma\frac{2}{9}\Gamma\frac{3}{9}.....\Gamma\frac{8}{9} = \frac{16\pi^4}{3}.$$

4. Prove that

$$\frac{\beta(m, n+1)}{n} = \frac{\beta(m+1, n)}{m}$$

$$= \frac{\beta(m, n)}{m+n}.$$

5. Prove that

$$2^{2n-1}\,\beta\,(n,\, n) = \frac{\sqrt{\pi}\,\Gamma n}{\Gamma n + \frac{1}{2}}, n > 0$$

6. Prove that

$$\Gamma\left(\frac{3}{2}+x\right)\Gamma\left(\frac{3}{2}-x\right) = \left(\frac{1}{4}-x^2\right)\pi \sec \pi x; -1 < 2x < 1$$

7. Prove that

$$\frac{\Gamma\frac{1}{3}\Gamma\frac{5}{6}}{\Gamma\frac{2}{3}} = \sqrt{\pi}2^{1/3}$$

8. Prove that

$$\beta(l, m)\ \beta(l + m, n) = \beta(m, n)\ \beta(m + n, l) = \beta(n, l)\ \beta(n + l, m)$$

9. Prove that

$$\beta(l, m)\ \beta(l + m, n)\ \beta(l + m + n, p) = \frac{\Gamma l\,\Gamma m\,\Gamma n\,\Gamma p}{\Gamma(l+m+n+p)}$$

10. Prove that

$$\beta\ (l, m) = \frac{1}{2}\int_0^1 \left[x^{l-1}(1-x)^{m-1} + x^{m-1}(1-x)^{l-1}\right]dx$$

11. Prove that

$$\int_0^p x^m\left(p^q - x^q\right)^n dx = \frac{p^{qn+m+1}}{q}\cdot\beta\left(n+1, \frac{m+1}{q}\right)$$

12. Prove that

$$\int_0^a (a-x)^{m-1} x^{n-1} dx = a^{m+n-1}\beta\left(m, n\right)$$

13. Prove that

$$\int_0^a \left(1-\frac{x}{n}\right)^n x^{t-1} dx = n^t\ \beta\left(t, n+1\right)$$

14. Prove that

$$\int_a^b (x-a)^{m-1}(b-x)^{n-1}\, dx = (b-a)^{m+n-1}\beta\left(m, n\right)$$

15. Prove that

(a) $\displaystyle\int_0^\infty x^2 e^{-x^2}\, dx = \frac{\sqrt{\pi}}{4}$

(b) $\displaystyle\int_0^\infty \frac{e^{-st}}{\sqrt{t}}\, dt = \sqrt{\frac{\pi}{s}}, s > 0$

(c) $\int_0^\infty 4\,x^4 e^{-x^4}\,dx = \Gamma\dfrac{5}{4}$

(d) $\int_0^\infty x^6 e^{-2x} dx = \dfrac{45}{8}$

(e) $\int_0^\infty x^5 e^{-x} dx = 120$

16. Prove that

$$\Gamma n = \int_0^1 \left(\log\frac{1}{x}\right)^{n-1} dx,\ n > 0$$

17. Prove that

$$\int_0^1 \frac{1}{\sqrt{-\log x}}\,dx = \sqrt{\pi}$$

18. Prove that

$$\int_0^1 x^{n-1}\left(\log\frac{1}{x}\right)^{m-1} dx = \frac{\Gamma m}{n^m},\ m, n > 0$$

19. Prove that

$$\int_3^1 (1 - x^n)^{1/n}\,dx = \frac{1}{n}\,\frac{\left(\Gamma\frac{1}{2}\right)^2}{2\Gamma\left(\frac{2}{n}\right)}$$

20. Prove that

$$\int_0^1 \frac{dx}{\sqrt{1 - x^n}} = \frac{\sqrt{\pi}\,\Gamma\left(\frac{1}{n}\right)}{n\Gamma\left(\frac{1}{2} + \frac{1}{n}\right)}$$

21. Prove that

(a) $\int_0^2 (4 - x^2)^{3/2}\,dx = 3\pi$

(b) $\int_0^3 \dfrac{dx}{\sqrt{3x - x^2}} = \pi$

(c) $\int_0^\infty \dfrac{x\,dx}{1 + x^6} = \dfrac{\pi}{3\sqrt{3}}$

(d) $\int_0^\infty \dfrac{x^2 dx}{1 + x^4} = \dfrac{\pi}{2\sqrt{2}}$

(e) $\int_0^2 \dfrac{x^2 dx}{\sqrt{1 - x^3}} = \dfrac{2}{3}$

(f) $\int_0^1 x^2 (1 - x)^3\,dx = \dfrac{1}{60}$

22. Prove that

$$\int_0^{\pi/2} \sqrt{\tan\theta}\, d\theta = \int_0^{\pi/2} \sqrt{\cot\theta}\, d\theta$$
$$= \frac{\pi}{\sqrt{2}}$$

23. Prove that

$$\int_0^{\pi/2} \frac{d\theta}{\sqrt{a\cos^4\theta + b\sin^4\theta}} = \frac{\left(\Gamma\frac{1}{4}\right)^2}{4\,(ab)\frac{1}{4}\sqrt{\pi}}$$

[**Hint:** Put $\tan\theta = x$ and then $bx^4 = ay$]

24. Prove that

(a) $\int_{-\infty}^{\infty} \cos\frac{\pi x^2}{2} = 1$

(b) $\int_0^{\infty} \cos x^2 dx = \frac{1}{2}\sqrt{\frac{\pi}{2}}$

25. Show that if $n > -1$,

$$\int_0^{\infty} x^n e^{-a^2x^2}\, dx = \frac{\Gamma\left(\frac{n+1}{2}\right)}{2a^{n+1}}$$

Hence or otherwise show that

$$\int_{-\infty}^{\infty} e^{-a^2x^2}\, dx = \frac{\sqrt{\pi}}{a}.$$

26. Prove that

$$\beta(m, n) = a^m b^n \int_0^{\infty} \frac{x^{m-1}}{(ax+b)^{m+n}}\, dx$$

and deduce that

$$\int_0^{\pi/2} \frac{\sin^{2m-1}\theta\cos^{2n-1}\theta}{\left(a\sin^2\theta + b\cos^2\theta\right)^{m+n}}\, d\theta = \frac{\beta(m, n)}{2a^m b^n}$$

$$\left[\textbf{Hint:}\, \beta(m, n) = \int_0^{\infty} \frac{y^{m-1}}{(1+y)^{m+n}}\, dy, \text{ put } y = \frac{ax}{b}\right]$$

27. Prove that

$$\Gamma x\, \Gamma(1-x) = \pi \operatorname{cosec}(\pi x)\,;\, 0 < x < 1$$

and deduce that

$$\int_0^1 \log \Gamma x\, dx = \frac{1}{2}\log 2\pi$$

$\left[\textbf{Hint: } I = \int_0^1 \log \Gamma x\, dx, \text{ then } I = \int_0^1 \log \Gamma(1-x)\, dx\right.$

$\left.\therefore I = \frac{1}{2}\int_0^1 \left(\log \Gamma x + \log \Gamma(1-x)\right) dx = \frac{1}{2}\int_0^1 \log \frac{\pi}{\sin \pi x}\, dx\right]$

ANSWERS

EXERCISE 12.1

1. (a) $\frac{1}{2}\beta\left(\frac{m+1}{2}, n+1\right)$

(b) $\frac{1}{5}\beta\left(\frac{3}{5}, \frac{1}{2}\right)$

(c) $\frac{1}{3}\beta\left(\frac{1}{3}, \frac{2}{3}\right)$

13

Determination of Areas (Quadrature)

13.1 Quadrature (Definition)

The process of finding the area bounded by a given curve is called Quadrature.

13.2 Area Formula for Cartesian Equations

To prove that the area bounded by the curve $y = f(x)$, the x-axis and ordinates $x = a$, $x = b$ is

$$\int_a^b y\, dx$$

where $y = f(x)$ is a continuous single-valued function and y does not change sign in the interval $a \leq x \leq b$.

Let $y = f(x)$ be the equation of curve AB. Let CA and CD be two ordinates at $x = a$ and $x = b$ respectively.

Suppose y is an increasing function of x in the interval $a \leq x \leq b$.

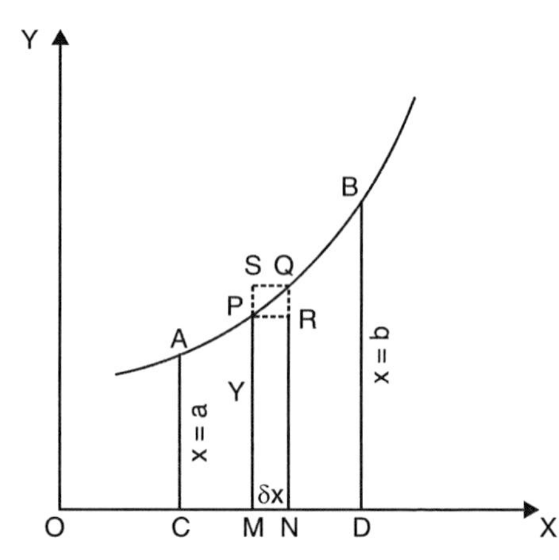

Let $P(x, y)$ be any point on the curve and $Q(x + \delta x, y + \delta y)$ be a neighbouring point on it. Draw their ordinates PM, QN. As x changes, the area $ACMP$ also changes and hence is clearly a function of x.

Let A denote the area $ACMP$, then the area

$$ACNQ = A + \delta A$$

so that area $PMNQ = \delta A$.

Complete the rectangle $PRQS$. Then the area $PRQS$ lies between the areas of the rectangles $PMNR$ and $SMNQ$, i.e. δA lies between $y\delta x$ and $(y + \delta y)\, \delta x$.

Dividing throughout by δx, $\dfrac{\delta A}{\delta x}$ lies between y and $y + \delta y$.

In the limiting position, when $Q \to P$, $\delta x \to 0$ and $\delta y \to 0$.

$\therefore \quad \text{Lt}_{\delta x \to 0} \dfrac{\delta A}{\delta x}$ lies between y and $\text{Lt}_{\delta y \to 0}(y + \delta y)$.

$\therefore \quad \dfrac{dA}{dx}$ lies between y and a quantity which tends to y.

$$\therefore \quad \frac{dA}{dx} = y$$

Integrating both sides *w.r.t.* x from $x = a$ to $x = b$, we have

$$\begin{aligned}\int_a^b y\, dx &= \int_a^b \frac{dA}{dx}\, dx \\ &= [A]_a^b \\ &= (\text{value of } A \text{ when } x = b) \\ &\qquad\qquad - (\text{value of } A \text{ when } x = a) \\ &= \text{area } ACDB - 0 \\ &= \text{area } ACDB\end{aligned}$$

Hence,

$$\text{area } ACDB = \int_a^b y\, dx$$

Note 1. The area bounded by the curve AB, the ordinates at A and B, and the x-axis is often called '*the area under the curve AB*'.

Note 2. *Sign of the area.* We know that if $y = f(x) > 0$ over the range $a \le x \le b$, then the area $\int_a^b f(x)\, dx$ is +ve and if $y = f(x) < 0$ in the range $a \le x \le b$, then the area $\int_a^b f(x)\, dx$ is –ve. The curve $y = f(x)$ in this case lies below the x-axis over the range $a \le x \le b$. Thus we consider the areas below the x-axis as –ve.

By the area in such cases, we mean the numerical value of the area.

13.3 To prove that the area of the curve $x = f(y)$ between y-axis and the lines $y = c, y = d$ is given by

$$\int_c^d x\, dy$$

Let $x = f(y)$ be the equation of curve AB. Let CA, DB be the abscissae at $y = c$, $y = d$ respectively.

Let $P(x, y)$ be any point on the curve and let $Q(x + \delta x, y + \delta y)$ be a neighbouring point on it.

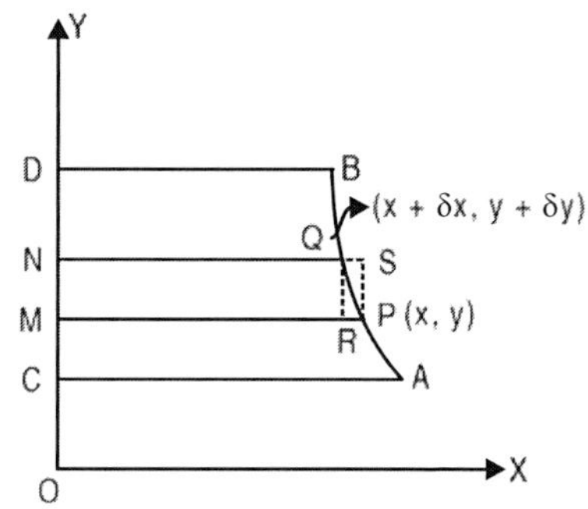

Draw PM, QN $\perp^{rs}$ on y-axis from P and Q.

As y changes, the area $ACMP$ also changes and hence is clearly a function of y. Let A denote the area $ACMP$ and $A + \delta A$ denote the area $ACNQ$, so that

$$\text{area } PMNQ = \delta A$$

Complete the rectangle $PRQS$. Then the area $PRQS$ lies between the areas of the rectangles $PMNQ$ and $PMNS$, i.e. δA lies between $x\delta y$ and $(x + \delta x)\,\delta y$.

Dividing throughout by δy, we have

$\dfrac{\delta A}{\delta y}$ lies between x and $x + \delta x$.

In the limiting position, when $Q \to P$, then $\delta x \to 0$, $\delta y \to 0$.

$\therefore\ \text{Lt}_{\delta y \to 0} \dfrac{\delta A}{\delta y}$ lies between x and $\text{Lt}_{\delta x \to 0}\,(x + \delta x)$.

i.e., $\dfrac{dA}{dy}$ lies between x and a quantity which tends to x.

$$\therefore \quad \frac{dA}{dy} = x.$$

Integrating both sides between the limits c to d, we have

$$\int_c^d x\, dy = \int_c^d \frac{dA}{dy}\, dy = [A]_c^d$$

$= (\text{value of } A \text{ when } y = d) - (\text{value of } A \text{ when } y = c)$

$= \text{area } ACDB - 0$

$= \text{area } ACDB.$

Hence area $ACDB = \int_c^d x\, dy.$

ILLUSTRATIVE EXAMPLES

Example 1. Find the area of the curve

$$a^2 x^2 = y^2 (2a - y)$$

Solution :

The equation of the curve is

$$a^2 x^2 = y^2 (2a - y) \qquad \ldots (1)$$

to trace the curve roughly to find the limits of integration.

(i) The curve is symmetrical about y-axis.

(ii) The curve passes through the origin. The tangents at the origin are $x^2 = 0$ or $x = 0$, $x = 0$ i.e. origin is a cusp.

(iii) The curve meets the y-axis at (0, 0) and (0, $2a$). Shifting the origin to (0, $2a$), the equation of the curve becomes

$$a^2 x^2 = (y + 2a)^2 (2a - y - 2a),$$

whence we have the tangent at the new origin as $y = 0$ i.e. new x-axis.

(iv) No asymptotes.

(v) The curve does not exist for values of $y > 2a$ or $y < 0$.

Thus the shape of the curve is as shown in the figure.

Hence, required area

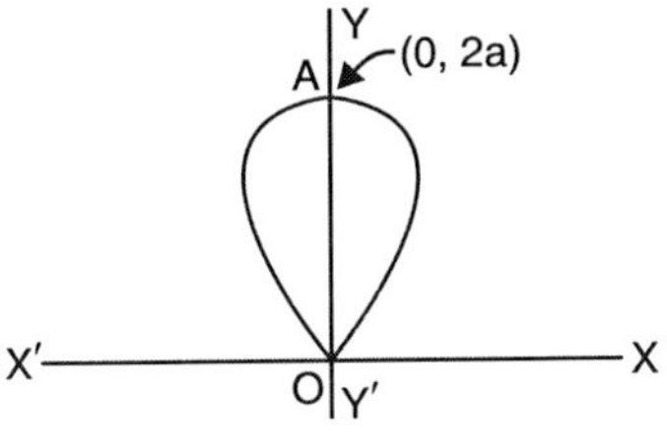

$$= 2 \text{ Area } OAB$$

$$= 2\int_{y=0}^{y=2a} x\, dy$$

$$= 2\int_0^{2a} \frac{y^{3/2}\sqrt{2a-y}}{a}\, dy$$

[Put $y = 2a \sin^2 \theta$

$\therefore\ dy = 4a \sin\theta \cos\theta\, d\theta$]

$$= 2\int_0^{\pi/2} \frac{(2a)^{3/2} \sin^3\theta\, (2a)^{1/2} \cos\theta \cdot 4a \sin\theta \cos\theta\, d\theta}{a}$$

$$= 32a^2 \int_0^{\pi/2} \sin^4\theta \cos^2\theta \, d\theta$$

$$= 32a^2 \frac{\Gamma\frac{5}{2}\Gamma\frac{3}{2}}{2\Gamma 4}$$

$$= 32a^2 \frac{\frac{3}{2}\cdot\frac{1}{2}\cdot\sqrt{\pi}\cdot\frac{1}{2}\cdot\sqrt{\pi}}{2.3.2.1}$$

$$= \pi a^2$$

Example 2. Find the area of the curve $y^2(2a - x) = x^3$ between the curve and its asymptotes.

Solution : The equation of the curve is

$$y^2(2a - x) = x^3 \qquad \text{... (1)}$$

to trace the curve roughly to find the limits of integration.

(i) The curve is symmetrical about x-axis.

(ii) The curve passes through the origin.

(iii) The tangents at the origin are $y^2 = 0$ or $y = 0$, $y = 0$ i.e. origin is a cusp.

(iv) The curve meets the x-axis at the origin only.

(v) The equation of asymptote is $x = 2a$.

(vi) The equation of the curve can be written as

$$y^2 = \frac{x^3}{2a - x}$$

which shows that for the values of $x > 2a$, y is imaginary i.e., the curve does not exist for values of $x > 2a$.

Similarly the curve does not exist for negative values of x.

(vii) Also as $x \to a$, $y \to \infty$.

Thus the shape of the curve is as shown in the figure.

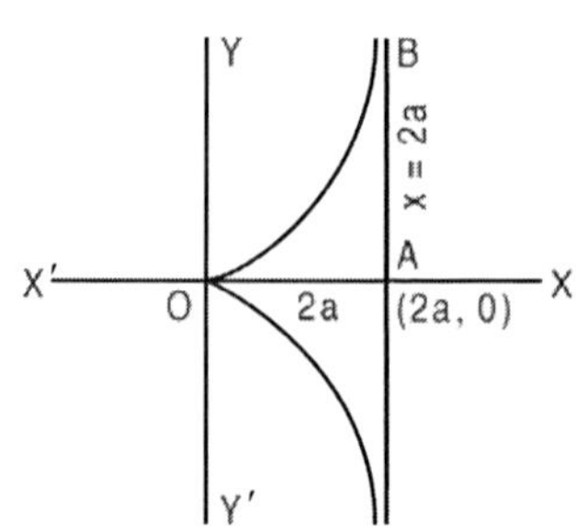

Hence, required area

$$= 2 \text{ Area } OAB$$

$$= 2\int_{z=0}^{2a} y \, dx$$

$$= 2\int_0^{2a} \frac{x^{3/2}}{\sqrt{2a - x}}\, dx \qquad \left[\text{Put } x = 2a \sin^2\theta \quad \therefore\ dx = 4a \sin\theta \cos\theta\, d\theta\right]$$

$$= 2\int_0^{\pi/2} \frac{(2a)^{3/2} \sin^3\theta\, 4a \sin\theta \cos\theta\, d\theta}{(2a)^{1/2} \cos\theta}$$

$$= 16a^2 \int_0^{\pi/2} \sin^4\theta\, d\theta$$

$$= 16a^2 \cdot \frac{3}{4} \cdot \frac{1}{2} \cdot \frac{\pi}{2}$$

$$= 3\pi a^2$$

Example 3. Find the area bounded by the parabola $y = 2x - x^2$ and x-axis.

Solution : The given curve (parabola) is

$$y = 2x - x^2$$

$$\Rightarrow \quad x^2 - 2x = -y$$

$$\Rightarrow \quad x^2 - 2x + 1 = 1 - y$$

$$\Rightarrow \quad (x - 1)^2 = -(y - 1)$$

This parabola being of the form $x^2 = -4ay$ is a downward parabola with vertex (1, 1).

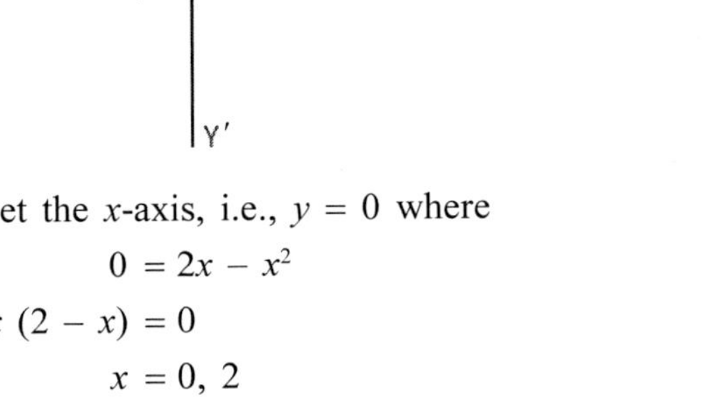

It meet the x-axis, i.e., $y = 0$ where

$$0 = 2x - x^2$$

$$\Rightarrow \quad x(2 - x) = 0$$

$$\Rightarrow \quad x = 0, 2$$

Hence the parabola meets the x-axis at O (0, 0) and A (2, 0). Thus the shape of the curve is as shown in the figure.

$$\text{Required Area} = \int_0^2 y\,dx$$

$$= \int_0^2 (2x - x^2)\,dx$$

$$= \left(\frac{2x^2}{2} - \frac{x^3}{3}\right)_0^2$$

$$= 4 - \frac{8}{3} = \frac{4}{3}$$

Example 4. Show that the area cut-off a parabola by any double ordinate is two-thirds of the corresponding rectangle contained by the double ordinate and its distance from the vertex.

Solution : Let the equation of the parabola be

$$y^2 = 4ax \qquad \text{... (1)}$$

and that of the double ordinate PP' be $x = c$.

The curve is symmetrical about the x-axis and for the part of the curve above the x-axis (taking +ve sign before the square root) from (1), we have

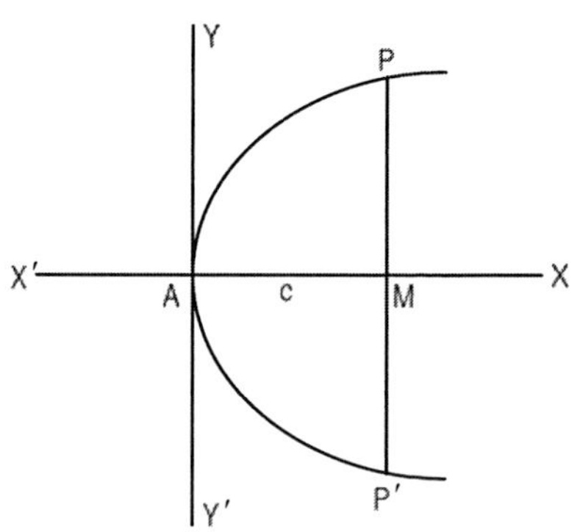

$$y = \sqrt{4ax}$$

$\therefore$ Area cut-off the parabola by the double ordinate PMP'

$$= \text{Area } PAP'$$

$$= 2 \text{ Area } PAM$$

$$= 2\int_0^c y\,dx$$

$$= 2\int_0^c \sqrt{4ax}\,dx$$

$$= 2\int_0^c 2\sqrt{a}\,\sqrt{x}\,dx$$

$$= 4\sqrt{a}\left(\frac{x^{3/2}}{3/2}\right)_0^c$$

$$= \frac{8}{3}\sqrt{a}\, c^{3/2} \qquad \text{... (2)}$$

Again, $\quad MP = \sqrt{4ax}$

$$= \sqrt{4ac} \qquad [\because AM = c]$$

$$= 2\sqrt{a}\,\sqrt{c}$$

$\therefore \quad PP' = 2MP = 4\sqrt{a}\,\sqrt{c}$

$\therefore$ Area of the rectangle formed by the double ordinate PMP' and its distance from the vertex, i.e.,

$$AM = PP' \times AM$$

$$= 4\sqrt{a}\,\sqrt{c} \times c = 4\sqrt{a}\,c^{3/2} \qquad \text{... (3)}$$

$\therefore$ Area cut-off the parabola by the double ordinate PP'

$$= \frac{8}{3}\sqrt{a}\, c^{3/2}$$

$$= \frac{2}{3}\left(4\sqrt{a}\, c^{3/2}\right)$$

$= \frac{2}{3}$ (Area of the rectangle formed by PP' and AM)

Example 5. Find the whole area of the ellipse

$$\frac{x^2}{a^2} + \frac{y^2}{b^2} = 1$$

Solution : The equation of the ellipse is

$$\frac{x^2}{a^2} + \frac{y^2}{b^2} = 1 \qquad \text{... (1)}$$

The ellipse is symmetrical about both the axes and so the whole area of the ellipse is four times the area under the curve in the first quadrant.

i.e., Whole area of the ellipse = 4 Area CAB

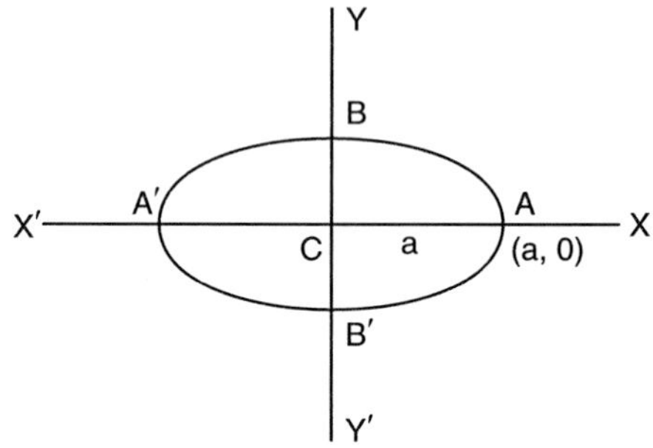

Now, for the area CAB, x varies from 0 to a and from (1).

$$\frac{y^2}{b^2} = 1 - \frac{x^2}{a^2} = \frac{a^2 - x^2}{a^2}$$

$$\therefore \quad y = \frac{b}{a}\sqrt{a^2 - x^2} \quad \text{[Taking +ve sign before the radical]}$$

$$\therefore \text{ Area } CAB = \int_0^a y\, dx$$

$$= \int_0^a \frac{b}{a}\sqrt{a^2 - x^2}\, dx$$

$$= \frac{b}{a}\left[\frac{x}{2}\sqrt{a^2 - x^2} + \frac{1}{2}a^2 \sin^{-1}\left(\frac{x}{a}\right)\right]_0^a$$

$$= \frac{b}{a}\left[0 + \frac{a^2}{2}\sin^{-1}(1) - 0 - 0\right]$$

$$= \frac{b}{a}\frac{a^2}{2}\cdot\frac{\pi}{2}$$

$$= \frac{\pi ab}{4} \qquad \left[\because \sin^{-1}(1) = \frac{\pi}{2}\right]$$

$\therefore$ Whole area of the ellipse

$$= 4 \text{ area } CAB$$

$$= 4\left(\frac{\pi ab}{4}\right)$$

$$= \pi ab$$

Example 6. Find the whole area of the astroid

$$x^{2/3} + y^{2/3} = a^{2/3}$$

Solution :

The equation of the astroid is

$$x^{2/3} + y^{2/3} = a^{2/3} \quad \text{... (1)}$$

to trace the curve roughly to find the limits of integration.

(i) The curve is symmetrical about both the axes.

(ii) The curve does not pass through the origin.

(iii) The curve meets the x-axis where $y = 0$, hence putting $y = 0$ in (1), we get

$$x^{2/3} = a^{2/3}$$

or $$x^2 = a^2$$

$\therefore$ $$x = \pm a$$

i.e. the points of intersection with x-axis are $(a, 0)$, $(-a, 0)$.

Similarly the curve meets the y-axis in the points

$$(0, a), (0, -a)$$

(iv) from (1)

$$y^{2/3} = a^{2/3} - x^{2/3} \quad \text{... (2)}$$

Now if $|x| > a$

$y^{2/3}$ is – ve

$\therefore$ y^2 is also – ve

and hence y is imaginary.

$\therefore$ There lies no portion of the curve beyond the lines $x = \pm a$.

Similarly, there lies no portion of the curve beyond the lines $y = \pm a$.

From (2), when $x = 0$, $y = a$ and as x increases from 0 to a, y decreases from a to 0.

Hence the shape of the curve is as shown in the figure.

Since the curve is symmetrical about both the axes,

$\therefore$ Whole area of the curve

= 4 × Area under the curve in the first quadrant.

i.e., Area $ABCD$

= 4 × Area OAB.

Now for the area OAB, i.e., area under the curve in the first quadrant, x varies from 0 to a.

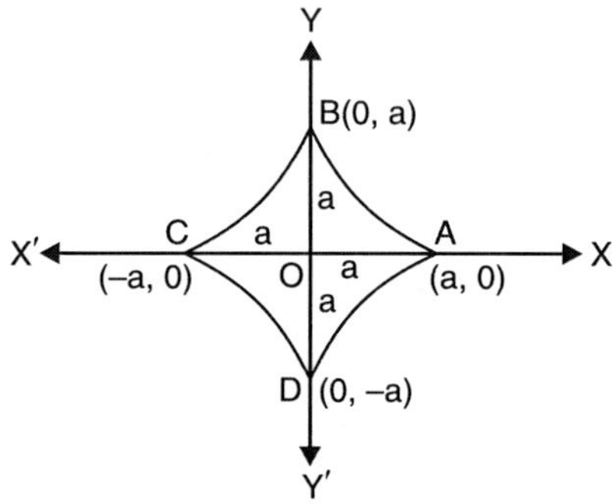

Now, from (1), $y^{2/3} = a^{2/3} - x^{2/3}$

$\therefore \quad y = (a^{2/3} - x^{2/3})^{3/2}$

$$\therefore \text{ Area } OAB = \int_0^a y\, dx$$

$$= \int_0^a \left(a^{2/3} - x^{2/3}\right)^{3/2} dx$$

[Put $x = a \sin^3 \theta$

$\therefore dx = 3a \sin^2 \theta \cos \theta \, d\theta$

when $x = 0, \theta = 0$

when $x = a, \theta = \pi/2$]

$$= \int_0^{\pi/2} \left(a^{2/3} - a^{2/3} \sin^2 \theta\right)^{3/2} 3a \sin^2 \theta \cos \theta \, d\theta$$

$$= \int_0^{\pi/2} a\left(1 - \sin^2 \theta\right)^{3/2} 3a \sin^2 \theta \cos \theta \, d\theta$$

$$= 3a^2 \int_0^{\pi/2} \sin^2 \theta \cos^4 \theta \, d\theta$$

$$= 3a^2 \frac{\Gamma\frac{3}{2}\Gamma\frac{5}{2}}{2\Gamma 4}$$

$$= \frac{3a^2}{2} \cdot \frac{\frac{1}{2} \cdot \sqrt{\pi} \cdot \frac{3}{2}\frac{1}{2} \cdot \sqrt{\pi}}{3.2.1}$$

$$= \frac{3\pi a^2}{32}$$

$\therefore$ Whole area of the curve

$$= 4 \times \text{Area } OAB$$

$$= 4 \times \frac{3\pi a^2}{32}$$

$$= \frac{3\pi a^2}{8}$$

Example 7. Find the area of the loop of the following curve

$$y^2 (a - x) = x^2 (a + x).$$

Solution : The equation of the curve is

$$y^2 (a - x) = x^2 (a + x) \quad \text{... (1)}$$

to trace the curve roughly to find the limits of integration.

(i) The curve is symmetrical about the x-axis.

(ii) The curve passes through the origin and the tangents at the origin are given by

$$y^2 = x^2$$

or, $\quad y = \pm x$

Since these tangents are real and different,

$\therefore$ Origin is a node.

(iii) The curve meets the x-axis at $y = 0$. Hence putting $y = 0$ in (1), we get

$$x^2 (a + x) = a$$

$\therefore \quad x = 0, - a$

i.e., the points of intersection are (0, 0), $(- a, 0)$.

Similarly, the curve meets the y-axis in the origin (0, 0).

(iv) The asymptote $\|$ to y-axis is given by

$$a - x = 0$$

i.e., $\quad x = a$

The curve has no other asymptote.

(v) From (1), we have (taking + ve square root)

$$y = x\sqrt{\frac{a+x}{a-x}} \qquad \text{... (2)}$$

when $x < -a$ or when $x > a$, we see that y is imaginary.

Hence no portion of the curve lies beyond the lines $x = \pm a$.

Hence the approximate shape of the curve is as shown in the figure and the loop lies between $x = -a$ and $x = 0$.

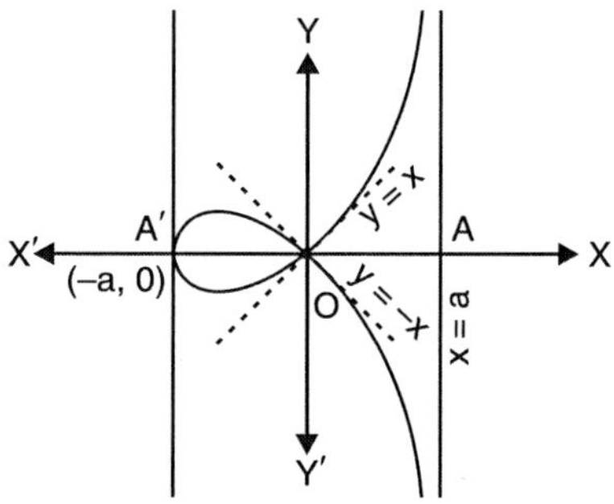

∴ Required area of the loop

$$= 2 \times \text{Area of the loop above the } x\text{-axis}$$

$$= 2\int_{-a}^{0} y\, dx$$

$$= 2\int_{-a}^{0} x\sqrt{\frac{a+x}{a-x}}\, dx \qquad \text{[from (2)]}$$

[Put $x = a \sin \theta$

∴ $dx = a \cos \theta \, d\theta$

when $x = 0$, $\theta = 0$

when $x = -a$, $\theta = -\pi/2$]

$$= 2\int_{-\pi/2}^{0} a \sin\theta \sqrt{\frac{(a + a\sin\theta)}{(a - a\sin\theta)}}\, a\cos\theta\, d\theta$$

$$= 2a^2\int_{-\pi/2}^{0} \sin\theta\cos\theta \sqrt{\frac{1+\sin\theta}{1-\sin\theta}}\, d\theta$$

$$= 2a^2\int_{-\pi/2}^{0} \sin\theta\cos\theta \sqrt{\frac{1+\sin\theta}{1-\sin\theta}}\sqrt{\frac{1+\sin\theta}{1+\sin\theta}}\, d\theta$$

$$= 2a^2 \int_{-\pi/2}^{0} \frac{\sin\theta \cos\theta\,(1+\sin\theta)}{\cos\theta}\, d\theta$$

$$= 2a^2 \int_{-\pi/2}^{0} \sin\theta\,(1+\sin\theta)\, d\theta$$

$$= 2a^2 \int_{-\pi/2}^{0} \left[\sin\theta + \frac{1-\cos 2\theta}{2}\right] d\theta$$

$$= 2a^2 \left[-\cos\theta + \frac{1}{2}\left(\theta - \frac{\sin 2\theta}{2}\right)\right]_{-\pi/2}^{0}$$

$$= 2a^2 \left[\left\{-\cos 0 + \frac{1}{2}(0-0)\right\} - \left\{-\cos\left(-\frac{\pi}{2}\right) + \frac{1}{2}\left(-\frac{\pi}{2} - \frac{\sin(-\pi)}{2}\right)\right\}\right]$$

$$= 2a^2 \left[(-1) - \left\{-\frac{\pi}{4}\right\}\right]$$

$$= 2a^2 \left[-1 + \frac{\pi}{4}\right]$$

$$= \frac{2a^2(\pi - 4)}{4}$$

$$= \frac{a^2(4-\pi)}{2} \text{ numerically} \qquad [\because \pi < 4]$$

Hence the area of the loop is $\dfrac{a^2}{2}(4-\pi)$.

Example 8. Find the area of the curve

$$x^2 (x^2 + y^2) = a^2 (y^2 - x^2)$$

between the curve and its asymptotes.

Solution : The equation of the curve is

$$x^2 (x^2 + y^2) = a^2 (y^2 - x^2) \qquad \dots (1)$$

to trace the curve roughly to find the limits of integration.

(i) The curve is symmetrical about both the axes.

(ii) The curve passes through the origin and the tangents at the origin are given by $y^2 - x^2 = 0$ or $y = \pm x$. The tangents being real and different, origin is a node.

(iii) The curve meets the x-axis and y-axis both only at the origin.

(iv) Equating to zero, the coefficient of y^2 in (1), the asymptotes parallel to y-axis are given by

$$x^2 - a^2 = 0$$

or, $$x = \pm a$$

The curve has no other asymptotes.

(v) From (1),

$$y^2 (a^2 - x^2) = x^2 (x^2 + a^2)$$

$$\therefore \qquad y = x\sqrt{\frac{a^2 + x^2}{a^2 - x^2}} \qquad \text{... (2)}$$

When $| x | > a$, y is imaginary.

$\therefore$ No portion of the curve lies beyond the lines $x = \pm a$. As x increases from 0 to a, y increases from 0 to ∞.

Thus the shape of the curve is as shown in the figure.

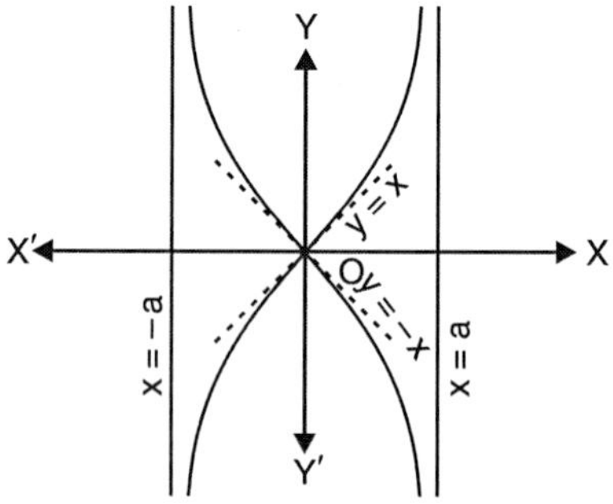

By symmetry, required area between the curve and its asymptotes

$= 4 \times$ Area between the curve in first quadrant and its asymptotes

$$= 4\int_0^a y\,dx$$

$$= 4\int_0^a x\sqrt{\frac{a^2+x^2}{a^2-x^2}}\,dx$$

[Put $x^2 = a^2 \cos\theta$

$\therefore\ 2x\,dx = -\,a^2 \sin\theta\,d\theta$

when $x = 0,\ \theta = \pi/2$

when $x = a,\ \theta = 0$]

$$= 4\int_{\pi/2}^{0}\sqrt{\frac{a^2(1+\cos\theta)}{a^2(1-\cos\theta)}}\left(-\frac{a^2\sin\theta}{2}\right)d\theta$$

$$= 4a^2\int_0^{\pi/2}\sqrt{\frac{2\cos^2\theta/2}{2\sin^2\theta/2}}\left(\frac{2\sin\frac{\theta}{2}\cos\frac{\theta}{2}}{2}\right)d\theta$$

$$= 4a^2\int_0^{\pi/2}\cos^2\frac{\theta}{2}\,d\theta$$

$$= 2a^2\int_0^{\pi/2}(1+\cos\theta)\,d\theta$$

$$= 2a^2(\theta+\sin\theta)_0^{\pi/2}$$

$$= 2a^2\left(\frac{\pi}{2}+1\right)$$

$$= a^2(\pi+2)$$

Example 9. Show that the area of the loop of the curve

$$y^2(a+x) = x^2(3a-x)$$

is equal to the area between the curve and its asymptotes.

Solution : The equation of the curve is

$$y^2(a+x) = x^2(3a-x) \qquad \text{... (1)}$$

to trace the curve roughly to find the limits of integration.

(i) The curve is symmetrical about the x-axis

(ii) The curve passes through the origin and the tangents at the origin are given by

$$y^2 = 3x^2$$

or $$y = \pm\sqrt{3}\,x$$

Since these tangents are real and distinct,

$\therefore$ Origin is a node.

(iii) The curve meets x-axis in the point (0, 0) and $(3a, 0)$ and y-axis at (0, 0).

Shifting origin to the point $(3a, 0)$, the equation (1) transforms to

$$y^2 (a + 3a + x) = (x + 3a)^2 (3a - x - 3a)$$

or $$y^2 (x + 4a) = - x (x + 3a)^2$$

$\therefore$ The tangent at the new origin is $x = 0$, i.e., the new y-axis [Equating lowest degree terms to zero].

Hence at the point $(3a, 0)$, the tangent to the curve is parallel to y-axis.

(iv) Equating to zero the coefficient of y^2 in (1), the asymptote parallel to y-axis is given by

$$x + a = 0$$

There is no other asymptote of the curve.

(v) From (1),

$$y = x\sqrt{\frac{3a - x}{a + x}} \qquad \text{... (2)}$$

[Taking +ve sign before the radical]

When $x > 3a$ or when $x < - a$, y is imaginary.

Thus the curve does not lie beyond the lines $x = - a$, $x = 3a$.

As x increases from 0 to $3a$, y first increases and then decreases to 0.

Thus there is a loop between $x = 0$, $x = 3a$.

Again, as x decreases from 0 to a, y also decreases from 0 to $- \infty$.

Thus the shape of the curve is as shown in the figure.

For the loop of the curve x varies from 0 to $3a$ and for the area of the curve between the curve and the asymptotes, x varies from $- a$ to 0.

$\therefore$ Area of the loop

$$= 2 \times \text{Area of the upper half of the loop}$$

$$= 2 \int_0^{3a} y \, dx$$

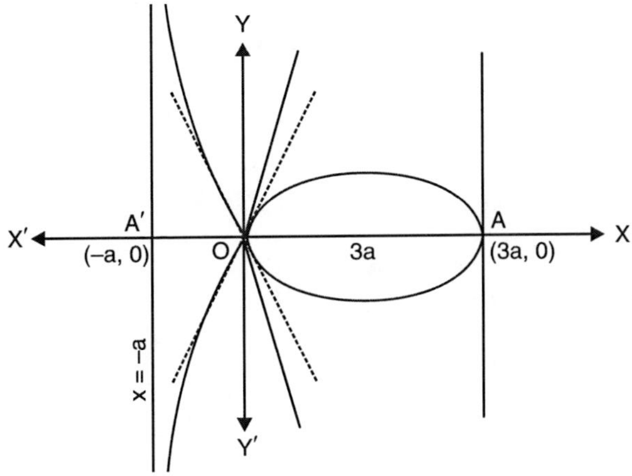

$$= 2\int_0^{3a} x\sqrt{\frac{3a-x}{a+x}}\,dx \qquad \text{[From (2)]}$$

$$= 2\int_0^{3a} x\sqrt{\frac{2a+(a-x)}{2a-(a-x)}}$$

[Put $a - x = 2a \cos \theta$
$\therefore\ dx = 2a \sin \theta\, d\theta$
when $x = 0,\ \theta = \pi/3$;
when $x = 3a,\ \theta = \pi$]

$$= 2\int_{\pi/3}^{\pi} (a - 2a\cos\theta)\sqrt{\frac{2a+2a\cos\theta}{2a-2a\cos\theta}}\ 2a\sin\theta\, d\theta$$

$$= 4a^2\int_{\pi/3}^{\pi} (2 - 2\cos\theta)\sqrt{\frac{1+\cos\theta}{1-\cos\theta}}\ \sin\theta\, d\theta$$

$$= 4a^2\int_{\pi/3}^{\pi} (1 - \cos\theta)\sqrt{\frac{1+\cos\theta}{1-\cos\theta}}\ \sqrt{\frac{1+\cos\theta}{1+\cos\theta}}\ \sin\theta\, d\theta$$

$$= 4a^2\int_{\pi/3}^{\pi} (1 - 2\cos\theta)\frac{1+\cos\theta}{\sqrt{1-\cos^2\theta}}\ \sin\theta\, d\theta$$

$$= 4a^2\int_{\pi/3}^{\pi} (1 - 2\cos\theta)(1+\cos\theta)\, d\theta$$

$$= 4a^2 \int_{\pi/3}^{\pi} \left(1 - \cos\theta - 2\cos^2\theta\right) d\theta$$

$$= 4a^2 \int_{\pi/3}^{\pi} \left[1 - \cos\theta - (1 + \cos 2\theta)\right] d\theta$$

$$= -4a^2 \int_{\pi/3}^{\pi} (\cos 2\theta + \cos\theta)\, d\theta$$

$$= -4a^2 \left[\frac{\sin 2\theta}{2} + \sin\theta\right]_{\pi/3}^{\pi}$$

$$= -4a^2 \left[0 - \left(\frac{1}{2}\sin\frac{2\pi}{3} + \sin\frac{\pi}{3}\right)\right]$$

$$= 4a^2 \left[\frac{1}{2}\cdot\frac{\sqrt{3}}{2} + \frac{\sqrt{3}}{2}\right] = 3\sqrt{3}\, a^2 \qquad \text{... (3)}$$

Again, the area between the curve and its asymptotes

= 2 × area between the curve and its asymptotes above the x-axis

$$= 2\int_{-a}^{0} y\, dx$$

$$= 2\int_{-a}^{0} x\sqrt{\frac{3a - x}{a + x}}\, dx \qquad \text{[From (2)]}$$

$$= 2\int_{-a}^{0} x\sqrt{\frac{2a + (a - x)}{2a - (a - x)}}\, dx$$

[Put $a - x = 2a\cos\theta$
$\therefore\ dx = 2a\sin\theta\, d\theta$
when $x = -a,\ \theta = 0$
when $x = 0,\ \theta = \pi/3$]

$$= 2\int_{0}^{\pi/3} (a - 2a\cos\theta)\sqrt{\frac{2a(1 + \cos\theta)}{2a(1 - \cos\theta)}}\cdot 2a\sin\theta\, d\theta$$

$$= 4a^2 \int_{0}^{\pi/3} (1 - 2\cos\theta)\frac{1 + \cos\theta}{\sqrt{1 - \cos^2\theta}}\sin\theta\, d\theta$$

$$= 4a^2 \int_{0}^{\pi/3} (1 - 2\cos\theta)(1 + \cos\theta)\, d\theta$$

$$= 4a^2 \int_0^{\pi/3} (1 - \cos\theta - 2\cos^2\theta)\, d\theta$$

$$= 4a^2 \int_0^{\pi/3} [(1 - \cos\theta) - (1 + \cos 2\theta)]\, d\theta$$

$$= -4a^2 \int_0^{\pi/3} (\cos 2\theta + \cos\theta)\, d\theta$$

$$= -4a^2 \left[\frac{\sin 2\theta}{2} + \sin\theta\right]_0^{\pi/3}$$

$$= -4a^2 \left[\left(\frac{1}{2}\sin\frac{2\pi}{3} + \sin\frac{\pi}{3}\right) - 0\right]$$

$$= -4a^2 \left[\frac{\sqrt{3}}{4} + \frac{\sqrt{3}}{2}\right]$$

$$= -3\sqrt{3}\, a^2$$

$$= 3\sqrt{3}\, a^2 \quad \text{(numerically)}$$

This is the same as (3),

Thus we prove the result.

Example 10. If A is the vertex, O the centre and $P(x, y)$ any point on the hyperbola

$$\frac{x^2}{a^2} - \frac{y^2}{b^2} = 1$$

prove that

$$x = a\cosh\left(\frac{2S}{ab}\right),$$

$$y = b\sinh\left(\frac{2S}{ab}\right)$$

where S is the sectorial area OPA.

Solution : The equation of the hyperbola is

$$\frac{x^2}{a^2} - \frac{y^2}{b^2} = 1$$

or $$\frac{y^2}{b^2} = \frac{x^2}{a^2} - 1 = \frac{x^2 - a^2}{a^2}$$

or $$y = \frac{b}{a}\sqrt{x^2 - a^2} \qquad \text{... (1)}$$

[Taking +ve sign with the square root]

Now, $$S = \text{Sectorial Area } OPA$$
$$= \text{Area } OMP - \text{area } AMP \qquad \text{... (2)}$$

But,

$$\text{area } OMP = \frac{1}{2} OM \cdot MP$$
$$= \frac{1}{2} x \cdot y$$
$$= \frac{1}{2} \cdot x \cdot \frac{b}{a}\sqrt{a^2 - x^2} \qquad \text{... (3)}$$

and,

$$\text{area } AMP = \int_a^x y\,dx$$
$$= \int_a^x \frac{b}{a}\sqrt{x^2 - a^2}\,dx \qquad [\because OA = a]$$
$$= \frac{b}{a}\left[\frac{1}{2} x\sqrt{a^2 - a^2} - \frac{1}{2} a^2 \cosh^{-1}\left(\frac{x}{a}\right)\right]_a^x$$
$$= \frac{b}{2a}\left[x\sqrt{x^2 - a^2} - a^2 \cosh^{-1}\left(\frac{x}{a}\right)\right]$$

$[\because \cosh^{-1}(1) = 0]$

$\therefore$ From (2),

$$S = \frac{1}{2}\frac{b}{a} x\sqrt{x^2 - a^2} - \frac{b}{2a}\left[x\sqrt{x^2 - a^2} - a^2 \cosh^{-1}\left(\frac{x}{a}\right)\right]$$
$$= \frac{ab}{2}\cosh^{-1}\left(\frac{x}{a}\right)$$

$$\therefore \cosh^{-1}\left(\frac{x}{a}\right) = \frac{2S}{ab}$$

$$\therefore \qquad x = a\cosh\left(\frac{2S}{ab}\right)$$

and from (1),

$$y = \frac{b}{a}\sqrt{x^2 - a^2}$$

$$= \frac{b}{a}\sqrt{a^2\left(\cosh^2\frac{2S}{ab} - 1\right)}$$

$$= \frac{b}{a}\cdot a\sinh\left(\frac{2S}{ab}\right) = b\sinh\frac{2S}{ab}$$

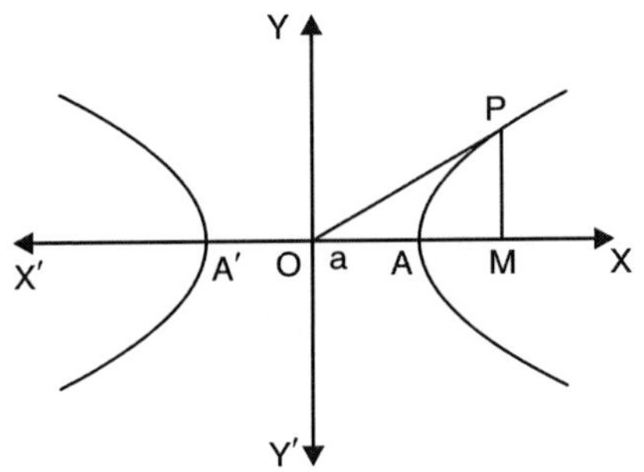

EXERCISE 13.1

1. Find the area enclosed by the curve $y = 3x - x^2$, x-axis and the lines $x = 0$ and $x = 3$.
2. Find the area enclosed by the curve $y^2 = x$ and the straight line $x = 4$.
3. Find the area bounded by the parabola $y = 2x - x^2$ and x-axis.
4. Find the area bounded by the curve $y = c \cosh x/c$, x-axis and the ordinates $x = 0$, $x = a$.
5. Find the areas bounded by the x-axis, the following curves and the specified ordinates:

   (a) $y = e^x$; $x = c$, $x = d$

   (b) $y = \log x$; $x = a$, $x = b$ $(b > a > 1)$

   (c) $y = \sin^2 x$; $x = 0$, $x = \pi/2$

   (d) $xy = k^2$; $x = c$, $x = d$

   (e) $y = xe^{x^2}$; $x = 0$, $x = a$

   (f) $y = 5 + \dfrac{x^2}{10}$; $x = 2$, $x = 10$.

6. Find the whole area of the circle $x^2 + y^2 = a^2$.

7. Find the whole area of the curve $y^2 = x^2 (4 - x^2)$.

8. Find the whole area of the curve $a^2y^2 = x^2 (a^2 - x^2)$.

9. Find the whole area of the curve $a^2y^2 = x^3 (2a - x)$.

10. Find the whole area of the curve $a^2x^2 = y^3 (2a - y)$.

11. Find the area of the parabola $y^2 = 4ax$ bounded by its latus rectum, and find its ratio with the area of the circle of radius a.

12. Find the area of the loop of the following curves :

(a) $y^2 = (x - 2)(x - 4)^2$

(b) $x(x^2 + y^2) = a(x^2 - y^2)$

(c) $a^2 y^2 = x^4 (b + x)$

(d) $ay^2 = x^2 (a - x)$

(e) $y^2 = x^4 (a + x)$

(f) $ay^2 = (x - a)(x - 5a)^2$

(g) $3ay^2 = x(x - a)^2$

13. Find the area between the following curves and their asymptotes :

(a) $x^2y^2 = a^2 (y^2 - x^2)$

(b) $x(x^2 + y^2) = a(x^2 - y^2)$

(c) $y^2 (a - x) = x^3$

(d) $xy^2 = 4a^2 (2a - x)$

14. Trace the curve $a^4y^2 = x^5 (2a - x)$ and prove that its area to the area of a circle of radius a is 5 : 4.

15. Show that the ordinate $x = a$ divides the area between $y^2 (2a - x) = x^3$ and its asymptotes in the ratio $3\pi - 8 : 3\pi + 8$.

16. In the ellipse $\dfrac{x^2}{a^2} + \dfrac{y^2}{b^2} = 1$, prove that $x = a \cos h \dfrac{2S}{ab}$, $y = b \sin h \dfrac{2S}{ab}$ where S is the sectorial area bounded by the ellipse, x-axis and the line joining (0, 0) to (x, y).

ANSWERS

EXERCISE 13.1

1. $\frac{9}{2}$

2. $\frac{32}{3}$

3. $\frac{4}{3}$

4. $c^2 \sin h\left(\frac{a}{c}\right)$

5. (a) $e^d - e^c$

(b) $b \log\left(\frac{b}{e}\right) - a \log\left(\frac{a}{e}\right)$

(c) $\frac{\pi}{4}$

(d) $k^2 \log \frac{d}{c}$

(e) $\frac{1}{2}\left(e^{a^2} - 1\right)$

(f) $\frac{1096}{15}$

6. πa^2

7. $\frac{32}{3}$

8. $\frac{4a^2}{3}$

9. πa^2

10. πa^2

11. $\frac{8}{3} a^2 2^{3/2}, \frac{8}{3\pi} \cdot 2^{3/2}$

12. (a) $\frac{32\sqrt{2}}{15}$

(b) $\frac{a^2}{2}(4 - \pi)$

(c) $\frac{32}{105} b^{7/2} a^{-3/2}$

(d) $\frac{8a^2}{15}$

(e) $\frac{32}{105} a^{7/2}$

(f) $\frac{256}{15} a^2$

(g) $\frac{8a^2}{15\sqrt{3}}$

13. (a) $4a^2$ (b) $\frac{a^2}{2}(\pi + 4)$ (c) $\frac{3}{4}\pi a^2$ (d) $4\pi a^2$

13.4 Area between Two Curves

The area bounded by the curves $y = f(x)$, $y = \phi(x)$ and the ordinates $x = a$, $x = b$ is

$$\int_a^b (y \text{ of upper curve} - y \text{ of lower curve})\, dx$$

Let APB, AQB be the curves

$$y = f(x), \; y = \phi(x)$$

respectively and MA, NB be the ordinates $x = a$, $x = b$.

$\therefore$ Area $APBQ$ between the two curves

$$= \text{Area } AMNBP - \text{Area } AMNBQ$$

$$= \int_a^b f(x)\,dx - \int_a^b \phi(x)\,dx$$

$$= \int_a^b \left[f(x) - \phi(x)\right] dx$$

$$= \int_a^b \left[y \text{ of upper curve} - y \text{ of lower curve}\right] dx$$

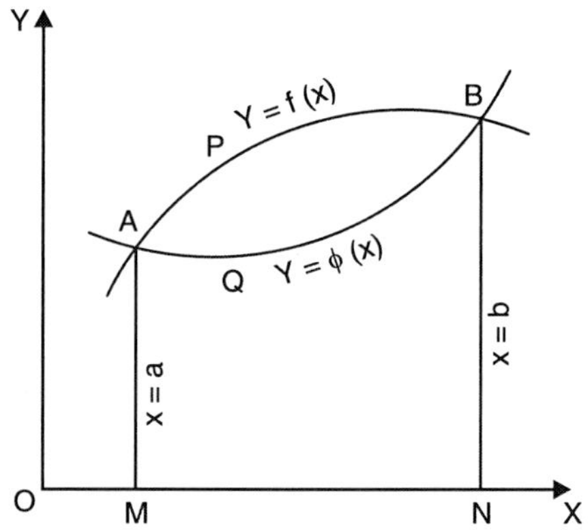

ILLUSTRATIVE EXAMPLES

Example 1. Prove that the area common to the two parabolas $x^2 = 4ay$ and $y^2 = 4ax$ is $\dfrac{16a^2}{3}$.

Solution : The equations of the two parabolas are

$$x^2 = 4ay \qquad \text{... (1)}$$

and $$y^2 = 4ax \qquad \text{... (2)}$$

Both the parabolas have their vertices at the origin. Their axes are along OY and OX respectively.

Solving (1) and (2) [eliminating y from these], we have

$$\frac{x^4}{16a^2} = 4ax$$

or $\quad x\,(x^3 - 64a^3) = 0$

$\therefore \quad x = 0$ or $4a$

when $\quad x = 0,\ y = 0$

when $x = 4a$, from (1) $y = 4a$.

Hence the two parabolas intersect in the points (0, 0), (4*a*, 4*a*).

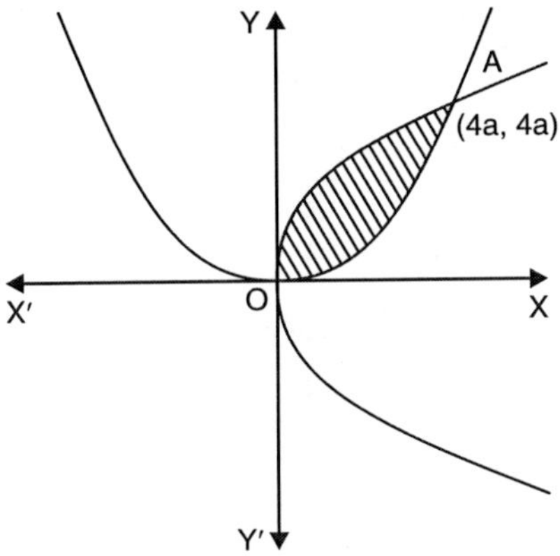

$\therefore$ Required area common to both the parabolas

$$= \text{Shaded area}$$

$$= \int_0^{4a} (y \text{ of upper curve } - y \text{ of lower curve})\, dx$$

$$= \int_0^{4a} \left(\sqrt{4ax} - \frac{x^2}{4a} \right) dx \qquad \text{[from (2) and (1)]}$$

$$= \left[2\sqrt{a}\, \frac{x^{3/2}}{\frac{3}{2}} - \frac{1}{4a} \frac{x^3}{3} \right]_0^{4a}$$

$$= \left[\frac{4\sqrt{a}}{3} x^{3/2} - \frac{1}{12a} x^3 \right]_0^{4a}$$

$$= \left\{ \frac{4\sqrt{a}}{3} (4a)^{3/2} - \frac{1}{12a} (4a)^3 \right\} - \{0\}$$

$$= \frac{32a^2}{3} - \frac{16a^2}{3} = \frac{16a^2}{3}$$

Example 2. Find the area common to the circle $x^2 + y^2 = 4$ and the ellipse $x^2 + 4y^2 = 9$.

Solution : Let P be the point of intersection in the first quadrant, of the circle and the ellipse, as shown in the figure. Draw $MP \perp$ x-axis.

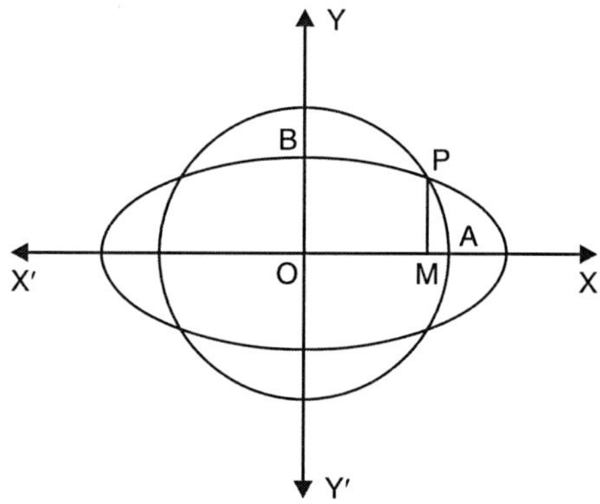

Eliminating y^2 from the two equations of the circle $x^2 + y^2 = 4$ and the ellipse $x^2 + 4y^2 = 9$, we have

$$x^2 + 4(4 - x^2) = 9$$

or,
$$3x^2 = 7$$

which gives

$$x = \sqrt{\frac{7}{3}} \text{ for } P$$

[Rejecting –ve value, as P is in the first quadrant]

Now for the ellipse

$$y = \frac{1}{2}\sqrt{9 - x^2}$$

and for the circle

$$y = \sqrt{4 - x^2}$$

Since the ellipse and circle are both symmetrical about both the axes.

$\therefore$ Required area common to the circle and ellipse

= 4 × Area common to circle and ellipse in the first quadrant

= 4 × Area $OAPB$

$$= 4\ [\text{Area } OBPM + \text{Area } PMA]$$

$$= 4\left[\int_0^{\sqrt{7/3}} (y \text{ of ellipse})\, dx + \int_{\sqrt{7/3}}^{2} (y \text{ of circle})\, dx\right]$$

$$= 4\left[\int_0^{\sqrt{7/3}} \frac{1}{2}\sqrt{9-x^2}\; dx + \int_{\sqrt{7/3}}^{2} \sqrt{4-x^2}\; dx\right]$$

$$= 4\left[\frac{1}{2}\left\{\frac{x}{2}\sqrt{9-x^2} + \frac{9}{2}\sin^{-1}\frac{x}{3}\right\}_0^{\sqrt{7/3}} + \left\{\frac{x}{2}\sqrt{4-x^2} + \frac{4}{2}\sin^{-1}\frac{x}{2}\right\}_{\sqrt{7/3}}^{2}\right]$$

$$\left[\because \int\sqrt{a^2-x^2}\; dx = \frac{1}{2}x\sqrt{a^2-x^2} + \frac{1}{2}a^2\sin^{-1}\left(\frac{x}{a}\right)\right]$$

$$= \left[\left\{\sqrt{\frac{7}{3}}\sqrt{9-\frac{7}{3}} + 9\sin^{-1}\frac{\sqrt{7}}{3\sqrt{3}}\right\} - \{0\}\right\}$$

$$+ 2\left[\{0 + 4\sin^{-1}1\} - \left\{\sqrt{\frac{7}{3}}\sqrt{4-\frac{7}{3}} + 4\sin^{-1}\frac{\sqrt{7}}{2\sqrt{3}}\right\}\right]$$

$$= \sqrt{\frac{7}{3}}\left\{\sqrt{\frac{20}{3}} - 2\sqrt{\frac{5}{3}}\right\} + 9\sin^{-1}\frac{\sqrt{7}}{3\sqrt{3}} + 8\frac{\pi}{2} - 8\sin^{-1}\frac{\sqrt{7}}{2\sqrt{3}}$$

$$= 0 + 9\sin^{-1}\sqrt{\frac{7}{27}} + 4\pi - 8\sin^{-1}\sqrt{\frac{7}{12}}$$

$$= 4\pi + 9\sin^{-1}\sqrt{\frac{7}{27}} - 8\sin^{-1}\sqrt{\frac{7}{12}}$$

Example 3. Show that the larger of the two areas into which the circle $x^2 + y^2 = 64a^2$ is divided by the parabola $y^2 = 12ax$ is

$$\frac{16a^2}{3}\left(8\pi - \sqrt{3}\right)$$

Solution : The equation of the circle is

$$x^2 + y^2 = 64a^2 \quad \text{... (1)}$$

Its centre is (0, 0) and radius is $8a$.

The equations of the parabola is

$$y^2 = 12ax \quad \text{... (2)}$$

Its vertex is (0, 0) and latus rectum is $12a$.

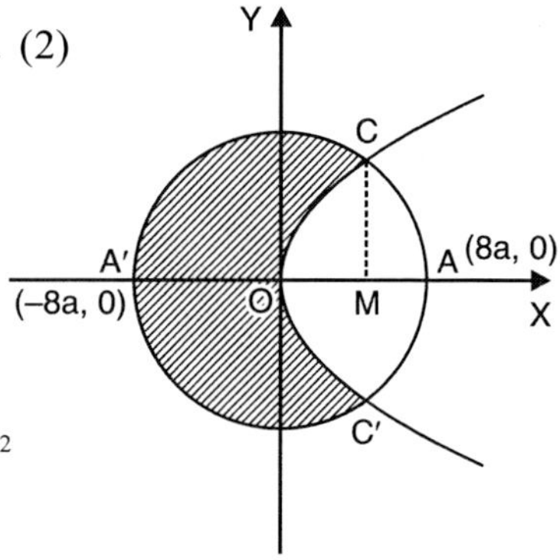

To find the points of intersection of (1) and (2),

eliminating y^2 from (1) and (2), we get

$$x^2 + 12ax = 64a^2$$

or $\quad x^2 + 12ax - 64a^2 = 0$

or $\quad (x + 16a)(x - 4a) = 0$

or $\quad x = -16a, 4a$

But $x = -16a$ is inadmissible because when $x = -16a$, from (2), y is imaginary.

$\therefore$ $x = 4a$, gives the abscissa of C, the point of intersection.

If the circle meets the x-axis in the points A and A', then these points are A ($8a$, 0) and A' ($-8a$, 0).

$\therefore$ Required shaded area

$$= \text{Area of circle} - \text{Area of } COC'A \quad \text{... (3)}$$

Now, area of circle

$$= \pi (8a)^2$$
$$= 64\pi a^2 \quad \text{... (4)}$$

and

$$\text{area } COC'A = 2 \text{ Area } COA$$
$$= 2 (\text{Area } COM + \text{Area } MCA)$$
$$= 2\left[\int_0^{4a} (y \text{ of parabola})\, dx + \int_{4a}^{8a} (y \text{ of circle})\, dx\right]$$
$$= 2\left[\int_0^{4a} \sqrt{12ax}\, dx + \int_{4a}^{8a} \sqrt{64a^2 - x^2}\, dx\right]$$

$$= 2\sqrt{12a}\left[\frac{x^{3/2}}{\frac{3}{2}}\right]_0^{4a} + 2\left[\frac{1}{2}x\sqrt{64a^2 - x^2} + \frac{64a^2}{2}\sin^{-1}\frac{x}{8a}\right]_{4a}^{8a}$$

$$= 2.2\sqrt{3}\,a\,\frac{2}{3}(4a)^{3/2} + 2\left[0 + 32a^2\sin^{-1}(1) - 2a\sqrt{48a^2} - 32a^2\sin^{-1}\frac{1}{2}\right]$$

$$= \frac{64}{\sqrt{3}}a^2 + 2\left[32a^2\cdot\frac{\pi}{2} - 8\sqrt{3}a^2 - 32a^2\cdot\frac{\pi}{6}\right]$$

$$= \left[\frac{64}{\sqrt{3}} - 16\sqrt{3}\right]a^2 + 32a^2\pi - \frac{32\pi a^2}{3}$$

$$= \frac{16}{\sqrt{3}}a^2 + \frac{64\pi a^2}{3}$$

$$= \frac{16a^2}{3}\left(\sqrt{3} + 4\pi\right) \qquad \text{... (5)}$$

Putting the values from (4) and (5) in (3), we get the required shaded area

$$= 64\,\pi a^2 - \frac{16a^2}{3}\left(\sqrt{3} + 4\pi\right)$$

$$= \frac{16a^2}{3}\left(12\pi - \sqrt{3} - 4\pi\right)$$

$$= \frac{16a^2}{3}\left(8\pi - \sqrt{3}\right)$$

Hence the result.

EXERCISE 13.2

1. Find the area included between the curves $y^2 = 4bx$ and $x^2 = 4ay$.
2. Find the area included between the parabola $x^2 = 4ay$ and the curve $y\,(x^2 + 4a^2) = 8a^3$.

3. Show that the area included between the parabolas

$$y^2 = 4a\,(x + a) \text{ and } y^2 = 4b\,(b - x)$$

is $\frac{8}{3}(a+b)\sqrt{ab}$.

4. Find the area common to the two curves

$$y^2 = ax \text{ and } x^2 + y^2 = 4ax.$$

5. Prove that the area enclosed by the curves

$$x^2 + y^2 = 2ax \text{ and } y^2 = ax$$

is $a^2\left(\frac{\pi}{4} - \frac{2}{3}\right)$.

6. Find the area of the smaller portion enclosed by the curves

$$y^2 = 8x \text{ and } x^2 + y^2 = 9.$$

7. Show that the area of the segment cut-off from the parabola $y^2 = 2x$ by the straight line $y = 4x - 1$ is $\frac{9}{32}$.

8. Show that the area of the segment cut-off from the parabola $y^2 = 4x$ by the straight line $2x - 3y + 4 = 0$ is $\frac{1}{3}$.

9. Find the area bounded by the parabola $x^2 = 8y$ and the line

$$x - 2y + 8 = 0.$$

10. Prove that the curves $y^2 = ax$ and $x^2 = 4y$ divided the area of the square bounded by $x = 0$, $x = 4$, $y = 0$, $y = 4$ into three equal parts.

11. Show that the area enclosed by the curves

$$xy^2 = a^2\,(a - x)$$

and $\quad y^2\,(a - x) = a^2x$ is $a^2\,(\pi - 2)$.

12. Two curves $y = 4x^2$ and $y^2 = 2x$ meet at the origin O and the point A, forming a loop. Show that the straight line OA divides the loop into two parts of equal area.

ANSWERS

EXERCISE 13.2

1. $\frac{16ab}{3}$ **2.** $\frac{2}{3}a^2(3\pi - 2)$

4. $a^2\left(3\sqrt{3}+\frac{4\pi}{3}\right)$ **6.** $\frac{2\sqrt{2}}{3}+\frac{9\pi}{2}-9\sin^{-1}\left(\frac{1}{3}\right)$

9. $25\frac{1}{3}$

13.5 Area Formula for Parametric Equations

(i) The area bounded by the curve

$$x = f(t),\ y = \phi(t),$$

the x-axis and the ordinates at the points where $t = a$, $t = b$ is

$$\int_a^b y\frac{dx}{dt}\,dt$$

The parametric equations of the curve are

$$\left.\begin{aligned} x &= f(t), \\ y &= \phi(t) \end{aligned}\right\}$$

$\therefore$ Required Area

$$= \int_{t=a}^{t=b} y\,dx$$

$$= \int_a^b y\frac{dx}{dt}\,dt$$

$$= \int_a^b \phi(t)\, f'(t)\,dt$$

(ii) The area bounded by the curve $x = f(t)$, $y = \phi(t)$, the y-axis and the abscissae at the points where $t = c$, $t = d$ is given by

$$\int_c^d x\frac{dy}{dt}\,dt$$

13.6 Area Formula for Polar Equations

The area bounded by the curve $r = f(\theta)$ and the radii vectors $\theta = \alpha$, $\theta = \beta$ is

$$\int_\alpha^\beta \frac{1}{2}r^2 d\theta$$

where $r = f(\theta)$ is finite, continuous, and single-valued function of θ in the interval $\alpha \le \theta \le \beta$.

Let AB be the curve $r = f(\theta)$ and OA, OB be the radii vectors $\theta = \alpha$, $\theta = \beta$.

Let $P(r, \theta)$ be any point on the curve. Let $Q\,(r + \delta r, \theta + \delta\theta)$ be a neighbouring point on the curve.

Then if A denotes the sectorial area OAP, then clearly A is a function of θ. Also sectorial area $OAQ = A + \delta A$, so that sectorial area

$$OPQ = \delta A$$

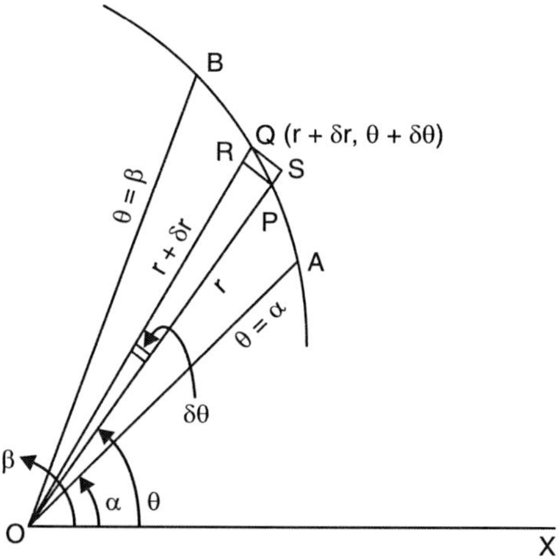

With O as centre and OP, OQ as radii, draw circular arcs to meet OQ, OP (produced) in R and S respectively.

Then the area OPQ lies between the circular sectorial areas OPR and OSQ,

i.e., δA lies between $\frac{1}{2}r^2\,\delta\theta$ and $\frac{1}{2}(r + \delta r)^2\,\delta\theta$.

[$\because$ area of the circular sector $= \frac{1}{2}$ (radius)^2 $\times$ circular measure of the angle of sector]

$\therefore\ \frac{\delta A}{\delta\theta}$ lies between $\frac{1}{2}r^2$ and $\frac{1}{2}(r + \delta r)^2$. Proceeding to limits as $Q \to P$.

i.e., as $\delta\theta \to 0\ \ \therefore\ \delta r \to 0$, we get

$\dfrac{dA}{d\theta}$ lies between $\dfrac{1}{2}r^2$ and a quantity which tends to $\dfrac{1}{2}r^2$.

$$\therefore \qquad \frac{dA}{d\theta} = \frac{1}{2}r^2$$

$$\therefore \quad \int_\alpha^\beta \frac{1}{2}r^2 d\theta = \int_\alpha^\beta \frac{dA}{d\theta}\, d\theta = (A)_\alpha^\beta$$

$$= (\text{Value of } A \text{ when } \theta = \beta) - (\text{Value of } A \text{ when } \theta = \alpha)$$

$$= \text{Area } OAB - 0$$

$$= \text{Area } OAB$$

Hence,

$$\text{Area } OAB = \frac{1}{2}\int_\alpha^\beta r^2 d\theta$$

Note 1. In some cases, it is more convenient to transform a given cartesian equation into polars rather than to solve for y. In such cases the above formula is applied after changing to polars.

Note 2. Determination of the limits of integration.

(i) In case of a loop, the limits of integration for finding its area are two successive values of θ which make $r = 0$.

(ii) If the curve is symmetrical about both the axes, the integral must be evaluated fom 0 to $\pi/2$ and the whole result be multiplied by 4.

(iii) If the curve is symmetrical about the x-axis, i.e., initial line only, the integral may be evaluated from 0 to π and the whole result multiplied by 2.

13.7 Area between Two Polar Curves

The area bounded by the curve $r = f(\theta)$ and $r = F(\theta)$ and the radii vectors $\theta = \alpha$, $\theta = \beta$ is

$$\int_\alpha^\beta \frac{1}{2}\left(r_1^2 - r_2^2\right) d\theta$$

where r_1 is the 'r' of the outer curve and r_2, the 'r' of the inner curve.

Let AB, CD be the two given curves $r = f(\theta)$ and $r = F(\theta)$ respectively and OCA, ODB the radii vectors $\theta = \alpha$, $\theta = \beta$ respectively.

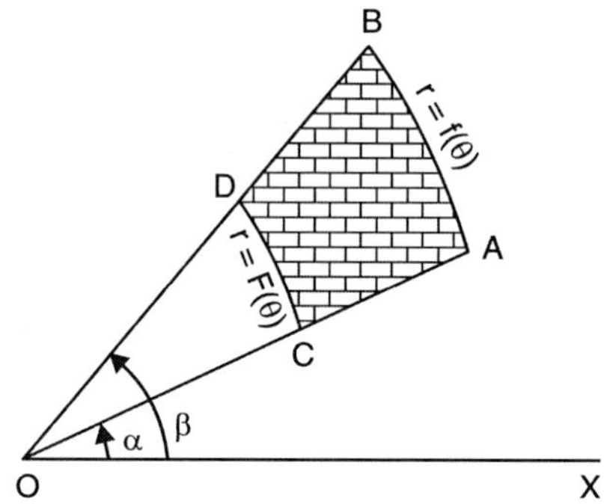

Then the area $ABCD$

$$= \text{area } OAB - \text{area } OCD$$

$$= \frac{1}{2}\int_{\alpha}^{\beta}\{f(\theta)\}^2\, d\theta - \frac{1}{2}\int_{\alpha}^{\beta}\{F(\theta)\}^2\, d\theta$$

$$= \frac{1}{2}\int_{\alpha}^{\beta}\left\{[f(\theta)]^2 - [F(\theta)]^2\right\} d\theta$$

$$= \frac{1}{2}\int_{\alpha}^{\beta}\left(r_1^2 - r_2^2\right) d\theta$$

where $r_1 = f(\theta)$ is the value of 'r' of the outer curve and $r_2 = F(\theta)$ is the value of 'r' of the inner curve.

13.8 Areas of closed curves given by parametric equations

The area of the closed curve $x = f(t)$, $y = \phi(t)$ is

$$\int_{t_1}^{t_2} \frac{1}{2}\left(x\frac{dy}{dt} - y\frac{dx}{dt}\right) dt$$

where t_1, t_2 are the value of t such that the point (x, y) travels once round the curve and $f(t)$, $\phi(t)$ are continuous functions of t in $t_1 \le t \le t_2$.

ILLUSTRATIVE EXAMPLES

Example 1. Find the area between the cycloid $x = a(\theta + \sin\theta)$, $y = a(1 - \cos\theta)$ and its base. Also find the area between the curve and the axis of x.

Solution : The parametric equations of the cycloid are

$$x = a(\theta + \sin\theta),\ y = a(1 - \cos\theta)$$

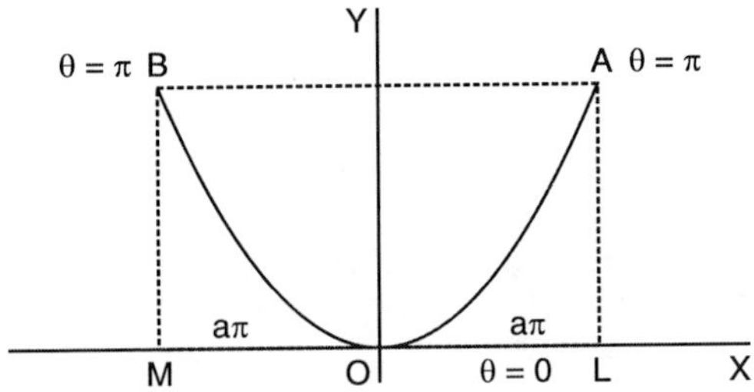

The cycloid is symmetrical about the y-axis, and the base is the line AB parallel to x-axis and at a distance $2a$ from it.

For the half of cycloid, θ varies from 0 to π.

The area between the curve and its base

$$= \text{area } BOA$$

$$= 2 \text{ area } OCA$$

$$= 2\int_0^\pi x \frac{dy}{d\theta}\, d\theta$$

$$= 2\int_0^\pi a(\theta + \sin\theta)(a\sin\theta)\, d\theta$$

$$= 2a^2\int_0^\pi (\theta\sin\theta + \sin^2\theta)\, d\theta$$

$$= 2a^2\int_0^\pi \theta\sin\theta\, d\theta + 2a^2\int_0^\pi \frac{1-\cos 2\theta}{2}\, d\theta$$

$$= 2a^2\left[\{\theta(-\cos\theta)\}_0^\pi - \int_0^\pi 1(-\cos\theta)\, d\theta\right] + a^2\left[\frac{\sin 2\theta}{2}\right]_0^\pi$$

$$= 2a^2\left[(-\theta\cos\theta)_0^\pi + (\sin\theta)_0^\pi\right] + a^2[\theta - \sin\theta\cos\theta]_0^\pi$$

$$= 2a^2[-\pi\cos\pi] + a^2(\pi)$$

$$= 2a^2\pi + a^2\pi$$

$$= 3a^2\pi$$

Again, area between the curve and x-axis

$$= 2 \text{ area } OAL$$

$$= 2\int_0^{\pi} y \frac{dx}{d\theta}\, d\theta$$

$$= 2\int_0^{\pi} a\left(1-\cos\theta\right) a\left(1+\cos\theta\right) d\theta$$

$$= 2a^2\int_0^{\pi} \left(1-\cos^2\theta\right) d\theta$$

$$= 2a^2\int_0^{\pi} \sin^2\theta\, d\theta$$

$$= 4a^2\int_0^{\pi/2} \sin^2\theta\, d\theta$$

$$= 4a^2 \cdot \frac{1}{2} \cdot \frac{\pi}{2}$$

$$= \pi a^2$$

Aliter. Area between the curve and x-axis

$= $ area of rectangle $ALMB$ – area between the curve and its base

$= AL \times LM - 3\pi a^2$

$= 2a \times 2a\pi - 3\pi a^2$

$= 4\pi a^2 - 3\pi a^2 = \pi a^2$

Example 2. Find the area of the curve $x = a\cos^3 t$, $y = b\sin^3 t$.

Solution : The equations of the curve are

$$x = a\cos^3 t,\ y = b\sin^3 t \qquad \ldots (1)$$

The curve is symmetrical about both the sides.

$\because$ $|x| \le a$ and $|y| \le b$.

$\therefore$ The curve lies within the rectangle bounded by the lines

$$x = \pm a,\ y = \pm b.$$

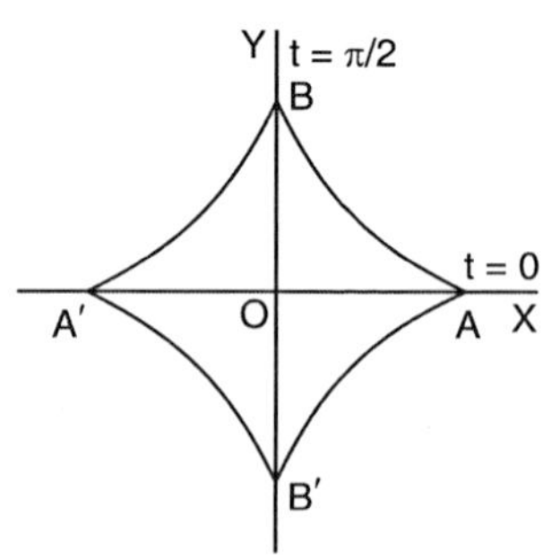

In the first quadrant, t varies from 0 to $\pi/2$.

$\therefore$ Required Area

$= 4 \times$ Area OAB

$$= 4\int_0^{\pi/2} y \frac{dx}{dt}\, dt$$

$$= 4\int_0^{\pi/2} b\sin^3 t \cdot 3a\cos^2 t(-\sin t)\,dt$$

$$= -12ab\int_0^{\pi/2} \sin^4 t\cos^2 t\,dt$$

$$= -12ab\frac{\Gamma\frac{5}{2}\Gamma\frac{3}{2}}{2\Gamma 4}$$

$$= -\frac{12ab}{2}\frac{\frac{3}{2}\cdot\frac{1}{2}\cdot\sqrt{\pi}\cdot\frac{1}{2}\cdot\sqrt{\pi}}{3.2}$$

$$= -\frac{12ab}{2}\cdot\frac{3\pi}{48}$$

$$= -\frac{3}{8}\pi ab$$

$$= \frac{3}{8}\pi ab \text{ (numerically)}$$

Example 3. Prove that the whole area between the four infinite branches of the tractrix

$$x = a\cos t + \frac{1}{2}a\log\tan^2\frac{t}{2},\ y = a\sin t$$

is πa^2.

Solution : The equations of the curve are

$$x = a\cos t + \frac{a}{2}\log\tan^2\frac{t}{2} \qquad \text{... (1)}$$

$$y = a\sin t \qquad \text{... (2)}$$

(i) Since x is an even function of t and y is an odd function of t, the curve is symmetrical about the x-axis.

(ii) Putting $y = 0$, we have $a\sin t = 0$ or $t = 0$.

But $t = 0$ does not make $x = 0$.

Hence the curve does not pass through the origin.

$\because \quad |\sin t| \leq 1$

$\therefore \quad |y| \leq a$

i.e., the curve lies between the lines $y = \pm a$.

(iii) When $y = 0$, $t = 0$, which makes x infinite, i.e., if $x \to \infty$, $y \to 0$.

Thus $y = 0$, i.e., x-axis is an asymptote of the curve.

(iv) Now,

$$\frac{dx}{dt} = a(-\sin t) + \frac{a}{2} \cdot \frac{1}{\tan^2 \frac{t}{2}} \cdot 2 \tan \frac{t}{2} \sec^2 \frac{t}{2} \cdot \frac{1}{2}$$

$$= a\left[-\sin t + \frac{1}{2 \sin \frac{t}{2} \cos \frac{t}{2}}\right]$$

$$= a\left(-\sin t + \frac{1}{\sin t}\right)$$

$$= a\left(\frac{1 - \sin^2 t}{\sin t}\right)$$

$$= \frac{a \cos^2 t}{\sin t}$$

and $$\frac{dy}{dt} = a \cos t$$

$\therefore$ $$\frac{dy}{dx} = \frac{dy/dt}{dx/dt}$$

$$= a \cos t \cdot \frac{\sin t}{a \cos^2 t}$$

$$= \tan t$$

The corresponding values of x, y for different values of t are

$t =$	$-\pi$	$-\pi/2$	0	$\pi/2$	π
$x =$	∞	0	$-\infty$	0	∞
$y =$	0	$-a$	0	a	0
$\frac{dy}{dx} =$	0	$-\infty$	0	∞	0

Thus it follows that when $t = 0$, the corresponding point is $(-\infty, 0)$, i.e., a point at ∞ on the –ve side of x-axis.

When $t = \pi$, the corresponding point is $(\infty, 0)$.

Also at $t = \pm \pi/2$, i.e., at the points $(0, -a)$ and $(0, a)$, since $\frac{dy}{dx} = \pm \infty$, $\therefore$ the tangent is $\parallel$ to y-axis.

In this case the line y-axis itself is the tangent to the curve. Thus the shape of the curve is roughly as shown in the figure.

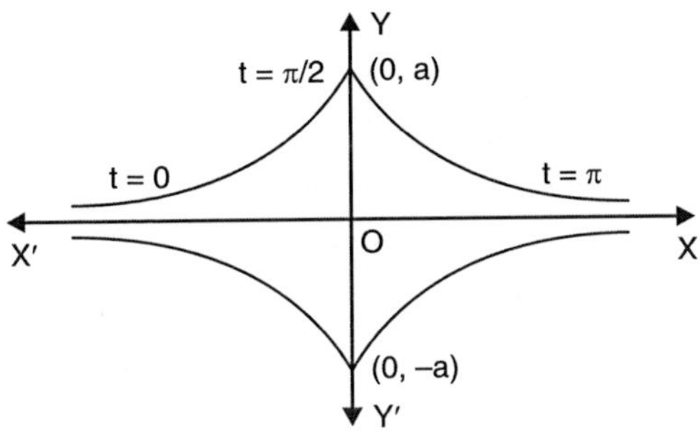

By symmetry,

Required area $= 4 \times$ area in the second quadrant

$$= 4 \times \int_0^{\pi/2} y \frac{dx}{dt}\, dt$$

$$= 4 \int_0^{\pi/2} a \sin t \frac{a \cos^2 t}{\sin t}\, dt$$

$$= 4a^2 \int_0^{\pi/2} \cos^2 t\, dt$$

$$= 4a^2 \frac{1}{2} \cdot \frac{\pi}{2} = \pi a^2$$

Example 4. Find the area of the loop of the curve

$$x = a\,(1 - t^2),\ y = at\,(1 - t^2).$$

Solution : The parametric equations of the given curve are

$$x = a\,(1 - t^2),\ y = at\,(1 - t^2) \qquad \text{... (1)}$$

to trace the curve roughly to find the limits of integration.

(i) Since x is an even and y is an odd function of t, therefore the curve is symmetrical about the x-axis.

(ii) $x = 0$ give $t = \pm 1$ which also makes $y = 0$.

$\therefore$ The curve passes through the origin. Since the curve passes through the origin for two different values of t, i.e., $+1$ and -1. $\therefore$ Origin is a node.

(iii) The curve meets x-axis where putting $y = 0$, we have

$$at\ (1 - t^2) = 0$$

$$\therefore \qquad t = 0 \text{ or } 1, -1$$

When $t = 0$, $x = a$;

When $t = \pm 1$, $x = 0$.

Thus the curve meets x-axis in the points $(0, 0)$ and $(a, 0)$.

(iv) The curve has no asymptotes, i.e., for no value of t, x (or y) tends to ∞ and y (or x) tends to a finite quantity.

(v)
$$\frac{dx}{dt} = -\ 2at$$

$$\frac{dy}{dt} = a\ (1 - 3t^2)$$

$$\therefore \qquad \frac{dy}{dt} = \frac{dy/dt}{dx/dt} = \frac{1-3t^2}{-2t} = \frac{3t^2-1}{2t}$$

Now $\frac{dy}{dx} = 0$ when $3t^2 - 1 = 0$, i.e., $t = \pm\frac{1}{\sqrt{3}}$.

When $t = \pm\frac{1}{\sqrt{3}}$, $x = \frac{2}{3}a$, $y = \pm\frac{2}{3\sqrt{3}}a$.

Thus at the points $\left(\frac{2}{3}a, \pm\frac{2}{3\sqrt{3}}a\right)$ the tangent is $\parallel$ to x-axis.

Again $\frac{dy}{dx} = \infty$, when $t = 0$.

Now when $t = 0$, $x = a$, $y = 0$. Thus at the points $(a, 0)$, the tangent is $\perp$ to x-axis.

Also $x \leq a$ always. Thus no portion of the curve lies beyond the line $x = a$.

As t increases from 0 to 1, x decreases from a to 0 and y first increases from 0 and then decreases to zero.

Again as $t \to \infty$, $x \to -\infty$ and $y \to -\infty$.

The shape of the curve is roughly as shown in the figure and for the upper half of the loop, t varies from 0 to 1.

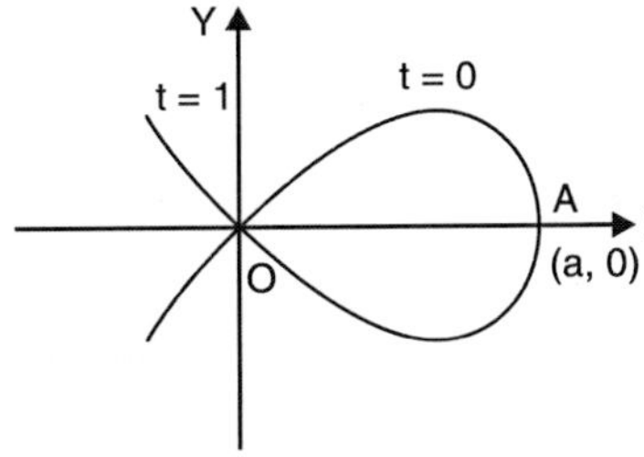

$\therefore$ Required area of the loop

$$= 2\int_0^1 y\frac{dx}{dt}\,dt$$

$$= 2\int_0^1 at\left(1-t^2\right)(-2at)\,dt$$

$$= -4a^2\int_0^1\left(t^2-t^4\right)dt$$

$$= -4a^2\left(\frac{t^3}{3}-\frac{t^5}{5}\right)_0^1$$

$$= -4a^2\left(\frac{1}{3}-\frac{1}{5}\right)=\frac{-8a^2}{15}$$

$$= \frac{8a^2}{15}\text{(in magnitude)}$$

Example 5. Show that the area bounded by the cissoid

$$x = a\sin^2 t,\ y = \frac{a\sin^3 t}{\cos t}$$

and is asymptote is $\dfrac{3\pi a^2}{4}$.

Solution : The equation of the curve are

$$x = a\sin t,\ y = a\frac{\sin^3 t}{\cos t} \qquad \text{... (1)}$$

to trace the curve roughly to find the limits of integration.

(i) Since x is an even function of t, and y is an odd function of t, the curve is symmetrical about the x-axis.

(ii) $x = 0$ gives $\sin^2 t = 0$ or $t = 0$ which also makes $y = 0$.

$\therefore$ The curve passes through the origin.

(iii) The curve meets both the axes only at the origin.

(iv) $$\frac{dx}{dt} = 2a\sin t\cos t$$

and $$\frac{dy}{dt} = a\frac{\cos t \cdot 3\sin^2 t\cos t - \sin^3 t(-\sin t)}{\cos^2 t}$$

$$= a\frac{\sin^2 t\left(3\cos^2 t + \sin^2 t\right)}{\cos^2 t}$$

$$= a\frac{\sin^2 t\left(1 + 2\cos^2 t\right)}{\cos^2 t}$$

$\therefore$ $$\frac{dy}{dx} = \frac{dy/dt}{dx/dt}$$

$$= \frac{a\sin^2 t\left(1+2\cos^2 t\right)}{\cos^2 t}\cdot\frac{1}{2a\sin t\cos t}$$

$$= \frac{\left(1+2\cos^2 t\right)\sin t}{2\cos^2 t}$$

$$\frac{dy}{dx} = 0 \text{ when } \sin t = 0$$

$$\left[\because 1 + 2\cos^2 t \neq 1 \text{ i.e. } \cos^2 t \neq -\frac{1}{2}\,(-\text{ve})\right]$$

or when $t = 0$, i.e., $x = 0$, $y = 0$.

Hence at the origin, the tangent is parallel to x-axis i.e., the x-axis itself.

Again, $\frac{dy}{dx} = \infty$ if $\cos t = 0$ or $t = \frac{\pi}{2}$

when $t = \pi/2$, $x = a$, $y = \infty$

Thus the line $x = a$ is an asymptote of the curve.

$$[\because \text{as } y \to \infty, x \to a]$$

(v) Since $x = a\sin^2 t$, x cannot be –ve.

Also x cannot be $> a$ $\quad [\because \sin^2 t \leq 1]$

Hence no portion of the curve lies to the left of y-axis and beyond the line $x = a$.

Thus for the upper half of the curve, t varies from 0 to $\frac{\pi}{2}$

$\therefore$ Required area between the curve and its asymptote

$$= 2 \times \text{Area of the upper half of the curve}$$

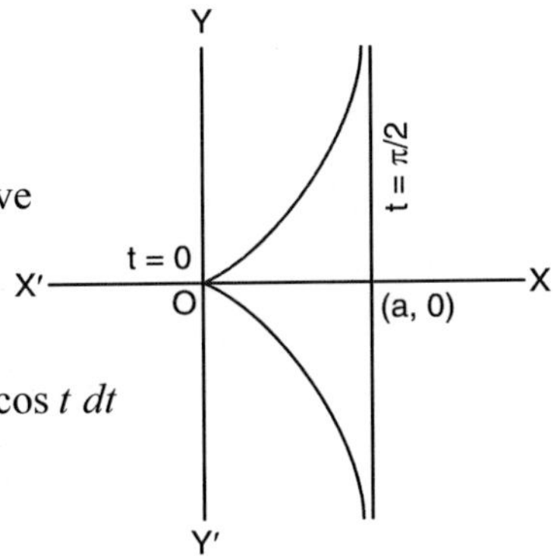

$$= 2\int_0^{\pi/2} y \frac{dx}{dt}\, dt$$

$$= 2\int_0^{\pi/2} a\frac{\sin^3 t}{\cos t}\, 2a \sin t \cos t \, dt$$

$$= 4a^2 \int_0^{\pi/2} \sin^4 t \, dt$$

$$= 4a^2 \frac{3}{4}\cdot\frac{1}{2}\cdot\frac{\pi}{2}$$

$$= \frac{3\pi a^2}{4}$$

Example 6. Find the area between the curve $r = a\theta \cos\theta$ and the radii vectors $\theta = 0$, $\theta = \pi/2$.

Solution : The given curve is

$$r = a\,\theta \cos\theta$$

Required sectorial area

$$= \frac{1}{2}\int_0^{\pi/2} r^2 d\theta$$

$$= \frac{1}{2}\int_0^{\pi/2} a^2\theta^2 \cos^2\theta \, d\theta$$

$$= \frac{a^2}{2}\int_0^{\pi/2} \theta^2 \frac{1+\cos 2\theta}{2}\, d\theta$$

$$= \frac{a^2}{4}\int_0^{\pi/2} \theta^2 d\theta + \frac{a^2}{4}\int_0^{\pi/2} \theta^2 \cos 2\theta \, d\theta$$

$$= \frac{a^2}{4}\left(\frac{\theta^3}{3}\right)_0^{\pi/2} + \frac{a^2}{4}\left[\left(\theta^2 \frac{\sin 2\theta}{2}\right)_0^{\pi/2} - \int_0^{\pi/2} 2\theta \cdot \frac{\sin 2\theta}{2}\, d\theta\right]$$

$$= \frac{a^2}{12}\frac{\pi^3}{8} + \frac{a^2}{4}\left[0 - \int_0^{\pi/2} \theta \sin 2\theta \, d\theta\right]$$

$$= \frac{a^2\pi^3}{96} - \frac{a^2}{4}\left[\left\{\theta\left(-\frac{\cos 2\theta}{2}\right)\right\}_0^{\pi/2} - \int_0^{\pi/2} 1 \cdot \frac{-\cos 2\theta}{2}\, d\theta\right]$$

$$= \frac{a^2\pi^3}{96} - \frac{a^2}{4}\left[\frac{\pi}{2}\cdot\frac{1}{2} + \frac{1}{2}\left(\frac{\sin 2\theta}{2}\right)_0^{\pi/2}\right]$$

$$= \frac{a^2\pi^3}{96} - \frac{\pi a^2}{16} - \frac{a^3}{16}(\sin\pi - \sin 0)$$

$$= \frac{a^2\pi^3}{96} - \frac{\pi a^2}{16} - 0$$

$$= \frac{\pi a^2}{16}\left(\frac{\pi^2}{6} - 1\right)$$

Example 7. Find the area of a loop of the curve $r^2 = a^2 \cos 2\theta$ and hence find its total area.

Solution : The curve is

$$r^2 = a^2 \cos 2\theta \qquad \text{... (1)}$$

Since the equation remains unchanged on changing θ to $-\theta$ or $\pi - \theta$, hence the curve is symmetrical about both the axes.

For the loop putting $r = 0$, we have

$$\cos 2\theta = 0 = \cos\left(\pm\frac{\pi}{2}\right)$$

$$\therefore \quad 2\theta = -\frac{\pi}{2}, \frac{\pi}{2}$$

$$\therefore \quad \theta = -\frac{\pi}{4}, \frac{\pi}{4} \qquad \text{[two consecutive values]}$$

Hence a loop lies between the radii vectors $\theta = -\pi/4$ and $\theta = \pi/4$. The curve consists of two equal loops and for half the loop in the first quadrant, θ varies from θ to $\pi/4$.

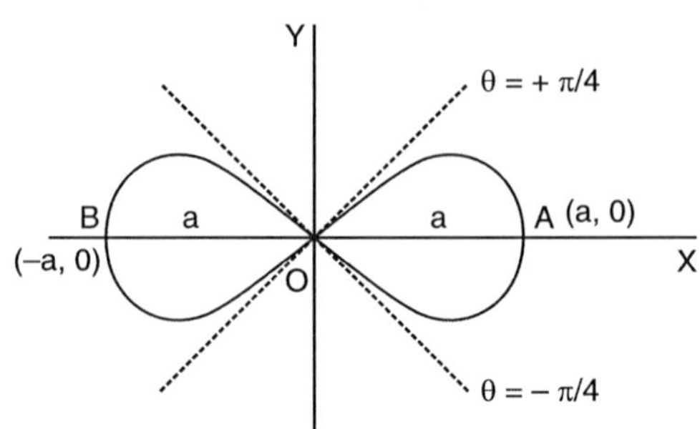

∴ Area of a loop

$$= 2\int_0^{\pi/4} \frac{1}{2} r^2 d\theta$$

$$= \int_0^{\pi/4} a^2 \cos 2\theta \, d\theta$$

$$= a^2 \left(\frac{\sin 2\theta}{2} \right)_0^{\pi/4} = \frac{a^2}{2}(1-0) = \frac{a^2}{2}$$

∴ Total area of the curve

$$= 2 \times \frac{a^2}{2}$$

$$= a^2$$

Example 8. Show that the area of a loop of $r = a \cos n\theta$ is $\frac{\pi a^2}{4n}$, n being integral. Also prove that the whole area is $\frac{\pi a^2}{4}$ or $\frac{\pi a^2}{2}$ according as n is odd or even.

Solution : The equation of the curve is

$$r = a \cos n\theta \qquad \ldots (1)$$

For a loop putting $r = 0$, we get

$$\cos n\theta = 0$$

$$\therefore \quad n\theta = -\frac{\pi}{2}, \frac{\pi}{2} \qquad \text{[two consecutive values]}$$

$$\therefore \quad \theta = \frac{-\pi}{2n}, \frac{\pi}{2n}$$

Thus one loop of the curve is obtained as θ varies from

$$-\frac{\pi}{2n} \text{ to } \frac{\pi}{2n}.$$

∴ Area of one loop

$$= \int_{-\pi/2n}^{\pi/2n} \frac{1}{2} r^2 d\theta$$

$$= \frac{1}{2} \int_{-\pi/2n}^{\pi/2n} a^2 \cos^2 n\theta \, d\theta$$

$$= \frac{a^2}{2} \int_{-\pi/2n}^{+\pi/2n} \frac{1 + \cos 2n\theta}{2} \, d\theta$$

$$= \frac{a^2}{4}\left[\theta + \frac{\sin 2n\theta}{2n}\right]_{-\pi/2n}^{\pi/2n}$$

$$= \frac{a^2}{4}\left[\frac{\pi}{2n} - \left(-\frac{\pi}{2n}\right) + \frac{1}{2n}\{\sin \pi - \sin(-\pi)\}\right]$$

$$= \frac{a^2}{4}\left[\frac{\pi}{n} + \frac{1}{2n}\cdot(0)\right]$$

$$= \frac{\pi a^2}{4n}$$

Case I. When n is odd, the curve has n loops.

$\therefore$ Total area of the curve

$$= n \times \frac{\pi a^2}{4n} = \frac{\pi a^2}{4}$$

Case II. When n is even, the curve has $2n$ loops.

$\therefore$ Total area of the curve

$$= 2n \times \frac{\pi a^2}{4n}$$

$$= \frac{\pi a^2}{2}$$

Example 9. Prove that the sum of the areas of the two loops of the limicon $r = a + b\cos\theta$ $(b > a)$ is equal to $\pi\left(a^2 + \frac{1}{2}b^2\right)$.

Solution : The equation of the curve is

$$r = a + b\cos\theta \ (b > a)$$

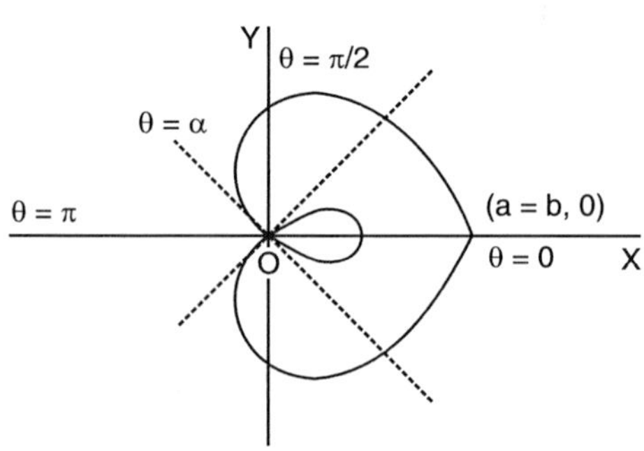

The curve is symmetrical about the initial line.

Let $\theta = \alpha$ when $r = 0$

$\therefore \quad a + b \cos \alpha = 0$

$$\therefore \quad \cos \alpha = -\frac{a}{b}$$

and the line $\theta = \alpha$ is the tangent at the pole.

For the larger loop, θ varies from 0 to α, and for the smaller loop, θ varies from α to π, above the initial line.

$\therefore$ Required sum of the areas of the two loops

$$= 2\left[\int_0^{\alpha} \frac{1}{2} r^2 d\theta + \int_{\alpha}^{\pi} \frac{1}{2} r^2 d\theta\right]$$

$$= 2\int_0^{\pi/2} \frac{1}{2} r^2 d\theta$$

$$\left[\because \int_a^b f(x)\,dx + \int_b^c f(x)\,dx = \int_a^c f(x)\,dx\right]$$

$$= \int_0^{\pi} (a + b\cos\theta)^2\, d\theta$$

$$= \int_0^{\pi} \left(a^2 + b^2 \cos^2\theta + 2ab\cos\theta\right) d\theta$$

$$= \int_0^{\pi} \left(a^2 + b^2 \cdot \frac{1 + \cos 2\theta}{2} + 2ab\cos\theta\right) d\theta$$

$$= \left[\left(a^2 + \frac{b^2}{2}\right)\theta + \frac{b^2}{4}\sin 2\theta + 2ab\sin\theta\right]_0^{\pi}$$

$$= \left(a^2 + \frac{b^2}{2}\right)\pi$$

Example 10. Find the area of the loop of the curve

$$x^3 + y^3 = 3axy$$

Solution : The given curve is

$$x^3 + y^3 = 3axy$$

changing to polars (by putting $x = r\cos\theta$, $y = r\sin\theta$), we have

$$r^2 (\cos^3\theta + \sin^3\theta) = 3ar^2 \sin\theta\cos\theta$$

or
$$r = \frac{3a\sin\theta\cos\theta}{\sin^3\theta + \cos^3\theta} \quad \text{... (1)}$$

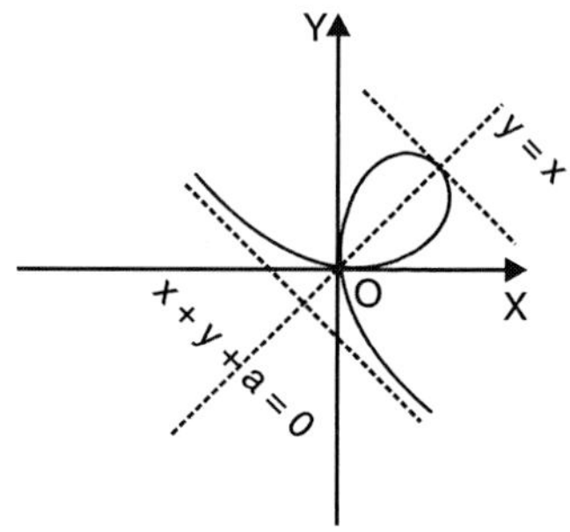

For a loop, putting $r = 0$, we get

$$\sin\theta\cos\theta = 0$$

i.e., $\sin\theta = 0$ and $\cos\theta = 0$

or $\theta = 0$ and $\pi/2$

[two consecutive values]

Hence as θ varies from 0 to $\pi/2$, we get the loop.

$\therefore$ Required area

$$= \int_0^{\pi/2} \frac{1}{2} r^2 d\theta$$

$$= \frac{9a^2}{2} \int_0^{\pi/2} \frac{\sin^2\theta\cos^2\theta\, d\theta}{(\sin^3\theta + \cos^3\theta)^2}$$

$$= \frac{9a^2}{2} \int_0^{\pi/2} \frac{\tan^2\theta\sec^2\theta\, d\theta}{(1+\tan^3\theta)^2}$$

[dividing the numerator and denominator by $\cos^6\theta$]

[Put $t = \tan^3\theta$

$\therefore\ dt = 3\tan^2\theta\sec^2\theta\, d\theta$

when $\theta = 0$, $t = 0$,

when $\theta = \pi/2$, $t \to \infty$]

$$= \frac{9a^2}{2} \int_0^{\infty} \frac{1}{(1+t)^2} \frac{dt}{3}$$

$$= \frac{3a^2}{2} \int_0^{\infty} (1+t)^{-2} dt$$

$$= \frac{3a^2}{2} \left[\frac{(1+t)^{-1}}{-1}\right]_0^{\infty}$$

$$= -\frac{3a^2}{2} \left(\frac{1}{1+t}\right)_0^{\infty}$$

$$= -\frac{3a^2}{2} \left(\frac{1}{\infty} - 1\right)$$

$$= -\frac{3a^2}{2}(0-1)$$

$$= \frac{3a^2}{2}$$

Example 11. Show that the area of the region included between the cardioids $r = a\,(1 + \cos\theta)$ and $r = a\,(1 - \cos\theta)$ is $\frac{a^2}{2}(3\pi - 8)$.

Solution : The equations of the two cardioids are

$$r = a\,(1 + \cos\theta) \qquad \text{... (1)}$$

and $$r = a\,(1 - \cos\theta) \qquad \text{... (2)}$$

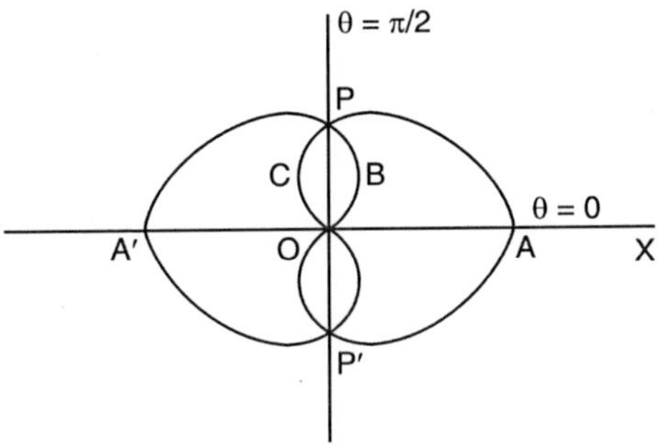

Solving (1) and (2) to find the points of intersection (eliminating r), we get

$$a\,(1 + \cos\theta) = a\,(1 - \cos\theta)$$

or $$2\cos\theta = 0$$

$\therefore$ $$\cos\theta = 0 = \cos(\pm\,\pi/2)$$

$\therefore$ $$\theta = \pm\,\pi/2$$

$\therefore$ For the point of intersection P, $\theta = \pi/2$.

Since both the cardioids are symmetrical about the initial line,

$\therefore$ By symmetry

Required area common to two cardioids

$$= 2 \text{ Area } OBPCO$$

$$= 4 \text{ Area } OBPO$$

where area $OBPO$ is the area of curve (2) between the radii vectors $\theta = 0$, $\theta = \pi/2$.

$\therefore$ Required area

$$= 4\int_0^{\pi/2} \frac{1}{2} r^2 d\theta$$

$$= 2\int_0^{\pi/2} a^2 (1 - \cos\theta)^2 \, d\theta$$

$$= 2a^2 \int_0^{\pi/2} (1 - 2\cos\theta + \cos^2\theta) \, d\theta$$

$$= 2a^2 [\theta - 2\sin\theta]_0^{\pi/2} + 2a^2 \int_0^{\pi/2} \cos^2\theta \, d\theta$$

$$= 2a^2\left(\frac{\pi}{2} - 2\right) + 2a^2 \cdot \frac{1}{2} \cdot \frac{\pi}{2}$$

$$= 2a^2\left(\frac{\pi}{2} - 2 + \frac{\pi}{4}\right)$$

$$= 2a^2\left(\frac{3\pi}{4} - 2\right)$$

$$= \frac{a^2}{2}(3\pi - 8)$$

Example 12. Show that the area common to the ellipses

$$a^2x^2 + b^2y^2 = 1 \text{ and } b^2x^2 + a^2y^2 = 1,$$

where $0 < a < b$ is $\dfrac{4}{ab} \tan^{-1}\left(\dfrac{a}{b}\right)$.

Solution : The first ellipse is

$$a^2x^2 + b^2y^2 = 1 \qquad \text{... (1)}$$

or $$\frac{x^2}{\left(\frac{1}{a^2}\right)} + \frac{y^2}{\left(\frac{1}{b^2}\right)} = 1$$

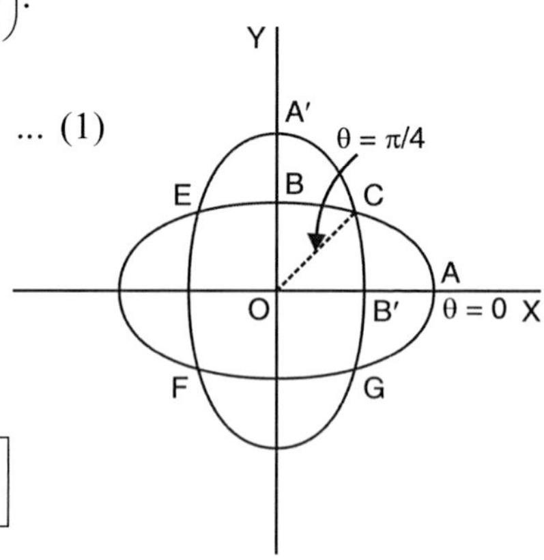

Its major axis lies along x-axis and minor axis along y-axis

$$\left[\because 0 < a < b \,(\text{given}) \therefore \frac{1}{a} > \frac{1}{b}\right]$$

The second ellipse is

$$b^2x^2 + a^2y^2 = 1 \qquad \text{... (2)}$$

or $$\frac{x^2}{\left(\frac{1}{b^2}\right)}+\frac{y^2}{\left(\frac{1}{a^2}\right)} = 1$$

$\because$ $$\frac{1}{a}>\frac{1}{b}$$

$\therefore$ Its major axis lies along y-axis and minor axis along x-axis.

Changing to polars (by putting $x = r\cos\theta$, $y = r\sin\theta$), we get

$$r^2 (a^2 \cos^2 \theta + b^2 \sin^2 \theta) = 1$$

or $$r^2 = \frac{1}{a^2\cos^2\theta+b^2\sin^2\theta} \quad \text{... (3)}$$

and $r^2 (b^2 \cos^2 \theta + a^2 \sin^2 \theta) = 1$

or $$r^2 = \frac{1}{b^2\cos^2\theta+a^2\sin^2\theta} \quad \text{... (4)}$$

To find the points of intersection of (3) and (4), eliminating r^2, we get

$$a^2 \cos^2 \theta + b^2 \sin^2 \theta = b^2 \cos^2 \theta + a^2 \sin^2 \theta$$

or $$(b^2 - a^2) \sin^2 \theta = (b^2 - a^2) \cos^2 \theta$$

or $$\sin^2 \theta = \cos^2 \theta$$

or $$\tan^2 \theta = 1$$

or at C, $$\tan \theta = 1$$

$\therefore$ $$\theta = \frac{\pi}{4}$$

Since on interchanging x and y in (1), we get (2).

$\therefore$ The area $OB'CB$ is symmetrical about the line

$$OC\ (y = x \text{ or } \theta = \pi/4)$$

$\therefore$ Required common area

$$= 4 \times \text{area } OB'CB$$

$$= 4 \times 2 \text{ area } OB'C$$

$$= 8\int_0^{\pi/4}\frac{1}{2}r^2 d\theta$$

$$= 4\int_0^{\pi/4}\frac{1}{b^2\cos^2\theta+a^2\sin^2\theta}d\theta \quad \text{[from (4)]}$$

$$= 4\int_0^{\pi/4} \frac{\sec^2\theta\, d\theta}{b^2 + a^2\tan^2\theta}$$ [dividing the numerator and denominator by $\cos^2\theta$]

[Put $\tan\theta = t$
$\therefore\ \sec^2\theta\, d\theta = dt$
when $\theta = 0,\ t = 0$
when $\theta = \pi/4,\ t = 1$]

$$= 4\int_0^1 \frac{dt}{b^2 + a^2t^2}$$

$$= \frac{4}{a^2}\int_0^1 \frac{dt}{t^2 + \dfrac{b^2}{a^2}}$$

$$= \frac{4}{a^2}\cdot\frac{1}{\left(\dfrac{b}{a}\right)}\tan^{-1}\left[\frac{t}{\left(\dfrac{b}{a}\right)}\right]_0^1$$

$$= \frac{4}{ab}\left[\tan^{-1}\left(\frac{a}{b}\right) - \tan^{-1}(0)\right]$$

$$= \frac{4}{ab}\tan^{-1}\left(\frac{a}{b}\right)$$

EXERCISE 13.3

1. Find the area included between the cycloid

$$x = a\,(\theta - \sin\theta),\ y = a\,(1 - \cos\theta)$$

and its base.

2. Find the area of the astroid $x = a\cos^3 t,\ y = a\sin^3 t$.

3. Find the whole area of the curve

$$x = a\frac{1-t^2}{1+t^2},\ y = \frac{2at}{1+t^2}$$

4. Find the area of a loop of the curve

$$x = a\sin 2t,\ y = a\sin t$$

5. Find the area of the loop of the curve

$$x = \frac{a\sin 3\theta}{\sin\theta},\ y = \frac{a\sin 3\theta}{\cos\theta}$$

6. Prove that the area of the curve

$$x = a \cos\theta + b \sin\theta + c,$$
$$y = a' \cos\theta + b' \sin\theta + c'$$

is equal to $\pi\,(ab' - a'b)$.

7. Find the area between the following curves and the radii vectors:

(a) $r = a\theta^{-1/2}$, $\theta = \alpha$ to $\theta = \beta$.

(b) $r = ae^{\theta \cot \alpha}$, $\theta = \beta$ to $\theta = \beta + \gamma$ $(\gamma < 2\pi)$.

(c) $r = ae^{m\theta}$, $\theta = \alpha$ to $\theta = \beta$.

(d) $\dfrac{l}{r} = 1 + \cos\theta, \theta = 0 \text{ to } \theta = \alpha$.

8. Find the whole area of the

(a) circle $r = 2a \cos\theta$

(b) cardioid $r = a\,(1 - \cos\theta)$

(c) cardioid $r = a\,(1 + \cos\theta)$

(d) curve $r^2 = a^2 \cos^2\theta + b^2 \sin^2\theta$

(e) curve $r = 3 + 2 \cos\theta$.

9. Find the area of a loop of the curve

(a) $r = a \sin 3\theta$ (three leaved rose)

(b) $r = a \cos 2\theta$ (four leaved rose)

(c) $r = a \sin\theta$ (four leaved rose)

Find also the total area in each case.

10. Find the area of a loop of the curve

$$r = a \cos 3\theta + b \sin 3\theta.$$

11. Find the area of one loop of $r = a \cos 4\theta$.

12. Find the area of a loop of the curve

$$r = \sqrt{3} \cos 3\theta + \sin 3\theta.$$

13. Calculate the ratio of the area of the larger to the area of the smaller loop of the curve

$$r = \frac{1}{2} + \cos 2\theta.$$

14. Show that the area contained between the circle $r = a$ and the curve $r = a \cos 5\theta$ is equal to three-fourths of the area of the circle.

15. Find the area of the loop of the following curves:

(a) $(x^2 + y^2)^2 = 4axy^2$ (b) $x^4 + y^4 = 4a^2xy$

(c) $x^5 + y^5 = 5ax^2y^2$ (d) $x^6 + y^6 = a^2x^2y^2$

(e) $x^4 + 3x^2y^2 + 2y^4 = a^2xy$

16. Prove that the area of the loop of the curve $x^3 + y^3 = 3axy$ is three times the area of a loop of the curve $r^2 = a^2 \cos 2\theta$.

17. Prove that the area of the loop of the curve $x^5 + y^5 = 5ax^2y^2$ is five times the area of a loop of the curve $r^2 = a^2 \cos 2\theta$.

18. Prove that the area common to the circles $r = a\sqrt{2}$ and $r = 2a \cos \theta$ is $a^2 (\pi - 1)$.

19. Prove that the area common to the circle $r = a$ and the cardioid $r = a (1 + \cos \theta)$ is

$$a^2\left(\frac{5\pi}{4} - 2\right).$$

20. Find the area outside the circle $r = 2a \cos \theta$ and inside the cardioid $r = a (1 + \cos \theta)$.

21. Find the area inside the circle $r = \sin \theta$ and outside the cardioid $r = 1 - \cos \theta$.

22. Find the area common to the ellipses

$$x^2 + 2y^2 = a^2 \text{ and } 2x^2 + y^2 = a^2.$$

23. Find the ratio of the two parts into which the parabola $2a = r (1 + \cos \theta)$ divides the area of the cardioid

$$r = 2a (1 + \cos \theta).$$

24. Find the area between the curve $r = a (\sec \theta + \cos \theta)$ and its asymptote.

25. Show that the area bounded by the curve $p = f(r)$ and the two radii vectors $r = a$, $r = b$ is

$$\frac{1}{2}\int_a^b \frac{pr}{\sqrt{r^2 - p^2}}\, dr.$$

ANSWERS

EXERCISE 13.3

1. $3\pi a^2$

2. $\dfrac{3\pi a^2}{8}$

3. πa^2

4. $\dfrac{a^2}{3}$

5. $\dfrac{3\sqrt{3}\,a^2}{2}$

7. (a) $\dfrac{a^2}{2}\log\dfrac{\beta}{\alpha}$

(b) $\dfrac{1}{4}a^2\tan\alpha\, e^{2\beta\cot\alpha}\left(e^{2\gamma\cot\alpha}-1\right)$

(c) $\dfrac{a^2}{4m}\left(e^{2m\beta}-e^{2m\alpha}\right)$

(d) $\dfrac{1}{4}e^2\left(\tan\dfrac{\alpha}{2}+\dfrac{1}{3}\tan^3\dfrac{\alpha}{2}\right)$

8. (a) πa^2

(b) $\dfrac{3\pi a^2}{2}$

(c) $\dfrac{3\pi a^2}{2}$

(d) $\left(a^2+b^2\right)\dfrac{\pi}{2}$

(e) 11π

9. (a) $\dfrac{\pi a^2}{12}, \dfrac{\pi a^2}{4}$

(b) $\dfrac{\pi a^2}{8}, \dfrac{\pi a^2}{2}$

(c) $\dfrac{\pi a^2}{8}, \dfrac{\pi a^2}{2}$

10. $\dfrac{\pi\left(a^2+b^2\right)}{12}$

11. $\dfrac{\pi a^2}{6}$

12. $\dfrac{\pi}{3}$

13. $\dfrac{4\pi+3\Gamma 3}{2\pi-3\Gamma 3}$

15. (a) $\dfrac{\pi a^2}{4}$

(b) $\dfrac{\pi a^2}{2}$

(c) $\dfrac{5a^2}{2}$ (d) $\dfrac{\pi a^2}{12}$

(e) $\dfrac{a^2}{4}\log 2$

20. $\dfrac{\pi a^2}{2}$ **21.** $1-\dfrac{\pi}{4}$

22. $2\sqrt{2}\,a^2\tan^{-1}\left(\dfrac{1}{\sqrt{2}}\right)$ **23.** $\dfrac{9\pi-16}{9\pi+16}$

24. πa^2

14

Determination of Lengths (Rectification)

14.1 Rectification

Definition. The process of finding the length of an arc of a curve between the two given points on it is called *rectification.*

14.2 Arc Formula for Cartesian Equations

To find the length of the arc of the curve $y = f(x)$ between the points where $x = a$, $y = b$.

Or

To show that the length of the arc of the curve $y = f(x)$ between the points where $x = a$, $y = b$ is given by

$$\int_a^b \sqrt{1 + \left(\frac{dy}{dx}\right)^2}\, dx$$

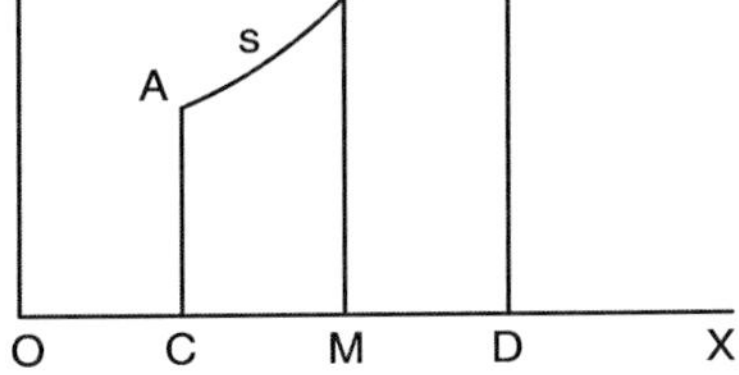

where y and $\frac{dy}{dx}$ are continuous and single valued functions in the interval $a \le x \le b$ and the integrand does not change sign in the interval.

Let AB be the curve $y = f(x)$ where A, B are the points whose abscissae are a and b respectively and CA, DB are their ordinates.

Let $P(x, y)$ be any point on the curve. Draw PM perpendicular to x-axis.

If s denotes the length of the arc AP measured from the fixed point A to the variable point P, then s is clearly a function of x.

From differential calculus, we know that

$$\frac{ds}{dx} = \sqrt{1+\left(\frac{dy}{dx}\right)^2} \qquad \ldots (1)$$

$$\therefore \quad \int_a^b \sqrt{1+\left(\frac{dy}{dx}\right)^2}\, dx = \int_a^b \frac{ds}{dx}\, dx$$

$$= [s]_a^b$$

$$= (\text{value of } s \text{ at } x = b) - (\text{value of } s \text{ at } x = a)$$

$$= \text{arc } AB - 0$$

$$= \text{arc } AB$$

Hence, $$\text{arc } AB = \int_a^b \sqrt{1+\left(\frac{dy}{dx}\right)^2}\, dx$$

Note 1. From (1), we have

$$s = \int \sqrt{1+\left(\frac{dy}{dx}\right)^2}\, dx$$

Note 2. If the equation of the curve is of the form $x = f(y)$, then the length of the arc between the points, where $y = c$, $y = d$ is given by

$$\int_c^d \sqrt{1+\left(\frac{dy}{dx}\right)^2}\, dy$$

14.3 Arc Formula for Parametric Equations

To show that the length of the arc of the curve $x = f(t)$, $y = \phi(t)$ between the points where $t = a$, $t = b$ is given by

$$\int_a^b \sqrt{\left(\frac{dx}{dt}\right)^2 + \left(\frac{dy}{dt}\right)^2}\, dt$$

where x and y are continuous and single-valued functions of t in the interval $a \le t \le b$.

Let AB be the curve $x = f(t)$, $y = \phi(t)$ where A, B are the two points $t = a$, $t = b$ respectively.

Let $P(x, y)$ be any point on the curve. Draw AC, BD and PM perpendicular on OX.

If s denotes the length of the arc from the fixed point A to the variable point P, then s is clearly a function of t.

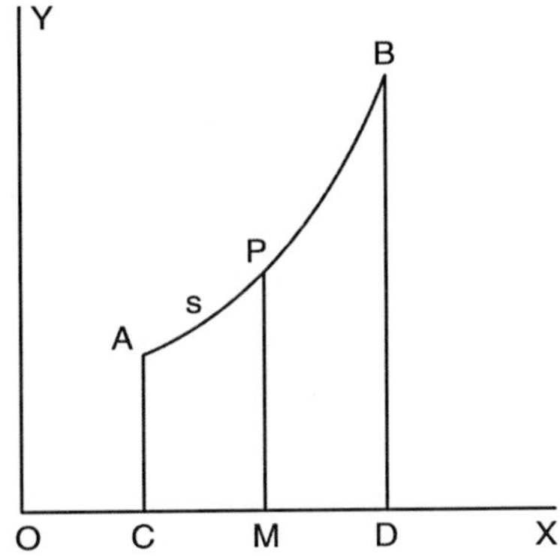

From differential calculus, we know that

$$\frac{ds}{dt} = \sqrt{\left(\frac{dx}{dt}\right)^2 + \left(\frac{dy}{dt}\right)^2}$$

$$\therefore \int_a^b \sqrt{\left(\frac{dx}{dt}\right)^2 + \left(\frac{dy}{dt}\right)^2}\, dt = \int_a^b \frac{ds}{dt}\, dt$$

$$= (s)_a^b$$

$$= (\text{value of } s \text{ when } t = b) - (\text{value of } s \text{ when } t = a)$$

$$= \text{arc } AB - 0$$

$$= \text{arc } AB$$

Hence, $$\text{arc } AB = \int_a^b \sqrt{\left(\frac{dx}{dt}\right)^2 + \left(\frac{dy}{dt}\right)^2}\, dt \qquad \dots (1)$$

Note 1. It has been assumed here that the integration does not change sign in the range of integration

$$a \le t \le b$$

Note 2. From (1),

$$s = \int \sqrt{\left(\frac{dx}{dt}\right)^2 + \left(\frac{dy}{dt}\right)^2}\, dt$$

14.4 Arc Formula for Polar Equations

To show that the length of the arc of the curve $r = f(\theta)$ between the points, where $\theta = \alpha$, $\theta = \beta$ is

$$\int_{\alpha}^{\beta}\sqrt{r^2+\left(\frac{dr}{d\theta}\right)^2}\,d\theta$$

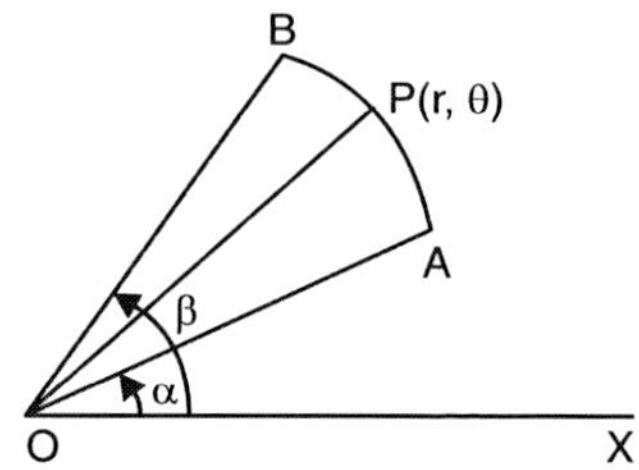

Let *AB* be the curve $r = f(\theta)$ and *A*, *B* the points where $\theta = \alpha$, $\theta = \beta$ respectively.

Let $P(r, \theta)$ be any point on the curve. If s denotes the length of the arc measured from the fixed point *A* to the variable point *P*, then clearly s is a function of θ.

From Differential Calculus, we know that

$$\frac{ds}{d\theta} = \sqrt{r^2+\left(\frac{dr}{d\theta}\right)^2} \qquad \dots (1)$$

$$\therefore \int_{\alpha}^{\beta}\sqrt{r^2+\left(\frac{dr}{d\theta}\right)^2}\,d\theta = \int_{\alpha}^{\beta}\frac{ds}{d\theta}\,d\theta$$

$$= (s)_{\alpha}^{\beta}$$

$$= (\text{value of } s \text{ when } \theta = \beta) - (\text{value of } s \text{ when } \theta = \alpha)$$

$$= \text{arc } AB - 0$$

$$= \text{arc } AB$$

Hence, $$\text{arc } AB = \int_{\alpha}^{\beta}\sqrt{r^2+\left(\frac{dr}{d\theta}\right)^2}\,d\theta$$

Note 1. From (1),

$$s = \int\sqrt{r^2+\left(\frac{dr}{d\theta}\right)^2}\,d\theta$$

Note 2. When the equation of the curve is of the form $\theta = f(r)$, the length of the arc from r_1 to r_2 is given by

$$\int_{r_1}^{r_2}\sqrt{1+r^2\left(\frac{d\theta}{dr}\right)^2}\,dr$$

14.5 Arc Formula for Pedal Equations

To show that the length of the arc of the curve $p = f(r)$ between the points where $r = a$, $r = b$ is

$$\int_a^b \frac{r\,dr}{\sqrt{r^2 - p^2}}$$

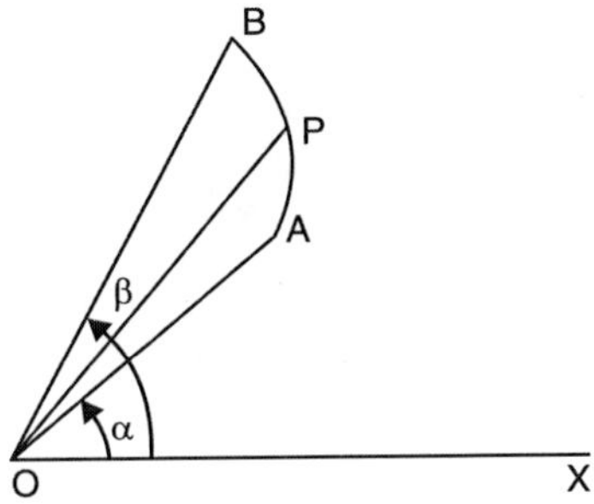

Let AB be the curve $p = f(r)$ and A, B be the points where $r = a$, $r = b$.

Let $P\,(p, r)$ be any point on the curve.

If s denotes the length of the arc AP measured from a fixed point A to the variable point P, then s is clearly a function of r.

From differential calculus, we know that

$$p = r \sin\phi \qquad \text{... (1)}$$

or $$\sin\phi = p/r$$

Also $$\frac{ds}{dr} = \sec\phi = \frac{1}{\cos\phi}$$

$$= \frac{1}{\sqrt{1-\sin^2\phi}}$$

$$= \frac{1}{\sqrt{1-\dfrac{p^2}{r^2}}}$$

$$= \frac{r}{\sqrt{r^2 - p^2}}$$

$$\therefore \quad \int_a^b \frac{r\,dr}{\sqrt{r^2-p^2}} = \int_a^b \frac{ds}{dr}\,dr = (s)_a^b$$

= (value of s when $r = b$) – (value of s when $r = a$)

= arc AB – 0

= arc AB

Hence, $$\text{arc } AB = \int_a^b \frac{r\,dr}{\sqrt{r^2 - p^2}}$$

14.6 Intrinsic Equation of a Curve (Definition)

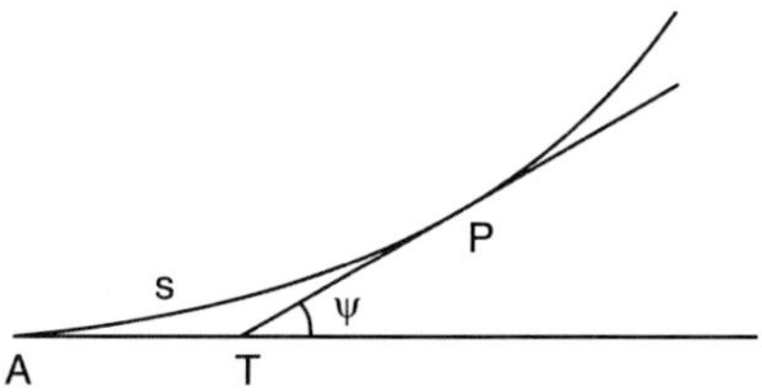

If s be length of the arc of a curve measured from a fixed point A on it to any point P on it, and ψ, the angle which the tangent at P to the curve makes with a fixed line (usually the tangent at the fixed point A) then the relation between s and ψ is called the intrinsic equation of the curve.

14.7 To find the intrinsic equation of a curve from the cartesian equation

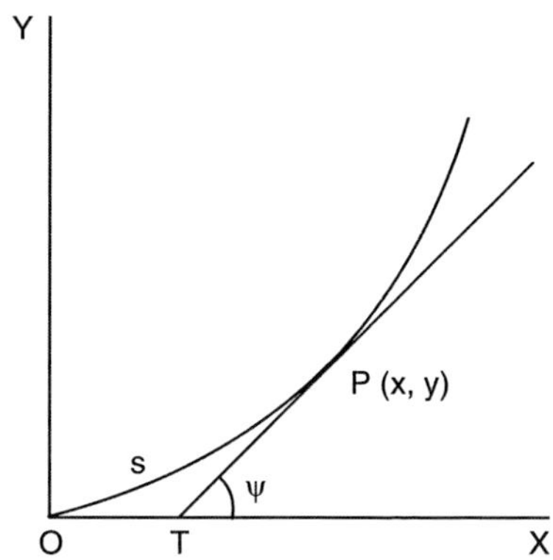

Let the cartesian equation of the curve be $y = f(x)$.

Let $P(x, y)$ be any point on it such that arc $OP = s$, O being the fixed point on the curve.

Let OT, the tangent at O, be taken as the x-axis and O as the origin. Let the tangent at P make an angle $PTX = \psi$ with x-axis.

$$\text{Now} \quad \tan \psi = \frac{dy}{dx} = f'(x) \qquad \dots (1)$$

$$\therefore \quad s = \int_0^x \sqrt{1 + \left(\frac{dy}{dx}\right)^2}\, dx$$

$$= \int_0^x \sqrt{1 + \{f'(x)\}^2}\, dx$$

$$= F(x) \text{ (say)} \qquad \dots (2)$$

Eliminating x from (1) and (2), we get a relation between s and ψ, which is the required intrinsic equation.

14.8 To obtain the intrinsic equation of a curve from the parametric equations

Let the parametric equations of the curve be

$$x = f(t),\ y = \phi(t) \quad \dots (1)$$

Let $P(x, y)$ be any point on it, such that arc $OP = s$, O being a fixed point on the curve. Let OT, the tangent at O to the curve, be taken as the x-axis, and O as the origin. Let the tangent at P make an angle $PTX = \psi$ with x-axis.

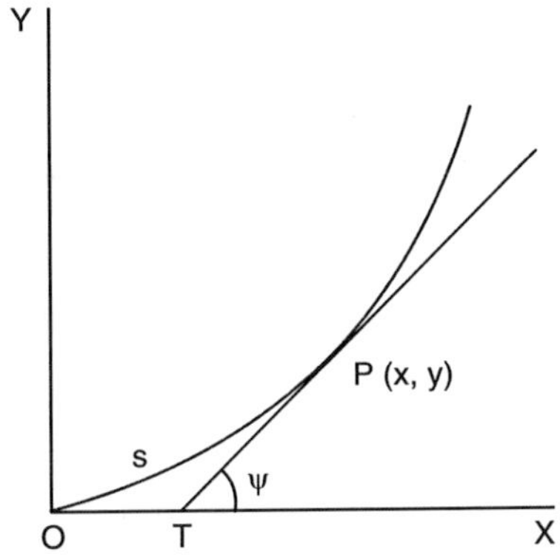

From (1),

$$\frac{dx}{dt} = f'(t), \frac{dy}{dt} = \phi'(t)$$

$$\therefore \quad \tan\psi = \frac{dy}{dx} = \frac{dy/dt}{dx/dt} = \frac{\phi'(t)}{f'(t)} \quad \dots (2)$$

Also

$$s = \int_0^t \sqrt{\left(\frac{dx}{dt}\right)^2 + \left(\frac{dy}{dt}\right)^2}\, dt$$

$$= \int_0^t \sqrt{\{f'(t)\}^2 + \{\phi(t)\}^2}\, dt$$

$$= F(t) \text{ say} \quad \dots (3)$$

Eliminating t from (2) and (3), we get a relation between s and ψ, which is the intrinsic equation of the curve.

14.9 To obtain the intrinsic equation of a curve from the polar equation

Let the polar equation of the curve be $r = f(\theta)$.

Let O be the pole, and the initial line be the tangent to the curve at the pole from which the arc is measured.

Let $P(r, \theta)$ be any point on the curve and PT, the tangent at P meeting the initial line in T.

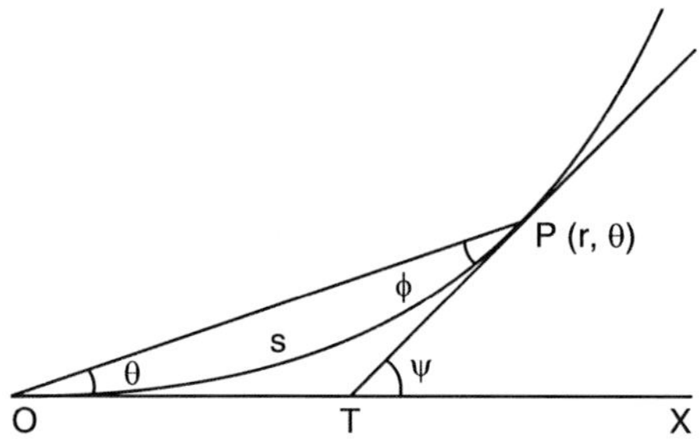

Let arc $OP = s$ and $\angle XTP = \psi$

$$\therefore \quad \frac{dr}{d\theta} = f'(\theta)$$

$$\therefore \quad s = \int_0^\theta \sqrt{r^2 + \left(\frac{dr}{d\theta}\right)^2}\, d\theta$$

$$= \int_0^\theta \sqrt{\{f(\theta)\}^2 + \{f'(\theta)\}^2}\, d\theta$$

$$= F(\theta) \text{ say} \qquad \ldots (1)$$

If ϕ be the angle between the tangent at P and its radius vector, then

$$\tan\phi = r\frac{d\theta}{dr} = \frac{r}{\frac{dr}{d\theta}} = \frac{f(\theta)}{f'(\theta)} \qquad \ldots (2)$$

Also $\qquad \psi = \theta + \phi \qquad \ldots (3)$

Eliminating θ, ϕ from (1), (2) and (3), we get a relation in s, ψ which is the intrinsic equation of the curve.

How to eliminate θ and ϕ?

First find the value of ϕ in terms of θ from (2), then find the value of ψ in terms of θ from (3), finally eliminate θ between the equation so obtained and the equation (1).

14.10 To obtain the intrinsic equation of a curve from the pedal equation

Let the pedal equation of the curve be $p = f(r)$.

$$\therefore \quad \frac{ds}{d\psi} = \rho = r\frac{dr}{dp} = \frac{r}{\frac{dp}{dr}} = \frac{r}{f'(r)} \qquad \ldots (1)$$

Also $$s = \int_0^r \frac{r}{\sqrt{r^2 - p^2}}\,dr$$

$$= \int_0^r \frac{r}{\sqrt{r^2 - \{f(r)\}^2}}\,dr \qquad \text{... (2)}$$

Eliminating r from (1) and (2), we get a relation between s and $\frac{ds}{d\psi}$, say $\frac{ds}{d\psi} = f_1(s)$

$$\therefore \qquad \frac{d\psi}{ds} = \frac{1}{f_1(s)}$$

or $$d\psi = \frac{ds}{f_1(s)}$$

$$\therefore \qquad \psi = \int \frac{ds}{f_1(s)}$$

which on integration gives us a relation between ψ and s i.e. the intrinsic equation of the curve.

ILLUSTRATIVE EXAMPLES

Example 1. Find the length of the arc of the curve

$$y = \log \frac{e^x - 1}{e^x + 1} \text{ from } x = 1 \text{ to } x = 2.$$

Solution : The equation of the curve is

$$y = \log \frac{e^x - 1}{e^x + 1}$$

$$\therefore \qquad y = \log (e^x - 1) - \log (e^x + 1)$$

$$\therefore \qquad \frac{dy}{dx} = \frac{e^x}{e^x - 1} - \frac{e^x}{e^x + 1}$$

$$= e^x \left[\frac{1}{e^x - 1} - \frac{1}{e^x + 1} \right]$$

$$= e^x \left[\frac{e^x + 1 - e^x + 1}{(e^x - 1)(e^x + 1)} \right]$$

$$= \frac{2e^x}{e^{2x} - 1}$$

$\therefore$ Required length of arc from $x = 1$ to $x = 2$ is

$$= \int_1^2 \sqrt{1 + \left(\frac{dy}{dx}\right)^2}\, dx$$

$$= \int_1^2 \sqrt{1 + \left(\frac{4e^{2x}}{\left(e^{2x} - 1\right)^2}\right)}\, dx$$

$$= \int_1^2 \sqrt{\frac{\left(e^{2x} - 1\right)^2 + 4e^{2x}}{\left(e^{2x} - 1\right)^2}}\, dx$$

$$= \int_1^2 \sqrt{\frac{\left(e^{2x} + 1\right)^2}{\left(e^{2x} - 1\right)^2}}\, dx$$

$$= \int_1^2 \frac{e^{2x} + 1}{e^{2x} - 1}\, dx$$

$$= \int_1^2 \frac{e^{x} + e^{-x}}{e^{x} - e^{-x}}\, dx$$ [Dividing the numerator and denominator by e^x]

$$= \left[\log\left(e^x - e^{-x}\right)\right]_1^2$$

$= \log (e^2 - e^{-2}) - \log (e - e^{-1})$

$= \log (e^2 - 1/e^2) - \log (e - 1/e)$

$= \log \{(e + 1/e)(e - 1/e)\} - \log (e - 1/e)$

$= \log (e + 1/e) + \log (e - 1/e) - \log (e - 1/e)$

$= \log (e + 1/e)$

Example 2. Find the length of the arc of the parabola $x^2 = 4ay$, from the vertex to an extremity of the latus rectum.

Solution : Let O be the vertex and L, an extremity of the latus rectum of the parabola $x^2 = 4ay$ or $y = \dfrac{1}{4a}x^2$

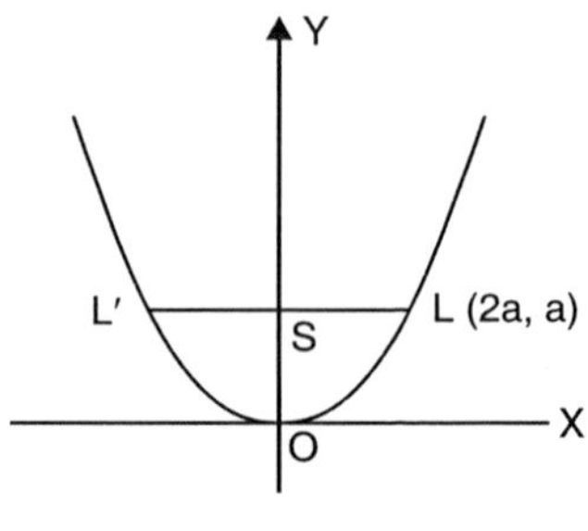

$$\therefore \qquad \frac{dy}{dx} = \frac{2x}{4a} = \frac{x}{2a}$$

For the length of the arc from O (0, 0) to L (2a, a), x varies from 0 to 2a.

$\therefore$ Required length of arc OL

$$= \int_0^{2a} \sqrt{1+\left(\frac{dy}{dx}\right)^2}\, dx$$

$$= \int_0^{2a} \sqrt{1+\frac{x^2}{a^2}}\, dx$$

$$= \frac{1}{2a}\int_0^{2a} \sqrt{x^2+4a^2}\, dx$$

$$= \frac{1}{2a}\left[\frac{1}{2}x\sqrt{x^2+4a^2}+\frac{4a^2}{2}\sinh^{-1}\left(\frac{x}{2a}\right)\right]_0^{2a}$$

$$= \frac{1}{2a}\left[\frac{2a}{2}\sqrt{4a^2+4a^2}+2a^2\sinh^{-1}(1)-0\right]$$

$$= \frac{1}{2a}\left[a\cdot 2\sqrt{2}\,a+2a^2\log\left(1+\sqrt{1+1}\right)\right]$$

$$\left[\because \sinh^{-1}x=\log\left(x+\sqrt{x^2+1}\right)\right]$$

$$= a\left[\sqrt{2}+\log\left(\sqrt{2}+1\right)\right]$$

Example 3. Show that the whole length of the curve

$x^2(a^2 - x^2) = 8a^2y^2$ is $\pi a\sqrt{2}$.

Solution : *To trace the curve roughly to find the limits of integration.*

(i) The curve is symmetrical about both the axes.

(ii) The curve passes through the origin and the tangents at the origin are given by

$$a^2x^2 = 8a^2y^2$$

or $$y = \pm\frac{1}{2\sqrt{2}}x,$$

showing that origin is a node.

(iii) The curve meets the x-axis where $y = 0$, so putting $y = 0$ in the given equation, we get

$$x^2(a^2 - x^2) = 0$$

or $$x = 0, \pm a$$

Hence the curve meets the x-axis at $(0, 0)$, $(a, 0)$, $(-a, 0)$.

The curve meets the y-axis where $x = 0$. So putting $x = 0$ in the given equation, we get

$$8a^2y^2 = 0$$

i.e. $$y = 0$$

i.e. at the origin (0, 0).

Shifting the origin to $(a, 0)$, the given equation transforms to

$$(x + a)^2 [a^2 - (x + a)^2] = 8a^2y^2$$

or $$8a^2y^2 = (x + a)^2 (-x^2 - 2ax)$$

$$= - x (x + 2a) (x + a)^2$$

and the tangent at the new origin is $-2a^3 x = 0$ or $x = 0$ i.e. the new y-axis.

Thus the tangent at $(a, 0)$ is $\parallel$ to y-axis.

(iv) The curve has no asymptotes.

(v) The given curve is

$$y^2 = \frac{1}{8a^2} x^2 (a^2 - x^2) \qquad \text{... (1)}$$

When $x > a$ numerically, y^2 is –ve,

$\therefore$ y is imaginary.

Thus no portion of the curve lies beyond the lines $x = a$, $x = -a$.

The shape of the curve is as shown in the figure. The curve consists of two symmetrical loops.

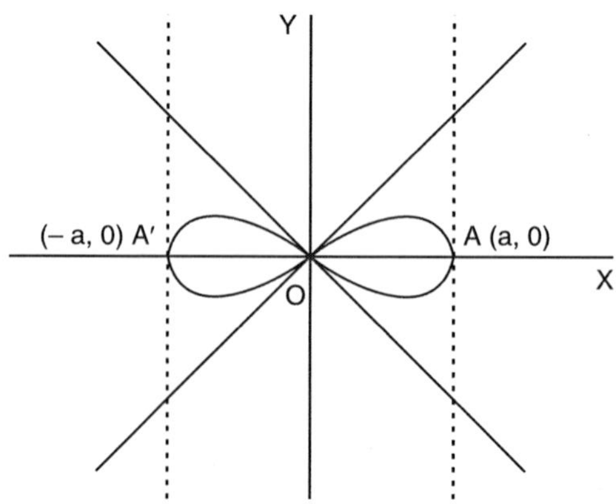

$\therefore$ Whole length of the curve

$$= 2 \times \text{length of a loop}$$

$$= 4 \times \text{arc of loop in first quadrant}$$

For half the loop in the first quadrant, x varies from 0 to a.

From (1)

$$y = \frac{1}{2\sqrt{2}\,a} x\sqrt{a^2 - x^2}$$

$$\therefore \quad \frac{dy}{dx} = \frac{1}{2\sqrt{2}\,a}\left[\sqrt{a^2 - x^2}\cdot 1 + x\cdot\frac{-2x}{2\sqrt{a^2 - x^2}}\right]$$

$$= \frac{1}{2\sqrt{2}\,a}\left[\frac{a^2 - x^2 - x^2}{\sqrt{a^2 - x^2}}\right]$$

$$= \frac{a^2 - 2x^2}{2\sqrt{2}\,a\sqrt{a^2 - x^2}}$$

$$\therefore \quad 1 + \left(\frac{dy}{dx}\right)^2 = 1 + \frac{(a^2 - 2x^2)^2}{8a^2(a^2 - x^2)}$$

$$= \frac{8a^4 - 8a^2x^2 + a^4 + 4x^4 - 4a^2x^2}{8a^2(a^2 - x^2)}$$

$$= \frac{4x^4 - 12a^2x^2 + 9a^4}{8a^2(a^2 - x^2)}$$

$$= \frac{(3a^2 - 2x^2)^2}{8a^2(a^2 - x^2)}$$

$\therefore$ Required whole length of the curve

$$= 4 \text{ arc } OA$$

$$= 4\int_0^a \sqrt{1 + \left(\frac{dy}{dx}\right)^2}\, dx$$

$$= 4\int_0^a \frac{3a^2 - 2x^2}{2\sqrt{2}\,a\sqrt{a^2 - x^2}}\, dx \qquad [\text{Put } x = a\sin\theta \quad \therefore \; dx = a\cos\theta\, d\theta]$$

$$= \frac{4}{2\sqrt{2}\,a}\int_0^{\pi/2} \frac{3a^2 - 2a^2\sin^2\theta}{a\cos\theta}\, a\cos\theta\, d\theta$$

$$= \sqrt{2}\, a \int_0^{\pi/2} [3 - (1 - \cos 2\theta)]\, d\theta$$

$$= \sqrt{2}\, a \int_0^{\pi/2} (2 + \cos 2\theta)\, d\theta$$

$$= \sqrt{2}\, a \left[2\theta + \frac{\sin 2\theta}{2} \right]_0^{\pi/2}$$

$$= \sqrt{2}\, a \left[\pi + \frac{1}{2} \sin \pi - 0 \right]$$

$$= \pi a \sqrt{2}$$

Example 4. Show that the length of an arc of the curve

$$x \sin \theta + y \cos \theta = f'(\theta),\ x \cos \theta - y \sin \theta = f''(\theta)$$

is given by

$$s = f(\theta) + f''(\theta) + c.$$

Solution : The curve is given by

$$x \sin \theta + y \cos \theta = f'(\theta) \quad \text{... (1)}$$

$$x \cos \theta - y \sin \theta = f''(\theta) \quad \text{... (2)}$$

Multiplying (1) by $\sin \theta$ and (2) by $\cos \theta$, and adding,

$$x (\sin^2 \theta + \cos^2 \theta) = \sin \theta\, f'(\theta) + \cos \theta\, f''(\theta)$$

or $$x = \sin \theta\, f'(\theta) + \cos \theta\, f''(\theta) \quad \text{... (3)}$$

Again multiplying (1) by $\cos \theta$ and (2) by $\sin \theta$, and subtracting,

$$y (\cos^2 \theta + \sin^2 \theta) = \cos \theta\, f'(\theta) - \sin \theta\, f''(\theta)$$

or $$y = \cos \theta\, f'(\theta) - \sin \theta\, f''(\theta) \quad \text{... (4)}$$

From (3)

$$\frac{dx}{d\theta} = \sin \theta\, f''(\theta) + f'(\theta) \cos \theta + \cos \theta\, f'''(\theta) - \sin \theta\, f''(\theta)$$

$$= [f'(\theta) + f'''(\theta)] \cos \theta$$

From (4)

$$\frac{dy}{d\theta} = \cos \theta\, f''(\theta) - \sin \theta\, f'(\theta) - \cos \theta\, f''(\theta) - \sin \theta\, f'''(\theta)$$

$$= -\, [f'(\theta) + f'''(\theta)] \sin \theta$$

$$\therefore \quad \left(\frac{dx}{d\theta}\right)^2 + \left(\frac{dy}{d\theta}\right)^2 = [f'(\theta) + f'''(\theta)]^2 (\cos^2\theta + \sin^2\theta)$$

$$= [f'(\theta) + f'''(\theta)]^2 \qquad \text{... (5)}$$

$\therefore$ The length of the arc is given by

$$s = \int \sqrt{\left(\frac{dx}{d\theta}\right)^2 + \left(\frac{dy}{d\theta}\right)^2}\, d\theta$$

$$= \int [f'(\theta) + f'''(\theta)]\, d\theta$$

$$= f(\theta) + f''(\theta) + c$$

where c is an arbitrary constant.

Example 5. Show that in the ellipse

$$x = a\cos\theta,\ y = b\sin\theta,$$

the perimeter may be expressed as

$$2a\pi\left[1 - \left(\frac{1}{2}\right)^2 \frac{e^2}{1} - \left(\frac{1.3}{2.4}\right)^2 \frac{e^4}{3} - \left(\frac{1.3.5}{2.4.6}\right)^2 \frac{e^6}{5} - .....\right]$$

where e is the eccentricity of the ellipse.

Solution : The equations of the ellipse are $x = a\cos\theta$, $y = b\sin\theta$.

$$\therefore \quad \frac{dx}{d\theta} = -a\sin\theta,$$

$$\frac{dy}{d\theta} = b\cos\theta$$

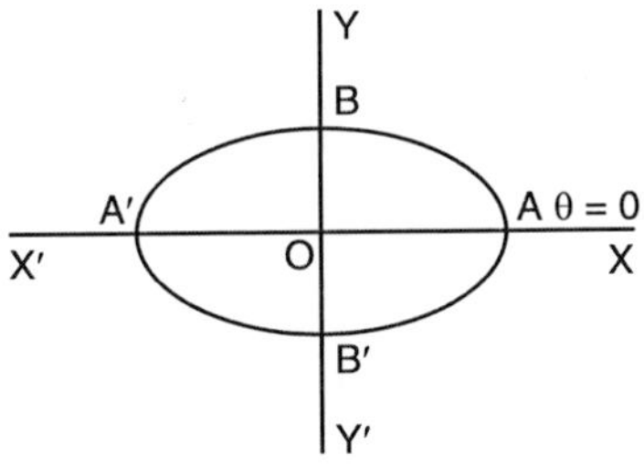

The ellipse is symmetrical about both the axes, and in the first quadrant, θ varies from 0 to $\pi/2$.

$\therefore$ Perimeter of the ellipse

$$= 4 \times \text{length of arc in first quadrant}$$

$$= 4\int_0^{\pi/2} \sqrt{\left(\frac{dx}{d\theta}\right)^2 + \left(\frac{dy}{d\theta}\right)^2}\, d\theta$$

$$= 4\int_0^{\pi/2} \sqrt{a^2\sin^2\theta + b^2\cos^2\theta}\, d\theta$$

$$= 4\int_0^{\pi/2} \sqrt{a^2 \sin^2\theta + a^2(1-e^2)\cos^2\theta}\, d\theta$$

$$= 4\int_0^{\pi/2} \sqrt{a^2 - a^2e^2\cos^2\theta}\, d\theta$$

$$= 4a\int_0^{\pi/2} \sqrt{1 - e^2\cos^2\theta}\, d\theta$$

$$= 4a\int_0^{\pi/2} (1 - e^2\cos^2\theta)^{+1/2}\, d\theta$$

$$= 4a\left[\int_0^{\pi/2}\left\{1 + \frac{1}{2}(-e^2\cos^2\theta) + \frac{\frac{1}{2}\left(\frac{1}{2}-1\right)}{2!}(-e^2\cos^2\theta)^2 + \frac{\frac{1}{2}\left(\frac{1}{2}-1\right)\left(\frac{1}{2}-2\right)}{3!}(-e^2\cos^2\theta)^3 + \ldots\right\}\right] d\theta$$

[on expanding by binomial theorem]

$$= 4a\int_0^{\pi/2}\left\{1 - \frac{e^2\cos^2\theta}{2} - \frac{e^4\cos^4\theta}{2.4} - \frac{1.3}{2.4.6}e^6\cos^6\theta - \ldots\ldots\right\} d\theta$$

$$= 4a\left[\int_0^{\pi/2} d\theta - \frac{e^2}{2}\int_0^{\pi/2}\cos^2\theta\, d\theta - \frac{e^4}{2.4}\int_0^{\pi/2}\cos^4\theta\, d\theta - \frac{1.3}{2.4.6}\int_0^{\pi/2} e^6\cos^6\theta\, d\theta - \ldots\ldots\right]$$

$$= 4a\left[\frac{\pi}{2} - \frac{e^2}{2}\cdot\frac{1}{2}\cdot\frac{\pi}{2} - \frac{1}{2.4}e^4\frac{3}{4}\cdot\frac{1}{2}\cdot\frac{\pi}{2} - \frac{1.3}{2.4.6}e^6\frac{5.3.1}{6.4.2}\frac{\pi}{2}\ldots\ldots\right]$$

$$= 4a\cdot\frac{\pi}{2}\left[1 - \frac{1}{2^2}e^2 - \frac{1.3}{2^2\cdot 4^2}e^4 - \frac{1^2\cdot 3^2\cdot 5^2}{2^2\cdot 4^2\cdot 6^2}e^6 - \ldots\ldots\right]$$

$$= 2a\pi\left[1 - \left(\frac{1}{2}\right)^2 e^2 - \left(\frac{1.3}{2.4}\right)^2\frac{e^4}{3} - \left(\frac{1.3.5}{2.4.6}\right)^2\frac{e^6}{5} - \ldots\ldots\right]$$

Example 6. Find the entire length of the cardioid $r = a(1 + \cos\theta)$ and show that the arc of the upper half is bisected by $\theta = \pi/3$.

Solution : The equation of the curve is

$$r = a(1 + \cos\theta) \qquad \text{... (1)}$$

(i) Since the equation remains unchanged on changing θ to $-\theta$, the curve is symmetrical about the initial line.

(ii) Since $|\cos\theta| \le 1$, $\therefore |r| \le 2a$.

Thus the curve lies entirely within the circle $r = 2a$.

(iii) Putting $r = 0$, we get $1 + \cos\theta = 0$

or $\cos\theta = -1 = \cos\pi$

$\therefore \quad \theta = \pi$

Hence the curve passes through the pole and the tangent at the pole is $\theta = \pi$.

(iv) The various values of r for some particular values of θ are :

θ :	0	$\frac{\pi}{3}$	$\frac{\pi}{2}$	$\frac{2\pi}{3}$	π
r :	$2a$	$\frac{3a}{2}$	a	$\frac{a}{2}$	0

Thus the shape of the curve is as shown in the figure. For the upper half of the curve, θ varies from 0 to π.

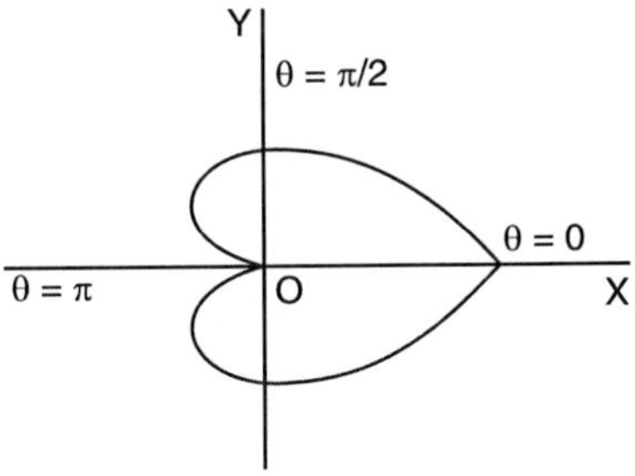

From (1),

$$\frac{dr}{d\theta} = -a\sin\theta$$

$$\therefore r^2 + \left(\frac{dr}{d\theta}\right)^2 = a^2(1 + \cos\theta)^2 + a^2\sin^2\theta$$

$$= a^2(1 + \cos^2\theta + 2\cos\theta + \sin^2\theta)$$

$$= a^2(2 + 2\cos\theta)$$

$$= 2a^2(1 + \cos\theta)$$

$$= 2a^2 \cdot 2\cos^2\theta/2$$

$$= 4a^2\cos^2\theta/2$$

$\therefore$ Required entire length of the curve

$$= 2\int_0^{\pi} \sqrt{r^2 + \left(\frac{dr}{d\theta}\right)^2}\, d\theta$$

$$= 2\int_0^{\pi} 2a \cos\frac{\theta}{2}\, d\theta$$

$$= 4a\left(\frac{\sin\frac{\theta}{2}}{\frac{1}{2}}\right)_0^{\pi} = 8a$$

Now, length of the upper half of the curve $= \frac{1}{2} \times 8a = 4a.$

Also length of the arc from $\theta = 0$ to $\theta = \pi/3$.

$$= \int_0^{\pi/3} \sqrt{r^2 + \left(\frac{dr}{d\theta}\right)^2}\, d\theta$$

$$= \int_0^{\pi/3} 2a \cos\frac{\theta}{2}\, d\theta$$

$$= 2a\left(\frac{\sin\frac{\theta}{2}}{\frac{1}{2}}\right)_0^{\pi/3} = 2a$$

$$= \frac{1}{2} \times 4a$$

$$= \frac{1}{2} \times \text{length of the upper half of the curve}$$

Example 7. Prove that the perimeter of the lemniscate

$$r^2 = a^2 \cos 2\theta \text{ is } \frac{a}{2\pi}\left(\Gamma\frac{1}{4}\right)^2.$$

Solution : Equation of the curve is

$$r^2 = a^2 \cos 2\theta \qquad \text{... (1)}$$

It is symmetrical about the pole, and the lines $\theta = 0$ and $\theta = \frac{\pi}{2}$.

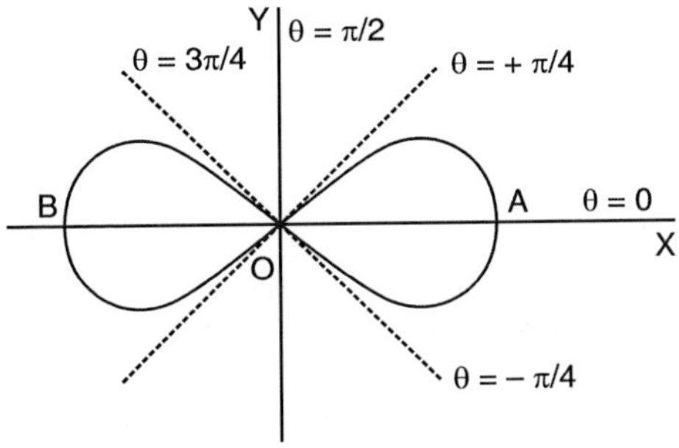

The curve passes through the pole and the tangents at pole are given by

$$\cos 2\theta = 0$$

i.e. $$2\theta = \frac{\pi}{2}, \frac{3\pi}{2}$$

i.e. $$\theta = \frac{\pi}{4}, \frac{3\pi}{4}$$

It has no asymptotes.

$\because$ Greatest value of $\cos 2\theta = 1$

$\therefore$ Greatest value of $r^2 = a^2$

$\Rightarrow \quad -a \leq r \leq a$

When $\theta = 0$, $r = a$

When $\theta = \pi/4$, $r = 0$

As θ increases from 0 to $\pi/4$, r is +ve and decreasing. When $\pi/4 < \theta < \pi/2$, r^2 is –ve.

$\therefore$ r is imaginary.

Thus the shape of the curve is as shown in the figure.

Taking logarithm, (1) becomes

$$2 \log r = 2 \log a + \log \cos 2\theta$$

Differentiating *w.r.t.* θ, we get

$$\frac{2}{r}\frac{dr}{d\theta} = 0 + \frac{1}{\cos 2\theta}(-2 \sin 2\theta)$$

$$\Rightarrow \quad \frac{1}{r}\frac{dr}{d\theta} = -\tan 2\theta$$

$$\Rightarrow \qquad \frac{dr}{d\theta} = -r \tan 2\theta$$

Perimeter of lemniscate

$$= 4 \times \text{arc } OA \text{ in the first quadrant}$$

$$= 4\int_0^{\pi/4} \sqrt{r^2 + \left(\frac{dr}{d\theta}\right)^2}\, d\theta$$

$$= 4\int_0^{\pi/4} \sqrt{r^2 + r^2 \tan^2 2\theta\, d\theta}$$

$$= 4\int_0^{\pi/4} \sqrt{r^2 \sec^2 2\theta}\, d\theta$$

$$= 4\int_0^{\pi/2} \sqrt{a^2 \cos 2\theta \sec^2 2\theta}\, d\theta$$

$$= 4a\int_0^{\pi/2} \sqrt{\sec 2\theta}\, d\theta$$

[Put $2\theta = \phi$

$\therefore \quad \theta = \phi/2$

$\therefore \quad d\theta = \frac{1}{2}\, d\phi$

when $\theta = 0,\ \phi = 0$

when $\theta = \theta/4,\ \phi = \pi/2$]

$\therefore$ Perimeter of lemniscate

$$= 4a\int_0^{\pi/2} \sqrt{\sec \phi}\, \frac{d\phi}{2}$$

$$= 2a\int_0^{\pi/2} \sin^0 \phi \cos^{-1/2} \phi\, d\phi$$

$$= 2a \frac{\Gamma\left(\frac{0+1}{2}\right)\Gamma\left(\frac{-\frac{1}{2}+1}{2}\right)}{2\Gamma\left(\frac{0-\frac{1}{2}+2}{2}\right)}$$

$$= 2a \frac{\Gamma\frac{1}{2}\,\Gamma\frac{1}{4}}{2\Gamma\frac{3}{4}}$$

$$= \frac{a\Gamma\frac{1}{2}\cdot\Gamma\frac{1}{4}\cdot\Gamma\frac{1}{4}}{\Gamma\left(1-\frac{1}{4}\right)\Gamma\frac{1}{4}}$$

$$= \frac{4a\sqrt{\pi}\left(\Gamma\frac{1}{4}\right)^2}{\dfrac{\pi}{\sin \pi/4}}$$

$$= \frac{a\sqrt{\pi}}{\pi\sqrt{2}}\left(\Gamma\frac{1}{4}\right)^2$$

$$= \frac{a}{\sqrt{2\pi}}\left(\Gamma\frac{1}{4}\right)^2$$

Example 8. Show that the intrinsic equation of the curve

$$r = a\,(1 + \cos\theta) \text{ is}$$

$$s = 4a \sin\left(\frac{\psi}{3} - \frac{\pi}{6}\right)$$

and hence or otherwise, prove that

$$s^2 + 9\rho^2 = 16a^2$$

where ρ is the radius of curvature at any point, and s the length of the arc intercepted between the vertex and the point.

Solution : The equation of the cardioid is

$$r = a\,(1 + \cos\theta)$$

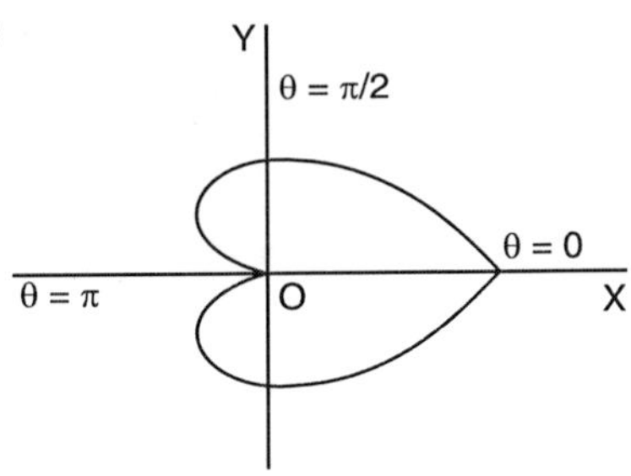

$$\therefore \quad \frac{dr}{d\theta} = -\,a \sin\theta$$

$$\therefore \quad \tan\theta = r\frac{d\theta}{dr}$$

$$= \frac{r}{\left(\dfrac{dr}{d\theta}\right)}$$

$$= \frac{a\left(1+\cos\theta\right)}{-a\sin\theta}$$

$$= \frac{2\cos^2\dfrac{\theta}{2}}{-2\sin\dfrac{\theta}{2}\cos\dfrac{\theta}{2}}$$

$$= -\cot\frac{\theta}{2}$$

$$= \tan\left(\frac{\pi}{2}+\frac{\theta}{2}\right)$$

$$\therefore \qquad \phi = \frac{\pi}{2}+\frac{\theta}{2} \qquad \ldots (1)$$

Also $\psi = \theta + \phi$

$$= \theta+\frac{\pi}{2}+\frac{\theta}{2} = \frac{\pi}{2}+\frac{3\theta}{2}$$

or $$\psi = \frac{\pi}{2}+\frac{3\theta}{2} \qquad \ldots (2)$$

Let s be measured from the point where $\theta = 0$, then we have

$$s = \int_0^\theta \sqrt{r^2+\left(\frac{dr}{d\theta}\right)^2}\, d\theta$$

$$= \int_0^\theta \sqrt{a^2\,(1+\cos\theta)+a^2\sin^2\theta}\, d\theta$$

$$= a\int_0^\theta \sqrt{1+\cos^2\theta+2\cos\theta+\sin^2\theta}\, d\theta$$

$$= a\int_0^\theta \sqrt{2+2\cos\theta}\, d\theta$$

$$= 2a\int_0^\theta \cos\frac{\theta}{2}\, d\theta$$

$$= 4a\left(\sin\frac{\theta}{2}\right)_0^\theta$$

$$= 4a\sin\frac{\theta}{2}$$

$$= 4a\sin\left(\frac{\psi}{3}-\frac{\pi}{6}\right) \qquad \text{[Using (2)]}$$

$\therefore$ The required intrinsic equation of the curve is

$$s = 4a\sin\left(\frac{\psi}{3}-\frac{\pi}{6}\right) \qquad \ldots (3)$$

From (3),

$$\rho = \frac{ds}{d\psi} = 4a\cos\left(\frac{\psi}{3}-\frac{\pi}{6}\right)\cdot\frac{1}{3}$$

or $$3\rho = 4a\cos\left(\frac{\psi}{3}-\frac{\pi}{6}\right) \quad \dots (4)$$

Squaring and adding (3) and (4), we have

$$s^2 + 9\rho^2 = 16a^2\left[\sin^2\left(\frac{\psi}{3}-\frac{\pi}{6}\right)+\cos^2\left(\frac{\psi}{3}-\frac{\pi}{6}\right)\right]$$
$$= 16a^2$$

EXERCISE 14.1

1. Show that the length of the arc of the curve $y = \log \sec x$ from $x = 0$ to $x = \pi/3$ is $\log(2 + \sqrt{3})$.

2. Find the length of the arc of the curve $y = ae^x$ from the point $(0, a)$ to the point (x_1, y_1).

3. Show that the length of an arc of the curve
$$x^2 = a^2(1 - e^{y/a})$$
measured from $(0, 0)$ to (x, y) is $a \log \dfrac{a+x}{a-x} - x$.

4. Find the length of the catenary $y = a\cosh(x/a)$ from $x = 0$ to $x = b$.

5. Show that in the catenary $y = c\cosh\left(\dfrac{x}{c}\right)$, the length of the arc from the vertex (where $x = 0$) to any point (x, y) is given by

(a) $s = c\sinh\left(\dfrac{x}{c}\right)$ (b) $s^2 = y - c^2$.

6. Find the length of the arc of the semi-cubical parabola $ay^2 = x^3$ from the vertex to the point (a, a).

7. Find the length of the arc of the parabola $y^2 = 4ax$.

(a) from the vertex to an extremity of the latus rectum.

(b) cut off by the latus rectum.

(c) cut off by the line $3y = 8x$.

8. Find the arc length of the curve $y = \dfrac{x^2}{2} - \dfrac{1}{4}\log x$ from $x = 1$ to $x = 2$.

9. Find the perimeter of the loop of the curve

(a) $9ay^2 = (x - 2a)(x - 5a)^2$

(b) $3ay^2 = x(x - a)^2$

(c) $3ay^2 = x^2(a - x)$.

10. Trace the curve $8a^2y^2 = x^2(a^2 - 2x^2)$ and show that the whole length of the curve is $a\pi$.

11. Show that the whole length of the curve $x^{2/3} + y^{2/3} = a^{2/3}$ is $6a$.

12. Find the length of the arc of the curve

(a) $x = e^\theta \sin\theta$, $y = e^\theta \cos\theta$ from $\theta = 0$ to $\theta = \pi/2$.

(b) $x = e^\theta\left(\sin\dfrac{\theta}{2} + 2\cos\dfrac{\theta}{2}\right)$,

$y = e^\theta\left(\cos\dfrac{\theta}{2} - 2\sin\dfrac{\theta}{2}\right)$ measured from $\theta = 0$ to $\theta = \pi$.

(c) $x = a\sin 2\theta(1 + \cos 2\theta)$, $y = a\cos 2\theta(1 - \cos 2\theta)$ from $(0, 0)$ to (x, y).

(d) $x = a(\cos t + t\sin t)$, $y = a(\sin t - t\cos t)$ from $t = 0$ to $t = 2$.

13. Find the length of an arc of the cycloid

$$x = a(\theta - \sin\theta),\ y = a(1 - \cos\theta).$$

14. Find the length of an arc of the cycloid

$$x = a(\theta + \sin\theta),\ y = a(1 + \cos\theta).$$

15. Find the perimeter of the loop of the curve

$$x = t^2,\ y = t - t^3/3.$$

16. Find the length of one quadrant of the curve

$$\left(\frac{x}{a}\right)^{2/3} + \left(\frac{y}{b}\right)^{2/3} = 1$$

17. Show that in the epicycloid

$$x = (a + b)\cos\theta - b\cos\left(\frac{a + b}{b}\theta\right);$$

$$y = (a + b)\sin\theta - b\sin\left(\frac{a + b}{b}\theta\right);$$

$$s = \frac{4b(a + b)}{a}\cos\left(\frac{a}{2b}\theta\right)$$

where s is measured from the vertex (where $\theta = \pi b/a$).

18. Show that the arc of the upper half of the curve $r = a\,(1 - \cos\theta)$ is bisected by $\theta = 2\pi/3$.

19. Show that the length of the arc of the hyperbolic spiral $r\theta = a$ taken from the point $r = a$ to $r = 2a$ is

$$a\left[\sqrt{5} - \sqrt{2} + \log\left(\frac{2+\sqrt{8}}{1+\sqrt{5}}\right)\right].$$

20. Find the perimeter of the curve $r = a\cos\theta$.

21. Find the length of the arc of the parabola $\frac{2a}{r} = 1 + \cos\theta$ cut off by its latus rectum.

22. Show that the whole length of the limacon $r = a + b\cos\theta$ $(a > b)$ is equal to that of an ellipse whose semi-axes are equal in length to the maximum and minimum radii vectors of the limacon.

23. Prove that the perimeter of the limacon $r = a + b\cos\theta$, if b/a be small, as approximately $2\pi a\left(1 + \frac{1}{4}\frac{b^2}{a^2}\right)$.

24. Show that the length of the arc of the hyperbola $xy = a^2$ between the limits $x = b$ and $x = c$ is equal to the arc of the curve $p^2\,(a^4 + r^4) = a^4 r^2$ between the limits $r = b$, $r = c$.

25. If s be the length of the curve $r = a\tanh\theta/2$ between the origin and $\theta = 2\pi$ and A the area between the same points, then show that

$$A = a\,(s - a\pi).$$

26. Show that the length of the loop of the curve $3x^2y - y^3 = (x^2 + y^2)^2$ is

$$2\int_0^1 \frac{dr}{\sqrt{1-r^6}}.$$

27. Show that the intrinsic equation of the semi-cubical parabola $3ay^2 = 2x^3$ is

$$9s = 4a\,(\sec^3\psi - 1).$$

28. Show that the intrinsic equation of the parabolic $y^2 = 4ax$ is

$$s = a\cot\psi\,\text{cosec}\,\psi + a\log(\cot\psi + \text{cosec}\,\psi).$$

29. For the astroid $x^{2/3} + y^{2/3} = a^{2/3}$, prove that

$$s = \frac{3a}{4}\cos^2\psi\,.$$

30. Prove that the intrinsic equation of the equiangular spiral $r = ae^{m\theta}$ when the arc is measured from $(a, 0)$ is

$$s = \frac{a\sqrt{1+m^2}}{m}\left[e^{m(\psi-\beta)} - 1\right]$$

where $\beta = \tan^{-1}\left(\frac{1}{m}\right)$.

ANSWERS

EXERCISE 14.1

2. $f(y_1) - f(a)$, where

$$f(y) = \log\left(\frac{y}{1+\sqrt{1+y^2}}\right) + \sqrt{1+y^2}$$

4. $a\sinh\frac{b}{a}$

6. $\frac{8}{27}\left(13\sqrt{13-8}\right)$

7. (a) $a\left[\Gamma 2 + \log\left(\Gamma 2 + 1\right)\right]$ (b) $2a\left[\Gamma 2 + \log\left(\Gamma 2 + 1\right)\right]$

(c) $a\left(\frac{15}{16} + \log 2\right)$

8. $\frac{3}{2} + \frac{1}{4}\log 2$

9. (a) $4\sqrt{3}\,a$ (b) $\frac{4a}{\sqrt{3}}$ (c) $\frac{4a}{\sqrt{3}}$

12. (a) $\sqrt{2}\left(e^{\pi/2} - 1\right)$ (b) $\frac{5}{2}\left(e^{\pi} - 1\right)$

(c) $\frac{4a}{3}\sin 3\theta$ (d) $2a$

13. $8a$

14. $8a$

15. $4\sqrt{3}$

16. $\frac{a^2 + ab + b^2}{a+b}$

20. πa

21. $2a\left[\sqrt{2} + \log\left(\sqrt{2} + 1\right)\right]$

15

Determination of Volumes and Surfaces of Solids of Revolution

15.1 Definitions

If a plane area is revolved about a fixed straight line lying in its own plane, then the body so generated by the plane area is called the *solid of revolution* and the surface generated by the boundary of the plane area is called the *surface of revolution.*

The fixed line about which the plane area rotates is called the *axis of revolution.*

For example, a right angled triangle when revolved about one of its sides (forming the right angle) generates a right circular cone.

Remember. The section of a solid of revolution by a plane perpendicular to the axis of revolution is a circle, having its centre on the axis of revolution.

15.2 Volume Formulae for Cartesian Equations

To show that the volume of the solid generated by the revolution about the x-axis, of the area bounded by the curve $y = f(x)$, the x-axis and the ordinates $x = a$, $x = b$ is $\int_a^b \pi y^2 dx$, where $y = f(x)$ is a finite, continuous and single valued function of x in the interval $a \leq x \leq b$.

Let AB be the curve $y = f(x)$ and CA, DB be the coordinates $x = a$, $x = b$ respectively.

Let $P(x, y)$ be any point on the curve AB.

Draw $PM \perp OX$.

$\therefore OM = x$ and $PM = y$

Let V denote the volume of the solid generated by the revolution about x-axis of the area $ACMP$.

As x increases i.e. MP moves towards the right, V also increases.

Thus the volume V depends on x and is therefore a function of x.

Let Q $(x + \delta x, y + \delta y)$ be a point on the curve. Then the volume of the solid generated by the revolution about x-axis of the area $ACNQ$, will be $V + \delta V$, so that the volume of the solid generated by the revolution about x-axis of the area $PMNQ$ is δV.

Complete the rectangle $PRQS$.

Then the volume of the solid generated by the revolution about the x-axis of the area $PMNQ$ lies between the right circular cylinders generated by the rectangles $PMNR$ and $SMNQ$ i.e., δV lies between $\pi y^2 \delta x$ and $\pi\ (y + \delta y)^2\ \delta x$.

or $\dfrac{\delta V}{\delta x}$ lies between πy^2 and $\pi\ (y + \delta y)^2$.

In the limiting position as

$Q \to P$, $\delta x \to 0$ and $\therefore\ \delta y \to 0$.

$\therefore\ \text{Lt}_{\delta x \to 0} \dfrac{\delta V}{\delta x}$ lies between πy^2

and $\text{Lt}_{\delta y \to 0}\, \pi\ (y + \delta y)^2$

or $\dfrac{dV}{dx}$ lies between πy^2 and a quantity which approaches to πy^2.

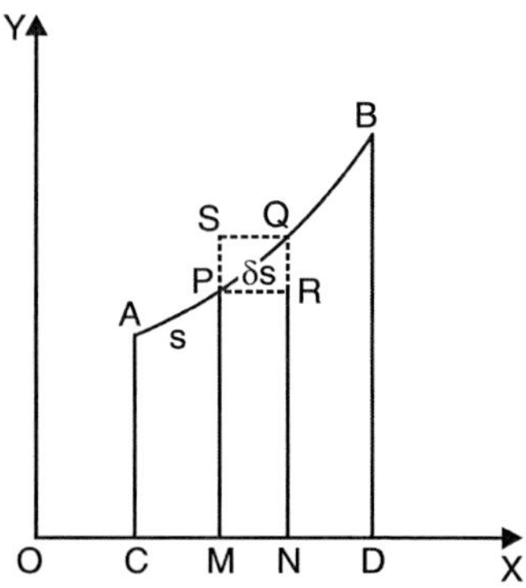

$$\therefore \qquad \frac{dV}{dx} = \pi y^2$$

$$\therefore \quad \int_a^b \pi y^2 dx = \int_a^b \frac{dV}{dx}\, dx = (V)_a^b$$

$= (\text{volume } V \text{ when } x = b)$

$\qquad - (\text{volume } V \text{ when } x = a)$

$=$ volume generated by the area $ACDB - 0$.

Hence the volume of the solid generated by the revolution of the area $ACDB$ about the x-axis is

$$\int_a^b \pi y^2 dx.$$

Corollary. Revolution about y-axis.

The volume of the solid generated by revolution about the y-axis of the area bounded by the curve $x = f(y)$, the y-axis and the abscissae $y = a$, $y = b$ is

$$\int_a^b \pi x^2 dy.$$

The result follows immediately on interchanging x and y in the above proposition.

An Important Advice (Remember)

(i) *If the generating curve is symmetrical about the x-axis* and it is required to find the volume generated by the revolution of the area about the x-axis, in such a case we shall revolve only one of the symmetrical portions, because the part of the curve above the x-axis generates the same volume as the part of the curve below x-axis when revolved about the x-axis. Thus the volume generated by the revolution of the area $DCOAB$ about OX = volume generated by the revolution of the area $OABM$ or $OCDM$ about OX.

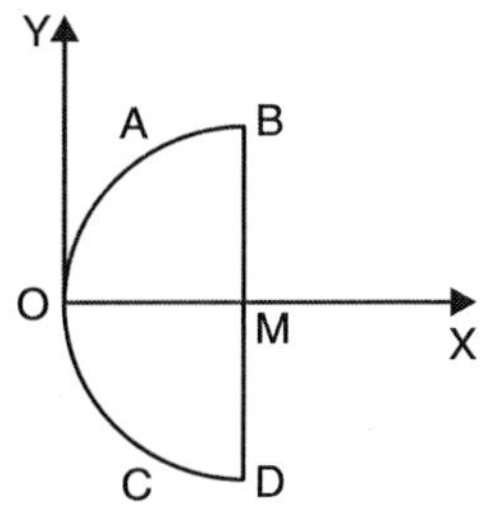

(ii) *If the curve is symmetrical about y-axis* and the same curve be made to revolve about the x-axis (the curve lying only on one side of the x-axis) then the volume generated = 2 × volume generated by the portion OAB lying to the right of y-axis.

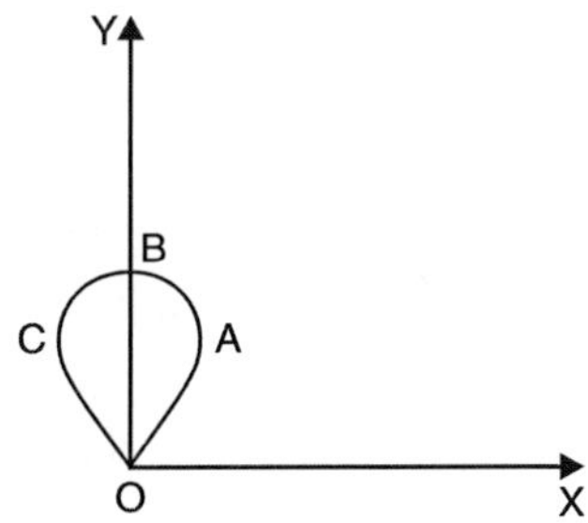

15.3 Prolate and Oblate Spheroids Definitions

(i) The solid formed by the revolution of the ellipse about the *major axis* is called a *prolate spheroid.*

(ii) The solid formed by the revolution of the ellipse about the *minor axis* is called an *oblate spheroid.*

15.4 Revolution about any axis

The volume of the solid generated by the revolution about any axis CD of the area bounded by the curve AB, the axis CD and the perpendiculars AC, BD on the axis, is

$$\int_{OC}^{OD} \pi (PM)^2 \, d(OM)$$

where O is a fixed point on the axis CD and PM is the perpendicular from any point P of the curve AB on CD.

Take the fixed point O on CD as origin and CD, the axis of revolution as x-axis.

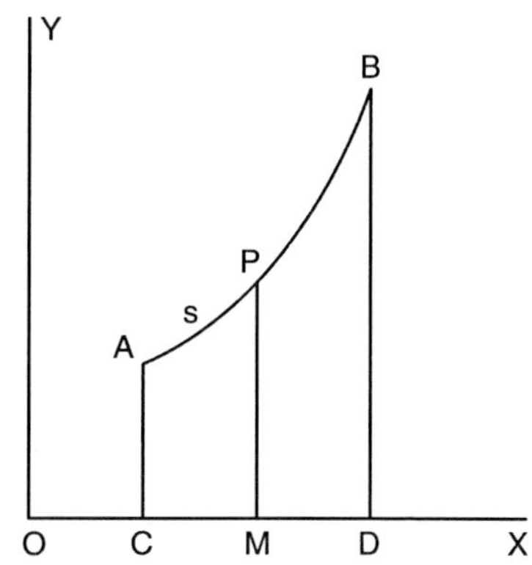

Let $OY \perp$ to CD be taken as y-axis.

Let $P\ (x, y)$ be any point on the curve referred to OC and OY as axes.

Draw $PM \perp OC$, so that $OM = x$ and $MP = y$.

If $OC = a$ and $OD = b$, then the required volume

$$= \int_a^b \pi y^2 dx = \pi \int_a^b (PM)^2 \, d(OM)$$

Remember:

Practical Method for Questions

(1) Take any point $P\ (x, y)$ on the curve.

(2) Draw $PM \perp$ on the line about which the curve is to be revolved and find the length of PM.

(3) Find the distance OM of the foot of $\perp$ from a fixed point O (say) on the line and take its differential.

(4) Then use the formula

$$\int \pi (PM)^2 \, d(OM)$$

with proper limits for integration.

15.5 Volume Formula for Parametric Equations

(i) The volume of the solid generated by the revolution about the x-axis, of the area bounded by the curve

$$x = f(t),\ y = \phi(t),$$

the x-axis and the ordinates, where $t = a$, $t = b$ is

$$\int_a^b \pi y^2 \frac{dx}{dt}\, dt$$

(ii) The volume of the solid generated by the revolution about the y-axis, of the area bounded by the curve

$$x = f(t),\ y = \phi(t),$$

the y-axis and the abscissae at the points, where $t = a$, $t = b$ is

$$\int_a^b \pi x^2 \frac{dy}{dt}\, dt.$$

15.6 Volume between Two Solids

The volume of the solid generated by the revolution about the x-axis of the area bounded by the curves

$$y = f(x),\ y = \phi(x)$$

and the ordinates $x = a$, $x = b$ is

$$\int_a^b \pi\left(y_1^2 - y_2^2\right) dx$$

where y_1 is the 'y' of the upper curve and y_2 that of the lower curve.

15.7 Volume Formula for Polar Curves

The volume of the solid generated by the revolution of the area bounded by the curve $r = f(\theta)$ and the radii vectors $\theta = \alpha$, $\theta = \beta$.

(i) about the initial line OX ($\theta = 0$) is

$$\int_\alpha^\beta \frac{2}{3}\pi r^3 \sin\theta\, d\theta$$

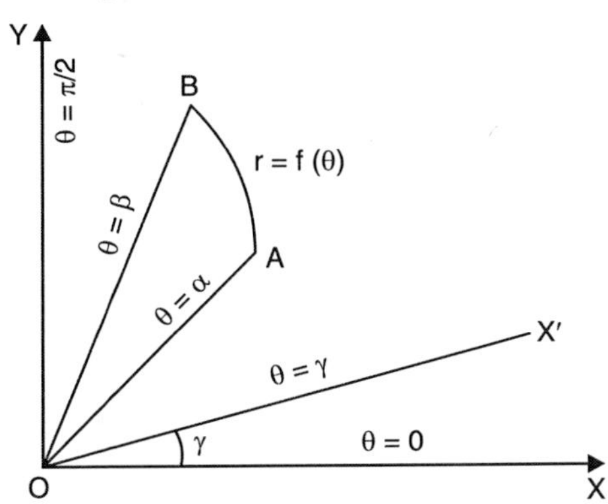

(ii) about the line OY $(\theta = \pi/2)$ is

$$\int_{\alpha}^{\beta} \frac{2}{3} \pi r^3 \cos\theta \, d\theta$$

(iii) about any line OX' $(\theta = \gamma)$ is

$$\int_{\alpha}^{\beta} \frac{2}{3} \pi r^3 \sin(\theta - \gamma) \, d\theta$$

ILLUSTRATIVE EXAMPLES

Example 1. The hyperbola $\frac{x^2}{a^2} - \frac{y^2}{b^2} = 1$ revolves about the axis of x. Show that the volume cut off from one of the two solids thus obtained by a plane perpendicular to x-axis, and distance h from the vertex, is

$$\frac{\pi b^2 h^2 (3a + h)}{3a^2}$$

Solution : The given hyperbola is

$$\frac{x^2}{a^2} - \frac{y^2}{b^2} = 1 \qquad \text{... (1)}$$

volume of the solid cut off by a plane $\perp$ to x-axis and at a distance h from the vertex is the same as the volume obtained by rotating the portion of the curve from $x = a$ to $x = a + h$ about the x-axis.

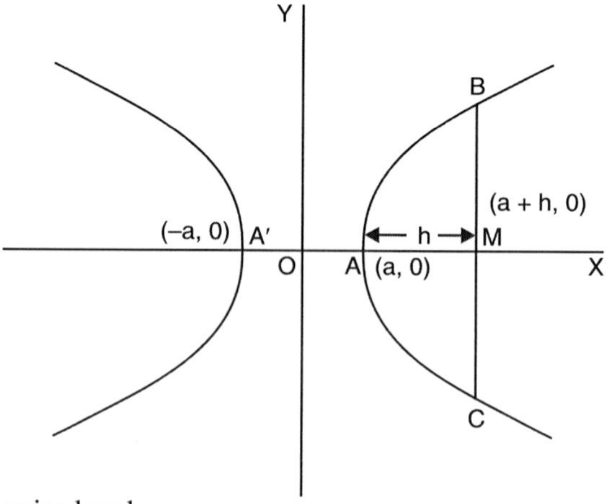

$\therefore$ Required volume

$$= \int_{a}^{a+h} \pi y^2 dx$$

$$= \pi \int_a^{a+h} \frac{b^2}{a^2}\left(x^2 - a^2\right) dx \qquad \left[\because \text{From (1)} \; y^2 = \frac{b^2}{a^2}\left(x^2 - a^2\right)\right]$$

$$= \frac{\pi b^2}{a^2}\left(\frac{x^3}{3} - a^2 x\right)_a^{a+h}$$

$$= \frac{\pi b^2}{a^2}\left[\frac{(a+h)^3 - a^3}{3} - a^2\left(\overline{a+h-a}\right)\right]$$

$$= \frac{\pi b^2}{a^2}\left[\frac{1}{3}\left(a^3 + 3a^2h + h^3 + 3ah^2 - a^3\right) - a^2 h\right]$$

$$= \frac{\pi b^2}{a^2}\left(\frac{3ah^2 + h^3}{3}\right) = \frac{\pi b^2 h^2 (3a+h)}{3a^2}.$$

Example 2. A segment is cut off from a sphere of radius a by a plane at a distance $a/2$ from the centre. Show that the volume of the segment is 5/32 of the volume of the sphere.

Solution: Let the equation of the circle be

$$x^2 + y^2 = a^2 \qquad \text{... (1)}$$

Let the plane PBP' cut the circle at a distance $a/2$ from the centre O of the circle.

Then the required volume of the segment is generated by revolving the area PBA of the circle (1) about the x-axis.

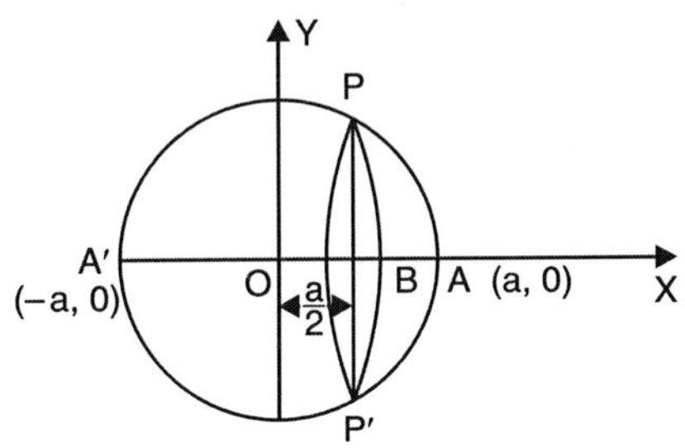

Now for the arc PA, x varies from $a/2$ to a.

$\therefore$ Required volume

$$= \int_{a/2}^{a} \pi y^2 dx$$

$$= \pi \int_{a/2}^{a} \left(a^2 - x^2\right) dx \qquad \text{[Using (1)]}$$

$$= \pi \left(a^2 x - \frac{x^3}{3}\right)_{a/2}^{a}$$

$$= \pi\left[\left(a^3 - \frac{a^3}{3}\right) - \left(\frac{a^3}{2} - \frac{a^3}{24}\right)\right]$$

$$= \pi a^2\left[1 - \frac{1}{8} - \frac{1}{2} + \frac{1}{24}\right]$$

$$= \pi a^3\left(\frac{24 - 8 - 12 + 1}{24}\right)$$

$$= \frac{5a^3}{24} = \frac{5}{32}\left(\frac{4}{3}\pi a^3\right)$$

$$= \frac{5}{32} \text{ (volume of the sphere of radius } a\text{)}$$

Example 3. Find the volume of the solid generated by revolving the ellipse $\frac{x^2}{a^2} + \frac{y^2}{b^2} = 1$ about the x-axis.

Solution : The equation of the ellipse is

$$\frac{x^2}{a^2} + \frac{y^2}{b^2} = 1$$

$$\Rightarrow \qquad y^2 = \frac{b^2}{a^2}\left(a^2 - x^2\right) \qquad \text{... (1)}$$

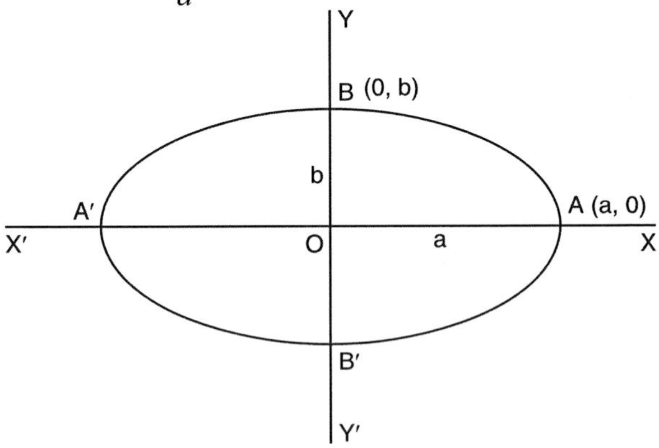

Since the ellipse is symmetrical about y-axis.

∴ Required volume generated by the ellipse by the revolution about x-axis

= 2 × volume generated by the arc BA in first quadrant about the x-axis

Now for the arc BA, x varies from 0 to a.

$\therefore$ Required volume

$$= 2\int_0^a \pi y^2 dx$$

$$= 2\pi \int_0^a \frac{b^2}{a^2}\left(a^2 - x^2\right) dx \qquad \text{[From (1)]}$$

$$= \frac{2\pi b^2}{a^2}\left(a^2 x - \frac{x^3}{3}\right)_0^a$$

$$= \frac{2\pi b^2}{a^2}\left(a^3 - \frac{a^3}{3} - 0\right)$$

$$= 2\pi \frac{b^2}{a^2} \cdot \frac{2a^3}{3}$$

$$= \frac{4}{3}\pi ab^2.$$

Example 4. Show that the volume of the solid generated by the revolution of the curve $(a - x)\, y^2 = a^2 x$ about its asymptote is $\frac{1}{2}\pi^2 a^3$.

Solution : The equation of the curve is

$$y^2 (a - x) = a^2 x \qquad \text{... (1)}$$

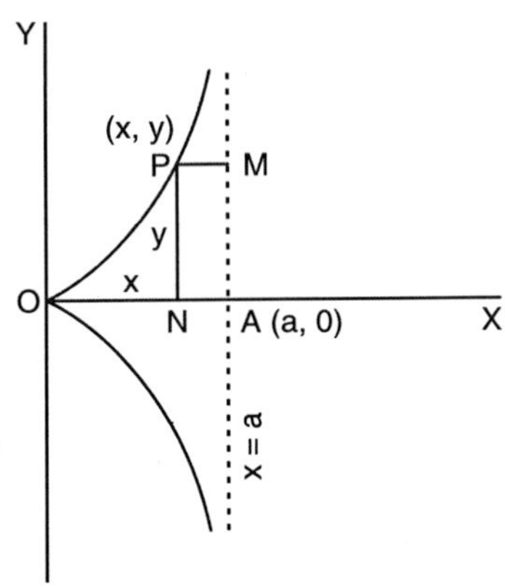

The curve is symmetrical about the x-axis and the asymptote in the line $x = a$.

Let $P(x, y)$ be any point on the curve. Draw PM perpendicular on the asymptote (the axis of revolution) and $PN \perp OX$.

Then $\quad PM = NA = OA - ON$

$\qquad\qquad = a - x$

and $\quad AM = PN = y$

where A is the point of intersection of the asymptote and the x-axis.

$\therefore$ Required volume

$$= 2\int \pi (PM)^2 \cdot d(AM) \qquad \text{... (2)}$$

$$= 2\int_0^\infty \pi (a-x)^2\, dy$$

$$= 2\pi \int_0^\infty \left[a - \frac{ay^2}{a^2+y^2}\right]^2 dy \qquad \text{[From (1)]}$$

$$= 2\pi \int_0^\infty \frac{a^6}{(a^2+y^2)^2}\, dy$$

[Put $y = a \tan \theta$
$\therefore\ dy = a \sec^2 \theta\, d\theta$
when $y = 0,\ \theta = 0,$
when $y \to \infty,\ \theta \to \pi/2$]

$$= 2\pi a^6 \int_0^{\pi/2} \frac{a \sec^2 \theta\, d\theta}{\left[a^2(1+\tan^2\theta)\right]^2}$$

$$= 2\pi a^3 \int_0^{\pi/2} \cos^2 \theta\, d\theta$$

$$= 2\pi a^3 \frac{1}{2}\cdot\frac{\pi}{2} = \frac{1}{2}\pi^2 a^3.$$

Example 5. Find the volume of the spindle shaped solid generated by revolving the astroid $x^{2/3} + y^{2/3} = a^{2/3}$ about the x-axis.

Solution : The equation of the curve is

$$x^{2/3} + y^{2/3} = a^{2/3} \qquad \text{... (1)}$$

The parametric equation of the curve are

$$x = a \cos^3 t$$
$$y = a \sin^3 t \qquad \text{... (2)}$$

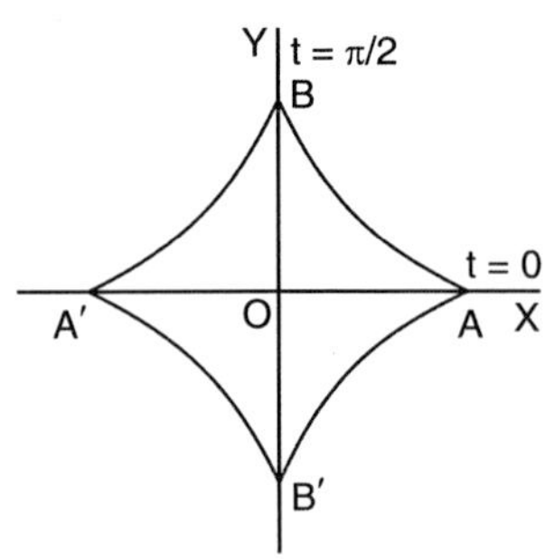

The curve is symmetrical about both the axes and for the portion of the curve in the first quadrant, t varies from 0 to $\pi/2$.

$\therefore$ Required volume

= 2 × volume generated by the arc in the first quadrant

$$= 2\int_0^{\pi/2} \pi y^2 \frac{dx}{dt}\, dt$$

$$= 2\pi \int_0^{\pi/2} a^2 \sin^6 t \left(-3a \cos^2 t \sin t\right) dt$$

$$= -6\pi a^3 \int_0^{\pi/2} \sin^7 t \cos^2 t \, dt$$

$$= -6\pi a^3 \frac{\Gamma\left(\frac{7+1}{2}\right)\Gamma\left(\frac{2+1}{2}\right)}{2\Gamma\left(\frac{7+2+2}{2}\right)}$$

$$= -3\pi a^3 \frac{\Gamma 4 \, \Gamma \frac{3}{2}}{\Gamma \frac{11}{2}}$$

$$= -3\pi a^3 \frac{3.2.1.\frac{1}{2}.\sqrt{\pi}}{\frac{9}{2}.\frac{7}{2}.\frac{5}{2}.\frac{3}{2}.\frac{1}{2}.\sqrt{\pi}}$$

$$= -3\pi a^3.\frac{32}{315} = -\frac{32\pi a^3}{105}$$

$$= \frac{32\pi a^3}{105} \text{ (in magnitude)}$$

Example 6. The cardioid $r = a\ (1 + \cos\theta)$ revolves about the initial line, find the volume of the solid generated.

Solution : The equation of the cardioid is

$$r = a\ (1 + \cos\theta)$$

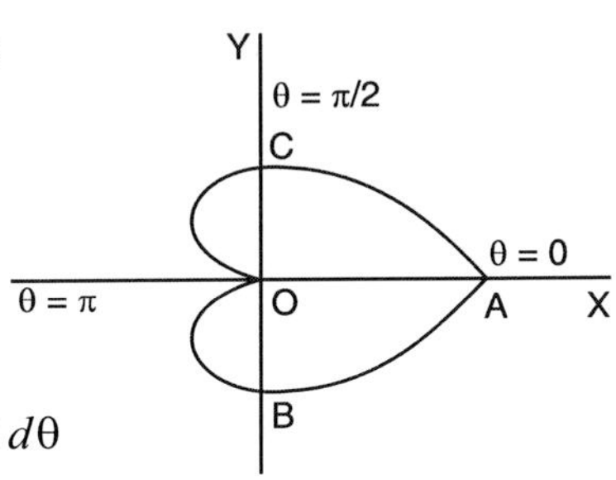

The cardioid is symmetrical about the initial line and for the upper half of the curve, θ varies from 0 to π.

$\therefore$ Required volume

$$= \int_0^{\pi} \frac{2}{3} \pi r^3 \sin\theta \, d\theta$$

$$= \frac{2}{3}\pi \int_0^{\pi} a^3 (1 + \cos\theta)^3 \sin\theta \, d\theta$$

$$= \frac{2}{3}\pi a^3 \left[\frac{(1+\cos\theta)^4}{-4}\right]_0^{\pi}$$

$$= -\frac{1}{6}\pi a^3\left[(1+\cos\theta)^4\right]_0^\pi$$

$$= -\frac{1}{6}\pi a^3(0-16)$$

$$= \frac{8}{3}\pi a^3.$$

Example 7. Find the volume of the spindle formed by the revolution of a parabolic arc about the line joining the vertex to one extremity of the latus rectum.

Solution : The equation of the parabola is

$$y^2 = 4ax$$

Let LSL' be the latus rectum and A the vertex of the parabola.

Then $\quad L \to (a, 2a)$

and $\quad A \to (0, 0)$

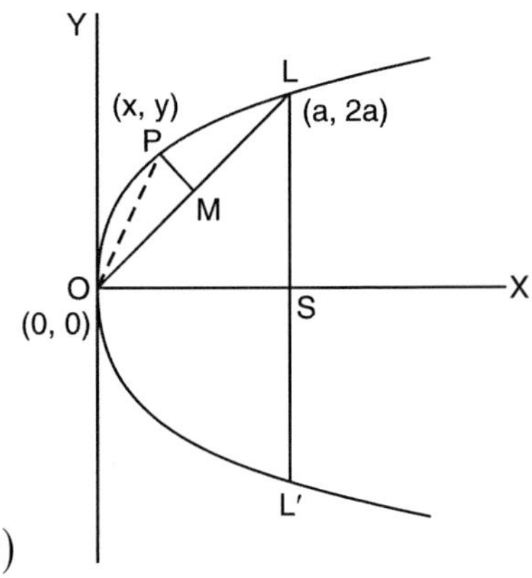

Now the equation of the line AL is

$$y - 0 = \frac{2a-0}{a-0}(x-0)$$

or $\quad 2x - y = 0$

Let P (x, y) be any point on the arc AL of the parabola. Draw $PM \perp AL$ and join AP. Then

$$PM = \perp \text{ distance of } P\ (x, y) \text{ from the line } 2x - y = 0$$

$$= \frac{2x-y}{\sqrt{4+1}}$$

$$= \frac{2x-y}{\sqrt{5}}$$

$$= \frac{2x-2\sqrt{ax}}{\sqrt{5}} \qquad [\because y^2 = 4ax]$$

$$= \frac{2\sqrt{x}\left(\sqrt{x}-\sqrt{a}\right)}{\sqrt{5}}$$

$$\therefore \qquad PM^2 = \frac{4x\left(x+a-2\sqrt{ax}\right)}{5}$$

Now $\quad AM^2 = AP^2 - PM^2$

$$= x^2 + y^2 - \frac{4x\left(x+a-2\sqrt{ax}\right)}{5}$$

$$= x^2 + 4ax - \frac{4}{5}x\left(x+a-2\sqrt{ax}\right) \qquad [\because y^2 = 4ax]$$

$$= \frac{1}{5}\left[5x^2 + 20ax - 4x^2 - 4ax + 8\sqrt{a}\,x^{3/2}\right]$$

$$= \frac{1}{5}\left[x^2 + 16ax + 8\sqrt{a}\,x^{3/2}\right]$$

$$= \frac{1}{5}\left[x + 4\sqrt{ax}\right]^2$$

$$\therefore \qquad AM = \frac{1}{\sqrt{5}}\left[x + 4\sqrt{a}\sqrt{x}\right]$$

$$\therefore \qquad d\,(AM) = \frac{1}{\sqrt{5}}\left(1 + 4\sqrt{a}\,\frac{1}{2\sqrt{x}}\right)dx$$

$$= \left(\frac{\sqrt{x}+2\sqrt{a}}{\sqrt{5}\,\sqrt{x}}\right)dx$$

$\therefore$ Required volume

$$= \int \pi\,(PM)^2\, d\,(AM)$$

$$= \pi\int_0^a \frac{4x\left(\sqrt{x}-\sqrt{a}\right)^2}{5}\,\frac{1}{\sqrt{5}}\left(\frac{\sqrt{x}+2\sqrt{a}}{\sqrt{x}}\right)d_x$$

[$\because$ For the arc AC, x varies from 0 to a]

$$= \frac{4\pi}{5\sqrt{5}}\int_0^a \sqrt{x}\left(\sqrt{x}-\sqrt{a}\right)^2\left(\sqrt{x}+2\sqrt{a}\right)d_x$$

[Put $x = at^2$

$\therefore\ dx = 2at\ dt$

when $x = 0,\ t = 0$

when $x = a,\ t = 1$]

$$= \frac{4\pi}{5\sqrt{5}}\int_0^1 \sqrt{a}\,t\left(\sqrt{a}\,t-\sqrt{a}\right)^2\left(\sqrt{a}\,t+2\sqrt{a}\right)2at\ dt$$

$$= \frac{8\pi a^3}{5\sqrt{5}} \int_0^1 t^2 (t+2)(t^2 - 2t + 1)\, dt$$

$$= \frac{8\pi a^3}{5\sqrt{5}} \int_0^1 t^2 (t^3 - 3t + 2)\, dt$$

$$= \frac{8\pi a^3}{5\sqrt{5}} \left[\frac{t^6}{6} - 3\frac{t^4}{4} + 2\frac{t^3}{3} \right]_0^1$$

$$= \frac{8\pi a^3}{5\sqrt{5}} \left[\frac{1}{6} - \frac{3}{4} + \frac{2}{3} \right]$$

$$= \frac{8\pi a^3}{5\sqrt{5}} \left(\frac{2-9+8}{12} \right)$$

$$= \frac{2\pi a^3}{15\sqrt{5}}.$$

Example 8. A basin is formed by the revolution of the curve $x^3 = 64y$ $(y > 0)$ about the axis of y. If the depth of the basin is 8 cm, how many cubic centimetres of water will it hold?

Solution : The equation of the generating curve is

$$x^3 = 64y \ (y > 0) \qquad \text{... (1)}$$

The curve is symmetrical in opposite quadrants. The shape of the curve is as shown in the figure.

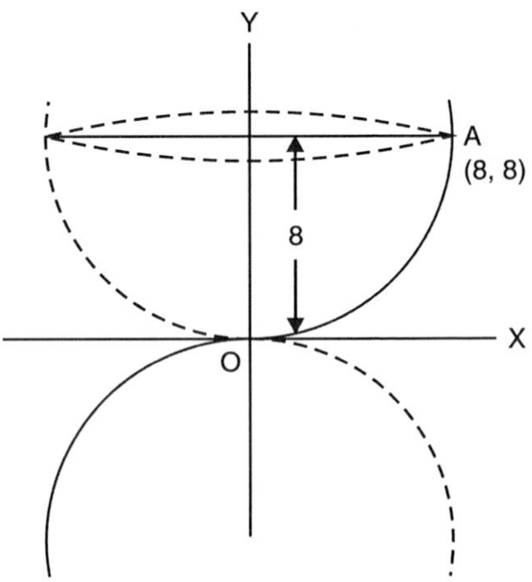

Since the height of the basin is 8 cm, so when $y = 8$, from (1),

$$x^3 = 64 \times 8 = 512$$

$$\therefore \quad x = 8$$

Thus A (8, 8) is the point on the curve (1) at a height of 8 cm.

Thus the basin is formed by the revolution of the arc OA about y-axis, where A is the point (8, 8).

∴ Required volume

$$= \int_0^8 \pi x^2 dy$$

$$= \int_0^8 \pi (64y)^{2/3} dy$$

$$= 16\pi \int_0^8 y^{2/3} dy$$

$$= 16\pi \left(\frac{3}{5} y^{5/3} \right)_0^8$$

$$= \frac{48}{5} \pi \left[(8)^{5/3} - 0 \right]$$

$$= \frac{48\pi}{5} \cdot 32 = \frac{1536\pi}{5} \text{ cubic curves.}$$

EXERCISE 15.1

1. Let B be a number > 1. What is the volume of solid generated by the area under the curve $y = e^{-x}$ between 1 and B (the axis of revolution being the x-axis) ? Does the volume approach to a limit as B becomes large ? If so, what is the limit?
2. Find the volume generated by rotating about the y-axis the area bounded by the coordinate axes and the graph of the curve $y = \cos x$ from $x = 0$ to $x = \pi/2$.
3. The part of the curve $y^2 = x^2 (1 - x^2)$ between $x = 0$ and $x = 1$ rotates about the x-axis. Obtain the volume of the solid thus generated.
4. Find the volume of a sphere of radius a.
5. Find the volume of a spherical cap of height h cut off from a sphere of radius a.
6. Find the volume of the solid generated by the revolution of an arc of the catenary $y = c \cosh (x/c)$ about the x-axis.
7. The area of the parabola $y^2 = 4ax$ lying between the vertex and the latus rectum is revolved about the x-axis. Find the volume generated.
8. A paraboloid of revolution is generated by rotating the parabola $y^2 = ax$ about OX. Find the volume generated by that portion of the curve which lies between $x = 0$ and $x = h$. If R is the

area of the cross-section at $x = h$, show that the volume is half that of a cylinder of base area R and length h.

9. Find the volume of the reel-shaped solid formed by the revolution about the y-axis of the part of the parabola $y^2 = 4ax$ cut off by the latus rectum.

10. Find the volume of the prolate spheroid generated by an ellipse whose major and minor axes are $(24\pi)^{1/3}$ and $(3\pi)^{1/3}$.

11. Prove that the volume of the solid generated by the revolution of an ellipse round its minor axis, is a mean proportional between those generated by the revolution of the ellipse and of auxilliary circle round the major axis.

12. Find the volume of the solid generated by revolving

$$x = a \cos \theta, \; y = b \sin \theta$$

about the y-axis.

13. The part of the ellipse

$$\frac{x^2}{a^2} + \frac{y^2}{b^2} = 1$$

cut off by a latus-rectum revolves about the tangent at the nearer vertex. Find the volume of the reel thus generated.

14. Find the volume generated by revolving the area bounded by the curve $y = xe^x$, ordinate $x = 1$ and the x-axis about the x-axis.

15. Find the volume of the solid formed by the revolution about the x-axis, of the loops of the following curves :

(a) $y^2 (a - x) = x^2 (a + x)$ (b) $y^2 (a + x) = x^2 (3a - x)$

(c) $y^2 (a + x) = x^2 (a - x)$ (d) $y^2 = x^2 (a - x)$.

16. Find the volume of the solid generated by the revolution of the curve $y (a^2 + x^2) = a^3$ about its asymptote.

17. Find the volume of the solid generated by the revolution of the area between the curve $xy^2 = 4a^2 (2a - x)$ and its asymptote about the asymptote.

18. The loop of the curve $2ay^2 = x (x - a)^2$ revolves about x-axis, find the volume of the solid so generated.

19. Find the volume of the solid obtained by revolving the loop of the curve $a^2y^2 = x^2 (2a - x) (x - a)$ about y-axis.

20. Find the volume of the solid formed by the revolution of the cissoid $y^2\ (2a - x) = x^3$ about its asymptote.

21. The ellipse $b^2x^2 + a^2y^2 = a^2b^2$ is divided with two points by the line $x = a/2$, and the smaller part is rotated through four right angles about this line. Prove that the volume generated is

$$\pi a^2 b\left[\frac{3\sqrt{3}}{4} - \frac{\pi}{3}\right].$$

22. Find the volume of the solid obtained by rotating the area bounded by the circle $x^2 + y^2 = a^2$ around the line $x = b\ (b > a)$.

23. A quadrant of a circle, of radius a, revolves about its chord. Show that the volume of the spindle generated is

$$\frac{\pi}{6\sqrt{2}}(10 - 3\pi)\,a^3.$$

24. Find the volume of the solid generated by revolution of the tractrix

$$x = a\cos t + \frac{a}{2}\log\tan^2\frac{t}{2}$$

$$y = a\sin t$$

about its asymptote.

25. Find the volume of the solid generated by the arc of the cissoid

$$x = 2a\sin^2 t,\ \ y = \frac{2a\sin^3 t}{\cos t}$$

about its asymptote.

26. Prove that the volume of the solid generated by the revolution about the x-axis of the loop of the curve

$$x = t^2,\ \ y = t - \frac{t^3}{3}\ \text{is}\ \frac{3\pi}{4}.$$

27. Find the volume of the solid formed by revolving the cycloid

$$x = a\ (\theta + \sin\theta),\ y = a\ (1 - \cos\theta)$$

(a) about the y-axis and

(b) about its base.

28. Find the volume of the solid formed by revolving the arc between the cycloid

$x = a\ (\theta - \sin\theta)$, $y = a\ (1 - \cos\theta)$, and its base

(a) about the y-axis and

(b) about its base.

29. Find the volume of the solid generated by the revolution of the lemniscate $r^2 = a^2 \cos 2\theta$ about

(a) the initial line and

(b) the line $\theta = \pi/2$.

30. Show that the volume generated by the revolution of the limacon

$$r = a + b\cos\theta \qquad (a > b)$$

about the initial line is

$$\frac{4}{3}\pi a\left(a^2 + b^2\right).$$

ANSWERS

EXERCISE 15.1

1. $\frac{\pi}{-2}\left[e^{-2B} - e^{-2}\right]$, yes, $\frac{\pi}{2e^2}$ **2.** $\pi(\pi - 2)$

3. $\frac{2\pi}{15}$ **4.** $\frac{4}{3}\pi a^3$

5. $\pi h^2\left(a - \frac{h}{3}\right)$ **6.** $\frac{c}{2}\left[\sinh\frac{2b}{c} - \sinh\frac{2a}{c}\right]$

7. $2\pi a^3$ **8.** $2\pi a h^2$

9. $\frac{4}{5}\pi a^3$ **10.** π^2

12. $\frac{4}{3}\pi a^2 b$

13. $\frac{2\pi b}{3a}\left[6a^2 b - b^3 - 3ab\sqrt{a^2 - b^2} - 3a^3 \sin^{-1}\frac{b}{a}\right]$

14. $\frac{\pi}{4}\left(e^2 - 1\right)$

15. (a) $2\pi a^3\left(\log 2 - \frac{2}{3}\right)$ (b) $\pi a^3(8\log 2 - 3)$

(c) $2\pi a^3\left(\log 2 - \frac{2}{3}\right)$ (d) $\frac{\pi a^4}{12}$

16. $\frac{1}{2}\pi^2 a^3$ **17.** $4\pi^2 a^3$

18. $\frac{\pi a^3}{27}$ **19.** $\frac{23\pi a^3}{60}$

20. $2\pi^2 a^3$ **22.** $\frac{\pi}{3}\left[6ab^2 + 4a^3 - 3a^2 b\pi\right]$

24. $\frac{2}{3}\pi a^3$ **25.** $2\pi^2 a^3$

27. (a) $\pi a^3\left(\frac{3}{2}\pi^2 - \frac{8}{3}\right)$ (b) $5\pi^2 a^3$

28. (a) $6\pi^3 a^3$ (b) $5\pi^2 a^3$

29. (a) $\frac{\pi a^3}{12}\left[\frac{3}{\sqrt{2}}\log\left(1+\sqrt{2}\right) - 1\right]$

(b) $\frac{\pi^2 a^3}{4\sqrt{2}}$.

15.8 To show that the curved surface of the solid generated by the revolution, about the x-axis, of the area bounded by the curve $y = f(x)$, the x-axis and the ordinates $x = a$, $x = b$ is

$$\int_{x=a}^{x=b} 2\pi y \, ds$$

where s is the length of the arc of the curve measured from a fixed point on it to any point (x, y).

Let AB be the curve $y = f(x)$ and A, B the points corresponding to $x = a$, $x = b$ respectively. Draw AC, $BD \perp$ to x-axis.

Let $P(x, y)$ be any point on the curve and let the arc AP be s. Draw $PM \perp OX$.

If S denotes the curve surface of the solid generated by the revolution of the area $ACMP$ about the x-axis, then clearly S is a function of s.

Let $Q(x + \delta x, y + \delta y)$ be a point on the curve in the neighourhood of D. Draw $QN \perp OX$, and let the arc AQ be $s + \delta s$, so that arc $PQ = \delta s$.

The curved surface of the solid of revolution of the area $PMNQ$ about the x-axis is δS. Draw PR and QS parallel to x-axis and each equal in length to the arc $PQ = \delta s$.

Now the lines PR and QS generate cylinder, when the arc PQ revolves about x-axis, whose base radii are PM and NQ. The area of the curved surface generated by the arc PQ lies between the areas of the curved surfaces of the cylinders whose base radii are PM and NQ.

i.e. δs lies between $2\pi y\ \delta s$ and $2\pi\ (y + \delta y)\ \delta s$.

$\therefore\ \dfrac{\delta S}{\delta s}$ lies between $2\pi y$ and $2\pi\ (y + \delta y)$. Proceeding to limit as $Q \to P$, i.e. as $\delta x \to 0$,

$$[\therefore \delta y \to 0,\ \delta s \to 0]$$

$\dfrac{\delta S}{\delta s}$ lies between $2\pi y$ and a quantity which approaches to $2\pi y$.

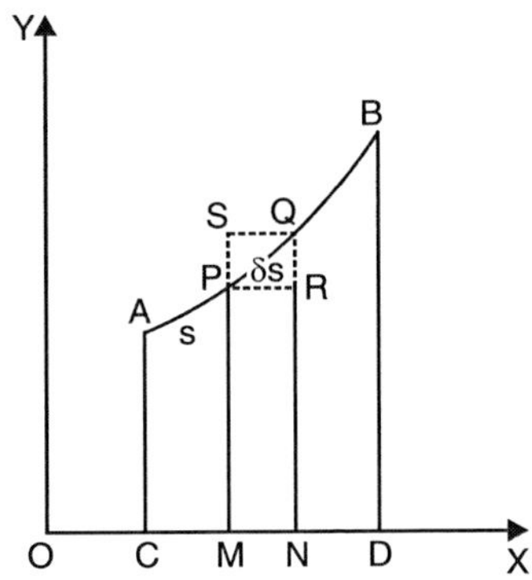

$$\therefore \quad \frac{dS}{ds} = 2\pi y$$

$$\therefore \int_{x=a}^{x=b} 2\pi y\ ds = \int_{x=a}^{x=b} \frac{dS}{ds}\ ds$$

$$= [S]_{x=a}^{x=b}$$

$= $ (volume of S when $x = b$) $-$ (volume of S when $x = a$)

$= $ area of the surface generated by the revolution of the arc $ACDB - 0$

$\therefore$ Surface area of the solid generated by the revolution of the area $ACDB$

$$= \int_{x=a}^{x=b} 2\pi y\ ds.$$

15.9 Surface Formula for Cartesian Equations

The curved surface of the solid generated by the revolution about the x-axis, of the area bounded by the curve $y = f(x)$, the x-axis and the ordinates $x = a$, $x = b$ is

$$\int_{x=a}^{x=b} 2\pi y \frac{ds}{dx}\ dx$$

where $$\frac{ds}{dx} = \sqrt{1 + \left(\frac{dy}{dx}\right)^2}$$

15.10 Surface Formula for Parametric Equations

The curved surface of the solid generated by the revolution about the x-axis of the area bounded by the curve $x = f(t)$, $y = \phi(t)$, the x-axis and the ordinates at the points, where $t = a$, $t = b$ is

$$\int_{t=a}^{t=b} 2\pi y \frac{ds}{dt}\, dt$$

where $$\frac{ds}{dt} = \sqrt{\left(\frac{dx}{dt}\right)^2 + \left(\frac{dy}{dt}\right)^2}$$

15.11 Surface Formula for Polar Equations

The curved surface of the solid generated by the revolution about the initial line, of the area bounded by the curve $r = f(\theta)$ and the radii vectors $\theta = \alpha$, $\theta = \beta$ is

$$\int_{\theta=\alpha}^{\theta=\beta} 2\pi y \frac{ds}{d\theta}\, d\theta,$$

where $$\frac{ds}{d\theta} = \sqrt{r^2 + \left(\frac{dr}{d\theta}\right)^2}$$

and $$y = r \sin\theta.$$

15.12 Revolution about y-axis

The curved surface of the solid generated by the revolution about the y-axis of the area bounded by the curve $x = f(y)$, the y-axis and the abscissae $y = a$, $y = b$ is

$$\int_{y=a}^{y=b} 2\pi x\, ds.$$

15.13 Revolution about Any Axis

The curved surface of the solid generated by the revolution, about an axis CD, of the area bounded by a curve AB, the axis CD and the perpendiculars AC, BD on the axis is

$$\int 2\pi (PM)\, ds$$

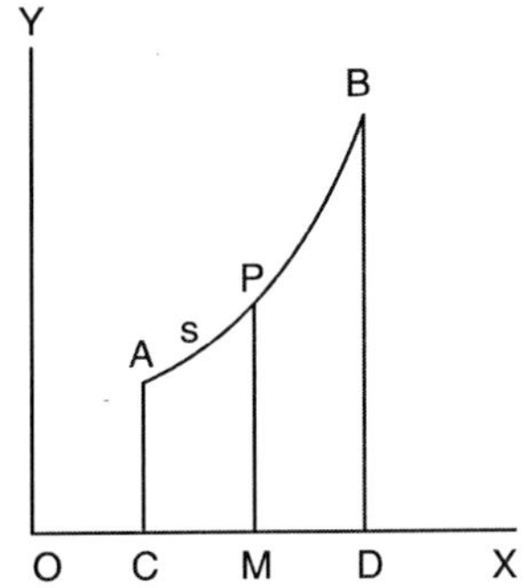

where PM is the $\perp$ from any point P of the curve on the axis, and arc $AP = s$, the limits of integration being the values of the independent variable at the ends of the revolving arc.

ILLUSTRATIVE EXAMPLES

Example 1. Find the curved surface of a sphere of radius a.

Solution : The sphere is generated by the revolution of a semicircle ABA' about its diameter AA'.

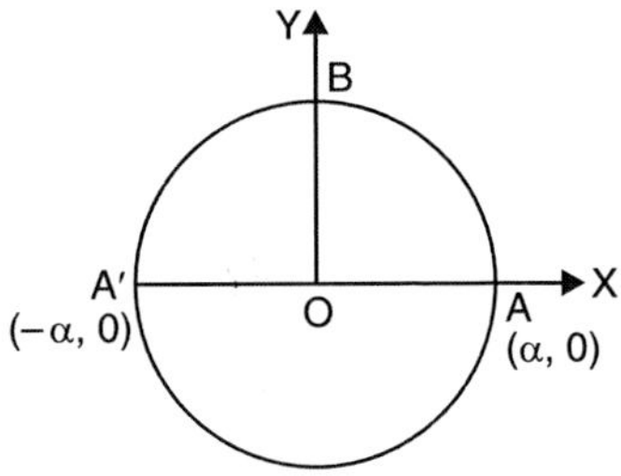

Let the equation of the generating curve (semicircle) be

$$x^2 + y^2 = a^2$$

or $$y = \sqrt{a^2 - x^2}$$

Now,

$$\frac{dy}{dx} = \frac{1}{2}\left(a^2 - x^2\right)^{-1/2}(-2x) = -\frac{x}{\sqrt{a^2 - x^2}}$$

$$\therefore \quad \frac{ds}{dx} = \sqrt{1 + \left(\frac{dy}{dx}\right)^2} = \sqrt{1 + \frac{x^2}{a^2 - x^2}} = \frac{a}{\sqrt{a^2 - x^2}}$$

For the semicircle ABA', x varies from $-a$ to a.

$\therefore$ Required volume

$$= \int_{-a}^{a} 2\pi y \frac{ds}{dx}\, dx$$

$$= 2\pi \int_{-a}^{a} \sqrt{a^2 - x^2}\, \frac{a}{\sqrt{a^2 - x^2}}\, dx$$

$$= 2\pi a \int_{-a}^{a} dx$$

$$= 2\pi a\,(a + a)$$

$$= 4\pi a^2.$$

Example 2. For the catenary $y = a \cosh (x/a)$, prove that

$$aS = 2V = \pi a\,(ax + sy)$$

where s is the length of the arc from the vertex, S and V are respectively the area of the curved surface and volume of the solid generated by the revolution of the arc about x-axis.

Solution : The equation of the catenary is

$$y = a\cosh\left(\frac{x}{a}\right)$$

$$\therefore \qquad \frac{dy}{dx} = \sinh\left(\frac{x}{a}\right)$$

$$\therefore \qquad \frac{ds}{dx} = \sqrt{1+\left(\frac{dy}{dx}\right)^2} = \sqrt{1+\sinh^2\frac{x}{a}} = \cosh\frac{x}{a}$$

At the vertex, $x = a$.

$$\begin{aligned}
\therefore \qquad s &= \text{length of the arc from vertex to any point } (x, y) \\
&= \int_0^x \frac{ds}{dx}\,dx \\
&= \int_0^x \cosh\frac{x}{a}\,dx \\
&= \left[a\sinh\frac{x}{a}\right]_0^x \\
&= a\left(\sinh\frac{x}{a} - 0\right) \\
&= a\sinh\frac{x}{a} \qquad \text{... (1)}
\end{aligned}$$

$$\begin{aligned}
S &= \text{surface area generated by the arc} \\
&= \int_0^x 2\pi y\frac{ds}{dx}\,dx \\
&= 2\pi\int_0^x a\cosh\frac{x}{a}\cdot\cosh\frac{x}{a}\,dx \\
&= 2\pi a\int_0^x \cosh^2\frac{x}{a}\,dx \\
&= \pi a\int_0^x \left[1+\cosh\left(\frac{2x}{a}\right)\right]dx \\
&= \pi a\left[x+\frac{a}{2}\sinh\left(\frac{2x}{a}\right)\right]_0^x \\
&= \pi a\left[x+\frac{a}{2}\sinh\left(\frac{2x}{a}\right)\right] \qquad \text{... (2)}
\end{aligned}$$

and $\qquad V$ = the volume generated by the arc by the revolution about x-axis

$$= \int_0^x \pi y^2 dx$$

$$= \pi \int_0^x a^2 \cosh^2 \frac{x}{a}\, dx$$

$$= \frac{\pi a^2}{2} \int_0^x \left(1 + \cosh \frac{2x}{a}\right) dx$$

$$\left[\because \cosh^2 \theta = \frac{1 + \cosh 2\theta}{2}\right]$$

$$= \frac{\pi a^2}{2} \left[x + \frac{a}{2} \sinh\left(\frac{2x}{a}\right)\right]_0^x$$

$$= \frac{\pi a^2}{2} \left[x + \frac{a}{2} \sinh\left(\frac{2x}{a}\right)\right] \qquad \text{... (3)}$$

From (2),

$$aS = \pi a^2 \left[x + \frac{a}{2} \sinh\left(\frac{2x}{a}\right)\right] \qquad \text{... (4)}$$

From (3),

$$2V = \pi a^2 \left[x + \frac{a}{2} \sinh\left(\frac{2x}{a}\right)\right] \qquad \text{... (5)}$$

From (1),

$$\pi a\,(ax + sy) = \pi a \left[ax + a^2 \sinh \frac{x}{a} \cosh \frac{x}{a}\right]$$

$$= \pi a \left[ax + \frac{a^2}{2} \cdot 2 \sinh \frac{x}{a} \cosh \frac{x}{a}\right]$$

$$= \pi a^2 \left[x + \frac{a}{2} \sinh\left(\frac{2x}{a}\right)\right] \qquad \text{... (6)}$$

From (4), (5) and (6), it follows that

$$aS = 2V = a\pi\,(ax + sy).$$

Example 3. Find the volume and surface of the right circular cone formed by the revolution of right-angled triangle about a side which contains the right angle.

Solution : Let the right angled triangle AOB be formed by the line $y = x \tan \theta$, the x-axis and the ordinate $x = h$. Then

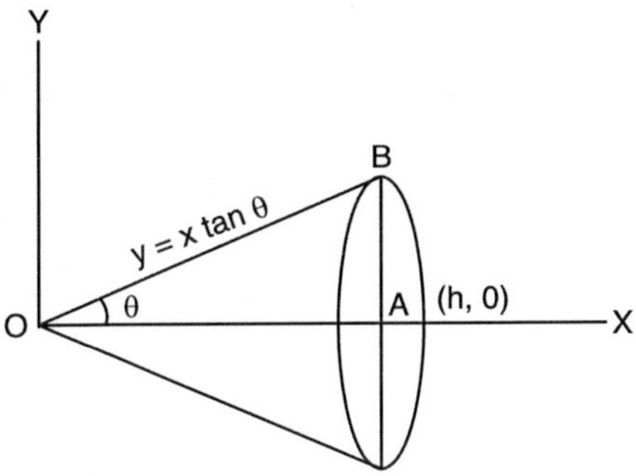

$OA = h$ is the height of the cone.

If $r = AB$ is the radius of the base, then

$$\frac{r}{h} = \frac{AB}{OA} = \tan \theta \qquad \text{... (1)}$$

and if $l = OB$ is the slant side,

then $$\sec \theta = \frac{l}{h} \qquad \text{... (2)}$$

∴ Required volume of the cone

$$= \int_0^h \pi y^2 dx$$

$$= \pi \int_0^h x^2 \tan^2 \theta \, dx \qquad [\because y = x \tan \theta]$$

$$= \pi \tan^2 \theta \left(\frac{x^3}{3} \right)_0^h$$

$$= \frac{\pi h^2 \tan^2 \theta}{3}$$

$$= \frac{1}{3} \pi h^3 \frac{r^2}{h^2}$$

$$= \frac{1}{3} \pi r^2 h \qquad \text{[using (1)]}$$

Now since $y = x \tan \theta$

$$\therefore \quad \frac{dy}{dx} = \tan \theta$$

$$\therefore \qquad \frac{ds}{dx} = \sqrt{1+\left(\frac{dy}{dx}\right)^2}$$

$$= \sqrt{1+\tan^2\theta}$$

$$= \sec\theta$$

$\therefore$ Required surface area of the cone

$$= \int_0^h 2\pi y \frac{ds}{dx}\,dx$$

$$= 2\pi \int_0^h x \tan\theta \cdot \sec\theta\,dx$$

$$= 2\pi \tan\theta \sec\theta \left(\frac{x^2}{2}\right)_0^h$$

$$= \pi h^2 \tan\theta \sec\theta$$

$$= \pi h^2 \frac{r}{h}\cdot\frac{l}{h} \qquad \text{[using (1) and (2)]}$$

$$= \pi r l.$$

Example 4. The portion between two consecutive cusps of the cycloid $x = a\,(\theta + \sin\theta)$, $y = a\,(1 + \cos\theta)$ is revolved about the x-axis. Prove that the area of the surface so formed is to the area of the cycloid as 64 : 9.

Solution : The equations of the cycloid are

$$\left.\begin{aligned} x &= a\left(\theta+\sin\theta\right) \\ y &= a\left(1+\cos\theta\right) \end{aligned}\right\}$$

The cycloid is symmetrical about the y-axis and for half of the cycloid, θ varies from O to π. If Δ denotes the area of the cycloid, then

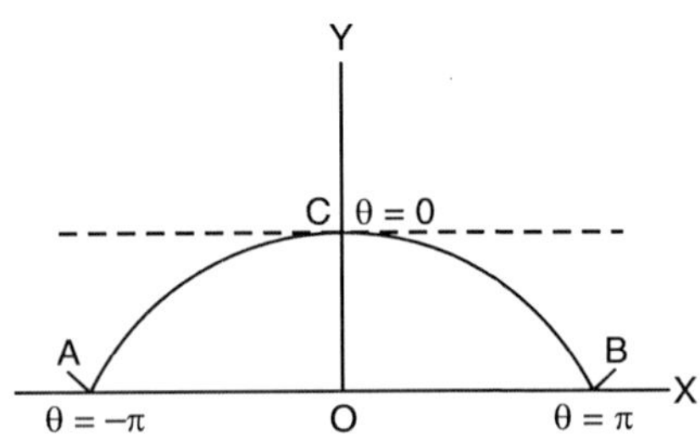

$$\Delta = 2\int_0^\pi y \frac{dx}{d\theta}\,d\theta$$

$$= 2\int_0^\pi a\left(1+\cos\theta\right) a\left(1+\cos\theta\right) d\theta$$

$$= 2a^2 \int_0^\pi \left(2\cos^2\frac{\theta}{2}\right)^2 d\theta$$

$$= 8a^2 \int_0^{\pi} \cos^4 \frac{\theta}{2} \, d\theta$$

[Put $t = \theta/2$

$\therefore\ dt = \dfrac{d\theta}{2}$

$\therefore\ d\theta = 2dt$]

$$= 8a^2 \int_0^{\pi/2} \cos^4 t \cdot 2\, dt$$

$$= 16a^2 \int_0^{\pi/2} \cos^4 t \, dt$$

$$= 16a^2 \cdot \frac{3}{4} \cdot \frac{1}{2} \cdot \frac{\pi}{2} = 3\pi a^2$$

Now $\quad \dfrac{dx}{d\theta} = a(1 + \cos\theta), \dfrac{dy}{d\theta} = -a \sin\theta$

$$\therefore \quad \frac{ds}{d\theta} = \sqrt{\left(\frac{dx}{d\theta}\right)^2 + \left(\frac{dy}{d\theta}\right)^2}$$

$$= \sqrt{a^2 (1 + \cos\theta)^2 + a^2 \sin^2\theta}$$

$$= a\sqrt{2 + 2\cos\theta}$$

$$= a\sqrt{2(1 + \cos\theta)}$$

$$= a\sqrt{4\cos^2\theta/2}$$

$$= 2a\cos\theta/2.$$

If S denotes the surface generated by the revolution of the cycloid about the x-axis, then

$$S = 2\int_0^{\pi} 2\pi y \frac{ds}{d\theta} \, d\theta$$

$$= 4\pi \int_0^{\pi} a(1 + \cos\theta) \cdot 2a\cos\frac{\theta}{2} \, d\theta$$

$$= 4\pi \int_0^{\pi} a \cdot \left(2\cos^2\frac{\theta}{2}\right) 2a\cos\frac{\theta}{2} \, d\theta$$

$$= 16\pi a^2 \int_0^{\pi} \cos^3\frac{\theta}{2} \, d\theta$$

$$= 16\pi a^2 \int^{\pi/2} \cos^3 t \cdot 2dt \qquad \text{where } t = \theta/2$$

$$= 32\pi a^2 \int^{\pi/2} \cos^3 t \, dt$$

$$= 32\pi a^2 \cdot \frac{2}{3} = \frac{64\pi a^2}{3}$$

$\therefore$ Required ratio

$$= \frac{S}{\Delta}$$

$$= \frac{\frac{64}{3}\pi a^2}{3\pi a^2}$$

$$= \frac{64}{9}.$$

Example 5. Find the surface of the solid generated by the revolution of the lemniscate $r^2 = a^2 \cos 2\theta$ about the initial line.

Solution : The equation of the lemniscate is

$$r^2 = a^2 \cos 2\theta \qquad \text{... (1)}$$

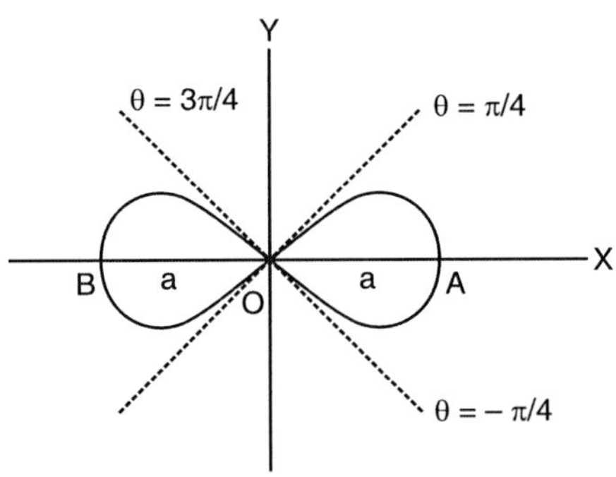

The curve is symmetrical about the initial line and the line $\theta = \pi/2$.

For a loop putting $r = 0$, we get

$$\cos 2\theta = 0 = \cos\left(\pm\frac{\pi}{2}\right)$$

$$\Rightarrow \qquad 2\theta = \pm\frac{\pi}{2}$$

$$\Rightarrow \qquad \theta = \frac{\pi}{4} \qquad \text{[two consecutive values]}$$

The curve consists of two equal loops and $\theta = -\pi/4$, $\theta = \pi/4$ are the tangents at the pole. In the first quadrant, for half of the loop, θ varies from 0 to $\pi/4$.

From (1)

$$2r\frac{dr}{d\theta} = -\,2a^2 \sin 2\theta$$

or

$$\frac{dr}{d\theta} = -\frac{a^2 \sin 2\theta}{r}$$

$$\therefore \qquad \frac{ds}{d\theta} = \sqrt{r^2 + \left(\frac{dr}{d\theta}\right)^2}$$

$$= \sqrt{a^2 \cos 2\theta + \frac{a^4 \sin^2 2\theta}{r^2}}$$

$$= \sqrt{a^2 \cos 2\theta + \frac{a^4 \sin^2 2\theta}{a^2 \cos 2\theta}}$$

$$= \frac{a}{\sqrt{\cos 2\theta}}$$

$\therefore$ Required surface

$$= 2\int_0^{\pi/4} 2\pi y \frac{ds}{d\theta}\, d\theta$$

$$= 4\pi\int_0^{\pi/4} r \sin\theta \frac{a}{\sqrt{\cos 2\theta}}\, d\theta$$

$$= 4\pi\int_0^{\pi/4} a\sqrt{\cos 2\theta}\, \sin\theta \frac{a}{\sqrt{\cos 2\theta}}\, d\theta$$

$$= 4\pi a^2\int_0^{\pi/4} \sin\theta\, d\theta$$

$$= 4\pi a^2 (-\cos\theta)_0^{\pi/4}$$

$$= 4\pi a^2\left(-\frac{1}{\sqrt{2}} + 1\right)$$

$$= 4\pi a^2\left(1 - \frac{1}{\sqrt{2}}\right)$$

Example 6. The part of the parabola $y^2 = 4ax$ cut-off by the latus rectum revolves about the segment at the vertex. Find the curved surface of the real thus generated.

Solution : The equation of the parabola is

$$y^2 = 4ax \qquad \text{... (1)}$$

The required curved surface is generated by the revolution of the arc LAL', cut-off by the latus rectum, about the tangent at the vertex, i.e., y-axis.

For half of the arc AL, x varies from 0 to a.

From (1),

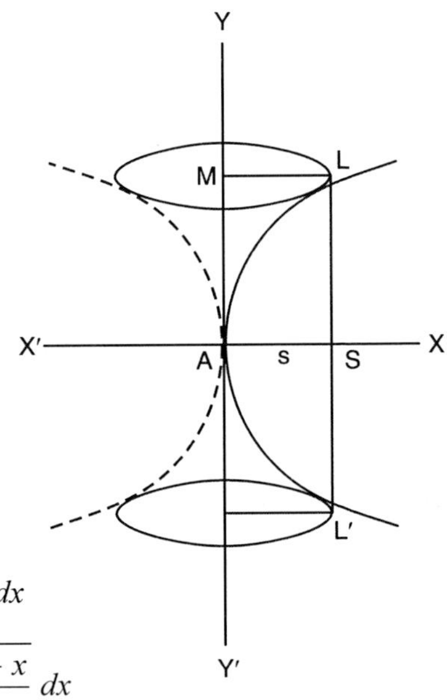

$$y = 2\sqrt{a}\sqrt{x}$$

$$\therefore \quad \frac{dy}{dx} = \frac{\sqrt{a}}{\sqrt{x}}$$

$$\therefore \quad \frac{ds}{dx} = \sqrt{1+\left(\frac{dy}{dx}\right)^2}$$

$$= \sqrt{1+\frac{a}{x}}$$

$$= \sqrt{\frac{x+a}{x}}$$

$\therefore$ Required surface

$$= 2\int_0^a 2\pi x \frac{ds}{dx}\, dx$$

$$= 4\pi\int_0^a x\sqrt{\frac{a+x}{x}}\, dx$$

$$= 4\pi\int_0^a \sqrt{x^2+ax}\, dx$$

$$= 4\pi\int_0^a \sqrt{\left(x+\frac{a}{2}\right)^2-\left(\frac{a}{2}\right)^2}\, dx$$

$$= 4\pi\left[\frac{1}{2}\left(x+\frac{a}{2}\right)\sqrt{\left(x+\frac{a}{2}\right)^2-\left(\frac{a}{2}\right)^2}\right.$$

$$\left.\frac{1}{2}\cdot\frac{a^2}{4}\cdot\cosh^{-1}\left(\frac{x+a/2}{a/2}\right)\right]_0^a$$

$$= 4\pi\left[\frac{1}{2}\cdot\frac{3a}{2}\cdot\sqrt{\frac{9a^2}{4}-\frac{a^2}{4}} - \frac{a^2}{8}\left(\cosh^{-1}3-\cosh^{-1}1\right)\right]$$

$$= 4\pi\left[\frac{3a}{4}\sqrt{2}\,a - \frac{a^2}{8}\left\{\log\left(3+\sqrt{9-1}\right) - \log\left(1+\sqrt{1-1}\right)\right\}\right]$$

$$\left[\because \cosh^{-1}x = \log\left\{x+\sqrt{x^2-1}\right\}\right]$$

$$= 3\sqrt{2}\,\pi a^2 - \frac{\pi a^2}{2}\log\left(3+2\sqrt{2}\right)$$

$$= \pi a^2\left[3\sqrt{2} - \frac{1}{2}\log\left(\sqrt{2}+1\right)^2\right]$$

$$= \pi a^2\left[3\sqrt{2} - \log\left(\sqrt{2}+1\right)\right]$$

Example 7. A quadrant of a circle of radius a revolves about its chord. Show that the surface of the spindle generated is

$$2\pi a^2\sqrt{2}\left(1-\frac{\pi}{4}\right).$$

Solution : The parametric equations of the circle are

$$x = a\cos\theta,\ y = a\sin\theta$$

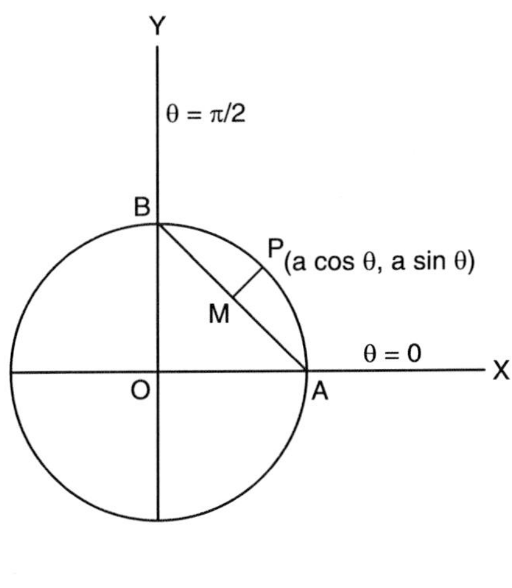

$$\therefore \qquad \frac{ds}{d\theta} = \sqrt{\left(\frac{dx}{d\theta}\right)^2 + \left(\frac{dy}{d\theta}\right)^2}$$

$$= \sqrt{a^2 \sin^2 \theta + a^2 \cos^2 \theta}$$

$$= a$$

Since $OA = OB = a$,

$\therefore$ the equation of the chord AB is

$$\frac{x}{a} + \frac{y}{a} = 1 \qquad \text{[Intercept form]}$$

or $\qquad x + y = a \qquad \ldots (1)$

Let P $(a \cos \theta, a \sin \theta)$ be any point on the arc AB. From P draw $PM \perp$ to chord AB i.e. (1).

$$\therefore \qquad PM = \frac{a \cos \theta + a \sin \theta - a}{\sqrt{2}}$$

$$= \frac{a}{\sqrt{2}} (\cos \theta + \sin \theta - 1)$$

Also for the arc AB, θ varies from 0 to $\pi/2$.

$\therefore$ Required surface

$$= \int_0^{\pi/2} 2\pi (PM) \frac{ds}{d\theta} d\theta$$

$$= 2\pi \int_0^{\pi/2} \frac{a}{\sqrt{2}} (\cos \theta + \sin \theta - 1) a \, d\theta$$

$$= \sqrt{2} \pi a^2 [\sin \theta - \cos \theta - \theta]_0^{\pi/2}$$

$$= \sqrt{2} \pi a^2 \left[1 - \frac{\pi}{2} + 1\right]$$

$$= \sqrt{2} \pi a^2 \left(2 - \frac{\pi}{2}\right)$$

$$= 2\sqrt{2} \pi a^2 \left(1 - \frac{\pi}{4}\right)$$

EXERCISE 15.2

1. Find the surface of a hemisphere of radius a.
2. Show that the surface of the spherical zone contained between two parallel planes is $2\pi ah$, where a is the radius of the sphere and h is the distance between the planes.

3. The arc AL of a parabola, where A and L are respectively the vertex and an extremity of the latus rectum, is revolved about its axis. Find the area of the surface generated.

4. (a) Find the area of the surface of the solid generated by the revolution about the x-axis of the area bounded by the parabola $y^2 = 4ax$, the x-axis and the ordinate $x = h$.

(b) Find the curved surface of the solid generated by the revolution about the x-axis of the area bounded by the parabola $y^2 = 4ax$, the ordinate $x = 3a$ and the x-axis.

5. Find the surface area of the solid formed by the revolution, about the axis of y, of the part of the curve $ay^2 = x^3$ from $x = 0$ to $x = 4a$ which is above the x-axis.

6. Find the surface generated by the revolution of the arc of the catenary $y = c \cosh x/c$ about the axis of x.

7. Find the surface generated by the revolution of the curve $y = c \cosh (x/c)$ about the x-axis, between the planes $x = a$ and $x = b$.

8. Find the surface of the solid generated by the revolution of the ellipse $x^2 + y^2 = 16$

(a) about its minor axis

(b) about its major axis.

9. Prove that the surface of the prolate spheroid formed by the revolution of the ellipse of eccentricity e about its major axis is equal to

$$2 \times \text{Area of the ellipse} \times \left[\sqrt{1-e^2} + \frac{1}{e}\sin^{-1} e\right].$$

10. Find the surface of the solid generated by the revolution of the astroid $x^{2/3} + y^{2/3} = a^{2/3}$ about the x-axis.

11. Prove that the surface area of the solid generated by the revolution of the loop of the curve

$$x = t^2,\ y = t - \frac{t^3}{3}$$

about the x-axis is 3π.

12. Prove that the surface of the solid generated by the revolution of the tractrix

$$x = a \cos t + \frac{1}{2} a \log \tan^2 \frac{t}{2}, y = a \sin t$$

about its asymptote is equal to the surface of a sphere of radius a.

13. Find the surface generated by the revolution of the cycloid

(a) $x = a(\theta - \sin \theta)$, $y = a(1 - \cos \theta)$ about the x-axis.

(b) $x = a(\theta + \sin \theta)$, $y = a(1 - \cos \theta)$ about the tangent at the vertex.

(c) $x = a(\theta + \sin \theta)$, $y = a(1 + \cos \theta)$ about its base.

14. Find the area of the surface of revolution formed by revolving the curve $r = 2a \cos \theta$ about the initial line.

15. The curve $r = a(1 + \cos \theta)$ revolves about the initial line. Find the surface of the figure so formed.

16. Find the surface of the solid formed by the revolution of the cardioid $r = a(1 - \cos \theta)$ about the initial line.

17. Find the surface of the solid generated by the revolution of the ellipse $4x^2 + 5y^2 = 20$ about the minor axis.

18. Prove that the surface of the oblate spheroid formed by the revolution of the ellipse of semi-major axis a and eccentricity e is

$$2\pi a^2 \left[1 + \frac{1 - e^2}{1 + e^2} \log \left(\frac{1 + e}{1 - e}\right)\right].$$

19. The arc of the cardioid $r = a(1 + \cos \theta)$ included between $-\pi/2 \le \theta \le \pi/2$ is rotated about the line $\theta = \pi/2$. Find the area of surface generated.

20. A circular arc revolves about its chord. Find the area of the surface generated, when 2α is the angle subtended by the arc at the centre.

ANSWERS

EXERCISE 15.2

1. $2\pi a^2$ **3.** $\frac{8\pi a^2}{3}(2\sqrt{2} - 1)$

4. (a) $\frac{8}{3}\pi\sqrt{a}\left[(a+h)^{3/2} - a^{3/2}\right]$

(b) $\frac{56}{3}\pi a^2$

5. $\frac{128\pi a^2}{1215}\left(125\sqrt{10}+1\right)$

6. $\pi c\left[x+\frac{c}{2}\sinh\left(\frac{2x}{c}\right)\right]$

7. $\pi c\left[(b-a)+\frac{c}{2}\sinh\left(\frac{2b}{c}\right)-\frac{c}{2}\sinh\left(\frac{2a}{c}\right)\right]$

8. (a) $32\pi\left[1+\frac{1}{4\sqrt{3}}\log\frac{2+\sqrt{3}}{2-\sqrt{3}}\right]$

(b) $8\pi\left[1+\frac{4\pi}{3\sqrt{3}}\right]$

10. $\frac{12}{5}\pi a^2$

13. (a) $\frac{64\pi a^2}{3}$ (b) $\frac{32\pi a^2}{3}$ (c) $\frac{64}{3}\pi a^2$

14. $4\pi a^2$

15. $\frac{32\pi a^2}{5}$

16. $\frac{32\pi a^2}{5}$

17. $10\pi\left[1+\frac{2}{\sqrt{5}}\log\left(\frac{\sqrt{5}+1}{\sqrt{5}-1}\right)\right]$

19. $\frac{96\pi a^2}{5\sqrt{2}}$

20. $4\pi a^2(\sin\alpha - \alpha\cos\alpha)$

16

Integration of Functions of Two and Three Variables

16.1 Double Integrals

Let $f(x, y)$ be defined for all points in a finite region A of the xy-plane. Let $\delta x\, \delta y$ be an elementary area of the region A surrounding the point (x, y). Then

$$\text{Lt}_{\delta x \to 0,\, \delta y \to 0} \sum \sum f(x, y)\, \delta x\, \delta y$$

is written as $\iint_A f(x, y)\, dx\, dy$ which is called the *double integral* of $f(x, y)$ over the region A.

If the region A is bounded by the curves

$$x = x_1,\ x = x_2,\ y = y_1,\ y = y_2$$

then $$\iint_A f(x, y)\, dx\, dy = \int_{y_1}^{y_2} \int_{x_1}^{x_2} f(x, y)\, dx\, dy \qquad \text{... (1)}$$

16.2 Evaluation of Double Integrals

(1) To evaluate (1) we proceeds as follows :

(a) If x_1, x_2, y_1, y_2 are constants, then the order of integration is immaterial, provided the limits of integration are changed accordingly.

Thus $\iint_A f(x, y)\, dx\, dy$

$$= \int_{y_1}^{y_2} \int_{x_1}^{x_2} f(x, y)\, dx\, dy$$

$$= \int_{x_1}^{x_2} \int_{y_1}^{y_2} f(x, y)\, dy\, dx$$

(b) If x_1, x_2 are functions of y, let $x_1 = \phi_1(y)$, $x_2 = \phi_2(y)$ and let y_1, y_2 be constants. Then

$$\iint_A f(x, y)\, dx\, dy = \int_{y_1}^{y_2} \int_{x_1}^{x_2} f(x, y)\, dx\, dy$$

(c) If y_1, y_2 are functions of x, let $y_1 = \phi_1(x)$, $y_2 = \phi_2(x)$ and let x_1, x_2 be constants. Then

$$\iint_A f(x, y)\, dx\, dy = \int_{x_1}^{x_2} \int_{y_1}^{y_2} f(x, y)\, dy\, dx$$

From (a), (b), (c) above, we observe that integration is first to be performed with respect to that variable having variable limits and finally with respect to the variable with constant limits.

(II) If $f(x, y) = 1$, then the double integral $\iint_A dx\, dy$ gives the area of the region A.

(III) To evaluate $\int_{y_1}^{y_2} \int_{x_1}^{x_2} f(x, y)\, dx\, dy = \int_{y_1}^{y_2} \left[\int_{x_1}^{x_2} f(x, y)\, dx \right] dy$ we integrate $f(x, y)$ *w.r.t.* x, treating y as a constant, getting a function of y (or a constant), say $F(y)$ and then $F(y)$ is integrated *w.r.t.* y.

16.3 Triple Integrals

Let $f(x, y, z)$ be defined for all points in a finite region V of space. Let $\delta x\, \delta y\, \delta z$ be an elementary volume of the region V surrounding the point (x, y, z). Then

$$\underset{\substack{\delta x \to 0 \\ \delta y \to 0 \\ \delta z \to 0}}{\text{Lt}} \sum \sum \sum f(x, y, z)\, \delta x\, \delta y\, \delta z$$

is written as $\iiint_V f(x, y, z)\, dx\, dy\, dz$ which is called the *triple integral* of $f(x, y, z)$ over the region V. If the region V is bounded by the surfaces $x = x_1$, $x = x_2$, $y = y_1$, $y = y_2$, $z = z_1$, $z = z_2$ then

$$\iiint_V f(x, y, z)\, dx\, dy\, dz = \int_{z_1}^{z_2} \int_{y_1}^{y_2} \int_{x_1}^{x_2} f(x, y, z)\, dx\, dy\, dz \quad \text{... (1)}$$

16.4 Evaluation of Triple Integrals

(I) To evaluate (1), we proceed as follows:

(a) If x_1, x_2, y_1, y_2, z_1, z_2 are all constants, then the order of integration is immaterial, provided the limits of integration are changed accordingly. Thus

$$\int_{z_1}^{z_2}\int_{y_1}^{y_2}\int_{x_1}^{x_2} f(x, y, z)\, dx\, dy\, dz$$

$$= \int_{y_1}^{y_2}\int_{z_1}^{z_2}\int_{x_1}^{x_2} f(x, y, z)\, dx\, dy\, dz$$

$$= \int_{x_1}^{x_2}\int_{y_1}^{y_2}\int_{z_1}^{z_2} f(x, y, z)\, dz\, dy\, dx \text{ etc.}$$

(b) If z_1, z_2 are functions of x and y; y_1, y_2 are functions of x while x_1, x_2 are constants then integration is to be performed first with respect to z, then with respect to y and finally with respect to x. Thus

$$\iiint_V f(x, y, z)\, dx\, dy\, dz$$

$$= \int_{x=a}^{x=b}\int_{y=y_1}^{y=y_2}\int_{z=\phi_1(x,y)}^{z=\phi_2(x,y)} f(x, y, z)\, dz\, dy\, dx$$

(II) If $f(x, y, z) = 1$, then the triple integral $\iiint_V dx\, dy\, dz$ gives the volume of the region V.

ILLUSTRATIVE EXAMPLES

Example 1. Choose the correct answer :

$$\int_0^1\int_0^1 (x^2 + y^2)\, dx\, dy$$

(i) 1 (ii) 0 (iii) $\frac{1}{3}$ (iv) $\frac{2}{3}$

Solution :

$$\int_0^1\int_0^1 (x^2 + y^2)\, dx\, dy = \int_0^1\left[\int_0^1 (x^2 + y^2)\, dx\right] dy$$

$$= \int_0^1 \left(\frac{x^3}{3} + y^2 x\right)_0^1 dy$$

$$= \int_0^1 \left(\frac{1}{3} + y^2\right) dy$$

$$= \left(\frac{y}{3} + \frac{y^3}{3}\right)_0^1$$

$$= \frac{1}{2} + \frac{1}{3} = \frac{2}{3}$$

Hence the correct answer is (iv) $\frac{2}{3}$.

Example 2. Evaluate $\int_0^2 \int_1^3 xy\,(1 + x + y)\, dx\, dy.$

Solution :

$$\int_0^2 \int_1^3 xy\,(1 + x + y)\, dx\, dy$$

$$= \int_0^2 \left[\int_1^3 xy\,(1 + x + y)\, dx \right] dy$$

$$= \int_0^2 \left[\int_1^3 \left(xy + x^2 y + xy^2 \right) dx \right] dy$$

$$= \int_0^2 \left(\frac{x^2 y}{2} + \frac{x^3 y}{3} + \frac{x^2 y^2}{2} \right)_1^3 dy$$

$$= \int_0^2 \left[\left(\frac{9y}{2} + \frac{27y}{3} + \frac{9y^2}{2} \right) - \left(\frac{y}{2} + \frac{y}{3} + \frac{y^2}{2} \right) \right] dy$$

$$= \int_0^2 \left(4y + \frac{26y}{3} + 4y^2 \right) dy$$

$$= \left(\frac{4y^2}{2} + \frac{26y^2}{3.2} + \frac{4y^3}{3} \right)_0^2$$

$$= \left(2y^2 + \frac{13}{3} y^2 + \frac{4y^3}{3} \right)_0^2$$

$$= \left(\frac{19y^2}{3} + \frac{4y^3}{3} \right)_0^2$$

$$= \frac{76}{3} + \frac{32}{3} = \frac{108}{3} = 36$$

Example 3. Evaluate $\int_0^1 \int_0^1 \frac{dx\, dy}{\sqrt{1 - x^2}\, \sqrt{1 - y^2}}$.

Solution :

$$\int_0^1 \int_0^1 \frac{dx\, dy}{\sqrt{1 - x^2}\, \sqrt{1 - y^2}}$$

$$= \int_0^1 \left[\int_0^1 \frac{dx}{\sqrt{1 - x^2}\, \sqrt{1 - y^2}} \right] dy$$

$$= \int_0^1 \left(\frac{1}{\sqrt{1 - y^2}} \sin^{-1} x \right)_0^1 dy$$

$$= \int_0^1 \frac{\pi}{2\sqrt{1-y^2}}\, dy$$

$$= \frac{\pi}{2}\left(\sin^{-1} y\right)_0^1$$

$$= \frac{\pi}{2}\left(\frac{\pi}{2}\right) = \frac{\pi^2}{4}$$

Example 4. Evaluate $\int_1^2 \int_0^x \frac{dy\, dx}{x^2 + y^2}$.

Solution :

$$\int_1^2 \int_0^x \frac{dy\, dx}{x^2 + y^2} = \int_1^2 \left(\int_0^x \frac{dy}{x^2 + y^2} \right) dx$$

$$= \int_1^2 \left\{ \frac{1}{x} \tan^{-1}\left(\frac{y}{x}\right) \right\}_0^x dx$$

$$= \int_1^2 \left[\frac{1}{x} \tan^{-1}\left(\frac{x}{x}\right) - \frac{1}{x} \tan^{-2}\left(\frac{0}{x}\right) \right] dx$$

$$= \int_1^2 \left(\frac{1}{x} \tan^{-1} 1 - 0 \right) dx$$

$$= \int_1^2 \frac{\pi}{4} \cdot \frac{1}{x}\, dx$$

$$= \frac{\pi}{4} (\log x)_1^2$$

$$= \frac{\pi}{4} \log 2$$

Example 5. Evaluate $\int_0^1 \int_0^{x^2} e^{y/x}\, dy\, dx.$

Solution :

$$\int_0^1 \int_0^{x^2} e^{y/x}\, dy\, dx = \int_0^1 \left[\int_0^{x^2} e^{y/x}\, dy \right] dx$$

$$= \int_0^1 \left(\frac{e^{y/x}}{1/x} \right)_0^{x^2} dx$$

$$= \int_0^1 \left(x e^{y/x} \right)_0^{x^2} dx$$

$$= \int_0^1 \left(xe^{x^2/x} - xe^{0/x} \right) dx$$

$$= \int_0^1 \left(xe^x - x \right) dx$$

$$= \int_0^1 \underset{\text{I}}{x} \underset{\text{II}}{\left(e^x - 1 \right)} dx$$

Integrating by parts, we get

$$= \left[x\left(e^x - x \right) \right]_0^1 - \int_0^1 1\left(e^x - x \right) dx$$

$$= e - 1 - \left(e^x - \frac{x^2}{2} \right)_0^1$$

$$= e - 1 - \left(e - \frac{1}{2} - 1 \right)$$

$$= \frac{1}{2}$$

Example 6. Evaluate $\int_0^1 \int_0^{\sqrt{1+x^2}} \frac{dy\,dx}{1 + x^2 + y^2}$.

Solution :

$$\int_0^1 \int_0^{\sqrt{1+x^2}} \frac{dy\,dx}{1 + x^2 + y^2} = \int_0^1 \left[\int_0^{\sqrt{1+x^2}} \frac{dy}{\left(1 + x^2 \right) + y^2} \right] dx$$

$$= \int_0^1 \left[\frac{1}{\sqrt{1+x^2}} \tan^{-1} \frac{y}{\sqrt{1+x^2}} \right]_0^{\sqrt{1+x^2}} dx$$

$$= \int_0^1 \frac{\pi}{4\sqrt{1+x^2}} dx$$

$$= \frac{\pi}{4} \left[\log\left(x + \sqrt{x^2 + 1} \right) \right]_0^1$$

$$= \frac{\pi}{4} \left[\log\left(1 + \sqrt{2} \right) - \log 1 \right]$$

$$= \frac{\pi}{4} \log\left(1 + \sqrt{2} \right)$$

Example 7. Evaluate $\int_{-c}^{c} \int_{-b}^{b} \int_{-a}^{a} \left(x^2 + y^2 + z^2 \right) dz\,dy\,dx.$

Solution :

$$\int_{-c}^{c}\int_{-b}^{b}\int_{-a}^{a}\left(x^2+y^2+z^2\right)dz\,dy\,dx$$

$$= \int_{-c}^{c}\int_{-b}^{b}\left[\int_{-a}^{a}\left(x^2+y^2+z^2\right)dz\right]dy\,dx$$

$$= \int_{-c}^{c}\int_{-b}^{b}\left(x^2z+y^2z+\frac{z^2}{3}\right)_{-a}^{+a}dy\,dx$$

$$= \int_{-c}^{c}\int_{-b}^{b}\left\{\left(x^2a+y^2a+\frac{a^3}{3}\right)-\left(-x^2a-y^2a-\frac{a^3}{3}\right)\right\}dy\,dx$$

$$= \int_{-c}^{c}\int_{-b}^{b}2\left(x^2a+y^2a+\frac{a^3}{3}\right)dy\,dx$$

$$= 2\int_{-c}^{c}\left[\int_{-b}^{b}\left(x^2a+y^2a+\frac{a^3}{3}\right)dy\right]dx$$

$$= 2\int_{-c}^{c}\left(x^2ay+\frac{y^2}{3}a+\frac{a^3}{3}y\right)_{-b}^{b}dx$$

$$= 2\int_{-c}^{c}\left\{\left(x^2ab+\frac{b^3}{3}a+\frac{a^3}{3}b\right)-\left(-x^2ab-\frac{b^3}{3}a-\frac{a^3b}{3}\right)\right\}dx$$

$$= 2\int_{-c}^{c}\left(2x^2ab+\frac{2b^3a}{3}+\frac{2a^3b}{3}\right)dx$$

$$= 2\cdot(2ab)\int_{-c}^{c}\left(x^2+\frac{b^2}{3}+\frac{a^2}{3}\right)dx$$

$$= 4ab\left(\frac{x^3}{3}+\frac{b^2}{3}x+\frac{a^2}{x}x\right)_{-c}^{c}$$

$$= 4ab\left[\left(\frac{c^3}{3}+\frac{b^2c}{3}+\frac{a^2c}{3}\right)-\left(-\frac{c^3}{3}-\frac{b^2c}{3}-\frac{a^2c}{3}\right)\right]$$

$$= 4ab\left[\frac{2c^3}{3}+\frac{2b^2c}{3}+\frac{2a^2c}{3}\right]$$

$$= \frac{8abc}{3}\left[c^2 + b^2 + a^2\right]$$

Example 8. Evaluate $\int_0^1 \int_{y^2}^1 \int_0^{1-x} x\, dz\, dx\, dy.$

Solution :

$$\int_0^1 \int_{y^2}^1 \int_0^{1-x} x\, dz\, dx\, dy = \int_0^1 \int_{y^2}^1 \left[\int_0^{1-x} x\, dz\right] dx\, dy$$

$$= \int_0^1 \int_{y^2}^1 (xz)_0^{1-x}\, dx\, dy$$

$$= \int_0^1 \left\{\int_{y^2}^1 x(1-x)\, dx\right\} dy$$

$$= \int_0^1 \left(\frac{x^2}{2} - \frac{x^3}{3}\right)_{y^2}^1 dy$$

$$= \int_0^1 \left\{\left(\frac{1}{2} - \frac{1}{3}\right) - \left(\frac{1}{2}y^4 - \frac{1}{3}y^6\right)\right\} dy$$

$$= \int_0^1 \left(\frac{1}{6} - \frac{1}{2}y^4 + \frac{1}{3}y^6\right) dy$$

$$= \left(\frac{1}{6}y - \frac{y^5}{10} + \frac{y^7}{21}\right)_0^1$$

$$= \frac{1}{6} - \frac{1}{10} + \frac{1}{21} = \frac{4}{35}$$

Example 9. Evaluate $\int_0^{\pi/2} d\theta \int_0^{a\sin\theta} dr \int_0^{a^2 - r^2/a} r\, dz.$

Solution :

$$\int_0^{\pi/2} d\theta \int_0^{a\sin\theta} dr \int_0^{a^2 - r^2/a} r\, dz$$

$$= \int_0^{\pi/2} d\theta \int_0^{a\sin\theta} dr\, (rz)_0^{a^2 - r^2/a}$$

$$= \int_0^{\pi/2} \int_0^{a\sin\theta} \frac{r\left(a^2 - r^2\right)}{a}\, dr$$

$$= \frac{1}{a} \int_0^{\pi/2} d\theta \int_0^{a\sin\theta} \left(ra^2 - r^3\right) dr$$

$$= \frac{1}{a}\int_0^{\pi/2} d\theta \left(\frac{r^2a^2}{2} - \frac{r^4}{4}\right)_0^{a\sin\theta}$$

$$= \frac{1}{a}\int_0^{\pi/2}\left(\frac{a^4\sin^2\theta}{2} - \frac{a^4\sin^4\theta}{4}\right)d\theta$$

$$= \frac{a^3}{4}\int_0^{\pi/2}\left(2\sin^2\theta - \sin^4\theta\right)d\theta$$

$$= \frac{a^3}{4}\left[2\cdot\frac{1}{2}\cdot\frac{\pi}{2} - \frac{3}{4}\cdot\frac{1}{2}\cdot\frac{\pi}{2}\right]$$

$$= \frac{5a^3\pi}{64}$$

EXERCISE 16.1

Evaluate the following :

1. $\int_0^1\int_0^2 (x+y)\,dx\,dy$

2. $\int_0^3\int_0^1 (x^2+3y^2)\,dx\,dy$

3. $\int_0^3\int_0^2 xy\,(1+x+y)\,dx\,dy$

4. $\int_0^a\int_0^b (x^2+y^2)\,dy\,dx$

5. $\int_0^a\int_0^b \frac{dx\,dy}{xy}$

6. $\int_0^1\int_0^2 (x+2)\,dx\,dy$

7. $\int_0^{\pi/2}\int_{\pi/2}^{\pi} \cos(x+y)\,dy\,dx$

8. $\int_1^2\int_3^4 (xy+e^y)\,dy\,dx$

9. $\int_3^4\int_1^2 (xy+e^y)\,dx\,dy$

10. $\int_{-1}^2\int_{x^2}^{x+2} dy\,dx$

11. $\int_0^1\int_{x^2}^{x} (x^2+3y+2)\,dy\,dx$

12. $\int_0^1\int_y^{y^2+1} x^2y\,dx\,dy$

13. $\int_0^1\int_x^{\sqrt{x}} (x^2+y^2)\,dy\,dx$

14. $\int_0^{\pi/2}\int_0^{4\sin\theta} r\,dr\,d\theta$

15. $\int_0^2\int_0^{\sqrt{2x-x^2}} x\,dy\,dx$

16. $\int_1^2\int_0^{y/2} y\,dy\,dx$

17. $\int_0^a\int_0^{\sqrt{a^2-y^2}} \sqrt{a^2-x^2-y^2}\,dy\,dx$

18. $\int_0^a\int_0^{\sqrt{a^2-y^2}} (a^2-x^2-y^2)\,dy\,dx$

19. $\int_0^1 \int_y^{\sqrt{y}} (x^2 + y^2)\, dy\, dx$

20. $\int_0^1 \int_0^{\sqrt{1-y^2}} y\, dy\, dx$

21. $\int_0^1 \int_0^2 \int_1^2 x^2 yz\, dz\, dy\, dx$

22. $\int_0^1 \int_0^1 \int_0^1 e^{x+y+z} dx\, dy\, dz$

23. $\int_0^a \int_0^a \int_0^a (yz + zx + xy)\, dx\, dy\, dz$

24. $\int_{-1}^1 \int_0^z \int_{x-z}^{x+z} (x + y + z)\, dy\, dx\, dz$

25. $\int_0^a dx \int_0^a dy \int_0^{a-x} xyz\, dz$

26. $\int_1^3 \int_{1/x}^1 \int_0^{\sqrt{xy}} xyz\, dz\, dy\, dx$

27. $\int_0^1 \int_0^{1-x} \int_0^{1-x-y} xyz\, dz\, dy\, dz$

28. $\int_1^e \int_0^{\log y} \int_1^{e^x} \log z\, dz\, dx\, dy$

29. $\int_0^{\pi/2} \int_0^{\pi/2} \int_0^{\sin z} x^2 \sin y\, dz\, dy\, dx$

30. $\int_0^{\log 2} \int_0^x \int_0^{x + \log y} e^{x+y+z} dx\, dy\, dz$

ANSWERS

EXERCISE 16.1

1. 3

2. 12

3. $30\frac{3}{4}$

4. $\frac{ab}{3}(a^2 + b^2)$

5. $\log a \cdot \log b$

6. 5

7. – 2

8. $\frac{21}{4} + e^4 - e^3$

9. $\frac{21}{4} + e^4 + e^3$

10. $\frac{9}{2}$

11. $\frac{7}{12}$

12. $\frac{67}{120}$

13. $\frac{8}{35}$

14. 2π

15. $\frac{\pi}{2}$ **16.** $\frac{7}{6}$

17. $\frac{\pi a^3}{6}$ **18.** $\frac{\pi a^4}{8}$

19. $\frac{3}{35}$ **20.** $\frac{1}{3}$

21. 1 **22.** $(e - 1)^3$

23. $\frac{3a^5}{4}$ **24.** 0

25. $\frac{a^6}{48}$ **26.** $\frac{13}{9} - \frac{1}{6}\log 3$

27. $\frac{1}{720}$ **28.** $\frac{1}{4}\left(1 + 8e - 3e^2\right)$

29. $\frac{2}{9}$ **30.** $\frac{3}{8}\log 2 - \frac{19}{9}$

16.5 The Region of Integration

A convenient and simple way to describe a region is by giving a system of inequalities, which the coordinates of a point must satisfy if it belongs to the region.

(i) If the region in the xy-plane is bounded by the lines $x = a$, $x = b$, $y = c$, $y = d$ $(a < b, c < d)$ then it can be expressed as $a \le x \le b$, $c \le y \le d$.

(ii) If the region in space is bounded by the planes

$x = x_1$, $x = x_2$, $y = y_1$, $y = y_2$, $z = z_1$, $z = z_2$

$(x_1 < x_2, y_1 < y_2, z_1 < z_2)$ then it can be expressed as

$x_1 \le x \le x_2$, $y_1 \le y \le y_2$, $z_1 \le z \le z_2$.

(iii) If the region in the xy-plane is the circle $x^2 + y^2 = a^2$, then it can be expressed as

$$\left.\begin{array}{ll} & -a \le x \le a, -\sqrt{a^2 - x^2} \le y \le \sqrt{a^2 - x^2} \\ \text{or as} & -\sqrt{a^2 - y^2} \le x \le \sqrt{a^2 - y^2}, -a \le y \le a \end{array}\right\}$$

because $x^2 + y^2 \le a^2 \Rightarrow y^2 \le a^2 - x^2$

$$\Rightarrow \quad -\sqrt{a^2 - x^2} \le y \le \sqrt{a^2 - x^2}$$

where $x^2 \le a^2$ i.e. $-a \le x \le a$

Similarly, we can prove the second form.

(iv) If the region in space is the sphere $x^2 + y^2 + z^2 = a^2$, then it can be expressed as

$$-\sqrt{a^2 - y^2 - z^2} \le x \le \sqrt{a^2 - y^2 - z^2}$$

$$-\sqrt{a^2 - z^2} \le y \le \sqrt{a^2 - z^2}$$

$$-a \le z \le a$$

OR

$$-a \le z \le a$$

$$-\sqrt{a^2 - x^2} \le y \le \sqrt{a^2 - x^2}$$

$$-\sqrt{a^2 - x^2 - y^2} \le z \le \sqrt{a^2 - x^2 - y^2} \quad \text{etc.}$$

ILLUSTRATIVE EXAMPLES

Example 1. Evaluate $\iint_D x^2 y^2 dx\, dy$, where D is the region bounded by $x = 0$, $y = 0$ and $x^2 + y^2 = 1$.

Solution : Here y varies from 0 to 1 and for any value of y between 0 and 1, x varies from 0 to $\sqrt{1-y^2}$.

Thus the region D can be expressed as

$$0 \le x \le \sqrt{1-y^2},\ 0 \le y \le 1$$

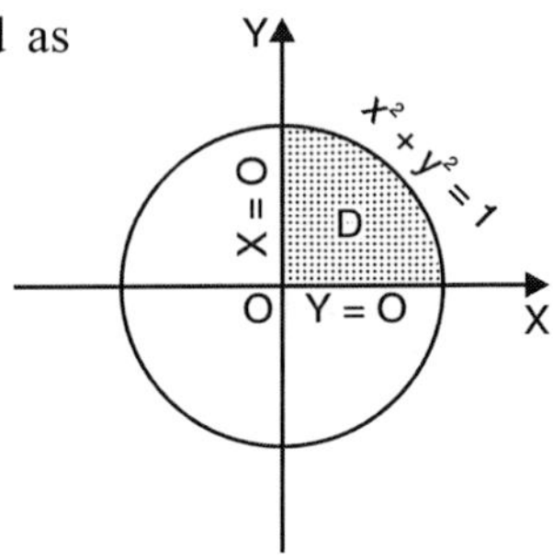

$$\therefore \quad \iint_D x^2 y^2 dx\, dy$$

$$= \int_0^1 \int_0^{\sqrt{1-y^2}} x^2 y^2 dx\, dy$$

$$= \int_0^1 \left(y^2 \frac{x^3}{3} \right)_0^{\sqrt{1-y^2}} dy$$

$$= \frac{1}{3} \int_0^1 y^2 (1-y^2)^{3/3} dy$$

[Put $y = \sin \theta$
so that $dy = \cos \theta \, d\theta$
when $y = 0$, $\theta = 0$
when $y = 1$, $\theta = \pi/2$]

$$\therefore \quad \iint_D x^2 y^2 dx\, dy$$

$$= \int_0^{\pi/2} \frac{1}{3} \sin^2\theta \cos^3\theta \cos\theta \, d\theta$$

$$= \frac{1}{3}\int_0^{\pi/2} \sin^2\theta \cos^4\theta \, d\theta$$

$$= \frac{\pi}{96}.$$

Example 2. Evaluate $\iint e^{2x+3y} dx\, dy$ over the triangle bounded by $x = 0$, $y = 0$ and $x + y = 1$.

Solution : The region R of integration is the shaded area shown in the figure.

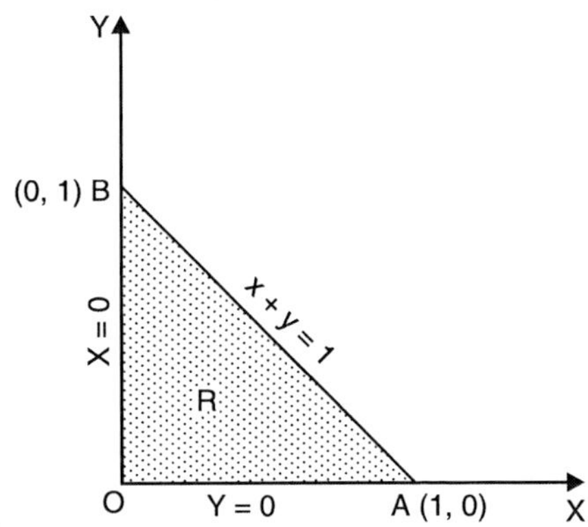

Here x varies from 0 to 1 and y varies from x-axis upto the line $x + y = 1$ i.e. from 0 to $1 - x$.

$\therefore$ The region R can be expressed as

$$0 \le x \le 1,\ 0 \le y \le 1 - x$$

$$\therefore \quad \iint_R e^{2x+3y} dx\, dy$$

$$= \int_0^1 \int_0^{1-x} e^{2x+3y} dy\, dx$$

$$= \int_0^1 \left(\frac{e^{2x+3y}}{3}\right)_0^{1-x} dx$$

$$= \frac{1}{3}\int_0^1 \left(e^{3-x} - e^{2x}\right) dx$$

$$= \frac{1}{3}\left[-e^{3-x} - \frac{1}{2}e^{2x}\right]_0^1$$

$$= \frac{1}{3}\left[e^2 + \frac{1}{2}e^2 - e^3 - \frac{1}{2}\right]$$

$$= -\frac{1}{3}\left[-e^2(e-1) + \frac{1}{2}(e-1)(e+1)\right]$$

$$= -\frac{e-1}{3}\left[-e^2 + \frac{e+1}{2}\right]$$

$$= \frac{e-1}{6}\left(2e^2 - e - 1\right)$$

$$= \frac{e-1}{6}\left(2e^2 - 2e + e - 1\right)$$

$$= \frac{e-1}{6}\left[2e(e-1) + 1(e-1)\right]$$

$$= \frac{(e-1)^2(2e+1)}{6}$$

Example 3. Evaluate $\iint_R y\,dy\,dx$, where R is the region bounded by the parabolas $y^2 = 4x$ and $y^2 = 4y$.

Solution : Solving $x^2 = 4y$ and $y^2 = 4x$, we get

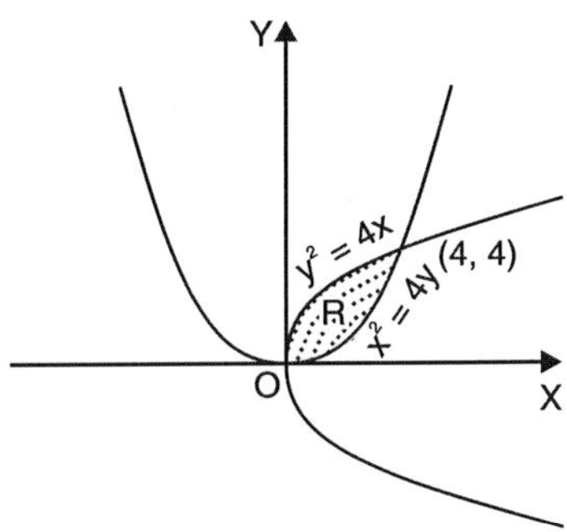

$$\left(\frac{x^2}{4}\right)^2 = 4x$$

$$\Rightarrow \quad x\,(x^3 - 64) = 0$$

$$\Rightarrow \quad x = 0,\ 4$$

when $x = 0$, $y = 0$;

when $x = 4$, $y = 4$.

$\therefore$ Coordinate of the point of intersection are (4, 4).

The region R can be expressed as

$$0 \le x \le 4, \frac{x^2}{4} \le y \le 2\sqrt{x}$$

$$\therefore \iint_R y\,dx\,dy = \int_0^4 \int_{x^2/4}^{2\sqrt{x}} y\,dy\,dx$$

$$= \int_0^4 \left(\frac{y^2}{2}\right)_{x^2/4}^{2\sqrt{x}} dx$$

$$= \int_0^4 \left(2x - \frac{x^4}{32}\right) dx$$

$$= \left(x^2 - \frac{x^5}{160} \right)_0^4$$

$$= 16 - \frac{32}{5} = \frac{48}{5}$$

EXERCISE 16.2

1. Find the area of the ellipse $\frac{x^2}{a^2} + \frac{y^2}{b^2} = 1$.

2. Evaluate $\iint xy\, dx\, dy$ over the rectangle bounded by $x = 2$, $x = 5$, $y = 1$, $y = 2$.

3. If A is the rectangle $0 \le x \le 1$, $1 \le y \le 3$, find $\iint_A x^2 y^2 dy\, dx$.

4. Evaluate $\iint x^2 y^2 dx\, dy$ over the circle $x^2 + y^2 = 1$.

5. Evaluate $\iint x^2 y^3 dx\, dy$ over the circle $x^2 + y^2 = a^2$.

6. Find the area of the region bounded by the circle $x^2 + y^2 = a^2$.

7. Evaluate $\iint (x + y + a)\, dx\, dy$ over the circular area $x^2 + y^2 \le a^2$.

8. Evaluate $\iint xy\, dx\, dy$ where the region of integration is the positive quadrant of the circle $x^2 + y^2 = a^2$.

9. Evaluate $\iint \frac{xy\, dx\, dy}{\sqrt{1 - y^2}}$ over the positive quadrant of the circle $x^2 + y^2 = 1$.

10. Prove that

$$\iint x^{2l-1} y^{2m-1} dx\, dy = \frac{c^{2(l+m)}\, \Gamma(l+1)\, \Gamma m}{4l\, \Gamma(l+m+1)}$$

for all positive values of x and y lying inside the circle

$$x^2 + y^2 = c^2.$$

11. Evaluate $\iint_R \sqrt{4x^2 - y^2}\; dx\, dy$ where R is the triangle bounded by the lines $y = 0$, $y = x$, $x = 1$.

12. Evaluate $\iint xy\, dx\, dy$ over the region in the positive quadrant for which $x + y \le 1$.

13. Evaluate

(a) $\iint_A (x^2 + y^2)\, dx\, dy$ (b) $\iint_A (2x + 3y)\, dx\, dy$

where A is the region bounded by $x = 0$, $y = 0$, $x + y = 1$.

14. Prove that the area of the region bounded by the line $x = \dfrac{1}{4}$ and the parabola $y^2 = 4x$ is $\dfrac{1}{3}$.

15. Find the area between the parabolas $y^2 = 4x$ and $x^2 = 4y$.

16. Evaluate $\iint xy(x + y)\, dx\, dy$ over the area between $y = x^2$ and $y = x$.

17. Compute the value of $\iint_R y\, dx\, dy$ when R is the region in first quadrant bounded by the ellipse $\dfrac{x^2}{a^2} + \dfrac{y^2}{b^2} = 1$.

18. Evaluate $\iiint xyz\, dx\, dy\, dz$ over the ellipsoid

$$\frac{x^2}{a^2} + \frac{y^2}{b^2} + \frac{z^2}{c^2} = 1.$$

19. Find the volume of the sphere $x^2 + y^2 + z^2 = a^2$.

20. Evaluate $\displaystyle\iiint \frac{dx\, dy\, dz}{(x + y + z + 1)^3}$ over the region

$$x \ge 0,\ y \ge 0,\ z \ge 0,\ x + y + z \le 1$$

(i.e. over the region bounded by the coordinate planes and the plane $x + y + z = 1$).

ANSWERS

EXERCISE 16.2

1. πab

2. $\dfrac{63}{4}$

3. $\dfrac{27}{4}$

4. $\dfrac{\pi}{24}$

5. 0

6. πa^2

7. πa^3

8. $\dfrac{a^4}{8}$

9. $\dfrac{1}{6}$

11. $\dfrac{1}{3}\left(\sqrt{\dfrac{3}{2}}+\dfrac{\pi}{3}\right)$

12. $\dfrac{1}{24}$

13. (a) $\dfrac{1}{6}$

(b) $\dfrac{1}{3}\left(e^3-\dfrac{3}{2}e^2+\dfrac{1}{2}\right)$

15. $\dfrac{16}{3}$

16. $\dfrac{3}{56}$

17. $\dfrac{ab^2}{3}$

18. 0

19. $\dfrac{4}{3}\pi a^3$

20. $\dfrac{1}{2}\log 2-\dfrac{5}{16}$

17

Change of Order of Integration

17.1 Sometimes it becomes difficult to evaluate double and triple integrals directly and in such cases, a change in the order of integration is found useful. In double integration if the limits of both the variables are constant, then we can always change the order of integration without any difficulty. But when the limits of y are functions of x and the limits of x are constant, then for direct evaluation of the double integral, we shall have to integrate first with respect to y (treating x as constant) and then with respect to x. However in case when the direct evaluation is difficult and a change in the order of integration seems to be desirable, then we shall have to find the new limits of x as function of y, and the limits of y as constants, by consideration of geometrical conditions.

ILLUSTRATIVE EXAMPLES

Example 1. Show that

$$\int_a^b \int_a^x f(x, y)\, dx\, dy = \int_a^b \int_y^b f(x, y)\, dy\, dx.$$

Solution :

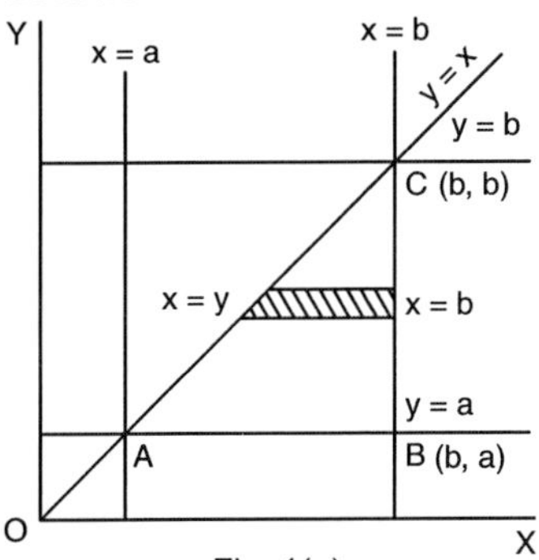

Fig. 1(a)

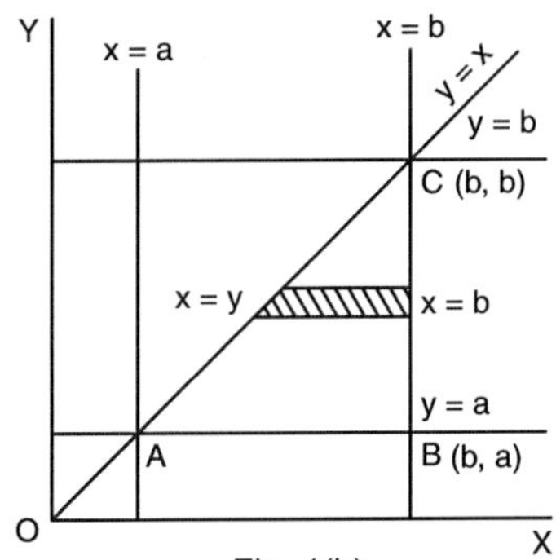

Fig. 1(b)

In the double integral on the left hand side, we see that y varies from the line $y = a$ to the line $y = x$ and x varies from the line $x = a$ to $x = b$. Thus the region of integration is the triangle ABC [Refer Fig. 1(a)]. If we reverse the order of integration, then we see that x varies from the line $x = y$ to the line $x = b$ and then y ranges from $y = a$ to $y = b$ [Refer Fig. 1(b)].

Hence $\int_a^b \int_a^x f(x, y)\, dx\, dy = \int_a^b \int_y^b f(x, y)\, dy\, dx.$

Example 2. Change the order of integration of $\int_0^a \int_{mx}^{lx} V\, dx\, dy.$

Solution : If we see the given double integral, we find that the whole region of integration is bounded by the lines $y = mx$, $y = lx$, $x = 0$ and $x = a$. Let us draw a line through A parallel to OX, dividing the region of integration OAB into two parts OAC and ACB. Let us consider the strips drawn parallel to the axis of x in each region. We see that

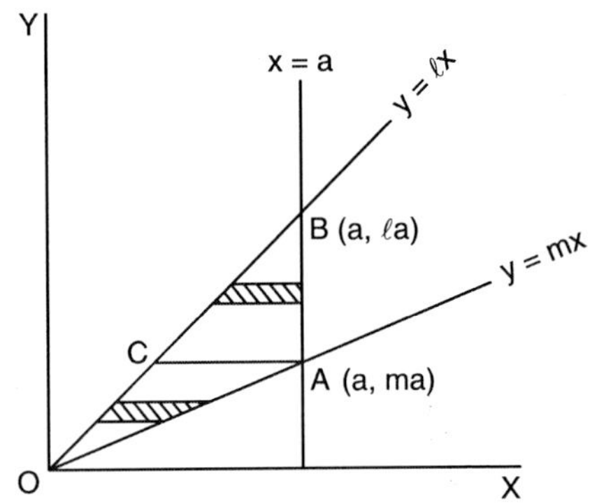

In the region *OAC*,

the integral after changing the order of integration becomes

$$\int_0^{ma} \int_{y/l}^{y/m} V\, dy\, dx$$

and **In the region *ACB*,**

the integral after changing the order of integration becomes

$$\int_{ma}^{la} \int_{y/l}^{a} V\, dy\, dx$$

Hence $\int_0^a \int_{mx}^{lx} V\, dx\, dy = \int_0^{ma} \int_{y/l}^{y/m} V\, dy\, dx + \int_{ma}^{la} \int_{y/l}^{a} V\, dy\, dx.$

Example 3. Change the order of integration in the double integral

$$\int_0^{a \cos \alpha} \int_{x \tan \alpha}^{\sqrt{a^2 - x^2}} f(x, y)\, dx\, dy.$$

Solution : The limits of integration in the given double integral show that the region of integration is bounded by the following curves

$$y = x \tan \alpha,\ y = \sqrt{a^2 - x^2},\ x = 0,\ x = a \cos \alpha.$$

$y = x \tan \alpha$ is a line passing through the origin which is the centre of the circle $x^2 + y^2 = a^2$, and is inclined at an angle α to x-axis. These two intersect at A $(a \cos \alpha, a \sin \alpha)$. Hence the region of integration is OAB as shown in the figure.

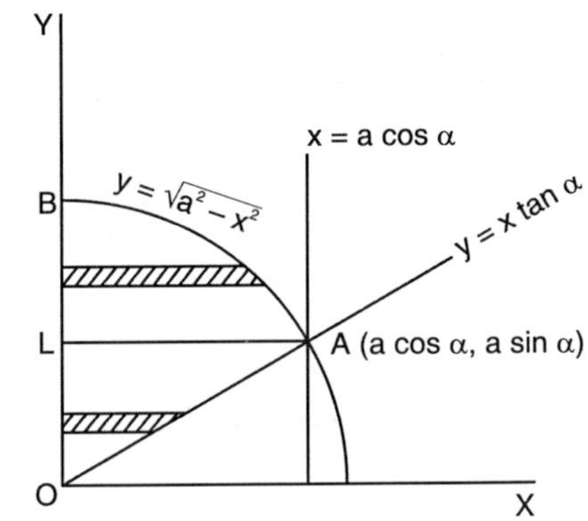

Through A draw a line parallel to x-axis, thus, dividing the region of integration into two parts say OAL and LAB.

In the region *OAL*

The strip parallel to x-axis has its extremities on $x = 0$ and $y = x \tan \alpha$. Hence limits of x are from $x = 0$ to $x = y \cot \alpha$. Since A is

$$(a \cos \alpha,\ a \sin \alpha),$$

the limits of y are from 0 to $a \sin \alpha$.

In the region *LAB*

The strip parallel to x-axis has its extremities on $x = 0$ and the circle $x^2 + y^2 = a^2$. Hence the limits of x are from 0 to $\sqrt{a^2 - y^2}$. The limits of y are clearly from $a \sin \alpha$ to a.

Thus

$$\int_0^{a \cos \alpha} \int_{x \tan \alpha}^{\sqrt{a^2 - x^2}} f(x, y)\, dx\, dy$$

$$= \int_0^{a \cos \alpha} \int_0^{y \cot \alpha} f(x, y)\, dy\, dx + \int_{a \sin \alpha}^{a} \int_0^{\sqrt{a^2 - y^2}} f(x, y)\, dy\, dx$$

Example 4. Change the order of integration in

$$\int_0^{2a} \int_{\sqrt{2ax - x^2}}^{\sqrt{2ax}} V\, dx\, dy.$$

Solution : The limits of integration in the given double integral show that the region of integration is bounded by

$$y = \sqrt{2ax - x^2}$$

i.e., $$x^2 + y^2 = 2ax$$

i.e., $$(x - a)^2 + y^2 = a^2 \text{ i.e.,}$$

a circle whose centre is $(a, 0)$ and radius a, $y = \sqrt{2ax}$ i.e., $y^2 = 2ax$ which is parabola, $x = 0$ and $x = 2a$. The parabola and circle touch each other at O $(0, 0)$, the common tangent there at being $x = 0$. The line $x = 2a$ meets the parabola $y^2 = 2ax$ at $y = 2a$ i.e., at the point B $(2a, 2a)$. Thus the region of integration is given by $OBACO$.

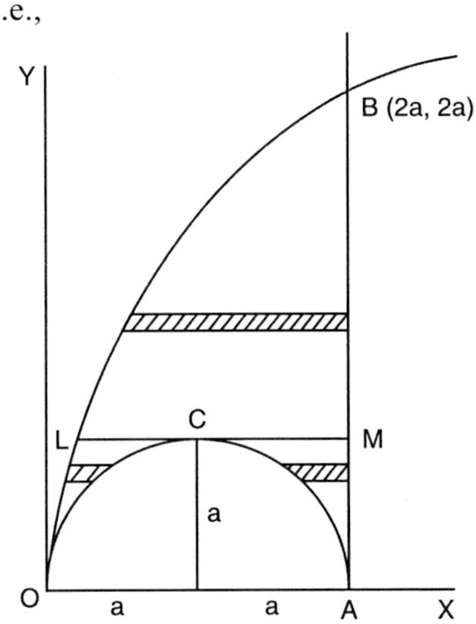

Through C, draw a line parallel to x-axis. Thus the region of integration is divided into three parts.

In the region *OLC*

The extremities of the strip parallel to x-axis lie on $y^2 = 2ax$ and $x^2 + y^2 = 2ax$, so that the limits of integration of x are $y^2/2a$ to $a - \sqrt{a^2 - y^2}$ because

$$x^2 + y^2 = 2ax$$

$$\Rightarrow \quad x^2 - 2ax + y^2 = 0$$

$$\Rightarrow \quad x = \frac{2a \pm \sqrt{4a^2 - 4y^2}}{2}$$

$$\Rightarrow \quad x = a \pm \sqrt{a^2 - y^2}$$

and we have to choose –ve sign because $x \leq a$ for the region. Also the constant limits of y are from 0 to a.

Hence the integral in this region after the change of order of integration becomes

$$\int_0^a \int_{y^2/2a}^{a-\sqrt{a^2-y^2}} V\, dy\, dx$$

In the region *AMC*

The extremities of the strip parallel to x-axis lie on the circle and the line $x = 2a$ and also $x \le a$ and hence the limits of x are from $a + \sqrt{a^2 - y^2}$ to $2a$. Also the constant limits of y are from 0 to a. Hence the integral in this region after the change of order of integration becomes

$$\int_0^a \int_{a+\sqrt{a^2-y^2}}^{a} V\, dy\, dx$$

In the region *LMB*

The extremities of the strip parallel to x-axis lie on the parabola $y^2 = 2ax$ and the line $x = 2a$. Hence the limits of x are from $y^2/2a$ to $2a$. Also the constant limits of y are from a to $2a$.

Hence the integral in this region after the change of order of integration becomes

$$\int_a^{2a} \int_{y^2/2a}^{2a} V\, dy\, dx$$

$$\therefore \quad \int_a^{2a} \int_{\sqrt{2ax-x^2}}^{\sqrt{2ax}} V\, dx\, dy$$

$$= \int_0^a \int_{y^2/2a}^{a-\sqrt{a^2-y^2}} V\, dy\, dx + \int_0^a \int_{a+\sqrt{a^2-y^2}}^{a} V\, dy\, dx + \int_a^{2a} \int_{y^2/2a}^{2a} V\, dy\, dx$$

Example 5. Change the order of integration in the double integral

$$I = \int_0^1 \int_y^1 x^2 \cos\left(x^2 - xy\right) dy\, dx$$

and hence evaluate it.

Solution : The limits given in the double integral show that the region of integration is bounded by $x = y$, $x = 1$, $y = 0$, $y = 1$. Thus the region of integration is the triangle OAB.

When we reverse the order of integration, we take an elementary strip parallel to y-axis. Then we see that the extremities of this strip lie on $y = 0$ and $y = x$. Hence the limits of y are from 0 to x. Also the constant limits of x in this region are from 0 to 1.

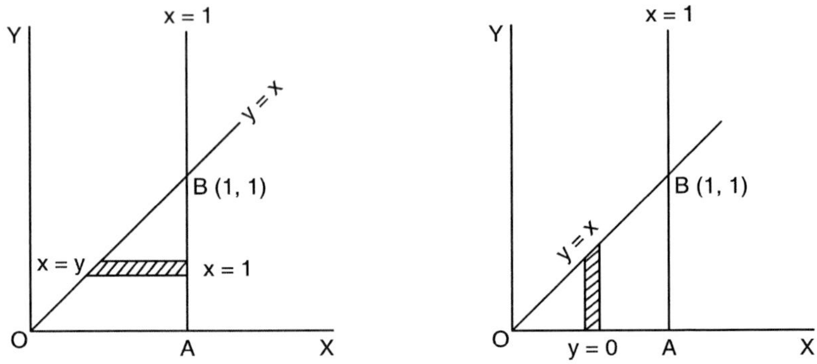

(a) **(b)**

$$\therefore \qquad I = \int_0^1 \int_y^1 x^2 \cos\left(x^2 - xy\right) dy\, dx$$

$$= \int_0^1 \int_0^x x^2 \cos\left(x^2 - xy\right) dx\, dy$$

$$= \int_{x=0}^1 \left\{ \frac{x^2 \sin\left(x^2 - xy\right)}{-x} \right\}_{y=0}^x dx$$

$$= \int_0^1 \left(-x \sin 0 + x \sin x^2\right) dx$$

$$= \int_0^1 x \sin x^2 dx = \left(-\frac{\cos x^2}{2}\right)_0^1 = \frac{1}{2}\left(1 - \cos 1\right)$$

EXERCISE 17.1

Change the order of integration in the following integrals :

1. $\int_0^a \int_0^x f(x, y)\, dx\, dy$

2. $\int_a^b \int_a^x f(x, y)\, dx\, dy$

3. $\int_a^\infty \int_0^{2x} f(x, y)\, dx\, dy$

4. $\int_0^4 \int_x^{2\sqrt{x}} f(x, y)\, dx\, dy$

5. $\int_1^2 \int_1^{x^2} \left(x^2 + y^2\right) dx\, dy$

6. $\int_0^3 \int_1^{\sqrt{4-y}} (x + y)\, dy\, dx$

7. $\int_0^a \int_{x^2/a}^{2a-x} f(x, y)\, dx\, dy$

8. $\int_0^a \int_0^{\sqrt{a^2 - x^2}} f(x, y)\, dx\, dy$

9. $\int_0^a \int_x^{a^2/x} f(x, y)\, dx\, dy$

10. $\int_0^{\pi/2} \int_0^{2a\cos\theta} f(r, \theta)\, d\theta\, dr$

11. $\int_0^{2a}\int_{x^2/4a}^{3a-x} V\, dx\, dy$ **12.** $\int_0^{\infty}\int_x^{\infty} \frac{e^{-y}}{y}\, dx\, dy$

Hence evaluate.

13. $\int_0^{a}\int_{\sqrt{ax-x^2}}^{\sqrt{ax}} f(x, y)\, dx\, dy$ **14.** $\int_0^{a}\int_{\sqrt{a^2-x^2}}^{x+2a} V\, dy\, dx$

15. $\int_0^{a}\int_{\frac{1}{2}\sqrt{a^2-x^2}}^{\sqrt{a^2-x^2}} V\, dx\, dy$ **16.** $\int_0^{a/2}\int_{x^2/a}^{x-x^2/a} V\, dx\, dy$

17. $\int_0^{a/2}\int_0^{a^2/x} V\, dx\, dy$

18. Show that

$$\int_0^a dx \int_0^{a-x} f(x, y)\, dy = \int_0^a dy \int_0^{a-y} f(x, y)\, dx$$

19. If $n \geq 0$, show that

$$\int_a^b\int_a^y (y-x)^n f(x)\, dy\, dx = \frac{1}{n+1}\int_a^b (b-x)^{n+1} f(x)\, dx$$

20. Prove that

$$\int_0^{4a}\int_{x^2/4a}^{2\sqrt{a-x}} dx\, dy = \int_0^{4a}\int_{y^2/4a}^{2\sqrt{ay}} dx\, dy$$

Indicate the region of integration and evaluate the integral. What does it represent?

ANSWERS

EXERCISE 17.1

1. $\int_0^a\int_y^a f(x, y)\, dy\, dx$ 2. $\int_a^b\int_y^b f(x, y)\, dy\, dx$

3. $\int_0^{\infty}\int_{y/2}^{\infty} f(x, y)\, dy\, dx$ 4. $\int_0^4\int_{y^2/4}^{y} f(x, y)\, dy\, dx$

5. $\int_1^4\int_{\sqrt{y}}^2 (x^2 + y^2)\, dy\, dx$ 6. $\int_1^2\int_0^{4-x^2} (x + y)\, dx\, dy$

7. $\int_0^a\int_0^{\sqrt{ay}} f(x, y)\, dy\, dx + \int_0^{2a}\int_0^{2a-y} f(x, y)\, dy\, dx$

8. $\int_0^a\int_0^{\sqrt{n^2-y^2}} f(x, y)\, dy\, dx$

9. $\int_0^a \int_0^y f(x, y)\, dy\, dx + \int_0^\infty \int_0^{a^2/y} f(x, y)\, dy\, dx$

10. $\int_0^{2a} \int_0^{\cos^{-1} r/2a} f(r, \theta)\, dr\, d\theta$

11. $\int_0^a \int_0^{2\sqrt{ay}} V\, dx\, dy + \int_0^{3a} \int_0^{3a-y} V\, dy\, dx$

12. $\int_0^\infty \int_0^y \frac{e^{-y}}{y}\, dy\, dx; 1$

13. $\int_0^{a/2} \int_{y^2/a}^{\frac{1}{2}\left[a - \sqrt{a^2 - 4y^2}\right]} f(x, y)\, dy\, dx$

$+ \int_0^{a/2} \int_{\frac{1}{2}\left[a + \sqrt{a^2 - 4y^2}\right]}^{a} f(x, y)\, dy\, dx + \int_{a/2}^{a} \int_{y^2/a}^{a} f(x, y)\, dy\, dx$

14. $\int_0^a \int_{\sqrt{a^2 - x^2}}^{a} V\, dy\, dx + \int_0^{2a} \int_0^a V\, dy\, dx + \int_{2a}^{3a} \int_{y-2a}^{a} V\, dy\, dx$

15. $\int_0^{a/2} \int_{\sqrt{a^2 - 4y^2}}^{\sqrt{a^2 - y^2}} V\, dy\, dx + \int_{a/2}^{a} \int_0^{\sqrt{a^2 - y^2}} V\, dy\, dx$

16. $\int_0^{a/4} \int_{\frac{a - \sqrt{a^2 - 4ay}}{2}}^{\sqrt{ay}} V\, dy\, dx$

17. $\int_0^a \int_0^y V\, dy\, dx + \int_0^\infty \int_0^{a^2/y} V\, dy\, dx$

20. Region enclosed between the parabolas $y^2 = 4ax$ and $x^2 = 4ay$.

Integral $= \dfrac{16a^2}{3}$. It represents the area of the region.